A GENERATION BETRAYED

Deconstructing Catholic Education in the
English-Speaking World

Eamonn Keane

Hatherleigh Press • New York

Published by Hatherleigh Press
An affiliate of W.W. Norton and Company
5-22 46th Avenue, Suite 200
Long Island City, NY 11101
www.hatherleighpress.com

Bulk purchases of this title should be directed to Special Sales Manager at 800-528-2550.

Library of Congress Cataloging-in-Publication Data

Keane, Eamonn.
   A generation betrayed : deconstructing Catholic education in the English-speaking world / by Eamonn Keane ; preface by Fabian Bruskewitz ; foreword by Donna Steichen ; introduction by Michael J. Wrenn.
    p. cm.
  Includes bibliographical references.
  ISBN 1-57826-088-4 (cloth : alk. paper)
   1. Christian education. 2. Catholic Church—Education. 3. Groome, Thomas H. 4. Schussler Fiorenza, Elisabeth, 1938- I. Title

BX926.3 .K43 2002
268'.82—DC21

             2002068653

Printed in Canada
10 9 8 7 6 5 4 3 2 1

Dedication

To my wife, Pat, on the celebration of our twenty-sixth wedding anniversary. Thanks be to God for all the graces he has bestowed on us and on our five children.

Acknowledgements

I wish to thank Gail Instance and all her co-workers at the *Population & Environment Research Institute* in Sydney, without whose help this book would not have been completed. I also thank Monsignor Michael Wrenn, Donna Steichen, Andrew Flach and Frederic Flach, M.D. for their support in bringing this project to completion. Finally, I thank Francis Young, Bob Denahy, John Young and Damian Tudehope for the various ways in which they helped to prepare this book for publication.

CONTENTS

PREFACE

It is difficult to exaggerate the value that one will be able to attribute to the fine work by Eamonn Keane, *A Generation Betrayed: Deconstructing Catholic Education in the English-Speaking World*. The need for this kind of work as well as for the work itself, is profound and immediate. Too often in the English-speaking world there has been an unfortunate reticence on the part of devoted and learned Catholic people in the face of the most appalling and outrageous attacks on the doctrine and discipline of the Church and upon Church order and Christian tradition. Eamonn Keane has given us in his critique of Thomas Groome's *Shared Christian Praxis,* and Elizabeth Schussler-Fiorenza's *Feminist Theology of Liberation,* not only a work of superb content and high intellectual order, but also an inspiration to confront courageously the malign and pervasive germs and viruses, which have in recent decades, infiltrated, and, in some instances, infected the various aspects of Catholic ecclesial life, particularly catechetics and Catholic education.

Effectively confronting falsehood and error, both in content and in proposed methodologies, is a constant necessity for the maintenance of vigorous Catholic life and Christian meaning, essential for all time, but vital for our current age, and for the present state of ecclesiastical development in the Catholic Church. Doctrinal and moral error which goes unrefuted and undisputed seems to metastasize with great speed in our contemporary atmosphere with its extraordinary communication technologies. The ability of our modern age to manipulate public opinion and form and shape the attitudes of modern men and women is multiplied in its effectiveness many times over by a long period of philosophical and theological misunderstanding in the matrix of which the tares are growing, sometimes with such rapidity that the good wheat is choked off. Instead of adhering to objective reality, modern human beings, particularly in our Western culture, no longer attempt to discern, or even accept that one can discern, the true and the false, the just and the unjust, the good and the bad, but rather modern man is persuaded only to compare advantages and inconveniences and to measure the practical utility of various thoughts and actions.

It is extremely important that this work of Eamonn Keane, and, it is to be hoped many similar works, will undertake to point again human intellectual development toward objective truth and those moral absolutes, which are not only the patrimony of the human race, but an essential part of the priceless treasure of divine revelation which has been given to humanity by the Maker of the universe in Sacred Scripture and Sacred tradition, mediated authentically and uniquely through the living Magisterium of the Catholic Church. The incalculably precious value, then, of this book of Eamonn Keane deserves to be appreciated in itself, but also deserves to be emulated by all who have the intellectual perception to use its example for their own work, whether in written or oral form, to take a stand for truth and moral good as has been done in "the olden times." Priests engaged in pastoral work will find the research of Eamonn Keane and the exceptional skill by which this is presented to be an important tool in their own lives and ministries.

Controversy and confrontational polemics for their own sake serve no purpose and can derive from base motives. However, controversy and confrontational polemics can also be as they are in this fine work a necessary defense of the truth and an important prophylactic for those in danger of intellectual, religious, and moral deception. The legal axiom of the ancients, "Silence gives consent," could be mistakenly construed as an attitude of devoted Catholics in the face of the deconstructing work of Thomas Groome and Elizabeth Schussler-Fiorenza without this brilliant undertaking of Eamonn Keane, who in this work of his appears to be a very effective channel of God's grace to the readers.

+Fabian W. Bruskewitz, D.D., S.T.D.
Bishop of Lincoln, Nebraska

FOREWORD

In this invaluable book, Eamonn Keane documents and meticulously refutes the errors that have turned the treasure-house of Catholic education into a toxic wasteland. He focuses attention on two prominent dissenters whose malign influence in the religious education field can scarcely be over-estimated: Thomas Groome, a professor of Catholic Religious Education and author of catechetical textbooks, and Elisabeth Schussler Fiorenza, a proto-typical feminist theologian.

Groome is considered a catechetical luminary, and is regularly invited to address religious education conferences, while Schussler Fiorenza's posture toward all of Catholicism is brutally confrontational. A Call To Action militant, and a zealous advocate of abortion, she joined her husband on the faculty of Harvard Divinity School only when her dissenting radicalism proved too much for the University of Notre Dame's usually complaisant theology department. Yet Mr. Keane establishes beyond dispute that Groome is in fact Schussler Fiorenza's disciple, and promotes the same dissenting notions. Both of them represent the corrosive stream of neo-modernist thought that has been trying to erode Catholic doctrine since the Enlightenment.

The Catholic Church, we believe, is divinely protected against the Gates of Hell. But not only against the Gates of Hell; she could not have survived two thousand years unless she were also protected against the sins and errors of her own children. Never has that endurance been tested more severely than in our time. Observers who do not look at the Church with eyes of faith inevitably conclude that she is dying.

Catholic education, for example, has sunk so deep in disarray that most students now stop practicing the faith as soon as they graduate. If the engines in sixty percent of the automobiles that rolled off Universal Motor's production line this year had stopped running the moment they

left the sales lot, officers of UMC would panic. If only thirty-eight percent of the wheat seed planted by Kansas farmers had sprouted this year,
seed company executives would stop all other activities until they discovered the cause of that disaster. And once it was found, the persons
responsible would face instant dismissal, or at least instant retraining. In
any company afflicted with massive failure, the chief objective must be
to ensure that such a catastrophe will never happen again, because no
corporate enterprise can survive protracted failure.

The Roman Catholic Church is also a corporate enterprise. She
exists not to enrich stockholders but to bring salvation to men's souls, a
far more significant purpose, in which failure is infinitely more tragic.
Increasingly over recent decades, we have seen Catholic education fail to
achieve its primary end – yet, incomprehensibly, those responsible have
seemed unable or unwilling to identify the cause and correct it.

As long ago as 1993, educational researcher Brother Marcellin Flynn
reported the grim findings uncovered in his twenty-one year study of
the faith and morals of senior students in Catholic high schools in Australia. Sunday Mass attendance fell precipitously, from sixty-nine percent
in 1972 to thirty-eight percent in 1990. Figures based on a 1996
National Church Survey in Australia recently released reveal that the
decline in the number of youth attending Mass has continued—now
down to 7 percent in the 20-29 age group. Year after year, in the course
of Bro. Flynn's study, Catholic students grew ever more accepting of
abortion, more permissive about sex outside of marriage, and more
accepting of euthanasia. By 1993, only twenty percent still thought premarital sex was sinful and only nineteen percent accepted Church teaching on contraception. Fifty-three percent approved abortion, at least in
hard cases like rape. Finally, when Br. Flynn tried to assess the students'
general knowledge of the faith, he found their ignorance of doctrinal
concepts, even of the vocabulary of religion, so bottomless that testing
was impossible.

Almost certainly, Brother Flynn's results could be replicated in any
Western country today. What students should but do not know is only
one side of the Catholic education problem, however. The other side is
that much of what they think they know is not true. Their opinions on
spiritual matters are apt to consist of a syncretist muddle of Christian
heresies, feminist neo-paganism, pantheist ecological fanaticism and
imperfectly understood Eastern religious notions, which they have
either absorbed from the "New Age" thought that pervades the sur-

rounding culture, or heard advanced directly in the classroom, even in the Catholic classroom.

In New South Wales, for example, many senior students in Catholic high schools are currently taking a "non-confessional" course in comparative religions entitled *Studies of Religion* which has been drawn up by the Board of Studies (an arm of the State Education Department). *This course relativises Christianity and reduces it to one socio-cultural phenomenon among others.* It tacitly repudiates Christianity's claim to uniqueness. Similarly creedless courses about religions as sociological phenomena are growing in popularity in the United States. Proponents claim they will deepen students' appreciation of their own faith, a recklessly optimistic prediction if they have virtually no knowledge of Catholic doctrine against which to judge the assertions of other religions, as Br. Flynn's study established and all experiential evidence supports. Such young people are far more likely to prove susceptible to religious indifference, at best, or at worst, to the syncretist cultural stew in which they are immersed.

This syncretism is the new religion that Elisabeth Schussler Fiorenza openly advocates. It constitutes variegated gnosticism for Catholics who never heard of gnosticism under its own label. She refers to her "Sophia-God" with feminine pronouns, and cites the heretical writings of ancient gnostics alongside Scriptural references, as though they were equally authoritative. In the present receptive social climate, her promotion of this gnostic vision may harm more young Catholics than her more ideologically conventional demands for feminist approved translations of Scripture and liturgy, or her vehement but duplicitous protests against exclusively male priesthood.

Those standard planks in the political edifice of feminism have slight appeal for lay Catholics. Most believers in the pews would prefer that there be no more tampering with the language of worship. As for the cause of women's ordination, Schussler Fiorenza revealed her distaste for it in her keynote address to the twentieth anniversary celebration of Women's Ordination Conference, in 1995, when she thundered, "Ordination means subordination!"

"The heart of the ordination rite is the promise of obedience," she warned. Instead of seeking "a piece of the clerical pie," she proposed that WOC should aim to transform society into a "discipleship of equals," where all the baptized will share priestly power. Her disavowal of ordination into what she calls "kyriarchy" was unanimously endorsed by the group's National Advisory Board, of which Schussler Fiorenza has long been a member. Nothing could reveal the fraudulent nature of religious feminism more clearly than this exploitation of a rejected cause.

The gnostic movement in the Church is not about God at all, nor about serving Jesus, nor about carrying one's cross. It is all about self, about seizing power and exacting vengeance. It is not religion but revolutionary politics. Yet as Eamonn Keane observes, the most notable characteristic of gnosticism has always been adaptability. Today, in what is in many ways a gnostic age, the greatest danger it presents is offering to answer the hunger for the spiritual with a false spirituality.

This book is exactly what has been needed for faithful Catholics in the field of religious education, who know something is wrong with the concepts they are encountering in certification classes, in-service programs, and in the materials they are given to use, but have not known how to identify and oppose those errors. It will be of inestimable value for those Catholics of good will who want to write specialized catechisms but are uncertain how to evaluate the concepts afloat in religious education these days. Eamonn Keane's analysis should be made as widely available as possible. The whole Church is in his debt.

Donna Steichen
Ojai, California

Donna Steichen is the author of *Ungodly Rage: The Hidden Face of Catholic Feminism* and *Prodigal Daughters: Catholic Women Come Home to the Church*, published by Ignatius Press.

INTRODUCTION

A Sorry and Sad Reminiscence of Thomas H. Groome

I can hardly believe that twenty-seven years have passed since the then Father Tom Groome came to visit me one beautiful summer evening in July at St. Joseph's Seminary, Dunwoodie. He had been introduced to me by one of the Auxiliary Bishops of the Archdiocese of New York. The stated purpose of the introduction was to elicit the possibility of Tom's serving as my assistant in the Department of Education in which I served as the Archdiocesan Director of the Office of Religious Education. Tom was working on a doctorate in Religious Education at the Union Theological Seminary in New York City.

Prior to his visit he had sent me a copy of his thesis outline which was aimed at translating Liberation Theology concerns into Catechetical methodology.

Being the son of Irish born parents, Limerick and Cavan, I naturally accorded Father Tom, himself a native born Irishman, a welcome befitting a Gael and a *Sagart a rúin* (Irish for 'a dear priest').

After exchanging pleasantries, we got down to a discussion of his thesis outline. He listened attentively as I attempted to convince him that what he was proposing had scant reference to what the Roman General Catechetical Directory of 1971 and the United States Bishops' document Basic Teachings for Religious Education of 1973 set forth as goals for the catechetical enterprise.

Our discussion went on for a good two and one-half hours until Tom let forth the following salvo: "You know, Michael, the problem with you is that you still believe in the myths which you learned when you sat on your father's knee and your mother's lap!"

I was really shocked by that remark which I will never forget. I replied, "That's blasphemy, Tom!" Besides the physical genes that we have inherited from our mother and father, there are also spiritual genes consisting of the religious inheritance handed down from one generation to the next – in this instance, for my parents, what they had learned from the Penny Catechism and during sacramental preparations by the Parish Priest in rural Ireland. My parents had indeed helped me to lisp my prayers, and later on during my adult years, what a joy it was when visiting them at home, to hear my Dad, sitting at the dining room table, early in the morning chanting, as it were, his favourite prayers from his particular breviary, **The Key of Heaven.**

I accompanied Father Groome down the empty corridors of St. Joseph's Seminary and bade him goodnight in the parking lot. As I made my way back to my quarters, I wondered what would come of Groome's efforts. I also concluded that the Auxiliary bishop who had recommended him to me must have done so without, at the time, realizing where Groome was coming from. Tom's charming ways and Irish wit were obviously what brought him to the attention of the good bishop.

Tom Groome would subsequently leave the priesthood, seek laicization and serve as a Professor of Religious Education at the Jesuit Boston College—*in direct contravention of the rescript for laicization which forbids former priests from teaching religion at any level!*

Groome and his ideas achieved tremendous success in the English speaking world largely due to his textbooks being published exclusively by the Sadlier Publishing Company of New York. Eamonn Keane's *A Generation Betrayed* is truly a superb critique of the pedagogical and theological ideas of Tom Groome. Eamonn has done us a great service. His mastery of Groome's content and methodology is, beyond a doubt, virtually on the same scholarly level as that of Father Donald Keefe, S.J., formerly professor of Dogma at Dunwoodie, who in 1992 wrote a shorter critique of Groome's *Christian Religious Education: Sharing Our Story and Vision* for the then Archbishop of Denver and now Curial Cardinal Francis Stafford. Allow me to whet your appetite for what will follow by quoting Father Keefe:

"Since its first publication a dozen years ago, this book has been widely used in Catholic catechetical formation, and has won for its author a prominent position among professional religious educators. This is an outcome more than unfortunate, for Groome's work betrays not so much the near-total ignorance of the Catholic Church which its cursory reading might suggest, but rather, a thoroughgoing strategy for the deconstruction of the *res Catholica*—a strategy whose success is now apparent in the freshmen classes of contemporary Catholic colleges and universities whose members display quite uniformly a complete unfamiliarity with, and frequently a disinterest in and disaffection from, the Catholic tradition in which they were for the most part reared. It is a consequence, which cannot be said to trouble Groome (218, 253). The finished product of Groome's version of religious education must typically evince a sublime ignorance of the historical particularity of Christianity and an inbred contempt for the claim of the historical Church to transcend 'historical conditioning' and the relativization of 'critical reflections'. Neither does this sorry outcome noticeably disturb Groome's equanimity, for from the stance of his educational theory, all of the doctrinal particularity once taught as integral to the historical Catholic tradition, insofar as undigested and unrelativized by *'shared praxis,'* is mere information, incapable of authentic assimilation by a free spirit apart from that critical reflection upon it which the *historical* concreteness of the res *Catholica* is *subordinated* to the absolute goal, the *'Vision' of an egalitarian utopia* whose intuitive and indeed ineffable clarity is the *telos* of all learning, the criterion of all truth. It is this flight from the historical particularity of the Catholic tradition that drives Groome's education-as-politics, controls its content, and defrauds his audience of their Catholic birthright.

"Groome and his disciples have long been active and worse, successful, in promoting this perversion of catechesis in Catholic precincts, to the point that some version of his 'shared praxis' is now normative for what most Catholic grammar, high school and college students learn from most Catholic catechists and religious educators. While this successful demolition of Catholic education reveals as much about the quality of the oversight maintained by the local ordinaries over Catholic education in their dioceses as it does about Groome, it is still worthwhile to detail his approach to religious education in order to make clear that it is a program for submitting the historical order of Catholic life and worship to a universal solvent, the teaching method which Groome trendily denominates 'shared praxis'.

"For 'praxis,' read idolatry of *method:* for 'shared,' read the mimetic servility which *idolatry* denotes. 'Shared praxis' is a programmatic return to the historical pessimism which relativizes all the historical mediation of God to man that is the historical worship of the historical Church; this 'praxis' consequently denies the significance of the ecclesial 'structure' which would stand in the way of the historical pessimism, the flight from historical particularity, that is inherent in idolatry as such. The way to this neopaganism was *charted by Hans Kung in On Being a Christian,* published some five years before Groome wrote his book which does little more than provide a concrete application of Kung's Hegelianism and its conjoined doctrinaire antisacramentalism."

An Official Committee of the United States Bishops recently confirmed what so many critics have said: that many popular Catholic texts are seriously at odds with the teachings of the Church. The Bishops' Ad Hoc Committee to oversee the use of the Catechism of the Catholic Church ticked off ten rather consistent deficiencies in Catechetical texts in use in the United States. What follows is taken directly from the report submitted to the US Bishops at their meeting in Kansas City in June 1997.

1. Insufficient attention to the Trinity and the Trinitarian structure of Catholic beliefs and teachings.

Relative to the Trinity, the texts fail most often in presenting it as the central mystery of the Christian faith. The intimate relationship and work of the Persons of the Trinity are not always presented clearly and consistently throughout the texts. The language used in referring to the Persons of the Trinity contributes at times to this lack of clarity. This is most evident in a recognized reluctance to use "Father" for the first person of the Trinity and, at times, to substitute "Parent God" for God the Father. Particularly, the relationship between Jesus and the Father is often weak. There are times where the word "God" is placed in a sentence where one would expect to find "Father" or "God the Father" since the reference is precisely to the relationship between first and second persons of the Trinity. Although the doctrine of the Trinity may be dutifully repeated throughout a series, it does not become the "inner life" or organizing principle of the texts.

2. Obscured presentation of the centrality of Christ in salvation history and insufficient emphasis on the divinity of Christ.

Texts fall short, at times, in presenting Jesus as the culmination of the Old Testament and fulfilment of God's plan for our salvation. The indispensable place of the Incarnation in the plan of salvation is not always sufficiently presented. Jesus as Saviour is often overshadowed by Jesus as teacher, model, friend, or brother.

Texts do not present the mystery of the Incarnation in its fullness. Often there appears to be an imbalance in the instruction on the divinity and humanity of Jesus Christ. There is present, at times, a negative undertone in speaking of the divine nature of Christ, as if divinity is equated with being "distant and unreal." The operative Christology "from below," which is evident in catechetical materials, needs balance in an equally positive reverence for divinity.

3. Indistinct treatment of the ecclesial context of Catholic beliefs and magisterial teachings.

Catechetical materials do not always clearly present the Church as established by Christ to continue both his presence and his work in the world. The teaching function of the Church and its apostolic nature, as well as the role of the hierarchy and the concept of the leadership of bishops and priests in teaching the Word of God are often under-treated.

The mark of unity in the Church is at times lost in a singular emphasis on the Church's catholicity and diversity.

4. Inadequate sense of a distinctively Christian anthropology.

By and large the catechetical texts do not seem to integrate the fundamental notions that man is by nature a religious being, that the desire for God is written in the human heart, that the human person is inherently spiritual and that man is irreducible to the merely material. Neither are the texts generally clear that it is precisely in Christ that man has been created in the image and likeness of God. Nor do they emphasise that Christ has restored to man the divine image of God, an image disfigured by sin. Rather, too often the impression is left that man is the first principle and final end of his own existence.

5. Insufficient emphasis on God's initiative in the world with a corresponding overemphasis on human action.

Texts do not always emphasise adequately that human action is intended to follow upon the priority of God's action and initiative in the world. When the methodological starting point is predominantly human experience, the texts at times easily leave the impression that human initiative is the prerequisite for divine action. God's initiative appears subordinate to human experience and human action.

6. Insufficient attention to the transforming effects of grace.

The catechetical texts do not seem to present a comprehensive understanding of grace. Once grace is described as God's love, usually not much more is said about it. That the preparation of man for the reception of grace is already a work of grace is not clearly presented. Grace is not generally treated as God's initiative which introduces humanity into the intimacy of Trinitarian life and makes us his adopted children and participants in his life. The texts are generally weak in treating the particular efficacy of the grace proper to the different sacraments.

7.   Inadequate presentation of the sacraments.

Catechetical texts most often do not treat the sacraments within the Paschal Mystery. They are not explicitly presented as the means by which the faithful share in the new life of Christ through the outpouring of the Holy Spirit. Sacraments are often presented as representative of events in human life of which God becomes a part, rather than signs and reality of divine life of which man becomes a part. This leads to a deficient understanding of the divine action and graced transformation that is at the heart of each of the sacraments. Particularly, the sacraments of Eucharist and Holy Orders evidence deficiency because the catechetical texts do not adequately present the character and role of the ordained minister in the life and ministry of the community.

8.   Deficient teaching on original sin and sin in general.

The texts do not clearly teach that original sin is the loss of original holiness and justice, transmitted by our first parents, and which wounds human nature in all people. How the doctrine of original sin informs our understanding of grace, baptism, human participation in sin, a world which continues to be broken and imperfect, redemption, and salvation is not often addressed. The texts need to speak of sin in a thematic way that presents the great struggle going on in the world and within each human heart - a struggle in which God's grace works within us to help us live more fully the new life we have received in the sacraments of initiation.

9.   Meagre exposition of Christian moral life.

At times there is an over-emphasis on personal identity and self-respect as if these were primary "sources" of morality. The source of morality found in God's revealed law, as taught by the Church and grounded in natural law, needs to be strengthened. Where texts could present the binding force of the Church's moral teaching in certain areas, they often do not. In addition, instruction on what is necessary for the formation of a correct conscience is at times inadequately, or even mistakenly, presented.

10. Inadequate presentation of eschatology.

The eschatological aspect of Catholic doctrine is often underemphasised. At times there is a negative lack of emphasis on the culmination of man's life in the eternal Kingdom of God coupled with a positive emphasis on the Kingdom of God as realizable in this world. The transcendent, trans-temporal and trans-historical nature of the Kingdom is not always present. The general judgement, the concept of hell, the eschatological dimensions of the Beatitudes, as well as the moral and sacramental orders, are not always adequately taught.

Results of surveys from various parts of the English-speaking world are now available which reveal a continuing decline in the practice of the faith by Catholics. This unfortunate state of affairs need not have happened if our Catholic faith, in all the splendour of its truth, had been properly and integrally communicated since the Second Vatican Council, the Extraordinary Synod of 1985 and, of course, the Catechism of the Catholic Church in English translation 8 years ago.

As far as I am concerned, Groome's pedagogical method of *shared praxis* which he developed in 1980 under the title *Christian Religious Education: Sharing Our Story and Vision* (Harper and Row, San Francisco 1980), was not based on any prior exhaustive educational research but only on a hunch. This is inconceivable methodologically in any accepted respectable field. Groome made no reference to any educational studies or research on which he might have attempted to validate his new method. This would be like a medical practitioner setting forth a new major medical innovation without ever having read the medical literature and without ever setting forth any medical empirical research to support his assertion. Or again, it is akin to a biblical scholar propounding a new Biblical method for interpretation but who apparently never read any other biblical scholars or their methods of interpretation.

As a keen observer of religious education for more than 30 years, I am emboldened to say that only in religious education can such a fly-by-night position be accepted by so many people and so uncritically throughout the English-speaking world.

Sad and sorry to say that Fr. Robert Drinan S.J, who finally was instructed by his Jesuit superiors with the acquiescence of the Holy See, to terminate his tenure in the Congress of the United States of America, is touted by Thomas Groome as a suitable model for a Grade 8 student research task on someone who is a "good Christian and citizen."

One wonders why Groome chose, in a Sadlier teachers manual, to weave a myth around this former member of the legislative branch of the Government of the United States. Would not Groome have known that Fr. Drinan consistently voted in favour of abortion legislation in this lower house of Congress?

While a member of this body, this Jesuit priest did more to cripple the Right To Life Movement in my country than most pro-abortion politicians. Out of office, Fr. Drinan saw fit to express approval for President Clinton's atrocious veto of a Bill that would have prohibited partial birth abortions.

As my revered Archbishop John Cardinal O Connor wrote and I quote: "I am deeply sorry, Fr. Drinan, but you're wrong. Dead wrong…you could have raised your formidable voice for life; you have raised it for death. Hardly the role of a lawyer. Surely not the role of a priest." The Archdiocesan paper of record of Fr. Drinan's Jesuit Province in New England, the *Boston Pilot,* called his stance, "shocking, schizophrenic, and even scandalous." *O Tempora, O Mores!*

It is my sincere hope that Eamonn Keane's exhaustive treatment of Groome's deconstruction of the faith which has had such an impact on religious education in Australia and elsewhere, not only by its content, but also by the deadly nature of its methodology will be studied far and wide beyond the Antipodes.

Please indulge me one final observation. I have been privileged to have lectured on two occasions in Australia and I remember that even before my first visit, I saw fit to write to James Cardinal Freeman, prior to his retirement, regarding the number of Australian priests and religious who were being educated at schools of religious education in the United States. I had observed these students at various conferences and seminars back in the Seventies and was startled at how readily they engaged in anti-Roman and anti-papal statements during the course of these events - these sentiments reflecting what their professors, in many cases former priests and religious, were teaching them. Sad to say, I received a reply from a priest-secretary, on his staff, acknowledging merely the reception of the letter by the late Eminence.

Again, it is my prayer and earnest best wish that Eamonn Keane's efforts in this masterful expose of the errors of Thomas H. Groome will

serve the truly worthwhile goals and outcomes in the catechetical task—
the methodology of which is meant to introduce and sustain Jesus as our
Way, our Truth and our Life!

**Rev. Msgr. Michael J. Wrenn, K.C.H.S., M.A., M.S.,
D.H.L.,S.T.D. (Honoris Causa)
Chevalier of the French Republic in the Order of Academic
Palms
Honorary Fellow of the Maryvale Institute of Religious Studies,
Birmingham, England
Dean of the Institute of Religious Studies,
St. Joseph's Seminary Dunwoodie,
Yonkers, New York**

Rev. Msgr. Michael Wrenn is the author of *Catechisms and Controversies*, co-author of
Flawed Expectations: The Reception of the Catechism of the Catholic Church published by Ignatius
Press. He was the founding Director of The Institute of Religious Studies begun in 1977 at
the direction of the Servant of God, Terence Cardinal Cooke.

1

Introducing Groome and Fiorenza

The *Instrumentum Laboris* (working document) for the Special Assembly of the Synod of Bishops for Oceania, which took place in Rome during November-December 1998, drew attention to concerns amongst Catholics for the state of Catholic education today. It stated that "teachers in Catholic schools often have lives or ideas that are publicly in conflict with church teaching"—something which it said is "a counter-sign" to the Church's witness and which "can be truly harmful for youth."[1] Other problems referred to in the *Instrumentum Laboris* included the difficulty faced by the Church in attracting young people, the challenges within the Church to the teaching of the Magisterium, confusion regarding the teaching of Vatican II, decline in sacramental practice and poor understanding of the Church's teaching on the sanctity of life.

The concerns listed above regarding Catholic education extend beyond Oceania to the entire English-speaking world. They strongly suggest that there is need for a thorough appraisal of catechetical and religious education methodologies and programs currently in use. Such an appraisal should seek to identify the theological underpinnings of such methodologies and programs with a view to discerning the degree to which they further the mission of the Church or whether they undermine it by serving as instruments for the propagation of ideologies hostile to Catholic doctrine. In this context, the purpose of this book is to draw attention to the danger of having the catechetical function of the Church in Australia and in other English-speaking countries subverted by the heavy reliance of some Catholic educators on the catechetical and theological ideas of Thomas Groome and Elisabeth Schussler Fiorenza.

Groome is a Professor of theology and religious education at Boston College, while Fiorenza is a Professor of Divinity at the Harvard Divinity School. Earlier in her career, Fiorenza was Professor of New Testament Studies and Theology at the Catholic University of Notre Dame in the United States. Both Groome and Fiorenza have a long history of dissent from the teaching of the Church's Magisterium.[2] When Pope John Paul II issued his apostolic letter *Ad Tuendam Fidem* (To Defend the Faith)—which authorised changes to the Code of Canon Law which the Holy Father said were necessary "to protect the faith of the Catholic Church against errors arising from certain members of the Christian faithful, especially from among those dedicated to the various disciplines of sacred theology."[3] Groome responded disparagingly to this Magisterial intervention by saying, "It's a pretentious attempt by the present pope to stifle conversation and dialogue." Having said this, he added, "I read the blessed thing and without being too melodramatic, I was on the verge of tears. It is a very sad day."[4]

Groome's disparaging comments about *Ad Tuendam Fidem* are not surprising given his track record of opposition to interventions by the Magisterium in the life of the Universal Church. For example, after the decision to produce the *Catechism of the Catholic Church (CCC)* was announced in 1985,[5] Groome protested that the decision to produce such a document "violates all the insights we've learned in psychology, anthropology (and other disciplines) over the last 100 years." Further to this, he stated that such a *Catechism* would be "totally contrary to church doctrine over the last 20 years" and he added that the decision to produce it was a political ploy to advance a conservative cause.[6] When the English translation of the *Catechism* was eventually produced, Groome noted, "with great regret," the fact that that the *Catechism* "does not reflect commitment to inclusive language."[7]

Fiorenza's response to *Ad Tuendam Fidem* echoed Groome's. She said, "Catholic theology had just gained some stature as an intellectual discipline. Now we'll go back to the old stereotype that Catholics can't think on their own."[8] In her keynote address to the annual gathering of *Call to Action* in the U.S. in late 1998, Fiorenza stated that *Ad Tuendam*

Fidem sought "to eliminate the remnants of the lawful freedom of inquiry, and the freedom to express it, that still exists in Catholic institutions."[9] She stated that this "papal decree attempts to silence women's claim to full membership of the church once and for all" and that it "reminds one of Dostoevsky's Grand Inquisitor, who must silence Jesus because of his own fear and lack of faith."[10] Further to this, Fiorenza added: "The language of the Inquisition, threatening penalization and expulsion from the church...is at work again in this apostolic letter. As the pope apologizes for the killing of witches several hundred years ago, the Vatican uses the same measures of silencing and exclusion against women today."[11]

Fiorenza also used her keynote address to the *Call to Action* gathering in 1998 to attack the teaching of the Magisterium regarding the hierarchical nature of the Church as something that is of Divine origin. She said, "The notion of the church as monarchical and hierarchical entered only when the church became Roman." It is ironic, she said, "that in defense of the Roman imperial structures—which, we may not forget, had crucified Jesus—the hierarchy has insisted that the church is not a democratic community."[12] Articulating her own vision of the Church as "a discipleship of equals," Fiorenza said: "We are the people of God made in her [sic] image and likeness. We are church. We are neither clergy, hierarchy and people, religious and secular. We are the people of God."[13] She added that, "in this struggle over the future of the church, understood either as a discipleship of equals or as the embodiment of the Grand Inquisition, we the people have an important role to play."[14]

Casting herself in the role of a champion of the poor, she went on to say, "At stake here are two different visions of faith. The church of Caesar—that means the Roman Caesar—powerful and rich, and the Church of Christ, loving, poor and spiritually rich."[15] Then, in a calling for a campaign of disobedience within the Church, Fiorenza said:

> We must not forget that we hold the power of the people. If we refuse consent to dominative teachings, the Vatican bureaucracy loses its power of control. Since ecclesiastic leadership has no longer the power of the state, it has only as much power as we the faithful grant to it. Without obedience, rules have no force; without the people of God, there is no church. Accordingly,

obedience should be put under the other sins we must avoid as much as possible.[16]

As well as being a militant pro-abortionist, Fiorenza rejects parts of Sacred Scripture and asserts that women should have access to all ministries in the Church including that of bishop and Pope. The fact that she has used passages from St. Mattew's Gospel in an attempt to lend a spiritual gloss to her trenchant support for abortion on demand,[17] has not in the least deterred Groome from referring to her as a "great Scripture scholar."[18]

Indeed, many of Groome's theological ideas appear to have been heavily influenced by Fiorenza's feminist theology of liberation. For example, Groome agrees with Fiorenza that the Catholic Church's refusal to admit women to the ranks of the ministerial priesthood is inherently 'unjust' and 'oppressive.' Coupled with this, Groome contradicts the teaching of the Magisterium that Christ instituted the male-only ministerial priesthood as one of the Church's constituent elements which is inextricably linked to its hierarchical structure.

Praise and Criticism for Groome

Shared Christian Praxis is the name Groome gives to his catechetical method which he has developed in several books. He first rose to international prominence with the publication in 1980, of his book, *Christian Religious Education: Sharing Our Story and Vision.*[19] Reviewing this book at the time of its publication, James Fowler stated that it was "likely to be the most significant single book in the field of Christian education for the next twenty years."[20] Professor John H. Westerhoff referred to *Christian Religious Education* as "a pioneering work of enduring significance by one of the most fertile minds in the field."[21]

Praising Groome's 1991 book titled *Sharing Faith,* Fr Richard McBrien, author of the controversial work *Catholicism,* said, "Thomas Groome is, in my judgement, the leading religious education theorist in the United States."[22] Iris V. Scully, editor of the *Encyclopedia of Religious Education,* in reviewing Groome's *Sharing Faith* said, "With this book, Thomas Groome has established himself as the leading theorist in religious education today."[23]

Sharing Faith received first place in the Catholic Press Association Awards for 1992. In reference to Groome's 1998 work titled *Educating for Life,* Rev. Theodore M. Hesburgh, President Emeritus of the University of Notre Dame in the U.S. said: *"Educating for Life* addresses the very soul of educators, it will inspire every teacher and parent. Written with ecumenical sensitivity by one of America's leading religious educators...This humanizinng proposal for education in our time is 'Catholic' in the richest sense of the term."[24]

While much of the case-study material to be cited in this book to illustrate the inadequacies of Groome's pedagogical method is drawn from the Australian scene, this fact should not, however, be seen as suggesting that Groome has less influence in the U.S. than he has in Australia. His pervasive influence in the U.S. is indicated by the fact that the catechetical establishment in that country has in recent times bestowed on him the highest awards it has to offer.

In 1997, the National Conference of Catechetical Leadership (NCCL) in the U.S. presented Groome with a special award for his work in catechesis. In a report on the granting of this award the *Boston College Chronicle* said:

> The NCCL is composed of bishops, pastors, diocesan and parish directors of religious education, scholars and publishers of catechetical materials. Among its activities, the NCCL is helping develop a set of performance standards to be used in certifying training programs for directors of religious education. Groome has authored several religious textbook series and is a national recognised authority on catechetics.[25]

In 2000, Groome was awarded the highest honour in the field of religious education in the U.S. when the National Association of Parish Catechetical Directors chose him to receive its Emmaus Award for Excellence in Catechesis 2000. According to a report in the *Boston College Chronicle*, this National Association of Parish Cathechetical Directors is "comprised of all parish-level religious education directors in the U.S., and under sponsorship of the U.S. Catholic Bishops."[26]

In Australia, Sr. Patricia Malone, Associate Professor of Religious Education at the Australian Catholic University in Sydney, has revealed that, "a number of key personnel in the Sydney Catholic Education Office studied under Groome at Boston College."[27] The Diocese of Parramatta in New South Wales has been working with Groome's *Shared Christian Praxis* for the last ten years and its diocesan religious education curriculum, *Sharing Our Story,* is explicitly based on it. This *Sharing Our Story* curriculum is used also in other Australian dioceses including Canberra-Goulburn and Wilcannia-Forbes.

A 1997 article co-authored by members of the Religious Education Department of the Parramatta Catholic Education Office stated that *Shared Christian Praxis* is "by far the most admirable faith forming religious education model available today because of its educational and theological precision."[28] This same article called for professional development of teachers which would allow them to undertake an "implementation" of *shared Christian praxis* which would be "faithful to Groome's thinking."[29] These authors also pointed out that Groome's method has been "highly influential" in the development of religious education curriculum in Victoria, Tasmania, South Australia and the Northern Territory.

Maurice Ryan, Head of the Department of Religious Education at the Australian Catholic University in Queensland, in speaking of Groome's work said, "The *shared Christian praxis* approach was one of the most significant developments in catechesis in the 1980s." Having said this, Ryan added:

> I will add my voice to the chorus of approval for Groome's approach: I agree with the Parramatta authors that it is the most admirable faith forming approach which exists today. When direct nurture of Christian faith is the goal of the Church's ministerial efforts, one should look no further than Groome's approach.[30]

In contrast to the praise lavished on Groome by those cited above, some commentators in the United States have expressed serious concerns about Groome's theology and pedagogical method. For example, in 1992 a blistering critique of Groome's *Christian Religious Education* was written by Fr. Donald Keefe, S.J., who at the time was serving as theological consultant to Archbishop (now Cardinal) Stafford in the Archdiocese of Denver. In his critique of Groome's work, Fr. Keefe said:

> Groome's work betrays not so much a near-total ignorance of the Catholic Church which its cursory reading might suggest,

but rather a thorough-going strategy for the deconstruction of the *res Catholica*...[The] historical concreteness of the *res Catholica* is subordinated to the absolute goal, the 'Vision' of an egalitarian utopia...It is this flight from the historical particularity of the Catholic tradition that drives Groome's education as politics, controls its content, and defrauds his students of their birthright."[3z]

In his review of *Christian Religious Education,* Fr. Keefe said that Groome had, "concocted his system from a mix of left-wing Hegelianism, a variant of Piaget's epistemology of the sort made familiar in the seventies by Laurence Kohlberg...and a liberation theology version of radical social criticism dependent upon Freire."[32] Fr. Keefe was particularly concerned to draw attention to what he saw as Groome's rejection "of the objectively and historically efficacious realism of Catholic sacramental worship"—something which he concluded "can hardly be other than deliberate"—given Groome's "training for and ordination to the Catholic priesthood."[33]

In this work, I will not traverse the ground already covered by Fr. Keefe in his critique of *Christian Religious Education.* Instead, I will base my critique of Groome's work almost exclusively on books he had published in the 1990s.

Praise for Fiorenza

In its review of Fiorenza's book *Bread Not Stone,* the New York Times said: "Elisabeth Schussler Fiorenza stands among the most articulate and respected theologians who have challenged the silence and marginality that have characterised the great majority of Christian women for nearly 2000 years."[34]

Much of the theological writing that has appeared in Australia in recent times contains references to the work of Fiorenza. In his book *Introducing Contemporary Theologies,* Neil Ormerod, who is Dean of Studies at the Centre for Spirituality (Sydney), devotes an entire chapter to Fiorenza whom he introduces as "a key figure within Feminist Theology."[35] Fiorenza was invited to write the 'Foreword' to a 1995 book titled *Freedom & Entrapment* which is a compilation of essays by various Australian religious feminists. A reading of this book indicates that Fiorenza has exercised a significant influence over many of the contributing authors.[36] In her 1997 book titled *Woman: Why Are You Weeping,* Margaret Mills reveals how many of the religious feminists who have infiltrated the Catholic education bureaucracy in South Australia have drawn heavily on the theological ideas of Fiorenza in developing their own deconstructionist ideas about the Catholic Church.[37]

A 1998 book titled *An Introduction to Catholic Theology,* produced by staff of the Catholic Institute of Sydney, cites examples from Fiorenza's work in order to illustrate the *'rhetorical approach'* to the interpretation of Sacred Scripture.[38] In a 1998 article titled *Feminism As A Liberating Theology,* Fr. Martin Kelly, M.S.C. follows Fiorenza in asserting that "the early Church flourished where it was marked by a discipleship of equals."[39] He states that "radical feminism" with its concern for "egalitarianism" makes possible "full humanity," and that "feminism mirrors the inclusive notion of the discipleship of equals typical of the early Jesus movement, and of Jesus' praxis." Fr. Kelly went on in typical Fiorenza-style to call on the Church to undertake a "thoroughgoing critique of its praxis and the false image of reality it legitimates by its own structures."[40] Following this, Fr. Kelly added, "The Church's 'official' theology excludes too much of people's lived reality and the faith experience of its members."[41]

An ardent disciple of Fiorenza in Australia is Sr. Elaine Wainwright, who until recently was Professor of Scripture at the Banyo Catholic Seminary in Queensland. Speaking of how she sees Fiorenza's place in the history of feminist theology, Wainwright says:

> At this point in the history of the *ekklesia* of women or Women-Church, the name Elisabeth Schussler Fiorenza is a 'household' word. She has provided us with language, with models and frameworks and with images and metaphors that have provoked and challenged, guided and supported our biblical and theological undertakings.[42]

Wainwright spent a sabbatical year in 1994 doing research at the Harvard Divinity School where Fiorenza is a Professor. In 1995, Wainwright coordinated Fiorenza's Australian lecture tour. On arriving in Sydney to deliver a public lecture at Santa Sabina College in Strathfield, Fiorenza described Pope John Paul II as "a child of his own culture, which was a Stalinistic culture, which essentially meant you had no freedom of speech."[43] Wainwright's 1998 book, titled *Shall We Look for Another: A Feminist Rereading of the Matthean Jesus,* is revealing in that it illustrates the extent to which its author's theological perceptions have been influenced by Fiorenza who is frequently cited as a substantiating authority for various contentious theological positions taken by Wainwright herself.[44]

Fiorenza also looms large in some catechetical texts published by Australian religious educators. For example, in a 1993 book on religious education, Kevin Treston, who lectures at the Australian Catholic University in Brisbane and who has had much to do with the inservicing of religious education teachers across the nation, posited that women theologians such as "Elisabeth Schussler Fiorenza are beginning to restore balance to a theology that was previously written from a male perspective."[45] In this book, the 'Foreword' to which was written by Thomas Groome, Treston went on to assert that "the Christian Churches, reflecting the sexual patterns of the cultural environment, have engaged in institutionalised discrimination against women through their structures and ministry." Having said this, Treston repeated an opinion very dear to Fiorenza which is that, "the radical vision of Jesus toward women was quickly lost in the primal Christian communities."[46]

In the 1993 book referred to above, Treston cast doubt on whether or not Jesus actually founded the Church. He said: "Scripture Scholars debate whether Jesus actually founded a church. What we are certain of is that he preached the reign of God and gathered a community of disciples to announce the good news of salvation."[47] He added that, "the only 'structure' initiated by Jesus was the institution of the twelve, and this structure disappeared after the death of Stephen."[48] Treston also asserted that "in the fourth century, the priesthood emerged from the office of the presbyter."[49] In his 'Foreword' to this book, Groome expressed the view that with its publication, Treston was making "a mighty contribution" to the "ongoing faith development of our catechists and teachers."[50]

In a book published in 2000 entitled *Visioning A Future Church,* Treston, after first stating that "the so-called 'shortage of priests' today is in reality a shortage of Roman flexibility in restoring the first traditions in the church about who presides over the Eucharist,"[51] went on to add that "Elisabeth Schussler Fiorenza reminds us how women worked alongside men as equal partners in early Christian ventures such as founding and leading churches."[52] He said that the Church's "credibility to speak on questions of justice is compromised" as long as it "continues to institutionalise sexism in its leadership structures,"[53] and added that he had "no doubt that ordination of women will eventually happen."[54] Finally, Treston asserted that "Catholic theology teaches that a sign of authentic teaching by the magisterium is when this teaching is accepted by the faithful" and that the same principle applies to "authoritative decisions" which he said "become effective only when they are received by the faithful."[55] As we will see in Chapter 5, this is a serious error which in a slightly different form has been widely propagated also by Groome.

Reference

1   Synod of Bishops—Special Assembly for Oceania, *Instrumentum Laboris*, n. 26. The *Instrumentum Laboris* was based on responses by Bishops, Church-based organisations and individual members of the laity to the Lineamenta (discussion document) for the Synod.

2   The word *Magisterium* refers to the office of teaching inscribed in the Church by Christ. This office is exercised by the Pope and the Bishops in communion with him when they act as teachers and preachers of the truths of faith and morals. The *Catechism of the Catholic Church* refers to the Magisterium's role in the life of the Church as follows: "The mission of the Magisterium is linked to the definitive nature of the covenant established by God with his people in Christ. It is this Magisterium's task to preserve God's people from deviations and defections and to guarantee them the objective possibility of professing the true faith without error. Thus, the pastoral duty of the Magisterium is aimed at seeing to it that the People of God abides in the truth that liberates" (n. 890).

3   Pope John Paul II, *Ad Tuendam Fidem* (Introduction).

4   Thomas H Groome, *The Wanderer*, July 16, 1998.

5   The *Catechism of the Catholic Church* owes its origin to a resolution of the Extraordinary Synod of Bishops in 1985. The Synod was convoked to commemorate the Second Vatican Council and to study its teachings in order to better adhere to and promote them in the Universal Church. In this context, the Synod Fathers expressed grave concern about the state of catechesis in the Church and about new difficulties which had arisen regarding the transmission of the faith to new generations. The Synod adopted a proposal by Cardinal Bernard Law of Boston for the publication of a catechism or compendium of Catholic teachings for the universal Church. Pope John Paul II interpreted the request by the Synod for a Catechism of the Universal Church as being expressive of a desire "acutely perceived in the whole Church, for greater clarity and doctrinal certainty in order to put an end to

teachings or interpretations of faith and morals that do not agree among themselves or with the universal Magisterium" (*L'Osservatore Romano*, July 7, 1986).

6   Thomas Groome, *National Catholic Reporter,* December 27, 1985.

7   Thomas Groome, Language for a Catholic Church, Sheed & Ward, Kansas City 1995, p. 37.

8   Elisabeth Schussler Fiorenza, The Wanderer, July 16, 1998.

9   Elisabeth Schussler Fiorenza, National Catholic Reporter, November 13, 1998, p. 7.

10 Ibid.

11 Ibid.

12 Elisabeth Schussler Fiorenza, *National Catholic Reporter,* November 13, 1998, p. 6.

13 Ibid.

14 Ibid. p. 7.

15 Ibid.

16 Ibid.

17 Cf. Elisabeth Schussler Fiorenza, *Discipleship of Equals: A Critical Feminist Ecclesiology of Liberation*, Crossroad, New York, 1993, p. 50.

18 Thomas Groome, *Educating For Life: A Spiritual Vision for Every Teacher and Parent,* Thomas More, RCL Company, Allen, Texas 1998, p. 185.

19 Thomas H. Groome, *Christian Religious Education: Sharing Our Story and Vision*, Harper & Row, San Francisco 1980.

20 James Fowler, front cover of *Christian Religious Education.*

21 John H. Westerhoff, back cover of *Christian Religious Education.*

22 This comment by Fr. McBrien appears in the list of reviews on the back cover of Thomas Groome's *Sharing Faith: A Comprehensive Approach to Religious Education & Pastoral Ministry,* Harper, San Francisco 1991.

23 Iris V. Scully, back cover of *Sharing Faith,* op. cit.

24 See back cover of Educating for Life, op. cit.

25 *Boston College Chronicle*, May 8, 1997 Vol. 5. No. 17

26 *Boston College Chronicle*, February 18, 1999, Vol. 7, No. 11.

27 Sr. Patricia Malone and Maurice Ryan, *Sound The Trumpet: Planning and Teaching Religion in the Catholic Primary School*, Social Science Press, Wentworth Falls (NSW) 1994, p. 54.

28 Michael Bezzina, Peter Gahan, Helen McLenaghan, Greg Wilson, *Shared Christian Praxis as a Basis for Religious Education*, Word of Life, Journal of Religious Education, Australian Catholic University, ACT, Vol. 45(3), 1997, p. 3.

29 Ibid. p 11.

30 Maurice Ryan, *Shared Christian Praxis: A Response to the Parramatta Experience,* Word in Life, Journal of Religious Education, Vol. 45 (3) 1997, pp. 12–13.

31 Fr Donald Keefe, S.J., *Critique* of Thomas H. Groome's *Christian Religious Education*, Archdiocese of Denver, December 1992. Fr Keefe now teaches at Dunwoody Seminary in New York.

32 Ibid.

33 Ibid.

34 Back cover of *Bread Not Stone: The Challenge of Feminist Biblical Interpretation*, Beacon Press, Boston 1984.

35 Neil Ormerod, *Introducing Contemporary Theologies: The What and the Who of Theology Today*, E.J. Dwyer, Sydney 1997, p. 165

36 *Freedom & Entrapment: Women Thinking Theology*, edited by Maryanne Confoy et al., Dove Publications, Victoria, Australia 1995.

37 Margaret E. Mills, *Woman: Why Are You Weeping,* News Weekly Books, Melbourne 1997, p. 108–109.

38 *An Introduction to Catholic Theology*, edited by Richard Lennan, Paulist Press, New York 1998, pp. 101–102 notes 10 and 11.

39 Fr Martin Kelly, M.S.C., *Feminism As A Liberating Theology*, published in *Compass: A Review of Topical Theology,* Vol. 32, Autumn 1998, p. 13. From the bibliography and footnoted references given in this article, the heavy influence of Fiorenza on the author's theological ideas is apparent.

40 Ibid. pp. 15–16.

41 Ibid. p. 16.

42 Elaine Wainwright, reviewing one of Fiorenza's books in *Women-Church 15: An Australian Journal of Feminist Studies in Religion*, August 1994, p. 42.

43 Elisabeth Schussler Fiorenza, reported in Sydney Morning Herald, August 23, 1995.

44 Elaine Wainwright, *Shall We Look for Another: A Feminist Rereading of the Matthean Jesus,* Orbis Books, Maryknoll, New York 1998.

45 Kevin Treston, A New Vision of *Religious Education: Theory, History, Practice, and Spirituality for DREs, Catechists, and Teachers,* Twenty-Third Publications, Connecticut 1993, p. 14.

46 Ibid.

47 Ibid. p. 63.

48 Ibid. p. 64.

49 Ibid.

50 Ibid. p. vi.

51 Kevin Treston, Visioning A Future Church, Creation Enterprises, Samford, Queensland, 2000, p. 80

52 Ibid. p. 83

53 Ibid.

54 Ibid. p. 87

55 Ibid. p.94

2

The Authoritative Interpretation
of Divine Revelation

Before going on in subsequent chapters to outline some of the philosophical and theological underpinnings of Groome's and Fiorenza's work as a prelude to an analysis of their methodologies, I will first set out in this chapter what I understand by the term *Divine Revelation* and how God has made provision for its authoritative interpretation. It is necessary to do this since later in this work I will be endeavouring to show that many of Groome's and Fiorenza's attacks on Catholic doctrine stem from a repudiation by them of the Catholic understanding of Divine Revelation and the role of the Magisterium in interpreting it authoritatively.

The Word of God

In a reaffirmation of the teaching of previous councils, the Council of Trent stated that the revealed truths of faith and morals are contained in "written books and in unwritten traditions that the apostles received from Christ himself or that were handed on...from the apostles under the inspiration of the Holy Spirit."[1] Reaffirming the teaching of the councils of Trent and Vatican I, the Second Vatican Council stated: "Sacred Tradition and Sacred Scripture make up a single sacred deposit of the Word of God which is entrusted to the Church. By adhering to it the entire holy people, united to its pastors, remains always faithful to the teaching of the apostles...."[2] The contents of Sacred Scripture and Sacred Tradition is also known as the "Deposit of Faith."[3]

According to Vatican II, Sacred Scripture "is the speech of God as it is put down in writing under the inspiration of the Holy Spirit."[4] In reference to Sacred Tradition, Vatican II stated: "To the successors of the apostles, sacred tradition hands on in its full purity God's word, which was entrusted to the apostles by Christ the Lord and the Holy Spirit. Thus, led by the light of the Spirit of truth, these successors can in their preaching preserve this Word of God faithfully, explain it, and make it more widely known."[5]

Accentuating the link that necessarily exists between Sacred Scripture and Sacred Tradition, the Council stated that the Church "does not derive her certainty about all revealed truths from the Holy Scriptures alone" but rather that "Scripture and Tradition must be accepted and honoured with equal sentiments of devotion and reverence."[6]

In view of the conflicting interpretations that arise regarding the meaning of the Word of God (Divine Revelation), how is one to discern truth from falsehood? The resolution of this question becomes imperative once one accepts that truth does in fact exist and that it is discernible in stages. In consequence of this, does not the very nature of Divine Revelation demand the presence in the world of an authoritative interpreter? In the event of there being no such authoritative interpreter of the Word of God present in the world, i.e. if the final court of appeal as to the substance of Divine Revelation is the partial and subjective understanding of the individual Christian, then how can such a person "make sure" that he or she is "in the faith" (2 Cor 13:5)? In such an event, who is to decide which of the conflicting interpretations are to be held by members of the Church so that together they will be "united in their convictions" with "a common purpose and common mind" (Phil 2:2)? If there is no authoritative interpreter of Divine Revelation present in the Church established by Christ, then there is nothing to prevent it distintegrating under the weight of a plurality of subjective and conflicting interpretations of the the contents of the Deposit of Faith.

'Thou art Peter and on this Rock I will Build My Church'

The question of teaching authority in the Church has been answered by Christ himself. In committing His Word to the Church, Christ gave Peter and the other Apostles the authority of office that was necessary for them to teach the truths of faith and morality in such a way as to command assent: "All authority in heaven and on earth has been given to me. Go therefore and make disciples of all nations... teaching them to observe all that I have commanded you" (Mt 28: 19-20).

The authority which Jesus bestowed on the Apostles as a group does not exist independently of the special authority he bestowed on Peter, the head of the group. In order that his Church would have one visible head and centre of unity, Jesus established Peter as the "rock" foundation upon which the Church is built. All the major strands of the New Testament—Synoptic, Johannine and Pauline—point in various ways to the primacy of Peter in the group of the Apostles.[7] Here, I will touch but briefly on a few of the perspectives which the New Testament offers on the special place of Peter in Jesus' plan for his Church.

In St. Matthew's Gospel, at a place called Caesarea Philippi, Jesus follows up his question "Who do people say that the Son of Man is?" (Mt 16: 13) with a more direct question addressed to the apostles: "But who do you say that I am?" (Mt 16: 15). The Gospel recounts that Simon responded in the name of the Twelve by saying: "You are the Christ, the Son of the living God" (Mt 16: 13-16). The *CCC* says that it was "on the rock of this faith confessed by St. Peter" that "Christ built his Church."[8] In accepting Simon's answer as true, Jesus attributed his insight to a special revelation from the heavenly Father: "Blessed are you Simon, son of Jonah. For flesh and blood has not revealed this to you but my heavenly Father" (Mt 16: 17). After thus acknowledging the origin of Simon's response, Jesus went on to say:

> And so I say to you: You are Peter, and on this rock I will build my Church, and the gates of the underworld will not prevail against it. I will give you the keys of the kingdom of heaven: whatever you bind on earth shall be considered bound in heaven; whatever you loose on earth shall be considered loosed in heaven." (Mt 16: 18-19).

The expression—"I say to you"—in the passage from St. Matthew's Gospel quoted above indicates that the power conferred by Christ on Peter "involves Jesus' sovereign authority" and that "it is a word of revelation in that it accomplishes what it says."[9] The new name given to Simon—*Kephas* in Aramaic and *Petros* in Greek—both mean "rock." Jesus' decision to give Simon this new name is indicative of his intention to confer on Peter a new mission. In commenting on the words Jesus addresses here to Simon Peter, Pope John Paul II said:

> Those words attest to Jesus' will to build his Church with an essential reference to the specific mission and power that in due time he would confer on Simon. Jesus described Simon Peter as the foundation on which the Church would be built. The Christ–Peter relationship is thus reflected in the Peter–Church relationship.[10]

Of great significance for understanding the Christ–Peter–Church relationship is the promise by Jesus to bestow on Peter the "keys of the kingdom of heaven." In biblical terms, it is the Messiah who possesses the keys of the kingdom. The Book of Revelation reproduces expressions from the prophet Isaiah in order to present Christ as "the holy one, the true, who holds the key of David, who opens and no one shall close, who closes and no one shall open." (Rev 3:7).

According to the *CCC,* the "power of the keys" bestowed by Christ on Peter "designates authority to govern the house of God, which is the Church," while the power to "bind and loose" connotes "the authority to absolve sins, to pronounce doctrinal judgements, and to make disciplinary decisions in the Church."[11] The *CCC* adds that Jesus entrusted this authority to the Church "through the ministry of the apostles and in particular through the ministry of Peter, the only one to whom he specifically entrusted the keys of the kingdom."[12]

At the Last Supper, after foretelling Peter's triple denial, Jesus went on to say to him: "Simon, Simon, behold Satan has demanded to sift all of you like wheat, but I have prayed that your own faith may not fail, and once you have turned back, you must strengthen your brothers" (Lk 22: 31-32). Peter needs Christ's prayer not only in view of the trial he will face later that night when he will deny Christ, but also later on when at times he will be led by the Holy Spirit to "strengthen his brothers" in the faith.

While in its immediate setting, Christ's mandate to Peter to "strengthen the brothers" refers to his duty in regards to the other apostles, in the broader context of the development of the Church it applies to the whole Christian community. We see this clearly in the account of the Council of Jerusalem given in the Acts of the Apostles. The Council was called to resolve a dispute over whether or not certain demands of the Jewish law were binding on converts to Christianity. Paul and Barnabas found themselves locked in debate with converted Pharisees, who argued that converts from paganism had to be circumcised. After the discussion, Peter stood up and stated his support for the position of Paul and Barnabas. This intervention by St. Peter was decisive in that it determined the outcome of the Council. St. Luke tells us that it was after Peter's speech to the Council that "the whole community fell silent, and they listened while Barnabas and Paul described the signs and wonders God had worked among the Gentiles through them." (Acts 5: 12). James, in his concluding address to the Council, alligned himself with Peter's judgement.

Speaking of the way Peter's intervention at the Council of Jerusalem settled a dispute over the proper direction for the Church to follow, Pope John Paul II said: "His [Peter's] authority thus played a decisive role in resolving an essential question for the Church's development and for the unity of the Christian community. The person and mission of Peter in the early Church are situated in this light."[13]

In giving His apostles the mandate to preach the Gospel throughout the world (cf. Mt 28: 19-20), Christ also promised them His Spirit to guide them "into all the truth" (Jn 16:13). It is only by the Apostles remaining in the truth that Christ's prayer for them at the Last Supper will be fulfilled: "That they may all be one. As you, Father, are in me and I am in you, may they also be one in us, so that the world may believe that you sent me" (Jn 17:21).

St. John tells us that Jesus after his Resurrection conferred on Peter the mandate to shepherd the Church: "Feed my lambs...Feed my sheep" (Jn 21: 15-17). Here, Jesus was confirming the promise He had made earlier to Peter at Caesarea Philippi (cf. Mt 16: 18-19). From all of this we see that Jesus established Peter as the visible head and centre of unity in the group of the apostles and thereby constituted him as Universal Shepherd of his Church.

By inscribing supreme authority over the whole Church in the office of Peter, Jesus was thus guaranteeing that His Church would remain forever in the truth delivered once and for all to the Apostles. In times of controversy regarding the content of divine revelation and all that pertains to it, Peter will have the authority to speak on behalf of Christ in such vein so as to "strengthen his brothers" in the truth that has been revealed once and for all (cf. Lk 10:16; 22:32).

The Catholic Church is apostolic, which means it is built on the lasting foundation of "the twelve apostles of the Lamb" (Rev 21:14).[14] The office of the apostles and that of Peter, their head, continues in the Church. Referring to this, Vatican II said: "Just as the office which the Lord confided to Peter alone, as first of the apostles, destined to be transmitted to his successors, is a permanent one, so also endures the office, which the apostles received, of shepherding the Church, a charge destined to be exercised without interruption by the sacred order of bishops."[15] The *CCC* says that the Church is kept faithful to the deposit of faith because "she is upheld infallibly in the truth" by Christ who "governs her through Peter and the other apostles, who are present in their successors, the Pope and the college of bishops."[16]

From what has been said above, it is clear that the task of authoritatively interpreting the contents of the deposit of faith has been entrusted by God to the Magisterium of the Church. Speaking of this, the *CCC* says: "The task of interpreting the Word of God authentically has been entrusted solely to the Magisterium of the Church, that is, to the Pope and to the bishops in communion with him."[17]

As was the case with Peter within the group of the apostles, the Pope as a member of the college of bishops always remains the Vicar of Christ. Speaking of this, Cardinal Charles Journet said: "Supreme authority over the universal Church rests wholly in the Sovereign Pontiff alone, and its exercise is therefore *personal*...The Pope is the Vicar of Christ to govern Christ's Church, he is not the vicar of the Church, he is the pastor of the flock. In the college, he preserves intact his office of Vicar of Christ...It is the college then which participates in a vital way in his authority."[18] In stating this, Cardinal Journet was echoing the teaching of the Second Vatican Council, which said: "The Roman Pontiff, by reason of his office as Vicar of Christ, namely, and as pastor of the entire Church, has full, supreme and universal power over the whole Church, a power which he can always exercise unhindered."[19]

Infallibile and Definitive Teaching

In order to preserve the Church in the purity of the faith handed on by the apostles, Christ willed to confer on the Church "a share in his own infallibility."[20] The word infallibility refers to an inability to err in believing or teaching revealed truth. The infallibility of the Church has several modes of expression. First, the whole Church is infallible in her belief when, "from the bishops to the last members of the laity it shows universal agreement in matters of faith and morals."[21] Secondly, in establishing the Church, Christ endowed its shepherds with the charism of infallibility in matters of faith and morals.[22] The infallibility of the Church's shepherds finds expression in the solemn definitions of Popes and Ecumenical Councils, as well as in the teaching of the Ordinary and Universal Magisterium.[23]

The fact that there exist various degrees in the exercise of the teaching authority of the Magisterium does not imply that firm assent is owed only to the supreme expressions of this authority. According to Pope John Paul II, this hierarchy of degrees of teaching authority "does not entitle one to hold that the pronouncements and doctrinal decisions of the Magisterium call for irrevocable assent only when it states them in solemn judgement or definitive act, and that, consequently, in all other cases one need only consider the arguments or reasons employed."[24]

To teach infallibly, the ordinary and universal Magisterium does not have to proclaim itself and it does not rely on extraordinary or solemn definitions. The Second Vatican Council listed the conditions necessary for the infallibility of the ordinary and universal magisterium. They are, that the Bishops: i) dispersed throughout the world but maintaining a bond between themselves and the Roman Pontiff, authoritatively teach on matters of faith and morals, and ii) agree that such a teaching be held definitively and absolutely.[25]

A key term to note in Vatican II's delineation of the conditions necessary for the ordinary universal Magisterium to teach infallibly is the word "definitively." As an indication of what it meant by this term, the Council inserted a footnote which referred to Vatican I's revised schema on the Church De Ecclesia Christi together with the commentary by Joseph Kleutgen which accompanied it.[26] In this commentary, Kleutgen defines as doctrines of the ordinary infallible Magisterium, "all those points which in matters of faith and morals are everywhere held or handed down as **undoubted** *(indubitata)* under bishops in communion with the Apostolic See."[27]

The authority of the college of Bishops however can never be exercised in separation from the Petrine office, which means that the Pope who is Head of the college can also teach on matters of faith and morals in a way that is definitive. Consequently, in a way other than through *ex cathedra* dogmatic definitions, the Pope can give expression to the *charism of infallibility* when, through the exercise of his ordinary papal Magisterium, he teaches a doctrine of faith and morals to be held definitively on the grounds that it has been constantly maintained and held by Tradition and transmitted by the ordinary universal Magisterium. Speaking of this, Archbishop Tarcisio Bertone, Secretary of the Congregation for the Doctrine of the Faith said:

> This latter exercise of the charism of infallibility does not take the form of a papal act of definition, but pertains to the ordinary, universal Magisterium which the Pope again sets forth with his formal pronouncement of *confirmation* and *reaffirmation* (generally in an Encyclical or Apostolic Letter)...A papal pronouncement of *confirmation* enjoys the same infallibility as the teaching of the ordinary, universal Magisterium, which includes the Pope not as a mere Bishop but as the Head of the Episcopal College.[28]

From what has been said above, it follows that whenever the Pope exercises his ordinary magisterium to teach a point of doctrine on faith or morals to be held definitively, the faithful must give to such teaching their irrevocable assent. This requirement follows from the institutional fact that the teaching authority of the Church is "exercised in the name of Jesus Christ."[29] In this context, it is interesting to note that in St. John's Gospel, the *Beloved Disciple* is tied to the office of Peter (cf. Jn 1:37-39; 13:22-30; 20;1-10; 21:1-23). Like the *Beloved Disciple*—who was first to arrive at the Empty Tomb but did not enter until Peter had first done so (cf. Jn 20:1-8)—so too must Catholics adhere firmly to the teaching of the Pope out of deference to the office he holds as Vicar of Christ and Successor of Saint Peter.

Regarding the authority of the Magisterium to specify what belongs to the Deposit of Faith, the Second Vatican Council said: "The task of giving an authentic interpretation of the Word of God, whether in its written form or in the form of Tradition, has been entrusted to the living teaching office of the Church alone. Its authority in this matter is exercised in the name of Jesus Christ."[30] When seen through the eyes of faith, the link God has established between Divine Revelation and its authoritative interpretation speaks clearly of His infinite Wisdom. Speaking of this, the Second Vatican Council said:

> It is clear therefore that, in the supremely wise arrangement of God, sacred Tradition, Sacred Scripture, and the Magisterium of the Church are so connected and associated that one of them cannot stand without the others. Working together, each in its own way, under the action of the Holy Spirit, they all contribute effectively to the salvation of souls.[31]

Cardinal John Henry Newman was acutely conscious of the implications for the life of faith of the answer one gives to the question of how in any given era one is to correctly discern the contents of the Tradition which has come down to us from the apostles. The answer which Newman gave to this question was instrumental in causing him to enter the Catholic Church. He said: "The gift of discerning, discriminating, defining, promulgating, and enforcing any portion of that tradition resides solely in the *Ecclesia docens*."[32] By the term *Ecclesia docens,* Newman means the teaching authority of the Church. This statement by Newman is based on the fact that while the faithful as a whole bear witness to the Gospel, this does not however render superfluous the role of the Magisterium.

Newman's keen awareness of the need at times for direct intervention by the Magisterium in order to specify the content of the Deposit of Faith was based on his observation that on occasions the *sensus fidelium* (the sense of the faithful) is not always clearly visible due to the impact of heretical ideas on the consciousness of some Catholics. In this regard, Newman cited the example of many Catholic laity, who during the Arian crisis of the fourth century allowed their faith to become contaminated by the teaching of corrupt Arian Bishops, "who got possession of the sees and ordained a heretical clergy."[33] The Arians, who were followers of an Alexandrian priest named Arius, denied the divinity of Christ and taught that God the Son was not eternal. They asserted that Christ had been made a partaker of the divine nature as a reward for the work of the redemption which he carried out.

Sacred Scripture and Sacred Tradition

Before concluding this section, I wish to briefly touch upon three important points which are the Canon of Sacred Scripture, the Church's attitude to biblical exegesis,[34] and the distinction between "Sacred Tradition" as a part of Divine Revelation and other traditions in the Church which are changeable.

The canon of Sacred Scripture includes 46 books of the Old Testament (counting Jeremiah and Lamentations as separate books) and 27 books in the New Testament. The leaders of the Protestant Reformation rejected the canonicity of certain books of the Bible and they maintained that a personal interpretation of Sacred Scripture was a sufficient rule of faith. The books not included by the Protestants are, namely, *1* and *2 Maccabees, Tobit, Judith, Sirach, Wisdom of Solomon, Baruch,* together with some additions to the books of *Daniel* and *Esther.* Regarding the New Testament, Martin Luther referred to the *Letter of James* as a "strawy epistle" because he saw an inconsistency between its teaching on the relationship between faith and good works and the teaching of St. Paul's *Letter to the Romans* on justification by faith.

Also, in strong contrast to the attitudes and practice of the early Church from the late first century onwards, the Reformers rejected Sacred Tradition as a source of Revelation. Responding to these errors, the Council of Trent taught that Sacred Tradition is as worthy of respect as are the books of the Bible and it condemned the notion that individuals can presume to interpret Sacred Scripture correctly, independently of the Church and its teaching authority. In doing this, the Council of Trent reaffirmed the listing of the canonical books of the Bible given by the Council of Florence—a listing which is exactly the same as the list given in the year 382 at the Council of Rome under Pope St. Damasus I.

After listing all the books belonging to the canon of Sacred Scripture, the Council of Trent went on to solemnly declare: "If any one does not accept these books as sacred and canonical in their entirety, with all their parts...let him be anathema."[35]

The substance of Trent's teaching was reaffirmed by the Second Vatican Council where it said: "For Holy Mother Church, relying on the faith of the apostolic age, accepts as sacred and canonical the books of the Old and the New Testaments, whole and entire, with all their parts, on the grounds that, written under the inspiration of the Holy Spirit (cf. Jn 20:31; 2 Tim. 3:16; 2 Pet. 1:19-21; 3: 15-16), they have

God as their author, and have been handed on as such by the Church herself."[36] Reaffirming this teaching, the *CCC* stated that "it was by the apostolic Tradition that the Church discerned which writings are to be included in the list of the sacred books."[37]

In his Encyclical Fides et Ratio (Faith and Reason), Pope John Paul II stated that today we are experiencing "a resurgence of fideism" which is an error that "fails to recognise the importance of rational knowledge and philosophical discourse for the understanding of faith, indeed for the very possibility of belief in God."[38] The Holy Father added that "one currently widespread symptom of this fideistic tendency is a 'biblicism' which tends to make the reading and exegesis of Sacred Scripture the sole criterion of truth", with the consequence that "the word of God is identified with Sacred Scripture alone, thus eliminating the doctrine of the Church."[39]

Regarding biblical exegesis, the Catholic Church is not opposed to the use of scientific methods in the interpretation of Sacred Scripture. In 1993, in an address to launch a document of the Pontifical Biblical Commission entitled *The Interpretation of the Bible in the Church,* Pope John Paul II affirmed the legitimacy and necessity of scientific biblical scholarship. He pointed out that exegesis must be attentive to the human aspects of the biblical texts and that it must be open to all the disciplines that shed light on the historical elements conditioning them. At the same time, the Holy Father insisted that the Divine element in Scripture must always be respected. Recalling that Holy Scripture is the Word of God in human words, Pope John Paul II stated that, "the exegete himself has to perceive the divine word in the texts."[40] After saying this, the Holy Father cautioned that another condition necessary for the exegete to bear fruit is that he carry out his work "in fidelity to the Church."[41]

To interpret Sacred Scripture correctly, "the reader must be attentive to what the human authors truly wanted to affirm and to what God wanted to reveal to us by their words."[42] To discover the sacred authors' intention, "the reader must take into account the conditions of their time and culture, the literary genres in use at the time, and the modes of feeling, speaking, and narrating then current."[43] Coupled with both of these requirements, the correct interpretation of Sacred Scripture also requires that it "be read and interpreted in the light of the same Spirit by whom it was written."[44]

In recalling the teaching of Vatican II, the *CCC* indicates three criteria for interpreting Sacred Scripture in accordance with the Spirit who inspired it. These criteria are: i) to be especially attentive "to the content and unity of the whole of Scripture," and ii) that Sacred Scripture be read "within the living Tradition of the whole Church," and iii) to be attentive to "the analogy of faith" which means that we must recognize "the coherence of the truths of faith among themselves and within the whole plan of Revelation."[45]

The word *doctrine* is derived from the Latin word *doctrina* which means to teach. Doctrines are not created by the Church. They refer to any truth taught by the Church as necessary for acceptance by the faithful such as the Divinity and Virginal Conception of Christ or that adultery is intrinsically evil. The propositions of faith form a body of doctrines called the **'Deposit of Faith'** *(depositum fidei)*. St. Paul tells his disciple Timothy to "guard the deposit" (1 Tim 6:20), "guard the noble deposit" (2 Tim 1:14).

The phrase doctrine of "faith and morals" means that a particular Church teaching can involve either a truth to be believed (eg. the Real Presence of Our Lord in the Eucharist) or a judgement about the rightness or wrongness of an action (eg. that adultery is seriously wrong). In other words, doctrine refers to divine teaching and divine law. That Our Lord is truly present in the Eucharist is divine teaching while the truth that acts of adultery are wrong is divine law. With respect to divine teaching and divine law, the Church has the responsibility to proclaim them faithfully but no authority whatsoever to change them.

Church "Discipline," on the other hand, is generally taken to refer to those regulations and rules which the Church puts in place in order to enable her to carry out her mission more effectively. In contrast to the unchangeable nature of doctrine, Church discipline can and does change. For a long period during its history, it was the discipline or law of the Church that Mass in the Latin Rite be said in the Latin language. However, since this discipline was of human rather than divine origin, the Church was able to change it so as to allow Mass in the Latin Rite to be said in vernacular languages such as English. When she judged it necessary to do so, the Church was able to change her discipline because it did not involve a change in the teachings of Christ or in the divine moral law.

I turn now to 'Sacred Tradition.' In its treatment of 'Tradition', the *CCC* is careful to distinguish 'Tradition' as a component of Revelation from "the various theological, disciplinary, liturgical, or devotional traditions" which "are born in the local churches over time." It pointed out that such "traditions" can be "retained, modified or even abandoned under the guidance of the Church's magisterium."[46] 'Tradition' as a component of the Word of God, however, "comes from the apostles and hands on what they received from Jesus' teaching and example and what they learned from the Holy Spirit."[47]

Between present and past 'Tradition' there can be no difference as regards the meaning of a doctrine possessed, but there can be growth in the Church's consciousness of the doctrine and improvements in the Magisterium's presentation of it. This process, known as the ***development of doctrine***, allows us to penetrate a particular Church teaching more deeply with accurate insights that will enable us to apply it more thoroughly to life.[48]

One of the great authorities on the development of doctrine was St. Vincent of Lerins who lived in the 5th century. In considering how development of doctrine occurs, St. Vincent gave the example of a child growing into an adult. What we see in the adult was always present in an undeveloped way in the child. If the child grows up and becomes a man, that is development, but if he becomes a tree that is alteration. Consequently, development of doctrine must never be confused with alteration.

Another person who contributed much to our understanding of how doctrine develops in the Church was Cardinal Newman who wrote a book on the question titled *Essay On The Development of Christian Doctrine*. In this work, Newman developed a set of criteria for distinguishing between the *Development* and the *Corruption* of a doctrine. Amongst these criteria Newman included the following: i) Preservation of Idea, ii) Continuity of Principles, iii) Logical Sequence, and iv) Preservative Additions.

For Newman, "the corruption" of a doctrine is "a development which undoes its previous advances."[49] Therefore, the loss of one of a doctrine's central ideas during the course of its development is tantamount to its corruption according to Newman.[50] Not only is the loss from a doctrine of one of its central principles a corruption, so also is any "alteration of the principles" upon which the doctrine in question has developed.[51] On the basis of these ideas, Newman summed up the method of distinguishing authentic doctrinal development from its counterfeit by saying that developments "which do but contradict and reverse the course of doctrine which has been developed before them, and out of which they spring, are certainly corrupt."[52]

Referring to the way in which Church doctrine must retain its original meaning in the course of its development, the First Vatican Council said that meaning of doctrine "must always be maintained which holy mother Church declared once and for all, nor should one ever depart from that meaning under the guise of or in the name of a more advanced understanding."[53] In harmony with this teaching, Vatican I condemned the opinion that doctrines once proposed by the Church "must with the progress of science be given a meaning other than that which was understood by the Church, or which she understands."[54] In its turn, Vatican II, in speaking of doctrinal development said:

> The tradition that comes from the apostles makes progress in the Church, with the help of the Holy Spirit. There is a growth in insight into the realities and words that are being passed on...Thus, as the centuries go by, the Church is always advancing towards the plenitude of divine truth, until eventually the words of God are fulfilled in her.[55]

As we shall see in later chapters, Groome and Fiorenza propose models and interpretations of Divine Revelation which are at variance with the Catholic Church's received doctrine and with its understanding of how doctrinal development takes place in the Church.

Reference

1   Council of Trent, *Decree Concerning the Canonical Scriptures,* Session IV, 1546.

2   Vatican II, *Dei Verbum,* n. 10.

3   Cf. *Catechism of the Catholic Church* (hereafter designated in footnotes as CCC), n. 84.

4   Vatican II, *Dei Verbum*, n. 9.

5   Ibid.

6   Vatican II, Dei Verbum, n. 9; cf. CCC. n. 82.

7   This question is dealt with in a most scholarly fashion in Chapter 3 of Cardinal Joseph Ratzinger's book Called To Communion: Understanding The Church Today (Ignatius Press, 1996).

8   CCC. n. 424.

9   Pope John Paul II, *General Audience,* November 25, 1992, in Catechesis on the Creed, Volume 4, Pauline Books & Media, Boston 1998, p. 247.

10 Pope John Paul II, *General Audience,* November 25, 1992. Ibid. p. 244.

11 CCC. n. 553.

12 Ibid.

13 Pope John Paul II, *General Audience,* January 13, 1993. In Catechesis on the Creed, Vol. 4. p. 268.

14 Cf. CCC. n. 869.

15 Second Vatican Council, *Lumen Gentium,* n. 20.

16 CCC. n. 869.

17 CCC. n. 100.

18 Cardinal Charles Journet, *L'Osservatore Romano,* October 10, 1968.

19 Second Vatican Council, *Lumen Gentium,* n. 22.

20 CCC. n. 889.

21 Vatican II, *Lumen Gentium,* n.12.

22 Cf. CCC. n. 89.

23 Cf. Vatican II, *Lumen Gentium,* n.25.

24 Pope John Paul II, *L'Osservatore Romano,* November 29, 1995.

25 Cf. Vatican II, *Lumen Gentium,* n. 25.

26 Footnote no. 40 of *Lumen Gentium 25.*

27 Joseph Kleutgen, commentary on Vatican I's Constitution II De Ecclesia Christi, Mansi, 53, 313. Cf. footnote 40 to Lumen Gentium 25.

28 Archbishop Tarcisio Bertone, S.D.B., *L'Osservatore Romano,* January 29, 1997

29 Cf. Second Vatican Council, Dei Verbum, n. 10.

30 Vatican II, *Dei Verbum,* n. 10

31 Vatican II, *Dei Verbum,* n. 10.

32 Cardinal Newman. *On Consulting The Faithful In Matters of Doctrine,* edited by John Coulson, Collins, London 1986, p. 63

33 Ibid. p. 75.

34 The term "biblical exegesis" refers to scientific methods for interpreting Scripture.

35 Council of Trent, Session IV, Decree Concerning the Canonical Scriptures.

36 Vatican II, Dei Verbum, n. 11

37 *CCC.* n. 120

38 Pope John Paul II, Fides et Ratio, n. 55.

39 Ibid.

40 Pope John Paul II, Address for launch of *The Interpretation of the Bible in the Church,* St. Paul Books and Media, Boston 1993, p. 19, n. 9.

41 Pope John Paul II, Address for launch of *The Interpretation of the Bible in the Church,* p. 20. n. 10

42 *CCC.* n. 109; cf. Vatican II, *Dei Verbum,* n. 12.

43 *CCC.* n. 110; cf. Vatican II, *Dei Verbum,* n. 12.

44 Vatican II, *Dei Verbum,* n. 12; cf. *CCC.* n. 11.

45   Cf. *CCC*. nn. 112–114; cf. Vatican II, Dei Verbum, n. 12.

46   *CCC*. n. 83

47   *CCC*. n. 83

48   Cf. Second Vatican Council, Lumen Gentium, n. 12.

49   Cardinal John Henry Newman, *Essay On The Development of Christian Doctrine,* Pelican Classics, Middlesex, 1974, p. 121.

50   Ibid. p. 122.

51   Ibid. p. 127.

52   Ibid. p. 141

53   Vatican Council 1: Dogmatic Constitution *Dei Filius,* ch. 4; *Conc. Oec. Decr.* (3), p. 809 (DS 3020)

54   Vatican Council 1: Dogmatic Constitution *Dei Filius,* can. 3; *Con. Oec. Decr.* (3), p. 811 (DS 3043).

55   Vatican II, *Dei Verbum,* n. 8

3

Philosophical and Theological Influences on Groome and Fiorenza

To better understand the general orientation of Groome's *Shared Christian Praxis* and Fiorenza's *Feminist Theology of Liberation,* it will help if we first look at some of the philosophical and theological ideas underpinning their writings. In this regard, we will look at Groome and Fiorenza separately starting in each instance with philosophical influences and proceeding from there to the theological ones.

Philosophical Influences on Groome

PAULO FREIRE

Groome's ideas on *praxis*-based education have been greatly influenced by the Chilean Marxist educationalist Paulo Freire.[1] In 1980, Groome acknowledged his debt to Freire by saying: "My first attempts to use a praxis approach in religious education began after meeting Freire and reading his foundational work, *Pedagogy of the Oppressed,* in 1972."[2] In 1991, Groome expressed the view that Freire "is the contemporary author most responsible for developing a praxis-based approach to education as a systematically understood option for educators—especially for those intending liberation and humanization."[3] In 1998,

Groome stated that Freire was, "likely the most prophetic voice on pedagogy of the twentieth century."[4]

Freire was a disciple of Antonio Gramsci (1891-1937) who founded the Italian Communist Party and whose major philosophical aim was the reconstruction of Marxism as a philosophy of praxis. Freire espoused the Marxist theory of class struggle as the key to history and built his educational philosophy upon its presuppositions.[5] Freire followed Gramsci in his interpretation of the theory of class struggle as necessarily involving a battle for the minds and hearts of people with a view to directing them to engage in emancipatory political action. Consequently, central to Freire's educational system is the objective of "conscientization," which refers to a process of "learning to perceive social, political, and economic contradictions, and to take action against the oppressive elements of reality."[6]

GEORG HEGEL

Hegel (1770-1831), conceived the subject matter of philosophy to be reality as a whole which he referred to as the Absolute.[7] He concluded that the Absolute must ultimately be regarded as pure Thought, or Spirit, or Mind in the process of self-development. Since Hegel did not believe in a transcendent, omniscient and omnipotent God who has existed from all eternity, then it would be erroneous to identify his idea of 'Spirit' with the God proclaimed by Christians. According to Hegel, "it is only in man that the spirit achieves self-consciousness and it knows only what man knows."[8]

Hegel used the term "Dialectic" to describe the logic that governs the development of the Absolute. The notion of the 'dialectic' means that progress is the result of a conflict of opposites. Later disciples of Hegel expressed this conflict of opposites in terms of the categories of thesis, antithesis, and synthesis. The thesis might be an idea, belief or historical movement. However, in the Hegelian system, every idea contains within itself incompleteness that generates opposition or antithesis. As a result of the conflict that arises between the thesis and antithesis, a third point of view or idea arises called the synthesis which in turn generates a further thesis.

On the basis of his understanding of reality as the product of dialectical processes, Hegel was opposed to all forms of dogma and authoritarianism. He analysed human progress towards understanding the Absolute on three levels—art, religion and philosophy—of which he believed philosophy was conceptually supreme because it could grasp the Absolute rationally. Hegel's ideas influenced Marx and Engels who used many of his ideas to construct their philosophical system of dialectical materialism.

While Hegel did not repudiate Christian terminology such as Trinity and Incarnation, he did however empty them of their dogmatic content in order to articulate his own understanding of reality.[9] Hegel's idea of the "infinite mind" is nothing more than the human mind at the end of its dialectical process in history—an idea which led philosopher Fr. Joseph M de Torre to refer to Hegel as "perhaps the most outstanding Gnostic in history."[10] Hegel did not believe in objective truths that are opposed to errors. He understood truth as a category which existed at the end of the evolutionary process of human consciousness—a supreme consciousness which is equated with God. Consequently, the God of Hegel was fully immanent in creation—equated with the supreme synthesis and consciousness of the human mind in the course of its historical evolution—which is why the great Catholic philosopher Jacques Maritain could refer to Hegel's philosophy as a form of pantheism.[11]

MARTIN HEIDEGGER

Groome is particularly interested in the application of hermeneutical methods to language and tradition and in this context he refers to Heidegger (1899-1976) as one of the "great exponents of *hermeneutics*."[12] The word 'hermeneutics' refers to the theory or practice of interpretation of texts in order to determine their actual meaning. While the term was originally applied to the science of biblical interpretation, the concept of hermeneutics has come to be extended by some modern philosophers to cover the whole of human existence. In the hands of philosophers such as Heidegger, it implies that while some interpretations are better than others, none can ever be final.[13]

Heidegger believed that philosophy had the task of investigating 'being'. In particular, he was concerned to investigate the nature of thought in existing human beings. In creating his philosophical system, Heidegger established a false dichotomy between 'Being' and 'Truth' by asserting that it was 'Being' alone and not truth that should concern philosophers. In his investigations into the nature of 'Being' and the meaning of existence to be derived from it, Heidegger rejected the doctrine of a Creator God. He believed that philosophy could provide man with a window into the true nature of his own being only if it was first purified of any contact with religion. Consequently, Heidegger believed that the notion of a 'Christian philosophy' is impossible.[14] In *Fides et Ratio,* Pope John Paul II pointed out that the notion of 'Christian philosophy' is in itself valid provided it is understood as "a Christian way of philosophising, a philosophical speculation conceived in dynamic union with faith."[15]

For Heidegger, man is merely a being on his way to death and consequently his existence is tied totally to this world and thus governed by pure temporality. In this setting, the life of an individual is understood as a sequence of choices made in the light of historical possibilities which bear no relationship to objective and universally binding moral norms.[16]

During the 1930s, Heidegger made no secret of his commitment to National Socialism and after World War II he failed to speak out in condemnation of Nazi atrocities. In his book titled *The Closing of the American Mind,* Alan Bloom, in speaking of Heidegger said: "His interest in new gods led him, as with Nietzsche, in his teaching to honour immoderation over moderation and to ridicule morality. Both [Neitzsche and Heidegger] helped to constitute that ambiguous Weimer atmosphere in which liberals looked like simpletons and anything was possible for people who sang of the joy of the knife in cabarets." Having said this, Bloom added: "Thus it was no accident that Heidegger came forward just after Hitler's accession to power to address the university community in Freiburg as the new rector, and urged commitment to National Socialism."[17] Alasdair MacIntyre, Professor of Philosophy at the University of Notre Dame, who has been referred to by *Newsweek* as "one of the foremost moral philosophers in the English-speaking world," has stated that Heidegger himself "discerned a close relationship between his own views and the philosophical politics of National Socialism."[18]

While admitting that much of Heidegger's philosophy is incompatible with Christianity, Groome nevertheless draws on him frequently by adopting many of his ideas and much of his terminology as foundational concepts in the development of *shared Christian praxis*.[19] Groome agrees with Heidegger that, "language is the house of Being" which sets "the parameters of our lives."[20] Consequently, in his published works, Groome is vitally concerned to "search for language capable of promoting a Christian religious education that is emancipatory."[21]

JURGEN HABERMAS

While Groome is critical of some aspects of the thought of Jurgen Habermas (b. 1929), he nevertheless acknowledges his dependence on him for the development of his *shared praxis* approach to religious education.[22] Habermas is one of the most influential contemporary representatives of the neo-Marxist social philosophy known as *Critical Theory*, which originated in Germany in the 1930s amongst a group of intellectuals who have come to be known as the *Frankfurt School.*

Habermas has written much about communication—from both its interpersonal dimension and from the perspective of language and tradition. He postulates that the reception of language and tradition have to be sifted by way of a critical theory (reflection) that will decipher and reveal the ideological distortions and false claims that they contain. This he believes is necessary in order to identify ways in which language and tradition embody ideological positions which give rise to "distorted communication." Such "distorted communication," posits Habermas, fosters the development of a false consciousness that "serves to legitimate relations of organised force" and thereby protects the interests of those in power.[23] In order to overcome such "distorted communication" and forge an emancipatory praxis, Habermas perceives of a need to submit all texts, knowledge and tradition—together with the structures of authority and domination in society—to a hermeneutic of suspicion in order to transpose the life praxis out of which they emerged as well as the unconscious compulsions which sustain them.

To interpret Sacred Scripture according to the principles of Habermas's critical theory, would mean that we are no longer only interested in understanding the historical meaning of biblical texts, but we must also search out their ingrained ideological content which it is asserted have operated to maintain structures of domination in ecclesiastically controlled environments. The same principle would apply to the transmission of Sacred Tradition, what has been handed down must be sifted in order to transpose ideological influences that serve to oppress rather than liberate.

Theological Influences on Groome

Apart from Fiorenza, other theologians who have influenced Groome in the development of his theological ideas include Fr. Karl Rahner, S.J., Leonardo Boff, Fr. Edward Schillebeeckx, Fr. Richard

McBrien, Fr. David Tracy and Paul Tillich. Few Catholic theologians of the twentieth century have more published works to their credit than Karl Rahner (1904-1984). Due to the widespread influence Fr. Rahner has had over recent decades, I will spend more time outlining some problems with his theology than I will in regard to the other theologians listed above.

KARL RAHNER

In an article published in the July 1994 edition of the *Homiletic and Pastoral Review,* Father Leonard Kennedy, C.S.B., who is Professor of Philosophy at St. Peter's Seminary at the University of Western Ontario in Canada, expressed the view that Karl Rahner "is a major contributor to the decline" of Catholicism in the Western world in recent decades.[24]

Rahner studied at Freiburg where, according to his own testimony, he "had the good fortune to have Martin Heidegger as a teacher."[25] From the late 1930s until 1967, Rahner taught theology at Innsbruck after which he taught for a few years at Munich and Munster. While much of his theological work is built on a philosophical system known as *Transcendental Thomism,* Rahner himself admitted that he never studied St. Thomas systematically and he testifies that the major philosophical influences on him were Heidegger and Fr. Marechal, S.J. (1878-1944).

In saying that Rahner's theological system "has a certain basis in Thomas himself," Fr. Avery Dulles, S.J. adds however that it is "heavily influenced by the transcendental idealism of Kant" and that it "has affinities with Heidegger's existential phenomenology and also...with Hegel's *Phenomenology of Spirit.*"[26] The transcendental method has come in for much criticism on the basis that it is metaphysically unsound. Metaphysics deals with the *science of being.* It has been defined "as the study of the ultimate cause and the first and most universal principles of reality."[27] In a Christian perspective, since God is the "ultimate cause" of all things, then "he is evidently a principal subject matter of metaphysics."[28] One Jesuit philosopher, Professor Robert J. Henle S.J., has stated that "the Transcendental Method results in an idealistic-oriented Platonizing metaphysics which is radically different from Thomistic metaphysics."[29] On the basis of his analysis of Transcendental Thomism in the light of its historical development, Fr. Henle concluded that it "has no philosophical right to be called Thomism" and that it is "internally inconsistent and metaphysically unsound."[30]

The watershed in Rahner's career seems to have been the publication in 1968 of Pope Paul VI's encyclical *Humanae Vitae* which upheld the traditional Catholic doctrine on the intrinsically evil nature of contraceptive acts. Rahner argued that since Pope Paul VI had not in *Humanae Vitae* proclaimed the immorality of contraceptive acts by way of an *ex-cathedra* definition, then the teaching could be regarded as reformable and thereby could not claim to carry that degree of authority necessary to bind the consciences of all Catholics. Rahner asserted that *Humanae Vitae* "is in principle capable of being revised" on the grounds that "an official pronouncement of the Church on doctrinal matters so long as it does not imply any definition, is susceptible to revision."[31]

In regard to the moral norm of *Humanae Vitae,* Rahner stated that "the individual and collective consciences of Catholic Christians neither have nor can assume any absolute certainty with regard to the objective correctness of the papal norm."[32] He asserted that the Second Vatican Council did "not in principle exclude the possibility of a theologian dissenting from a statement of teaching of this kind" and he further advised married couples that they need not fear "incurring any subjective guilt," nor need they regard themselves "as in a state of formal disobedience to the Church's authority" were they to "sincerely form their consciences" in a way "which deviates from the papal norm."[33] Rahner delineated certain criteria by which he claimed such Catholics could form their conscience in opposition to the moral norm of *Humanae Vitae.* He advised that any Catholic who formed his conscience according to this same criteria need feel "no obligation to subject the judgement of his conscience which he has arrived at in this way to fresh questioning each time he receives the sacrament of penance."[34]

Rahner argued that "any bishop" can "honourably and in all subjective honesty point out to the faithful over whom he presides the weight and importance to be attached to a papal pronouncement" such as *Humanae Vitae,* while at the same time "he can put the question to the conscience of the individual believer whether he can have, or actually has, a sufficient conviction, supported by serious arguments, to make it lawful for him in conscience, either in theory or in practice, to deviate from the papal norm."[35] In saying this, Rahner stressed that "a bishop need not and should not act either as though the papal pronouncement were absolute and incapable of revision..."[36]

Despite many reaffirmations of the doctrine of *Humanae Vitae* by the Magisterium in the period between 1974 and the early 1980s, Rahner nevertheless persisted in his dissent. In the last years of his life he gave interviews some of which have been gathered into the book *Faith in a Wintry Season*. Here, on the basis of what he saw as a problem of "overpopulation," Rahner argued that a "new directive" from Rome on the contraceptive question "would be desirable."[37] Indeed, Rahner appears to have adopted a neo-Malthusian view of population growth, even to the extent of referring to the modern world as one characterised by "a human race that is growing gigantically and at a terrifying rate."[38]

In his dissent from *Humanae Vitae,* Rahner failed to consider whether or not the doctrine it affirmed had been taught definitively by the universal and ordinary magisterium—something that would mean the teaching was irreformable. The moral norm of *Humanae Vitae* transmits a doctrine which has been taught by: i) the Fathers of the Church both East and West,[39] ii) the constant and unvarying magisterium of the Roman Pontiffs down the centuries, iii) Synods of Bishops,[40] iv) the Canon Law of the Church,[41] v) an Ecumenical Council, vi) the two universal Catechisms that have appeared so far in the course of the Church's history.[42]

To understand the magnitude of Rahner's error in his dissent from *Humanae Vitae,* it will be useful to recall some key moments during this century when the essential nucleus of the doctrine was reaffirmed by the Magisterium. Of special significance are the words of Pope Pius XI in *Casti Connubii* where he said: "No reason, however grave, may be put forward by which anything intrinsically against nature may become conformable to nature and morally good...[The] conjugal act is destined primarily by nature for the procreation of offspring, those who in exercising it, deliberately deprive it of its natural power and purpose, sin against nature and commit a deed which is disgraceful and intrinsically immoral."[43] Having said this, Pius XI added: "Any use whatsoever of matrimony exercised in such a way that the act is deliberately frustrated in its natural power to generate life, is an offence against the law of God and of nature, and those who indulge in such are branded with the guilt of grave sin."[44]

In order to stress the binding nature of the doctrine he was reaffirming in *Casti Connubii*, Pius XI addressed a special word to priests in which he said:

Therefore, priests who hear confessions and others who have the care of souls are admonished by Us, in the exercise of Our sovereign authority and Our care for the salvation of the souls of all, that they must not allow the souls committed to their charge to be in error concerning this most serious law of God, and, what is much more important, that they must themselves be on their guard against these false doctrines and in no way connive at them. [45]

In his *Allocution* to Italian midwives on October 29, 1951, Pope Pius XII reaffirmed the teaching of *Casti Connubii*. He said: "Our predecessor, Pius XI...solemnly restated the basic law of the conjugal act and conjugal relations. 'Every attempt on the part of the married couple during the conjugal act or during the development of its natural consequences to deprive it of its inherent power and to hinder the procreation of a new life is immoral. No 'indication' or need can change an action that is intrinsically immoral into an action that is moral and lawful." Having thus reaffirmed the received doctrine, Pope Pius XII went on to say: "This prescription holds good today just as much as it did yesterday. It will hold tomorrow and always, for it is not a mere precept of human right but the expression of the natural and Divine Law."

The Second Vatican Council taught that acts directed at the regulation of birth must be evaluated on the basis of "objective criteria...drawn from the nature of the human person and of human action."[46] It added that the objective norms of conjugal morality were directed at keeping the exercise of the marital act within "the context of true love" by safeguarding its "total meaning of mutual self-giving and human procreation."[47] Consequently, the Council added that in matters of birth regulation the faithful "are forbidden to use methods disapproved of by the Magisterium."[48] In order to ensure that no trace of ambiguity remained in regard to the Church's teaching on this question, the Fathers of Vatican II went on to recall by way of a footnote the teaching of Pope Pius XI in *Casti Connubii* and of Pius XII in his *Allocution* to Italian midwives.[49] A few weeks after *Humanae Vitae* was published, the Vatican Press published an article by Cardinal Pericle Felici in which he stated that the Fathers of Vatican II insisted on the inclusion of footnote 14 in *Gaudium et Spes 51* in order to ensure that the Council's teaching on the regulation of birth would be interpreted in continuity with the teaching of Pius XI and Pius XII on the same question.[50]

The Catholic Church could never teach that contraceptive acts are not intrinsically evil since to do so would involve a discontinuity of principles expressed through a contradiction of the essential idea in what has been transmitted by the teaching of the Magisterium as the binding doctrine of the Church. Pope John Paul II has on several occasions alluded to the irreformable nature of the doctrine of *Humanae Vitae*. Speaking of it to a group of moral theologians he said: "It is not in fact a doctrine invented by man: it was stamped on the very nature of the human person by God the Creator's hand and confirmed by him in revelation. Calling it into question therefore, is equivalent to refusing God himself the obedience of our intelligence." Having said this, Pope John Paul II added: "By describing the contraceptive act as intrinsically illicit, Pope Paul VI meant to teach that the moral norm of Humanae Vitae is such that it does not admit exceptions. No personal or social circumstances could ever, can now or will ever render such an act lawful in itself."[51]

The **irreformable** and **definitive** nature of the Church's teaching on the immorality of contraceptive acts was reaffirmed in a document issued by the *Pontifical Council for the Family* in February 1997. The document *(Vademecum)* was prepared at the request of Pope John Paul II and is intended to assist priests to use the Sacrament of Penance as a means of aiding married people to correctly form their conscience in the area of conjugal morality. In relation to contraception, this document states:

> The Church has always taught the intrinsic evil of contraception, that is, every marital act intentionally rendered unfruitful. **This teaching is to be held as definitive and irreformable.** Contraception is gravely opposed to marital chastity; it is contrary to the good of the transmission of life, (the procreative aspect of matrimony), and to the reciprocal self-giving of the spouses (the unitive aspect of matrimony); it harms true love and denies the sovereign role of God in the transmission of human life.[52]

Rahner's dissent from *Humanae Vitae* contributed to the acceptance by many theologians of the erroneous belief that Catholics owed irrevocable assent only to those doctrines that have been solemnly defined by a Council or by the Roman Pontiff speaking *ex-cathedra*. In his dissent, Rahner made the error of overlooking the fact that the Pope can, without using a technical formula, appeal to his ministry of strengthening his brethren in the truth in order to confirm and reaffirm a teaching that has already been infallibly set forth by the ordinary and universal Magisterium.

Towards the end of his life, Rahner was making ever more incoherent statements about sexual morality. In reference to how the Church's "sexual norms" might be made reasonable for young people, he said: "The Church in earlier times did not always come up with individual norms which were precisely the right ones, or which were genuinely and vitally human, this fact is, of course, a proof that detailed norms are not always above doubt in every instance."[53] To this he added: "I presume there can be differences of opinion in the Church as to how, in individual instances, premarital sexuality can and should be expressed in a genuinely human way, that is, in a way that is truly according to the will of God. Possibly, there are still further traditional attitudes in the Church's moral teaching which are not completely fair to a genuinely human, and hence Christian, sexuality."[54] Finally, in regard to sexual morality in general, Rahner said: "I think persons must figure out for themselves how they are going to proceed in individual instances."[55]

Rahner made no apology for the fact that his dissent from the Church's moral doctrine was the cause of confusion to many Catholics in the formation of their conscience. He said:

> Whether it is congenial or uncongenial, in spite of all complaints that we are rendering many people in the Church insecure in their moral conscience, it must be said that there are not a few concrete principles and patterns of behaviour which formerly—and quite rightly in the circumstances—counted as binding, concrete expressions of the ultimate Christian moral principles, but today are not necessarily binding always and in every case.[56]

Many of Rahner's moral ideas can be traced to the adoption by him of a faulty anthropology which led him to believe that the range of the Church's authority to teach definitively on moral questions extends to "hardly any particular or individual norms of Christian morality" since "the concrete nature of man in all its dimensions...is itself subject to a most far-reaching process of change."[57] After drawing a distinction "between that which belongs to human nature as of metaphysical necessity" and that "which belongs to human nature as it exists in concrete history," Rahner went on to conclude that "inevitably there emerges in concrete human morality that disquieting interaction which we have often spoken of between changeable and unchangeable moral norms which cannot fully be distinguished from each other."[58]

Dr John M. Finnis, Professor of Law and Legal Philosophy at Oxford University, says that after Rahner "had abandoned the traditional view of specific moral absolutes" he went on to speak of a "faith instinct" in "relation to moral judgements." This idea, says Professor Finnis, eventually led followers of Rahner such as Joseph Fuchs, S.J. and Richard McCormick, S.J. to "find an instinct" which "contradicts and discredits the faith, or at least some of the constant and most firm teachings, of the church."[59]

McCormick has argued from Rahner's authority that the moral norm of *Humanae Vitae* could not possibly be proposed infallibly by the Magisterium since it relates to concrete human nature which is subject to change.[60] In a critique of *Veritatis Splendor,* McCormick referred to Rahner as "the greatest theologian of this century."[61] In this article, McCormick stated that *Veritatis Splendor* rejected the "teleological directions" taken by certain moral theologians, such as Franz Bockle, Charles Curran, Joseph Fuchs, Bernard Haring, Louis Janssens, Peter Knauer, Giles Milhaven, Bruno Schuller and McCormick himself, on the basis of "their impoverished anthropology."[62] Having stated this, McCormick went on to add that *Veritatis Splendor* also had Karl Rahner "in its cross hairs" since "it is Rahner's anthropology that the cited theologians share."[63]

The influence of Rahner's notion that moral norms are subject to alteration because concrete human nature is subject to change is clearly evident in the work of Fr. Charles Curran. After speaking approvingly of theologians "who have tried to nuance the interpretation of *Humanae vitae* in such a way that one can accept the morality of artificial contraception in some circumstances without accusing the encyclical of being totally wrong," Fr. Curran went on to say:

Karl Rahner recognises that one can dissent from an authoritative, noninfallible papal teaching. However, he suggests that there might be another way to understand the teaching of *Humanae vitae.* The pope is here proposing an ideal norm which cannot always be effectively realised in all its moral obligations in every situation in human life or by every individual or social group. It is conceivable at least in principle that only later will the ideal which is now being taught be understood as having the force of moral obligation in actual concrete reality.[64]

Following his dissent from *Humanae Vitae,* Fr. Curran went on to eventually posit that there can be legitimate grounds for dissent from any specific moral teaching of the Magisterium including abortion and euthanasia.[65]

In *Veritatis Splendor,* Pope John Paul II referred to dissent from the Church's moral teaching as a *"genuine crisis."*[66] In his Encyclical *Fides et Ratio,* the Holy Father stated that "moral theology requires a right philosophical vision of human nature and society, as well as general principles of ethical decision-making."[67] Professor John Finnis has pointed out that Rahner himself "never ventured to make clear what he thought changeable and what constant in human nature" and that he seemed to equate "faith instinct" with "sheer will, operating without or beyond reason."[68]

Professor Germain Grisez holds that Rahner's concept of human freedom suffers from the same "incoherence" as that of Kant.[69] Coupled with this, Grisez and Russel Shaw have been critical of Rahner for his promotion of "intuitionism" under the guise of a certain "moral instinct of faith" which serves as a means of arriving at moral decisions. With "intuitionism", judgements of conscience do not proceed from principles but tend instead to invoke community standards and calculations based on such notions as "greater goods and lesser evils."[70] Also, Grisez and Shaw have been critical of Rahner for promoting an understanding of "Fundamental Option" which misrepresents the teaching of the Council of Trent and which is opposed to Catholic doctrine.[71]

Cardinal Joseph Ratzinger says that to a great extent Rahner "adopted the concept of freedom that is proper to idealistic philosophy, a concept that in reality, is appropriate to the absolute Spirit—to God— but not to man."[72] In reference to Rahner's notion that "He who...accepts his existence...says...Yes to Christ,"[73] that is, to be a Christian is to accept oneself, Cardinal Ratzinger says: "In this spiritual transposition of transcendental deduction—which was its hidden starting point—I see a resolution of the particular into the universal that is at variance with the newness of Christianity and reduces Christian liberation to pseudoliberation."[74]

As well as dissenting from *Humanae Vitae,* Rahner also helped muddy the waters in the debate about the relationship between science, abortion, morality and law. In June 1976, the then Government of West Germany adopted legislation which effectively legalised every request for abortion. The German physician and author, Alfred Haussler M.D., stated that the resistance to permissive abortion legislation in Germany had weakened in the wake of dissent from *Humanae Vitae* by theologians such as Rahner. He also criticised Rahner for imprudently publishing a "scientifically wrong" article in 1970 which asserted that there were "biological developments" in the early embryo which were "prehuman."[75]

In speaking of abortion, Rahner said: "The direct killing of the fetus is objectively against God's law, and against the dignity of the person."[76] Having said this, Rahner added that "it is an entirely different question whether the state should criminally prosecute such an objective offense against the Christian moral law."[77] In the same context, Rahner stated that "the question of the moral judgement about abortion and the question of penal prosecution of abortion are two entirely different things," further to which it was necessary, he said, to take into account that a person such as a doctor "may engage in abortion in good faith."[78]

Regarding the relationship between law and morality, it was rather imprudent of Rahner to reduce the question of abortion to one of "Christian moral law." Abortion is first of all a question of natural law since reason can perceive that the direct and intentional killing of an innocent human being is gravely wrong.[79]

In order to maintain public order and to promote the common good, the State has the responsibility to make laws which regulate the rights and duties of individuals. In doing so, legislators are not free to act arbitrarily due to the fact that "among the laws which men make are some which deal with what is good or bad by its very nature; and they require man to do right and avoid wrong and make their observance binding on pain of some suitable penalty."[80] Civil law "must ensure that all members of society enjoy respect for certain fundamental rights which innately belong to the person"—"rights which every positive law must recognise and guarantee," "first and fundamental" among which "is the inviolable right to life of every innocent human being."[81]

To Argue that penal sanctions should not be invoked against abortionists is equivalent to asserting that there should be no penal sanctions against murder.

While "it is true that the civil law cannot expect to cover the whole field of morality or to punish all faults," a failure by legislators to apply penal sanctions against abortion would be an admission "that the legislator no longer considers abortion a crime against human life, since murder is still always severely punished."[82] Consequently, "the legal toleration of abortion...can in no way claim to be based on respect for the conscience of others, precisely because society has the right and duty to protect itself against the abuses which can occur in the name of conscience and under the pretext of freedom."[83] Hence, state law must protect the innocent from the unjust actions of others irrespective of their personal moral or religious beliefs—including doctors who, according to Rahner, perform abortions "in good faith."

Rahner's rejection of *Humanae Vitae* was followed by dissent from other areas of Catholic doctrine. Speaking of this, Rev. Professor Leonard Kennedy, C.S.B. said: "Rahner's rejection of Humanae Vitae led him to reject other Catholic teachings and to come to a vision of a do-it-yourself Church."[84] One of these areas where Rahner dissented from the doctrine of the Church and where he seems to have influenced the thinking of many other dissenters was in relation to the question of the male-only ministerial priesthood.

In 1975, Pope Paul VI, by way of a response to the Archbishop of Canterbury *Concerning the Ordination of Women to the Priesthood,* reaffirmed the received Catholic teaching on the impossibility of conferring priestly ordination on women. In 1976, the Sacred Congregation for the Doctrine of the Faith published, with the approval of Pope Paul VI, a *Declaration on the Question of the Admission of Women to the Ministerial Priesthood.* Entitled *Inter Insigniores,* this Declaration stated that the Church did not have the power to ordain women and that its practice of reserving the ministerial priesthood to men only was based on the behaviour of Christ, the practice of the Apostles and the constant Tradition of the Church.

Rahner's dissent from *Inter Insigniores* followed the same pattern as his dissent from *Humanae Vitae.* He said that "despite papal approval" and the fact that *Inter Insigniores* "is an authentic declaration of the Roman authorities on faith," the "Declaration is not a definitive decision; it is in principle reformable and it can...be erroneous."[85] After stating that the *Declaration* has "an authentic but not defining character," Rahner went on to advise that any Catholic theologian or believer "has not only the right but also the duty of examining it critically and under certain circumstances of contradicting it"—even "to the point of regarding it as objectively erroneous in its basic thesis."[86]

Rahner faulted *Inter Insigniores* for holding up the practice of Jesus and the Apostles as a basis for the Church's teaching on the impossibility of conferring the ministerial priesthood on women. He argued that "at least the possibility must be envisaged of explaining the practice of Jesus and the Apostles simply on sociological and cultural conditions of their time."[87] Rahner argued further that due to the nature of Judaism in Jesus' time, which he said "was based on a male domination," it "is quite impossible to think that Jesus and his Apostles (and with them their Hellenistic congregations under the influence of Judaism) could have abolished or even have been permitted to abolish this male preponderance in their congregations."[88]

In dissenting from *Inter Insigniores,* Rahner asserted that "the transition from the concept of the apostle and the Twelve to the concept of the priest (and bishop) in the Declaration is too simple to fit in with our present-day knowledge of the origins, structure and organisation of the primitive Church."[89] Indeed, Rahner asked whether "it is possible to look at all to Jesus and the Apostles for a plan in regard to the structure of the communities which...could really be related to later times unambiguously and for ever."[90] Further to this, Rahner argued that the question of women's ordination and its connection with the practice of the early Church "must be considered from the standpoint of leadership in the congregations and not from that of strictly sacramental powers." In respect of these sacramental powers, Rahner asserted "that there is no immediate evidence of a special power over the Eucharist in the New Testament."[91]

Rahner concluded his statement of dissent from the Church's doctrine on the male only ministerial priesthood by saying: "It does not seem to be proved that the actual behaviour of Jesus and the Apostles implies a norm of divine revelation in the strict sense of the term."[92] The practice of the non-ordination of women, said Rahner, "can certainly be understood as 'human' tradition like other traditions in the Church which were once unquestioned, had existed for a long time and nevertheless became obsolete as a result of sociological and cultural change."[93]

In the interviews recounted in *Faith in a Wintry Season,* Rahner again expressed his mind on the question of the ordination of women by stating that despite the Declaration *Inter Insigniores* the question was still open and that only time would tell who was right—the Magisterium or its opponents such as himself.[94] He said: "Personally, I can easily imagine that one day, through a further development of society's thinking, the Catholic Church will acknowledge the ordination of women with eucharistic powers to preside over communities."[95]

I will not reply here to Rahner's dissent from the Church's doctrine on the male-only ministerial priesthood as this question will be taken up again in later chapters dealing with the writings of Groome and Fiorenza.

In addition to his dissent from the Church's doctrine on the male-only ministerial priesthood, Rahner also stated that "a Catholic in good standing can certainly hold the opinion that the declaration of Pope Leo XIII concerning the presumed invalidity of Anglican orders (1896) is incorrect, even according to Catholic understanding of the sacraments."[96] Here again Rahner was contradicting the definitive teaching of the Church. According to the *Congregation for the Doctrine of the Faith,* "the declaration of Pope Leo XIII in the Apostolic Letter *Apostolicae Curae* on the invalidity of Anglican ordinations" is a truth taught by the Magisterium which "must be held definitively."[97]

Leonardo Boff and Liberation Theology

Groome's *shared Christian praxis* draws heavily on concepts derived from certain forms of liberation theology. In 1984, the *Congregation for the Doctrine of the Faith* (CDF) issued an *Instruction* on Liberation Theology whose "precise purpose" was stated as: "To draw the attention of pastors, theologians, and all the faithful to the deviations, and risks of deviation, damaging to the faith and to Christian living, that are brought about by certain forms of liberation theology which use, in an insufficiently critical manner, concepts borrowed from Marxist thought."[98] The *Instruction* also pointed out that Marxist-inspired liberation theologies draw the conclusion that class struggle "divides the Church herself, and that in light of this struggle even ecclesial realities must be judged."[99] The publication of this CDF *Instruction* was ordered by Pope John Paul II. Speaking of the authority belonging to such

Magisterial documents, the *Instruction on the Ecclesial Vocation of the Theologian* said:

> The Roman Pontiff fulfils his universal mission with the help of various bodies of the Roman Curia and in particular with that of the Congregation for the Doctrine of the Faith in matters of doctrine and morals. Consequently, the documents issued by this Congregation expressly approved by the Pope participate in the ordinary magisterium of the successor of Peter.[100]

In *Fides et Ratio,* Pope John Paul II referred to the CDF *Instruction on Liberation Theology* in order to point to the "danger of an uncritical adoption by some liberation theologians of opinions and methods drawn from Marxism." In doing this, the Holy Father also recalled the "specific task and service" performed by the CDF to "the Roman Pontiff's universal Magisterium" when it issues documents such as the *Instruction on Liberation Theology.*[101]

Leonardo Boff is one of the leading liberation theologians to have come out of South America. In an article co-authored with his brother, Boff openly expressed his dependence on Marxist ideas by stating: "Liberation theology uses Marxism as an instrument...liberation theology feels no obligation to account to social scientists for any use it makes—correct or otherwise—of Marxist terminology and ideas... Liberation theology freely borrows from Marxism."[102]

In the late 1980s, Boff wrote a *Theological Reflection On Socialism* in which he said: "The Socialist Revolution of 1917 marked something new in the history of humanity. The revolution was not alien to the Holy Ghost, in spite of all the contradictions the revolution encompassed." This *Reflection On Socialism* was first published in the November–December 1988 issue of the Brazilian Catholic Journal *Vozes.* The Journal is operated by the Franciscan Order and at the time Boff was himself an editor. In 1991, Boff's Franciscan Superiors removed him as editor of *Vozes* and ordered him to stop publicising his views for one year. This move to censure Fr. Boff was supported by Cardinal Nicolas Lopez Rodriquez who was President of the Latin American Bishops' Council. Some time after this happened, Boff left the priesthood.

A characteristic of Boff's work is that he often uses conventional theological language but empties it of its doctrinal content. He recommends Freire's pedagogical method as the most apt educational instrument for the diffusion of his own liberationist ideas. Also, he develops a model of the Church which he says is based on a "Communitarian Christianity" and places it in opposition to the hierarchically structured Church founded by Christ. He claims the ecclesiastical structure of the Catholic Church cannot be traced back any further than the third century. Finally, in terms of the theory of class struggle, Boff casts the "Roman Catholic Church" in the role of an oppressor.[103]

Boff's theology is a mishmash of Marxist theory and a defective Christology which was influenced by the ideas of Rudolf Bultmann and Karl Rahner under whom he studied in Munich. In describing Boff's Christology, Hans Urs von Balthasar said:

> Boff seems to develop a Christology strongly influenced by Bultmann, with whom he suggests that we know very little about the historical Jesus. However, he believes that we can interpret the primary intention of Jesus as that of someone who understood himself in his role as liberator of the poor and oppressed...The liberation—the 'Kingdom of God'—which Jesus expected to result from it—had failed to come about, as expressed by the authentic cry on the Cross: 'Why hast thou forsaken me?' The doctrine of substitution is rejected by Boff as well as by Rahner. It is up to us present-day Christians to adopt and execute what Jesus had wished and begun.[104]

In his book *From Death To Life,* Cardinal Christoph Schonborn, O.P. places Boff in the company of scholars such as Reimarus, Reuss, Schweitzer and Loisy—all of whom propagated the error that Jesus' disciples, and even Jesus himself, lived in an eschatological "high tension," expecting the imminent eruption of the kingdom of God and the overthrowing of this world. This error reached its high point in the writings of Rudolf Bultmann, who equated the Kingdom of God with the end of the world. Cardinal Schonborn points out that Boff assumed the correctness of Bultmann's theory.[105]

Boff's liberation theology has influenced Groome's ecclesiology. Coupled with this, it is interesting to note that Groome quotes approvingly Boff's statement that the Church's law on priestly celibacy "is tantamount to an unlawful violation of the rights of the faithful" and he agrees with Boff also that women should be ordained to the ministerial priesthood.[106]

Fr. Rodger Charles S.J., has stated that Boff's brand of liberation theology amounted to nothing less than "a total rejection of [the Catholic Church's] self-understanding through the centuries down to and through the Second Vatican Council."[107]

In his book *Covenantal Theology,* Fr. Donald Keefe S.J., makes reference to Boff by saying:

> Boff, following Rahner's lead…argues that the humanity of the *Theotokos* [Greek term for Mary as the 'Mother of God'] is hypostatically united to the Holy Spirit, thereby presenting a feminine expression of God in history corresponding to that masculine expression found in the Incarnation of the *Logos.*[108]

Edward Schillebeeckx

Groome's writings indicate that his ideas on sacramental theology have been heavily influenced by the work of Edward Schillebeeckx.[109] Regarding social history, Fr. Schillebeeckx asserts there are no such things as hard "facts" but "only interpreted facts."[110] In this regard, it is important to note that Schillebeeckx has relied heavily on the philosophical ideas of Jurgen Habermas in constructing his theology. This view of history gives Schillebeeckx great leverage in his interpretation of early Christian sources. He holds that the pre-Pauline Christian communities were characterised by a thorough egalitarianism centred on communities of "free fellowships."[111] Schillebeeckx argues that these household churches were not hierarchically structured but rather represented "a brotherhood and sisterhood of equal partners" which were governed along "democratic" lines.[112]

Schillebeeckx believes that over time these democratically structured house churches gave way to more hierarchically structured communities. He claims to have unearthed New Testament material to support such a claim and he asserts that "Paul and Luke have clearly different views of church structures."[113] He asserts that it was only at the end of the first century when it was finally decided that ultimate authority in the communities would reside in those believers "who took the title *'episkopos'* (presbyter) and deacon", and that "from this time on women have to keep silent in services."[114] On the basis of this "reinterpretation" of Christian origins, Schillebeeckx goes on to say that this evolution in the structural form of the early Christian community represented a surrender to "the non-Christian pagan, patriarchal household code of the Graeco-Roman family...Christians took over hierarchy."[115]

The most radical aspect of Schillebeeckx's reconstruction of New Testament data is that he understands the appointment of the "Twelve" as having merely symbolic eschatological meaning which leaves him free to assert that "the Christian communities did not receive any kind of church order from the hands of Jesus."[116] Having thus deprived the church of it's divinely instituted hierarchucal structure, Schillebeeckx is free to assert that all ministries in it grew out of "what developed spontaneously from below...in accordance with the sociological laws of group formation."[117] Indeed, Schillebeeckx follows his ideas through to their logical conclusion and affirms that "one can never give an absolute cut-and-dried formulation of what is specifically normative for Christians, since this can only be found in changing historical forms."[118]

In reference to Schillebeeckx's book titled *The Church with a Human Face: A New and Expanded Theology of Ministry,* Fr. Donald Keefe, S.J. says:

> Schillebeeckx has thus proceeded...to contest the Tridentine emphases, repeated at Vatican II, upon the relation of the sacrament of orders, and the apostolic succession, to the Eucharist, and has concluded to a notion of the relation of the Church to the Eucharist in which the faith of the Church is the cause of the Eucharistic presence: this of course rules out the notion of the Eucharist as the representation of the One Sacrifice, and thus of the need for ordination to offer that sacrifice. Thereby the Letters To The Churches of Ignatius of Antioch, written *ca.*110, have become an embarrassment: Schillebeeckx has cooly relegated them to a later period, in order that they may be the product of an ecclesial development that would hardly have been possible so early in the second century.[119]

Finally Schillebeeckx was one of the 163 theologians who, in 1989, signed the *Cologne Declaration.* This *Declaration* objected to what it saw as an "inadmissible" attempt to "enforce" the Pope's "competence in the field of doctrinal teaching alongside that of jurisdiction." Coupled with this, it objected to the more active role Pope John Paul II had taken in the appointment of bishops in Austria and Switzerland. In particular, it opposed the authority with which Pope John Paul II was reaffirming the doctrine of *Humanae Vitae* asserting that he was doing so "without consideration for the degrees of certainty and the different weight of Church statements."[120]

RICHARD MCBRIEN

To buttress his own theological positions, Groome occasionally draws on the work of Fr. Richard McBrien who he refers to as "a leading American theologian."[121] McBrien is well known for his book *Catholicism,* against the first edition of which the Australian Bishops issued a monitum stating it was not suitable as a reference text for teachers. In his booklet *Ministry,* McBrien asserts that in the early Church there were "two diverging patterns of ministry: (a) 'charismatic,' as in the original Jerusalem community and later in Corinth; and (b) 'structured' based on the synagogue model."[122]

McBrien asserts that over the course of the first few centuries, the institutional model of the Church won out over the charismatic as Christians sought to fix the structure of their community along the pattern of the prevailing municipal and political organisational structures.[123] He asserts that "in the early Church there was no hard and fast distinction between clergy and laity" but rather that such a distinction emerged "with the establishment of Christianity as the state religion in the fourth century."[124]

In 1996, the National Conference of Catholic Bishops' Committee on Doctrine in the United States censured the 3rd edition of McBrien's *Catholicism* for "certain shortcomings." The committee was concerned about McBrien's treatment of the Virgin Birth of Jesus, the perpetual virginity of Mary, the ordination of women, his treatment of moral issues such as homosexuality and contraception, and about his tendency to place the teaching of the Church on the same level as the opinion of dissenting theologians.[125] Dr. Robert Fastiggi, who is an associate professor of religious studies at St. Edward's University in Austin, Texas, sums up McBrien's methodology well where he says:

What one often finds is a discussion of a traditional Catholic dogma cast in ambiguous terms by a skilful turn of phrase or a clever sleight of hand. Thus, the uncritical reader is given the false impression that McBrien's discussion of the dogma is safely rooted within the parameters of Catholic orthodoxy without realizing that the author has frequently undercut the full meaning and authority of the dogma itself.[126]

The distinguished theologian, Fr. John Hardon, S.J., has cited Richard McBrien as an example of "still professed Catholic writers" who "are re-interpreting the Church's teaching on the sacraments with a license and a devastating consequence that has no counterpart in the last half millennium." Having said this, Fr. Hardon added:

I will never forget the conference I attended of the Midwestern Theological Society. The keynote speaker was Richard McBrien. Through one hour of learned discourse, he gave the audience one reason after another why the Catholic priesthood was not a sacrament instituted by Our Lord at the Last Supper. It was a later second century innovation. A logical consequence of this position is to question whether Christ had instituted any of the sacraments.[127]

DAVID TRACY

Groome refers to David Tracy as "a great theologian of our day."[128] Tracy has posited that "neo-orthodoxy" is not viable for futuristic Catholicism because it tends "to bolster concepts of God and Christian revelation which are neither internally coherent, nor able to illuminate our own ineluctable commitment to the ultimate meaningfulness of every struggle against oppression and for social justice and agapic love."[129]

On February 21, 1972, the Sacred Congregation For The Doctrine Of The Faith (SCDF) issued a statement on *Errors Concerning the Mysteries of the Incarnation and the Trinity* which sought to draw attention to "the mystery of the Son of God made man, and the mystery of the Most Holy Trinity." This Majesterial statement was to reaffirm the teaching of Chalcedon which "decreed for belief that the Son of God according to His Divinity was begotten of the Father before all ages, and according to His human nature was born in time of the Virgin Mary". This SCDF statement was targeted at so-called "non-Chalcedonian" Christologies which—according to the distinguished theologian Fr. Jean Galot, S.J.—found expression in the works of theologians such as David Tracy and Hans Kung.[130]

Tracy, together with Richard McBrien, was one of the signatories of Charles Curran's protest against *Humanae Vitae* which appeared in the August 4, 1968 edition of the *National Catholic Reporter.* On Ash Wednesday, February 28, 1990, an advertisement titled *"A Call for Reform in the Catholic Church"* was published in the *New York Times.* Calling for such things as the ordination of women, "open dialogue" in regard to Church teaching on sexual morality and nomination of bishops by the laity, this advertisement again included David Tracy amongst its signatories.

PAUL TILLICH (1886-1965)

Groome refers to Paul Tillich as "the great Lutheran theologian."[131] Tillich was very concerned to define the way in which Christianity related to secular culture and to social problems. In this regard, his work had an affinity to various liberation theologies. In attempting to make Christianity more acceptable to secular man, Tillich posited that Christians could draw inspiration from the Scriptures without having to accept as true the miracles they report. In other words, Tillich advocated an approach to Scripture that being predicated on scepticism did not require a supernatural frame of reference.

Tillich advocated the recreation of Christian symbols which he said "die because they can no longer produce response in the group where they originally found expression."[132] In Catholic faith and worship, the word "symbol" has diverse meanings. For example, in the *CCC* we read: "A symbol of faith is a summary of the principal truths of the faith and therefore serves as the first and fundamental point of reference for catechesis."[133]

Tillich believed that changing historical conditions required the destruction of received Christian symbols. In particular, he was concerned with reshaping Christianity's perception of God. Consequently, he advocated that we move beyond the Trinitarian understanding of God—which, he said, represented "the glorification of an absurdity in numbers" which had become "a powerful weapon for ecclesiastical authoritarianism and the suppression of the searching mind."[134] Tillich believed historical consciousness had now reached the stage where the deity needs to be primarily understood as the "ground of being" which "points to the mother-quality of giving birth, carrying and embracing and, at the same time, of calling back."[135] In this, Tillich emphasized God's immanence to the exclusion of his transcendence. Consequently, in Tillich's theology, God's presence in the world is emphasized while his superiority to the world is lost sight of to the extent that he is seen as identical with the totality of this world.[136]

Alasdair MacIntyre is of the view that Tillich's work is essentially atheistic.[137] He says that Tillich reduces the reality of God to nothing more than our own "ultimate concern." In "relying on his own doctrine of God," says MacIntyre, Tillich evacuates belief in God "of all its traditional content" and reduces it to nothing more than "moral seriousness."[138]

Philosophical Influences On Fiorenza

Fiorenza approaches reality from the perspective of that branch of the women's liberation movement which has deep roots in neo-Marxist social theory. She testifies that some of her most important theological positions were developed "in conversation with the critical theory of J. Habermas."[139] She acknowledges her debt to "critical theory as developed in the Frankfurt School" for providing her with "a hermeneutical understanding" of Christian tradition as "a source not only of truth but also untruth" that has "perpetuated violence, alienation and oppression."[140] Fiorenza also draws on the work of Paulo Freire using his "definition of oppression" to articulate her own understanding of how women are culturally oppressed.[141]

SIMONE DE BEAUVOIR

In constructing her theology, Fiorenza has drawn much inspiration from the work of Simone de Beauvoir. She posits that de Beauvoir's book *The Second Sex* is "still paradigmatic" for feminist attempts to analyse the way "Christian churches" have contributed to the development of "sexist ideology." Fiorenza asserts that it is by way of this same "sexist ideology" that the Christian churches have been able to perpetuate "women's inferiority."[142]

De Beauvoir was a long-time companion of the French existentialist philosopher Jean-Paul Sartre (1905-1980). Sartre's major concern as a philosopher was with the question of "freedom." He claimed that existence precedes essence and that the exercise of "freedom" was the means by which the human person defined himself or herself. Positing that "human beings are nothing but what they make of themselves,"[143] Sartre held that human beings are faced with a project of possibilities whereby they can decide what is to be made of them. Underpinning his claims in this regard was his belief that there is no God and therefore no creator to conceive of a "human nature." Consequently, he asserted that obstacles to one's self-realisation are posed by both belief in God and by other people. A failure to negotiate these obstacles to self-realisation is known as "alienation." Sartre inevitably brought his atheistic understanding of human existence to its logical conclusion by asserting that there are no immutable moral values to determine how the human person should act and behave.

Towards the end of his life, Sartre attempted to reconcile his existentialist philosophy with Marxism. In this he was influenced by de Beauvoir who sought to integrate Marxist tenets with a form of liberalism understood as a program of life wherein individual liberty is seen as the decisive and absolute value. Apart from this, Sartre's influence on the intellectual development of de Beauvoir was very extensive—especially his philosophical works entitled *Imagination* (1936) and *The Psychology of Imagination* (1940). In these works, Sartre argued that consciousness can negate the world as it is and replace it with a possible alternative so that the human being has a capacity for negation which is "the power not to be what it is and to be what it is not."[144]

De Beauvoir attempted to apply Sartre's existentialism to the situation of women in the world. In contemporary feminist literature, the most frequently quoted words of de Beauvoir are:"One is not born, but rather becomes, a woman. No biological, psychological, or economic fate determines the figure that the human female presents in society; it is civilisation as a whole that produces this creature."[145] Commenting on these words of de Beauvoir, Fr Manfred Hauke says: "Conceiving oneself as a woman is thus something completely free. Just as there is, for Sarte, no predetermined essence of man, so it is even more true , for de Beauvoir, that there exists no 'essence of woman' with specific qualities that must be presupposed when making one's own life choices."[146]

De Beauvoir believed that in patriarchal societies, women live in a state of permanent alienation because they are defined in relation to men: "She [woman] is defined and differentiated with reference to man and not he with reference to her; she is the incidental, the inessential as opposed to the essential. He is the Subject, he is the Absolute—she is the Other."[147] At times de Beauvoir expressed hope in the emergence of an androgynous human being that would end the alienation of women in patriarchal societies, while on other occasions she seems to hold up masculinity as the goal to be striven for. In one place she spoke of ten-to twelve-year-old girls as "children who lack something of being boys."[148] She asserted that the problem of female alienation could be moderated by rearing girls in the same way as boys are reared. She stated that "if the little girl were brought up from the first with the same demands and rewards, the same severity and the same freedom, as her brothers, taking part in the same studies and the same games, promised the same future," and if she was "authorized to test her power in work and sports, competing actively with the boys", that then "she would not find the absence of the penis—compensated by the promise of a child—enough to give rise to an inferiority complex."[149]

De Beauvoir believed that capitalism and the institutionalisation of the right to private property worked to subjugate women economically—it amounted, she said, to "the great historical defeat of the feminine sex."[150] Coupled with this, after asserting that being "wife, mother and housekeeper," subjects a woman to economic "vassalage" that deprives her of "recognition as an individual," she advised that escape from this alienating state be had through women seeking "gainful employment" in work outside the home.[151] Holding up Communist Russia as the place where women were most liberated, de Beauvoir said: "It is in Soviet Russia that the feminist movement has made the most sweeping advances...Faithful to Marxist tradition, Lenin bound the emancipation of women to that of the workers; he gave them political and economic equality."[152]

De Beauvoir claimed that women—by being subject to conceiving, gestating, giving birth to and nurturing children—were thereby placed in a position of less independence and autonomy than men. She said:

Woman is of all mammalian females at once the one who is most profoundly alienated and the one who most violently resists this alienation; in no other is enslavement of the organism to reproduction more imperious or more unwillingly accepted... In comparison with her the male seems infinitely favoured: his sexual life is not in opposition to his existence as a person. [153]

Consonant with her degraded view of female biology and physiology, de Beauvoir believed that women must be able to protect themselves against unwanted pregnancies by whatever means necessary. Consequently, she lampooned the Catholic Church's arguments against abortion[154] and openly boasted of having undergone two abortions herself.[155] She applauded Communist Russia for having introduced in 1924 "the facility of divorce and the legalising of abortions" which she said had "assured woman's liberty with relation to the male."[156] De Beauvoir rejoiced in the possibilities opened up by artificial insemination—saying that it "completes the evolutionary advance that will enable humanity to master the reproductive function" thereby allowing it to place "woman" in a position "to assume the economic role that is offered her and will assure her of complete independence."[157]

Theological Influences on Fiorenza

Theologically, Fiorenza draws on a wide range of authors from both English and non-English speaking backgrounds. Some of these authors with which people in the English-speaking world are familiar include David Tracy, Hans Kung, Rudolf Bultmann, Edward Schillebeeckx, Rosemary Radford Ruether, Leonardo Boff and Carol Christ. Most significantly, however, Fiorenza's religious feminist ideology reveals a heavy dependence on the ideas of Elizabeth Cady Stanton and Mary Daly.

ELIZABETH CADY STANTON

Stanton (1815-1902) was a founder of the women's rights movement in the United States. She was the first president of the National Woman Suffrage Association and for a time she coedited the feminist journal *Revolution*. Stanton was convinced that the emancipation of women would be impossible unless the Bible was first rejected as revelation and until it came to be more widely interpreted from a feminist point of view.[158] To this end, Stanton published the first feminist edition of the Bible which she titled *The Women's Bible*.

In 1994, Fiorenza was the chief contributing author and editor of *Searching the Scriptures: A Feminist Commentary,* which she dedicated to Stanton. Fiorenza began this book with a quotation from Stanton which reads:

> Now, to my mind, the Revising Committee of the 'Women's Bible,' in denying divine inspiration for such demoralizing ideas shows a more worshipful reverence for the great Spirit of All Good than does the Church. We have made a fetich of the Bible long enough. The time has come to read it as we do all other books, accepting the good and rejecting the evil it teaches.[159]

Following the above quotation, Fiorenza in her introduction to *Searching the Scriptures* praised Stanton for having drawn attention to the way in which people have "internalised scripture's misogynist teachings as the Word of God" and used its authority "against women struggling for emancipation."

MARY DALY

Fr. Manfred Hauke points out that in the index of persons section in one particular German dictionary of feminist theology, the name most frequently cited after Jesus is that of Mary Daly.[160] For many years up until the late 1990s, Daly taught theology at Boston College. She was finally dismissed for refusing to allow men to enroll in her classes. Reporting on her dismissal, Professor James Hitchcock stated that for many years Boston College had defended Daly "against charges that she was undermining Catholic doctrine in her courses and her writing."[161]

In speaking of the New Testament theme of "Antichrist", Daly says: "What if the idea has arisen out of the male's unconscious dread that women will rise up and assert the power robbed from us?" She adds, "the Antichrist dreaded by the Patriarchs may be the surge of unconsciousness, the spiritual awakening, that can bring us beyond Christolatry into a fuller stage of conscious participation in the living God."[162] In this perspective, says Daly, "the Antichrist and the Second Coming of Women are synonymous" whereby "this Second Coming is not a return of Christ but a new arrival of female presence, once strong and powerful, but enchained since the dawn of patriarchy."[163] Finally on this point, Daly posits that this "Second Coming" of women "means that the prophetic dimension in the symbol of the great Goddess...is the key to salvation from servitude to structures that obstruct human becoming..."[164]

Fiorenza acknowledges her debt to Daly for having arrived at an understanding that the "imposed submission" of women to men in "Christian patriarchy" is responsible for "turning women against themselves" and condemning them to live as "marginal beings."[165] In 1996, in challenging women to "break the silence" in regard to all the ways that patriarchy has "excluded" them "from defining the world and the meaning of human life and society," Fiorenza repeated Mary Daly's rallying call that women must reclaim "the power of the naming that was stolen from us."[166]

Reminiscent of Simone de Beauvoir, whose work exercised a formidable influence on her, Daly's first major publication was titled *The Church and the Second Sex*. Here, Daly followed de Beauvoir in asserting that one is not conceived and born as a woman but rather becomes one in response to environmental influences.[167] To suit her theological purposes, Daly plays off one Scriptural passage against another—e.g. Jesus against St. Paul—as though there was no inner harmony in the message of the Bible.[168] In her book *Beyond God the Father*, Daly claimed that the Bible was irredeemably sexist. She said: "If God in 'his' heaven is a Father ruling 'his' people, then it is in the 'nature' of things...that society be male-dominated."[169] In 1974, Daly summarised "the significance of the women's revolution as anti-Christ and its import as anti-Church."[170]

Reference

1   My criticism of neo-Marxist liberation theologies should not be construed as implicit approval for all forms of capitalism. Liberal Capitalism, which accompanied the Industrial Revolution, generated grave injustices. It was thoroughly materialistic in that it considered "profit as the key motive for economic progress, competition as the supreme law of economics, and private ownership of the means of production as an absolute right that has no limits and carries no corresponding social obligation" (Pope Paul VI, *Populorum Progressio*, n. 26). Capitalism of this sort inevitably gives rise to the "international imperialism of money" (ibid.). In teaching that the right to private property is a natural right necessary to ensure human liberty, the Church simultaneously insists that this right is not absolute since it must not

be understood in isolation from complementary principles such as the universal purpose of created things (Cf. Vatican II, *Gaudium et Spes*, n. 69; Pope John Paul II, *Centesimus Annus*, n. 6). In *Centesimus Annus*, Pope John Paul II pointed out that the market economy becomes morally acceptable only when it is "circumscribed within a strong juridical framework which places it at the service of human freedom in its totality" (n. 42). Indeed, Pope John Paul II invited people of goodwill to consider "an alternative" to liberal capitalism and socialism: "a society of free work, of enterprise and of participation...which demands that the market be appropriately controlled by the forces of society and by the state so as to guarantee that the basic needs of the whole of society are satisfied" (CA. n. 35).

2   Thomas H Groome, *Christian Religious Education*, op. cit. p. 175.

3   Thomas H Groome, *Sharing Faith*, op. cit. p. 484; cf. pp. 156–159, 184, 244.

4   Thomas H Groome, *Educating for Life*, op. cit. p. 103.

5   Cf. Paulo Freire, *Pedagogy of the Oppressed*, Penguin Books, Middlesex 1972, pp. 101, 113.

6   Paulo Freire, *Pedagogy of the Oppressed*, op. cit. p. 15 n.1 together with Chapter 3.

7   Direct references to Hegel in Groome's books are: *Christian Religious Education*, pp. 5, 127, 150, 153, 162–65, 166, 173, 179; *Sharing Faith*, pp. 72, 101, 475n.38; *Educating for Life*, p. 144.

8   Cf. *The Concise Encyclopedia of Western Philosophy and Philosophers*, edited by J.O. Urmson & Jonathan Ree, Routledge, London 1991, p. 127.

9   Cf. *The Concise Encyclopedia of Western Philosophy and Philosophers*, op. cit. p. 129.

10   Fr. Joseph M De Torre, *The Humanism of Modern Philosophy*, Southeast Asian Science Foundation, Manilla 1989, p. 148.

11   Jacques Maritain, Christianity and Democracy: *The Rights of Man and Natural Law*, Ignatius Press, San Francisco 1986, p. 15.

12   Thomas H. Groome, *Sharing Faith*, p. 228. Other direct references to Heidegger in Groome's books are: *Christian Religious Education*, pp. 4, 12, 13, 17; *Sharing Faith*, pp. 76–79, 98, 452–53n.5, 457—58n.61.

13   On this point see *The Concise Encyclopedia of Western Philosophy and Philosophers*, op. cit. pp. 130–131.

14   Cf. Fr. Joseph M De Torre, *The Humanism of Modern Philosophy*, op. cit. p. 245.

15   Pope John Paul II, *Fides et Ratio*, n. 76.

16   This point will become very significant later on when we come to look at some problems with the theology of Karl Rahner who was a student of Heidegger's and whose ideas have influenced Groome in the development of his theological positions.

17   Allan Bloom, *The Closing of the American Mind,* Penguin Philosophy, London 1988, pp. 154, 311.

18   Alasdair MacIntyre, in *The MacIntyre Reader,* edited by Kelvin Knight, Polity Press, Cambridge, UK, 1998, p. 265.

19   See especially *Sharing Faith,* op. cit. pp. 76-79, 98, 452-453n.5, 457-458n.61.

20   Thomas H Groome, *Christian Religious Education,* op. cit. p. 4.

21   Ibid.

22   Cf. *Christian Religious Education,* op. cit. pp. 169-175. Other direct references to Habermas in Groome's books are: *Christian Religious Education,* pp. 130, 168, 170-76, 180-82, 188, 204; *Sharing Faith,* pp. 102-3, 107-8, 476n.45-46 and 48, 477-78n.68, 478n.73; *Educating for Life,* 45, 198, 296, 317.

23   Jurgen Habermas, *A Review of Gadamer's Truth and Method, in 'Hermeneutics and Modern Philosophy',* edited by Brice R. Wachterhasuer, State University of New York Press, Albany 1986, p. 272.

24   Rev. Professor Leonard Kennedy, *Legacy of Karl Rahner,* Homiletic and Pastoral Review, July, 1994, p. 63.

25   Karl Rahner, S.J., *Faith in a Wintry Season,* Crossroad, New York, 1990, pp. 15 and 51.

26   Fr. Avery Dulles, S.J., *The Craft of Theology: From Symbol to System* (New Expanded Edition), Crossroad, New York 1996, p. 124.

27   Tomas Alvira et.al., Metaphysics, Philosophy Books Series, Sinag Tala Publ., Manila, 1991, p. 4.

28   Ibid.

29   Fr. Robert J. Henle, S.J., *Transcendental Thomism: A Critical Assessment, in One Hundred Years Of Thomism: A Symposium,* edited by Victor B. Brezik, C.S.B., Centre For Thomistic Studies, University of St. Thomas, Houston, 1981, p. 110. Fr. Henle served as President of Georgetown University from 1969-1976 and as Academic Vice President of Saint Louis University prior to that.

30   Ibid. 110.

31   Karl Rahner, S.J. *On the Encyclical 'Humanae Vitae,' in Theological Investigations,* Vol. 11, Darton, Longman & Todd, London 1974, p. 272-73.

32   Ibid. p. 276.

33   Ibid. pp. 284-285.

34   Ibid. p. 286.

35   Ibid. p. 281.

36   Ibid.

37   Karl Rahner, S.J., *Faith in a Wintry Season: Conversations and Interviews with Karl Rahner,* edited by Paul Imhof and Hubert Biallowons, Crossroad, New York 1990 p. 72.

38   Karl Rahner, in *The Content of Faith, The Best of Karl Rahner's Theological Writings,* edited by Karl Lehmann and Albert Raffelt, Crossroad, New York, 1993,

p. 588. Thomas Malthus' view that there is a negative correlation between population growth and human flourishing is now a totally discredited theory.

39　Contraceptive acts were condemned in the catechetical instructions of St. Clement of Alexandria (cf. *Paedagogus*, II, 9-10). This work was a synthesis for catechetical purposes of the tradition of Christian moral education in the East and in North Africa in the generation after the Apostles. Contraceptive practices were condemned by St. Jerome and St. Augustine in the West and by St. Epiphanius and St. John Chrysostom in the East.

40　The doctrine of *Humanae Vitae* was reaffirmed by the 1980 Synod of Bishops on the Family.

41　For several centuries up until 1917, the Canon Law of the Church condemned as gravely sinful, any act by a man or a woman "so that he cannot generate, or she cannot conceive, or offspring be born."

42　*The Catechism of the Council of Trent* stated: "Married persons who, to prevent conception or procure abortion, have recourse to medicine, are guilty of a heinous crime." The *Catechism of the Catholic Church* reaffirmed the doctrine of *Humanae Vitae* by saying: "Every action which, whether in anticipation of the conjugal act, or in its accomplishment, or in the development of its natural consequences, proposes, whether as an end or as a means, to render procreation impossible is intrinsically evil" (n. 2370).

43　Pope Pius XI, *Casti Connubii,* n. 54.

44　Ibid. n. 56.

45　Ibid. n. 57.

46　Vatican II, *Gaudium et Spes,* n. 51.

47　Ibid.

48　Ibid.

49　Cf. Footnote 14 attached to *Gaudium et Spes,* n. 51.

50　Cf. Cardinal Pericle Felici, *L'Osservatore Romano,* September 26, 1968.

51　Pope John Paul II, *L'Osservatore Romano,* 12 December 1988.

52　Pontifical Council for the Family, *Vademecum: For the Use of Confessors,* n.4., *L'Osservatore Romano,* December 12, 1997 (emphasis added).

53　Karl Rahner, S.J., *Faith in a Wintry Season,* op. cit. p. 112

54　Ibid.

55　Ibid. p. 113

56　Karl Rahner, *Shape of the Church to Come,* Seabury Press, New York, 1974, p. 64.

57　Karl Rahner, S.J., *Theological Investigations,* Vol. XIV, trans. David Bourke (Darton, Longman & Todd), London 1976, pp. 14-15.

58　Ibid. p. 16

59　Professor John M. Finnis, *Moral Absolutes: Tradition, Revision and Truth,* Catholic University of America Press, Washington, D.C. 1991, p. 100.

60 Richard McCormick, cf. "Current Theology: Notes on Moral Theology," *Theological Studies* 40 (1979), pp. 89-90. On this point see also Germain Grisez in *The Teaching of Humanae Vitae, A Defense: Is its Teaching Infallible? Are its Norms Defensible?* by John C.Ford, S.J, Germain Grisez, Joseph Boyle, John Finnis, William May (Ignatius Press, San Francisco 1988, p. 17).

61 Richard A. McCormick, S.J., *Some Early Reactions To Veritatis Splendor,* Theological Studies, Vol. 55, No. 3, 1994, p. 486.

62 Ibid. p. 485.

63 Ibid. p. 486.

64 Charles Curran, *Transition and Tradition in Moral Theology,* University of Notre Dame Press, London 1979, p. 46

65 Cf. Charles E. Curran, *Ten Years Later,* 'Commonweal' 105, July 7, 1978, p. 426. See also Curran's *New Perspectives in Moral Theology,* University of Notre Dame Press, Indiana 1974, pp. 19-22, 41-42, 192-193, 211, 271-276.

66 Pope John Paul II, *Veritatis Splendor,* n. 5.

67 Pope John Paul II, Fides et Ratio, n. 68.

68 Professor John M. Finnis, *Moral Absolutes: Tradition, Revision and Truth,* op. cit. pp. 24, 100.

69 Cf. Germain Grisez *The Way of the Lord Jesus: Christian Moral Principles,* Vol. 1, Franciscan Herald Press, 1983, Chicago 1983, p. 404n11. In this very long footnote, Grisez develops in some depth his critique of Rahner's notion of "Fundamental Option." Also, in this book Grisez critiques Rahner's notion of changing "concrete human nature" and its relationship to moral norms (cf..Appendix 3, p. 859).

70 Cf. Germain Grisez and Russel Shaw, *Fulfilment in Christ: A Summary of Christian Moral Principles,* University of Notre Dame Press, Indiana 1991, pp. 41 and 70-71.

71 Cf. Ibid. p. 195.

72 Cardinal Joseph Ratzinger, *Principles of Catholic Theology: Building Stones for a Fundamental Theology,* Ignatius Press, San Francisco 1987, pp. 170-71. Professor William May, in the revised edition of his book *An Introduction to Moral Theology,* refers his readers to "an excellent and devastating critique of Rahner's anthropology" by Cornelio Fabro (Our Sunday Visitor, Indiana, 1994, p. 246n16).

73 Karl Rahner, Grundkurs des Glaubens. *Einfuhrung in den Begriff des Christentums* (Freiburg: Herder, 1976), pp. 225-26; cited by Cardinal Ratzinger in Principles of Catholic Theology, op. cit. p. 167

74 Cardinal Joseph Ratzinger, *Principles of Catholic Theology: Building Stones for a Fundamental Theology,* Ignatius Press, San Francisco 1987, p. 167.

75 Alfred Haussler, M.D., *The Betrayal of the Theologians, Human Life International,* Washington, 1982; Rahner's comments on "pre-human" stages of post-fer-

tilisation development appeared in Naturwissenschaft und Theologie, brochure 11, 1970, p. 86.

76 Karl Rahner, S.J., *Faith in a Wintry Season,* op.cit. p. 98.

77 Ibid..

78 Ibid. p. 72

79 Cf. *Declaration on Procured Abortion, Sacred Congregation for the Doctrine of the Faith,* n. 14.

80 Pope Leo XIII, *Encyclical Libertas Praestantissimum.*

81 Pope John Paul II, *Evangelium Vitae,* n. 71.

82 *Declaration on Procured Abortion, Sacred Congregation for the Doctrine of the Faith,* 1974, n. 20.

83 Pope John Paul II, *Evangelium Vitae,* n. 71.

84 Rev. Professor Leonard Kennedy, *Legacy of Karl Rahner,* op. cit. p. 65.

85 Karl Rahner, *Theological Investigations: Concern for the Church,* Vol. XX, (Darton, Longman & Todd, London, 1981), p. 37.

86 Ibid. p. 38.

87 Ibid. p. 40.

88 Ibid. p. 43..

89 Ibid. p. 40.

90 Ibid.

91 Ibid. p. 43.

92 Ibid. p. 45.

93 Ibid.

94 Karl Rahner, S.J., *Faith in a Wintry Season,* op. cit. p. 101.

95 Ibid.

96 Ibid. p. 171.

97 Cf. *Doctrinal Commentary on the Concluding Formula of 'Professio fidei,' Congregation for the Doctrine of the Faith,* June 29, 1998, published in L'Osservatore Romano, July 15, 1998.

98 *Instruction On Certain Aspects Of The Theology Of Liberation,* CDF, 1984. This statement of purpose appears in the introduction to the document.

99 *Instruction On Certain Aspects Of The Theology Of Liberation,* CDF, 1984, Part IX, n.2.

100 *CDF The Ecclesial Vocation of the Theologian,* n. 18. Cf. Code of Canon Law, cc. 360-361; Pope Paul VI, Apost. Const. Regimini Ecclesiae Universae, August 15, 1967, nn. 29-40, AAS 59 (1967), 879-899; Pope John Paul II, Apost. Const. Pastor Bonus, June 28, 1988, AAS 80 (1988), 873-874. The authoritative status of such documents emanating from the CDF was reaffirmed again recently by Pope John Paul in Fides et Ratio (cf. n. 54 together with footnote 70).

101 Pope John Paul II, *Fides et Ratio,* n. 54.

102 Boff Brothers, cited by Rev. Professor J. H. Gillis in *Liberation Theology: A Debate,* Challenge Magazine, Canada, May 1990, p. 24

103 Everything I have here attributed to Boff is to be found in the concluding chapter of his book Good News to the Poor, Orbis Books, U.S.A., 1992.

104 Hans Urs von Balthasar. *Test Everything: Hold Fast To What Is Good.* Ignatius Press, San Francisco, 1989, pp. 41–42. Von Balthasar's identification of a nexus between Boff's defective Christological ideas and those of Rahner is not surprising. As we will see later, Groome's Christology is also defective. For example, he approves Rahner's suggestion for a reformulation of the teaching of the Council of Chalcedon on the 'Person of Christ'—something with which there are serious problems as we shall see in Chapter 8. For a critique of Rahner's Christology, see *Cardinal Ratzinger's Principles of Catholic Theology,* op. cit. pp.162–170. For an outline of the doctrinal problems that arise from Rahner's attempted reformulation of the dogma of Chalcedon, see *The Mystery of Jesus Christ: A Christology and Soteriology Textbook* by F. Ocariz et.al., Four Courts Press, Dublin 1994, pp. 85 and 127–129.

105 Bishop Christoph Schonborn, O.P. *From Death To Life: The Christian Journey,* Ignatius Press, San Francisco 1995. Cf. Book Review by Edith Myers, Homiletic and Pastoral Review, January 1996, p. 77.

106 Thomas Groome, *Sharing Faith,* op. cit. pp. 328, 517n.111

107 Rodger Charles, S.J., *Christian Social Witness and Teaching: The Catholic Tradition from Genesis to Centesimus Annus,* vol. 2, From Biblical Times to the late Nineteenth Century, Gracewing, Leominster, 1998, p.312.

108 Fr. Donald Keefe, S.J., *Covenantal Theology: The Eucharistic Order of History (revised edition),* Presidio Press, California, 1996, p. 188.

109 Cf. *Sharing Faith,* pp. 309nn. 21 and 21, 341–42, 310n.29, 519.n18.

110 Fr Edward Schillebeeckx, O.P., *The Church With A Human Face: A New and Expanded Theology of Ministry,* Crossroad, New York 1985, p. 40

111 Ibid. p. 46

112 Ibid. pp. 47 and 49

113 Ibid. p. 51

114 Ibid. pp. 66 and 67

115 Ibid. p. 68.

116 Fr Edward Schillebeeckx, O.P., *Ministry: Leadership in the Community of Jesus Christ,* Crossroad, New York 1981, p. 5; The Church With A Human Face: A New and Expanded Theology of Ministry, Crossroad, New York 1985, p. 74.

117 Fr Edward Schillebeeckx, O.P., *Ministry: Leadership in the Community of Jesus Christ,* op. cit. p. 5.

118 Fr Edward Schillebeeckx, O.P., *The Church With A Human Face,* op. cit. p. 2.

119 Fr. Donald Keefe, S.J., *Covenantal Theology: The Eucharistic Order of History,* op. cit. p. 108.

120 *The Cologne Declaration,* Tablet, U.K., February 4, 1989.

121 Thomas Groome, *Educating for Life,* op. cit. p. 57.

122 Fr Richard McBrien, *Ministry, Harper & Row,* San Francisco 1987, p. 30.

123 Cf. Ibid. p. 33.

124 Ibid. p. 38.

125 The review of *McBrien's* book by the Bishops' Committee On Doctrine was published in the April 18, 1996 edition of Origins.

126 Dr. Robert Fastiggi, *Homiletic and Pastoral Review,* June 1998, pp. 48-49.

127 Fr. John Hardon, S.J., Sacraments: Channels of Divine Grace, Catholic Faith Magazine, May/June 1996. Also available on http://www.catholic.net/-RCC/Periodicals/Faith/0506-96/article1.html).

128 Thomas H. Groome, *Educating for Life,* op. cit. P. 142.

129 David Tracy, *Blessed Rage for Order: The New Pluralism in Theology,* Seabury Press, New York 1975, p. 245.

130 Cf. Jean Galot, Christo contestato, Florence, 1979. See also F. Ocariz et. al., *The Mystery of Jesus Christ: A Christology and Soteriology Textbook,* op. cit. p. 68, 65n.

131 Thomas Groome, *Educating for Life,* op. cit. p. 91.

132 Paul Tillich, *Dynamics of Faith,* Harper & Row, New York 1967, p. 43.

133 *CCC.* n. 188.

134 Paul Tillich, *Systematic Theology,* Volume 3, Nisbett & Co., London, 1964, p. 310.

135 Ibid. p. 313. Tillich's understanding of God as the "ground of being" should not be understood as necessarily synonymous with the Catholic doctrine of God as "subsistent Being" which means that God is "the absolute fullness of Being and therefore of every perfection" (Cf. Pope John Paul II, A Catechesis on *The Creed: God Father and Creator,* Volume I, Pauline Books and Media, Boston 1996, pp. 115, 121).

136 Here I have summarised Fr. Manfred Hauke's evaluation of Tillich's theology which he gives in his book God or Goddesses (Ignatius Press, San Francisco, 1995, pp. 82-83, 146). Hauke is a very highly regarded theologian. He is the author of the book Women in the Priesthood: A Systematic Analysis in the Light of the Order of Creation and Redemption (Ignatius Press, San Francisco, 1988). Referring to this book, Hans Urs Von Balthasar said that it was "undoubtedly the definitive work available on this important topic."

137 Alasdair MacIntyre, in *The Honest To God Debate,* edited by David L. Edwards, SCM Press Ltd, Bloomsbury Street, London, 1963, p. 217.

138 Ibid. pp. 219-220

139 Elizabeth Schussler Fiorenza, *Sharing Her Word: Feminist Biblical Interpretation in Context,* Beacon Press, Boston 1998, p.7.

140 Elizabeth Schussler Fiorenza, Discipleship of Equals, op. cit. pp. 62-63. What Fiorenza means by "Christian tradition" is not always clear, I will address this problem later when I look at Groome's understanding of the term.

141 Elizabeth Schussler Fiorenza, *Discipleship of Equals,* op. cit. p. 55.

142 Ibid. p. 58.

143 Jean-Paul Sarte, *Is Existentialism a Humanism,* Zurich 1947, p. 14.

144 On this point, see Concise Encyclopedia of Western Philosophy and Philosophers, Routledge, London 1991, p. 287-88.

145 Simone de Beauvoir, *The Second Sex, Vintage Books,* New York 1974, p. 301.

146 Fr Manfred Hauke, God or Goddess? *Feminist Theology: What Is It: Where Does It Lead?* Ignatius Press, San Francisco 1995, p. 29.

147 Simone de Beauvoir, *The Second Sex,* op. cit. p. xix.

148 Ibid. pp. 807-808.

149 Ibid. p. 36.

150 Cf.. Ibid. p. 60 and see also pp. 63, 92, 98, 103, 114, 127-28.

151 Cf. Ibid. pp. 699, 755

152 Ibid. p. 142.

153 Ibid. p. 36.

154 Ibid. pp. 540-543.

155 In regard to de Beauvoir's two abortions, Fr Manfred Hauke points out that her decision in this area was probably heavily influenced by pressure from Sarte who did not want her to have children. Fr. Hauke tells of how de Beauvoir was greatly oppressed by Sartre who "betrayed her by his philandering." Fr. Hauke adds that one reason why de Beauvoir disparaged women who aspired to having "a faithful husband and children" might have been the fact that her relationship with Sartre deprived her of both (cf. God or Goddesses? op.cit. pp. 28-33).

156 Simone de Beauvoir, *The Second Sex,* op. cit. p. 143.

157 Simone de Beauvoir, *The Second Sex,* op. cit. p. 136.

158 On this point see *The Emerging Feminist Religion* by Cornelia R. Ferreira, Life Ethics Centre, Toronto 1989, p. 6.

159 Elizabeth Cady Stanton, cited by Elizabeth Schussler Fiorenza in Searching the *Scriptures: A Feminist Commentary,* Crossroad, New York 1994.

160 Fr Manfred Hauke, *God or Goddesses?* Ignatius Press, San Francisco 1995, p. 78

161 Professor James Hitchcock, *Fellowship of Catholic Scholars* Quarterly, Vol. 22, No. 3, Summer 1999, p. 27.

162 Mary Daly, *Beyond God the Father: Towards a Philosophy of Women's Liberation,* Beacon Press, Boston 1973, p. 96

163 Ibid.

164 Ibid.

165 Elisabeth Schussler Fiorenza, *Discipleship of Equals,* op. cit. page 58 (including note 9) as well as page 61 (note 16).

166 Elisabeth Schussler Fiorenza, *The Power of Naming: A Concilium Reader in Feminist Liberation Theology*, Orbis Books, New York 1996, p. 168.

167 Cf. *The Church and the Second Sex,* New York, 1968, p. 71-72

168 Cf. *The Church and the Second Sex,* New York, 1968, pp. 77-81, 198

169 Mary Daly, *Beyond God the Father,* op. cit. p.13

170 Mary Daly, *Beyond God the Father,* Beacon Press, Boston 1973, p. 140

4

Fiorenza's Methodology

In outlining, in the previous chapter, some of the philosophical ideas that have influenced Fiorenza and Groome in the development of their ideas, I was not suggesting that Catholic theologians and religious educators should not study philosophy with a view to using it as an aid to better express Catholic doctrine. In his Encyclical *Fides et Ratio,* Pope John Paul II called on theologians "to enter into a demanding critical dialogue with both contemporary philosophical thought and with philosophical tradition in all its aspects, whether consonant with the word of God or not."[1] In this Encyclical, the Holy Father stated that "the Church considers philosophy an indispensable help for a deeper understanding of faith and for communicating the truth of the Gospel."[2] Relating this to catechesis, the Pope added: "In addition to theology, reference to *catechesis* is also important, since catechesis has philosophical implications which must be explored more deeply in the light of faith."[3] Through the "study of the structure of knowledge and personal communication, especially the various forms and functions of language," philosophy can assist theology to both receive and better communicate the contents of the deposit of faith.[4]

Pope John Paul II points out that the relationship between theology and philosophy stems from the fact that the primary source for theology is the truth conferred by Revelation which "is a truth to be understood in the light of reason."[5] In saying that Christians can fruitfully engage philosophy in their proclamation of the Gospel, the Holy Father cited in *Fides et Ratio* an example from the New Testament to illustrate his point. He said: "The Acts of the Apostles provides evidence that Christian proclamation was engaged from the very first with the philosophical currents of the time. In Athens, we read, Saint Paul entered into discussion with 'certain Epicurean and Stoic philosophers' (Acts 17:18)."[6] Pope John Paul II followed up this point by stating that the Fathers of the Church adopted a similar stance in regard to philosophy: "It was on this basis that the Fathers of the Church entered into fruitful dialogue with ancient philosophy, which offered new ways of proclaiming and understanding the God of Jesus Christ."[7]

A Need For Discernment

In pointing to the benefits to be derived for the proclamation of the Gospel from a positive engagement between philosophy and the disciplines of theology and catechesis, Pope John Paul II was careful in *Fides et Ratio* to point out also that "the teaching of the Saviour is perfect in itself and has no need of support, because it is the strength and the wisdom of God."[8] Being this "wisdom of God," it therefore follows that "the knowledge which the Church offers to man has its origin not in any speculation of her own, however sublime, but in the word of God which she has received in faith (cf. *1 Th* 2:13)."[9] Therefore, while philosophy can be of assistance to theology and catechesis, nevertheless "the truth made known to us by Revelation is neither the product nor the consummation of an argument devised by human reason" and hence "philosophy is not meant in the first place to bolster and complete Christian truth."[10] Therefore, "theology's source and starting-point must always be the word of God revealed in history, while its final goal will be an understanding of that word which increases with each passing generation."[11] Consequently, when harnessing philosophical ideas to the work of theology, care must be taken to ensure that philosophy does not claim a "self-sufficiency of thought" that refuses "the truth offered by divine revelation"—since to do so would mean that philosophy would do "itself damage" by precluding "access to a deeper knowledge of truth."[12]

While the Church "sees in philosophy the way to come to know fundamental truths about human life,"and while it "considers philosophy an indispensable help for a deeper understanding of faith and communicating the truth of the Gospel," at the same time the Church also recognises that present in any given philosophical system there can be elements "which are incompatible with her own faith,"[13] Consequently, since some philosophies can "obscure" or "deny" the contents of faith,[14] it is thereby necessary to adopt critical caution when importing philosophical ideas into catechetical or theological methodologies, lest in doing so we compromise the integrity of the truth to be communicated. In *Fides et Ratio,* Pope John Paul II drew attention to the need for such a discernment when in reference to the attitude of the Church Fathers to various philosophies he said: "Faced with various philosophies, the Fathers were not afraid to acknowledge those elements in them that were consonant with Revelation and those that were not. Recognition of the points of convergence did not blind them to the points of divergence."[15] Coupled with this, the Holy Father cited the example of Saint Paul and Saint Irenaeus who did not hesitate to "sound the alarm" when they were "confronted with a cultural perspective which sought to subordinate the truth of revelation to the interpretation of the philosophers."[16]

The Methodology of Fiorenza

In their published works, Groome and Fiorenza frequently contradict Catholic doctrine. This is sometimes due to a failure on their part to make a proper discernment in the use of philosophical and theological ideas they borrow from elsewhere. For the rest of this chapter, I will deal only with the methodology of Fiorenza.

To position herself along the theological spectrum, Fiorenza says: "My work joins the discussion on theological hermeneutics from the intellectual location within post-Vatican II European Catholicism, which is quite distinct from American immigrant Catholicism."[17] She says, "The hermeneutical center of feminist biblical interpretation is the women-church (*ekklesia gynaikon),* the movement of self-identified women and women-identified men in biblical religion."[18] She understands the "*ekklesia* of women" as "part of the wider women's movement in society and in religion that conceives itself not just as a civil rights movement but as a women's liberation movement."[19] She adds that "as a Christian" she does not "use the expression women-church" in an "exclusionary" sense but rather "as a political oppositional term to patriarchy."[20]

Two terms which appear frequently in Fiorenza's work are *kyriarchy* and *discipleship of equals.* To understand the term *kyriarchy* as it is used by

Fiorenza, it is necessary to first understand the meaning of the terms *androcentrism* and *patriarchy. Androcentrism* refers to the assumption that the experience of males is normative for both men and women—something which, it is claimed, gives rise to 'androcentric' or 'noninclusive' language. *Patriarchy* refers to systems of social organisation ruled by men wherein women are expected to be submissive to males at all levels.

As regards the term *kyriarchy,* Fiorenza uses it to refer to what she sees as the place of elite males in maintaining interlocking structures of domination characteristic of patriarchal society. She believes the term qualifies the terms *androcentrism* and *patriarchy* by delineating "power imbalances in gender relations."[21] She says that "*Kyriarchy* connotes a social-political system of domination and subordination that is based on the power and rule of the lord/master/father," and she believes the term to be "historically more adequate and theologically more appropriate than the word 'hierarchy' which is commonly used in English to designate a pyramidal system of power relations."[22] In other words, Fiorenza uses the term *kyriarchy* as a substitute term for *patriarchy* to refer to the hierarchy of the Catholic Church.

What all of the above indicates is that Fiorenza's theology is eminently political. Following Paulo Freire, she believes an important function of her work to be the fostering of a "feminist process of *'conscientization'* or learning" that will lead to the recognition of "sociopolitical, economic, cultural and religious contradictions."[23]

Regarding the term *Discipleship of Equals,* Fiorenza uses it to refer to the way in which she imagines the early Church was organised. Based on her attempted reconstruction of the early "Christian movement"—a term she uses in preference to "early Church"—Fiorenza asserts that it was "egalitarian" and "inclusive of women's leadership." She claims this early Christian movement, "challenged and opposed the dominant patriarchal ethos" in the Greco-Roman world through its "praxis of equal discipleship." [24]

Fiorenza holds that "Feminist theology begins with the systematic exploration of women's experience," especially, "the experience of women struggling against patriarchal oppression."[25] In consequence of this, she approaches the interpretation of Sacred Scripture from a feminist liberationist perspective which revolves around four key elements which are: i) a hermeneutics of suspicion, ii) a hermeneutics of proclamation, iii) a hermeneutics of remembrance, iv) a hermeneutics of creative actualization.[26]

A *hermeneutics of suspicion* means that in approaching the Bible we must take as a "starting point the assumption that biblical texts and their interpretations are androcentric and serve patriarchal functions."[27] Applying a hermeneutics of suspicion to Sacred Scripture means reading it in such a way as to "elaborate as much as possible the patriarchal, destructive aspects and oppressive elements of the bible."[28] For Fiorenza, the adoption of a hermeneutics of suspicion calls for the rejection of "all sexist traditions even if they are deeply rooted in Christian Scriptures and traditions."[29] She says that "The first and never-ending task of a hermeneutics of suspicion...is to elaborate as much as possible the patriarchal, destructive aspects and oppressive elements of the bible," something which she says is necessary in order "to detect the antipatriarchal elements and functions of biblical texts, which are obscured and made invisible by androcentric language and concepts."[30]

A *hermeneutics of remembrance* seeks to realise in the present the vision of women who struggled to maintain the early "Christian movement" as an egalitarian "discipleship of equals." In Fiorenza's words, a *hermeneutics of remembrance* "moves from the biblical texts about women to the reconstruction of women's history."[31] Such a reconstruction or re-visioning of women's history opens up new possibilities for the present.

A *hermeneutics of proclamation* means that elements in Sacred Scripture judged to be androcentric and oppressive to women should not be included in the proclamation of the Gospel or in the lectionary. Speaking of this, Fiorenza says: "A *hermeneutics of proclamation* insists that texts which reinscribe patriarchal relations of domination and exploitation must not be affirmed and appropriated. In theological terms, they should not be proclaimed as the word of G-d [sic] but must be exposed as the words of men."[32] She says: "If the locus of revelation is not the androcentric text but the life and ministry of Jesus and the movement of women and men called forth by him, then we must develop critical-historical methods for feminist readings of the biblical texts."[33] In other words, Fiorenza postulates that those biblical texts which she interprets as oppressive to women may not have the authority of Sacred Scripture.

Finally, a *hermeneutics of creative actualisation* (or *liberative vision and imagination*), "involves the church of women in the imaginative articulation of women's biblical story and its ongoing history and community."[34] In a subsequent development of this idea, Fiorenza states that, "the social function of imagination and fantasy is to introduce possibilities...for we can work toward actualizing only that which we have first imagined."[35] Outlining the way such an interpretive hermeneutic might be applied to the canon of Sacred Scripture, Fiorenza says:

> To displace the marginalising dynamics of the androcentric bib-lical source-text or artefact, a critical feminist interpretation must take the texts about women out of their contextual frame-works and reassemble them like the mosaic stones in a feminist design which, rather than recuperating the marginalising or oppressive tendencies of the text, is able to counteract it.[36]

In pursuing such a critical feminist reconstruction of Sacred Scripture, Fiorenza makes no attempt to cloak its subjectivist nature. She says: "Such a feminist critical method could be likened to the work of a detective insofar as it does not rely solely on historical 'facts' nor invents its evidence, but is engaged in an imaginative reconstruction of historical reality."[37]

A good example of what Fiorenza means by "imaginative recon-struction of historical reality" is the way she interprets the differences between two Gospel stories: the first, where St. Luke tells of a woman "who was a sinner" anointing the "feet" of Jesus with her tears and dry-ing them with her hair (cf. Lk 8: 36-56); and the second, where St. Mark gives an account of a woman who poured costly ointment on the "head" of Jesus in response to which action he directed that wherever the Gospel is proclaimed the story of what this woman had done in anointing, "my body beforehand for its burial...will be told also in remembrance of her" (cf. Lk 14: 3-9). St. Matthew has a woman anoint the "head" of Jesus (Mt 26: 7) while in St. John's Gospel the woman anoints the "feet" of Jesus (Jn 12: 3). In St. Matthew and St. John the anointing occurs at Bethany. St. John is the only Evangelist to mention the woman's first name which he gives as Mary.

In the time of Jesus, to anoint the "feet" of a guest entering one's home was a commonplace occurrence. Given this fact, Fiorenza won-ders why St. Luke mentions the insignificant detail of the anointing of Jesus' "feet" in contradistinction to St. Mark who tells us that it was Jesus' "head" that had been anointed by the woman—an action which Fiorenza claims had great symbolic significance and which "must have been understood immediately as a prophetic recognition of Jesus, the Anointed, the Messiah, the Christ."[38] Fiorenza says that "It is much more likely that in the original story the woman anointed Jesus' head" and she infers that in the retelling of the story St. Luke substituted the word "feet" for "head" in order placate the sensitivities of his "patriarchal Greco-Roman audience."[39] Further to this, Fiorenza asserts that in reshaping this account of Jesus' anointing, St. Luke "shifts the focus of the story from woman as disciple to woman as sinner."[40] Fiorenza accuses all three synoptic Gospels of suppressing the woman's name: "The name of the betrayer is remembered, but the name of the faithful disciple is forgotten because she was a woman."[41]

This attempt by Fiorenza to 'expose' what she believes to be the 'androcentric' and 'patriarchal' prejudice underlying the final shape given to the Gospels, has to be understood in terms of her overall objective which is to recreate the early Christian community as a "discipleship of equals" where both men and women had equal access to all ministries in the Church. Her reconstruction of St. Luke's Gospel to conform exactly to what is recounted in St. Mark is all part of this overall strategy. In particular, in reconstructing the Gospel accounts of Jesus' anointing, Fiorenza is seeking to give to these events a significance for the ordering of Christian community and worship equal to that of the sacramental charge to celebrate the Eucharist conferred by Christ on the apostles at the Last Supper. Fiorenza makes her intent in this regard clear when she says:

> Both Christian feminist theology and biblical interpretation are in the process of rediscovering that the Christian gospel cannot be proclaimed if the women disciples and what they have done are not remembered. They are in the process of reclaiming the supper at Bethany as women's Christian heritage in order to correct symbols and ritualisations of an all-male Last Supper that is a betrayal of true Christian discipleship and ministry.[42]

A grave danger lurking in Fiorenza's *hermeneutic of creative actualisation* is that truth will become confused with fantasy. Imagination departs from reality, either for recreation or creation, and then returns to reality again. Fantasy, on the other hand, is expressive of a desire to escape into the world of the unreal in which the creature presumes to control the world and the creator. While there is scope in theology and catechesis for a creative presentation of the doctrines of the faith, there is no scope whatsoever for fantasy.

In reference to the canon of Sacred Scripture, Fiorenza, after first stating that "the motivation for the authoritative collection was not only religious but also political," goes on to add: "Struggles between orthodoxy and heresy, as well as the political goal of establishing the unified church as the consolidating power of the Roman Empire, drove the exclusionary selection of the canonisation process."[43] Fiorenza posits that "the canon reflects an androcentric selection process" which has "functioned to inculcate a kyriarchal imperial church order" in consequence of which "feminist biblical scholarship cannot remain within the limits drawn by the established canon."[44]

Fiorenza contends that only those parts of the Bible that are not opposed to her egalitarian and liberationist views should be accepted as authoritative—which means she approaches the Sacred Scriptures seeking to identify a canon within the canon. She argues that "only the nonsexist and non-androcentric traditions of the Bible and the nonoppressive traditions of biblical interpretation have the theological authority of revelation if the Bible is not to continue as a tool for the oppression of women."[45] She holds that such a "hermeneutics of suspicion" needs to be applied to "oppressive" Biblical texts in order that they be "demythologized as androcentric codifications of patriarchal power and ideology that cannot claim to be the revelatory Word of God."[46]

In her 1998 book *Sharing Her Word,* Fiorenza quoted Vatican II's *Dogmatic Constitution on Divine Revelation (Dei Verbum)* as having stated that the bible "contains revelation, namely in the form of a written record; but that not all of Scripture is revelation."[47] A council of the Church would never make such a statement as it would conflict with the teaching of the Church on the inspiration and inerrancy of Sacred Scripture.[48] But how then has Fiorrenza managed to attribute such a statement to Vatican II? In referencing this quotation which she claimed came from Dei Verbum, Fiorenza wrote: "W. Abbott and J. Gallaher, eds., *The Documents of Vatican II* (New York: America Press, 1966), 108."[49] Note, how in giving this reference to what she claimed was the teaching of Vatican II, Fiorenza did so by giving a page number from the Abbot collection of Vatican II documents rather than the actual paragraph number in *Dei Verbum* itself which would be the usual method for giving such a reference. When we turn to page 108 of the Abbott collection of Vatican II documents, what we find is not the Council document *Dei Verbum* at all, but rather an introductory commentary on it by R.A.F. MacKenzie, S.J. It is Fr. MacKenzie and not *Dei Verbum* who stated that "Not all Scripture is revelation."

The Abbott edition of the Vatican II documents, together with its accompanying commentaries, was published in 1966. Some commentators have drawn attention to serious inaccuracies in Abbott's translation of the texts of Vatican II,[50] as well as to confusing elements in its accompanying commentaries. In 1975, a more accurate translation of the Vatican II documents was produced by Austin Flannery, O.P.—it is from Flannery's work that the *CCC* draws all its citations from Vatican II documents.

While the Flannery edition of the Vatican II documents did not contain confusing introductory commentaries as did the Abbot edition, it did however contain a revealing preface written by Cardinal John Wright. Here, in referring to earlier translations of Vatican II documents such as Abbott's, Cardinal Wright said that the rapidity with which earlier translations had been produced assured "frequent infelicities, not to say inaccuracies, in translation." Cardinal Wright added that some of the first translations "were frequently accompanied by commentary or reactions usually friendly and helpful to further lines of independent thought, but frequently irrelevant and even confusing to one seeking to learn exactly what the Council *said* rather than what someone outside the Council *thought* about the matter."[51]

Continuing now with Fiorenza's assault on the integrity of the canon of Sacred Scripture. In order "to undo the exclusionary kyriarchal tendencies of the ruling canon and to renew the debate on the limits, functions and extent of the canon," Fiorenza believes it is necessary "to explore extra-canonical writings" and to make them "available to a wider audience."[52] By the term "extra-canonical writings," Fiorenza has in mind gnostic texts such as the *Gospel of Mary,* the *Acts of Thecla* and the *Gospel of Thomas*—all of which either feature or allude to female figures holding leadership roles equal or superior to those held by Saint Peter and the other apostles in the early "Christian movement."[53] In adopting such a methodology, Fiorenza is thereby implicitly asserting that such heretical texts should be taken as trustworthy sources of information about the role of women in the early Church.[54] The corollary of this is, that in pursuing her "theological reconstruction" of Christian origins, Fiorenza is forced to the conclusion that the New Testament does not bear faithful witness to the true position of women in the early Church. She says: "Our canon of Scriptures reflects a patriarchal selection process and has functioned to bar women from ecclesial leadership."[55]

Due to her belief that the canon of Sacred Scripture cannot provide adequate evidence to substantiate her claim that the early Church was structured as a "discipleship of equals," Fiorenza is driven "to challenge the traditional interpretive models for the reconstruction of early Christianity and to search for new models that can integrate both egalitarian and 'heretical' traditions."[56] In her 1983 book *In Memory of Her,* Fiorenza pursued such an integration of "egalitarian" and "heretical" traditions by drawing on gnostic texts in an attempt to marshall historical data to validate her assertion that in the early Church women held leadership roles equivalent or maybe even superior to that of Peter and the other apostles.[57]

In her 1993 book *Discipleship of Equals,* Fiorenza again drew on heretical sources in order to lend plausability to her claim that in the early Church women had access to all its ministries. Applying a hermeneutic of suspicion to the Gospel of Luke, she said:

> The Lukan stress on Peter as the primary Easter witness must be situated within the early Christian discussion of whether Peter or Mary of Magdala qualifies as the first resurrection witness. This discussion understands Peter to be in competition with Mary Magdalene insofar as he complains constantly that Christ has given so many revelations to a woman.[58]

Such a reconstruction of life in the early Christian community is without support from any orthodox Christian sources. Unperturbed by this, Fiorenza goes on and uses heretical sources to bolster her case. She says:

> The Gospel of Thomas reflects this competition between Peter and Mary Magdalene. The gnostic writing *Pistis Sophia* and the apocryphal Gospel of Mary further develops this motif. In the Gospel of Mary it is asked how Peter can be against Mary Magdalene because she is a woman if Christ has made her worthy of his revelations...While the Gospel of Mary argues for the authority of Mary Magdalene on the grounds that Christ loved her more than all the other disciples, the Apostolic Church

Order argues for the exclusion of women from the priesthood by letting Mary Magdalene herself reason that the weak, namely, women, must be saved by the strong, namely, men. This dispute about the resurrection witness of Mary Magdalene shows, however, that Mary, like Peter, had apostolic authority in some Christian communities even into the third and fourth centuries.[59]

Fiorenza states that "a feminist history of the first centuries could demonstrate," that "Paul, the post-Paul tradition, and the Church Fathers reversed the emancipatory processes of their society." This, she asserts, led to the "elimination of women from ecclesial leadership," which she claims was achieved through "women's domestication under male authority in the home or in the monasteries."[60] However, to substantiate this claim, Fiorenza again draws upon heretical sources for support. She says:

> Less known, however, is how strong the women's movement for emancipation was in various Christian groups. For instance, in Marcionism, Montanism, Manicheism, Donatism, Priscillianism, Messalianism, and Pelagianism, women had authority and leading positions. They were found among the bishops and priests of the Quintillians...Women flocked to the medieval reform movements and were leaders among the Waldensians, the Anabaptists, the Brethren of the Free Spirit, and especially the Beguines.[61]

Fiorenza's attitude to Sacred Tradition is no different from her attitude to Sacred Scripture. In stating that "tradition is a source not only of truth but also of untruth, repression, and domination,"[62] Fiorenza does not specify what she means by "tradition." Is she referring to reformable disciplinary, liturgical and devotional 'traditions', or does she mean instead to include within her frame of reference the 'Tradition' of the Church. Taken in the context of the entire book from which these quotations are drawn, it is clear that Fiorenza is definitely referring to the 'Tradition' of the Church irrespective of whatever else she intends by her use of the word 'tradition'. That this is so is made clear by Fiorenza in her treatment of the Church's doctrine on a male-only ministerial priesthood.

To achieve the emancipation of women in the Church, Fiorenza argues that "A reconceptualisation of church and ministry is necessary."[63] She states that women have a "right to be admitted to all minis-terial functions in the Church, including the episcopal and papal offices."[64] She says that "since the gifts of the Spirit are not restricted to a certain group within the community," then "everyone is able and authorized in the power of the Spirit to preach, to prophesy, to forgive sins."[65] She holds that "all members of the people of God, by virtue of their baptismal 'priesthood', have the capability and right to exercise liturgical and ecclesiastical leadership functions."[66] Fiorenza is of the view that "Eucharistic con-celebrations [sic]"—together with "the lay-ing on of hands in the ordination rite"—"are manifestations of the Church as an 'old boys club" which she suggests leads many Christians to "believe that God is a male patriarch and that the male sex of Jesus Christ is salvific."[67] She holds that the teaching of the Magisterium on a male-only ministerial priesthood "denies the universality of incarnation [sic] and salvation in order to maintain and legitimate the patriarchal structures of the Church."[68]

In speaking of the theological enterprise, Vatican II said: "Sacred theology relies on the written Word of God, taken together with sacred Tradition, as on a permanent foundation."[69] Given the fact that Fiorenza calls into question the integrity of the canon of Sacred Scripture and that she rejects the Magisterium's delineation of the contents of the Apostolic Tradition, then what claim can she possibly have without being absurd to the title 'Catholic theologian'?

Reference

1   Pope John Paul II, *Fides et Ratio*, n. 105.
2   Ibid. n. 5
3   Ibid. n. 99
4   Ibid. n. 65
5   Ibid. n. 35
6   Ibid. n. 36
7   Ibid. n. 36
8   Pope John Paul II, *Fides et Ratio*, n. 38. The Holy Father made this statement by way of a quotation from Saint Clement of Alexandria.
9   Pope John Paul II, *Fides et Ratio*, n. 7.
10 Ibid. nn. 15 and 38.
11 Ibid. n. 73.
12 Ibid. n. 75.
13 Ibid. nn. 5 and 50.
14 Ibid. n. 84.
15 Ibid. n. 41.

16 Ibid. n. 37.

17 Elisabeth Schussler Fiorenza, *Sharing Her Word,* op. cit. p. 85.

18 Elizabeth Schussler Fiorenza, in *Feminist Interpretation of the Bible,* edited by Letty Russell, Westminster Press, Philadelphia 1985, p. 126.

19 Ibid.

20 Ibid. pp. 126–27

21 Elisabeth Schussler Fiorenza, *Sharing Her Word,* op. cit. p. 16.

22 Ibid. p. 190n.52.

23 Elisabeth Schussler Fiorenza, *But She Said, Beacon Press,* Boston 1992, p. 53 together with footnote 6 for reference to Freire.

24 Elisabeth Fiorenza, *In Memory of Her,* SCM Press, London 1983.

25 Elizabeth Schussler Fiorenza, *Discipleship of Equals,* op. cit. p. 213 and 244.

26 Elisabeth Schussler Fiorenza, *Bread Not Stone: The Challenge of Feminist Biblical Interpretation,* Beacon Press, Boston 1984, p. 15. See also But She Said, op. cit. pp. 52–76.

27 Elisabeth Schussler Fiorenza, *Bread Not Stone,* op. cit. p. 15.

28 Elisabeth Schussler Fiorenza, "The Will to Chose or to Reject: Continuing Our Critical Work" in *Feminist Interpretations of the Bible,* edited by Letty Russel (Philadelphia: Westminster 1985, p. 130).

29 Elizabeth Schussler Fiorenza, *Discipleship of Equals,* op. cit. p. 127.

30 Elisabeth Schussler Fiorenza, "The Will to Chose or to Reject: Continuing Our Critical Work" in *Feminist Interpretations of the Bible,* op. cit. pp. 130–131.

31 Elisabeth Schussler Fiorenza, *Bread Not Stone,* op, cit. p. 15.

32 Elisabeth Schussler Fiorenza, *But She Said,* op. cit. p. 54. Explaining her reason for spelling 'God' as 'G-d', Fiorenza says: "Since our language is not capable of adequately expressing the Divine, making all our names and titles for G-d insufficient, I seek to indicate this theological insight by writing the standard designation of the Divine in a 'broken' form rather than to adopt the lengthy 'Goddess/God'" (Discipleship of Equals, op. cit. p. 10. note. 13).

33 Elisabeth Fiorenza, *In Memory of Her,* op. cit. p. 41.

34 Elisabeth Schussler Fiorenza, *Bread Not Stone,* op. cit. p. 15.

35 Elisabeth Schussler Fiorenza, *But She Said,* op. cit. p. 54. See footnote 10 for sources of Fiorenza's quotation on this point.

36 Elisabeth Schussler Fiorenza, *But She Said,* op. cit. p. 32.

37 Elisabeth Schussler Fiorenza, *In Memory of Her,* op. cit. p. 41.

38 Ibid. p. xiv.

39 Ibid. pp. xiii–xiv.

40 Ibid. p. xiii.

41 Ibid. p. xiii.

42 Ibid. p. xiv.

43 Elisabeth Schussler Fiorenza, *Searching The Scriptures: A Feminist Commentary,* Volume Two, Crossroad, New York 1994, p. 5.

44 Ibid. p. 8.

45 Elisabeth Schussler Fiorenza, *Towards a Feminist Biblical Hermeneutics, in Readings in Moral Theology* No 4, edited by Charles Curran and Richard A. McCormick, Paulist Press, New York 1984, p. 376.

46 Elisabeth Schussler Fiorenza, *In Memory of Her,* op. cit. p. 32.

47 Elisabeth Schussler Fiorenza, *Sharing Her Word,* op. cit. p. 85.

48 The question of the inspiration and inerrancy of Sacred Scripture will be taken in Chapter 11 of this book.

49 Elisabeth Schussler Fiorenza, *Sharing Her Word,* op.cit. p. 202n.18.

50 See for example the critique of some aspects of the Abbott translation in Robert H. *Vascoli's What God Has Joined Together: The Annulment Crisis in American Catholicism,* Oxford University Press, 1998, pp. 30-31.

51 Cardinal John Wright, in Vatican II: The Conciliar and Post Conciliar Documents, Austin Flannery, O.P., Dominican Publications, Dublin, 1975, pp. xxiii-xxiv.

52 Elisabeth Schussler Fiorenza, *Searching The Scriptures: A Feminist Commentary,* Volume Two, Crossroad, New York 1994, p. 5.

53 See chapters 30, 32, 34, 38 and 39 of *Searching The Scriptures: A Feminist Commentary,* Volume Two, edited by Elisabeth Schussler Fiorenza, Crossroad, New York 1994.

54 For example, see pages 304-309 of *In Memory of Her where Fiorenza* draws support for her position from the Gospel of Mary Magdalene, the Sophia Jesus Christi, the Gospel of Philip, the Dialogue of the Redeemer, the Gospel of Thomas and the Pistis Sophia.

55 Elisabeth Schussler Fiorenza, *Discipleship of Equals,* op. cit. p. 167.

56 Ibid. p. 174.

57 Cf. Elisabeth Schussler Fiorenza, *In Memory of Her,* op. cit. pp. 243-351.

58 Elisabeth Schussler Fiorenza, *Discipleship of Equals,* op. cit. p. 164.

59 Ibid.

60 Ibid. p. 69.

61 Ibid. p. 70.

62 Ibid. p. 62. Admission to the ministerial priesthood is a privilege which comes by way of a call from Christ rather than by way of some perceived "right" as Fiorenza asserts. Also, Fiorenza seems to understand the ordained priesthood more in terms of 'power' than of 'service' which is its truest meaning.

63 Elisabeth Schussler Fiorenza, *Discipleship of Equals,* op. cit. p. 32.

64 Ibid. p. 37.

65 Ibid. p. 34.

66 Ibid.

67 Elisabeth Schussler Fiorenza, *The Power of Naming,* op. cit. p. 162.

68 Ibid.

69 Vatican II, *Dei Verbum,* n. 24.

5

Theological Underpinnings of Groome's Pedagogical Method

In this Chapter, I will outline Groome's approach to the interpretation of Divine Revelation and briefly look at how this undergirds his pedagogical method. In Chapters 6-8, I will examine some of the more significant theological errors of Groome and Fiorenza with a view to carrying out a more systematic evaluation of their work in Chapters 9 and 10.

First, a few words on the meaning of the word *praxis*. The term's usage has a long history—stretching from the philosophers of ancient Greece, through Marxism, and into the philosophy of Karol Wojtyla (Pope John Paul II). In Chapter 10, I will try to situate Groome's understanding and use of the word *praxis* in relation to the meaning it carries in the work of Aristotle, Marx and Wojtyla. For the present, we will make do with dictionary definitions of the term such as: i) "exercise or discipline for a specific purpose; practical application of rules as distinguished from theory,"[1] ii) "practice, esp. as opposed to theory,"[2] iii) "the practising of an art or skill. (Greek, = doing)."[3]

Turning directly now to Groome's *shared Christian praxis*. While Freire sought to create an educational system for use with the oppressed of Latin America, Groome has set himself the task of creating a more comprehensive 'liberating' pedagogy of faith. He says: "Freire invented a pedagogy for the oppressed, and I had a more obvious task of trying to create a pedagogy for oppressors."[4] Consonant with his commitment to recycling Freire's ideas in both a social and ecclesial context, Groome believes that an overriding objective of religious education should be the development of a critical consciousness that will foster an 'emanci-patory praxis' and thereby contribute to the emergence of a more egal-itarian society and Church. In consequence of his commitment to such a 'vision', Groome perceives all education as eminently political in nature: "I contend that the essential characteristic of all education is that it is a political activity."[5]

In tandem with his understanding of education as essentially politi-cal, Groome endorses "liberation theologies" because he believes they "heighten the emancipatory intent of Christian faith" in a way that "unmasks what has been used to oppress and victimize."[6] In reference to "feminist liberation theology," Groome is of the view that it "reflects and contributes to the rising feminist consciousness throughout the world" and that it "mounts a devastating criticism of the patriarchy of the Church and challenges the ways Jewish and Christian traditions have been interpreted to legitimate the oppression of women and dom-ination by men."[7]

If someone wanted to use the educational system to spread abroad the liberationist ideas of people such as Freire, Boff and Fiorenza, one could not find a pedagogical method more suited to such a purpose than Groome's *shared Christian praxis*. In this context, it is revealing how some of Groome's disciples are also staunch supporters of Boff and Freire-type liberation and educational ideas. For example, Dr. Michael Bezzina, Director of Religious Education and Educational Services at the Parramatta Catholic Education Office, published a paper in 1996 calling for a renewal of Catholic Education in Australia based on a Boff and Freire-type liberation theology and pedagogy.[8] As was noted in Chapter 1 of this book, Bezzina co-authored an article in 1997 which called for the professional development of teachers which would allow them to undertake an "implementation" of *shared Christian praxis* which would be "faithful to Groome's thinking."[9]

Groome understands *shared Christian praxis* in integral terms in that it is intended to address the entire "being" of the person to be edu-cated.[10] He is concerned to promote an education that goes beyond cognition to "conation" or "wisdom." According to Groome, conation reflects the "holistic intent of a knowing/desiring/doing that engages and shapes the whole 'being' of people as agents-subjects in the world."[11] Groome states his understanding of conation to have emerged "from the recognition that we humans have a fundamental eros that moves us to realise our 'being' in relationship with others in the world."

He adds that the vocation to become "agent-subjects-in-right relation-ship" can "be frustrated by personal choices and by situations or social structures that militate against one so becoming."[12]

Groome's understanding of the nature of "being" bears the imprint of Marxist ideas. Though distancing himself from Marx's atheism and materialism, Groome nevertheless insists that Marx's "insight that our 'knowing' and thus our very 'being' is powerfully shaped by our socio/cultural context must be honoured in a pedagogy for conation."[13] In line with this, Groome is very concerned to ensure that his pedagogy for conation invite "participants to develop a critical consciousness on their 'being' in the world, to see the reconstruction needed."[14] In tune with all of this, Groome defines *Shared Christian Praxis* as:

> A participative and dialogical pedagogy in which people reflect critically on their own historical agency in time and place and on their socio-cultural reality, have access together to Christian Story/Vision, and personally appropriate in community with the creative intent of renewed praxis in Christian faith towards God's reign for all creation.[15]

After a relevant "Focusing Activity', *shared Christian praxis* follows five movements which are:

Movement 1: Naming/Expressing 'Present Praxis'.
Movement 2: Critical Reflection on Present Action
Movement 3: Making Accessible Christian Story and Vision
Movement 4: Dialectical Hermeneutic to Appropriate Christian
                 Story/Vision to Participants' Stories and Visions
Movement 5: Decision/Response for Lived Christian Faith.[16]

According to Groome, the *Focusing Theme* "turns people to their own 'being' in place and time, to their present praxis, and establishes a focus for the curriculum."[17] This *focusing activity* establishes "a generative theme for the teaching/learning event."[18] Regarding Movement 1, Groome says:

Movement 1 invites participants to 'name' or express in some form their own or society's 'present action,' typically of a generative theme or around an engaging symbol, as they participate in and experience that praxis in their historical context. Depending on the focused generative theme, this expression of consciousness of present action varies in both content and form.[19]

Movement 2, says Groome, "encourages 'critical reflection' by participants on what was expressed as 'present action' in Movement 1" and its intent is to "bring participants to a critical consciousness of present praxis: its reasons, interests, assumptions, prejudices, and ideologies (reason); its socio-historical and biographical sources (memory); its intended, likely, and preferred consequences (imagination)."[20] Groome states that "critical reflection on present praxis is constituted by an emancipatory interest in that it intends to 'decode' the historical reality that our location in place and time mediates to us 'coded' (Freire)" so as to "uncover the personal and social biases, ideologies, and so on in present praxis and in our own naming of it."[21] Finally, Groome says that "critical reflection encourages 'disbelief' as well as belief, 'disbelief' especially toward the controlling myths, both inside and outside us, that maintain structures of domination..."[22]

Explaining what he means by the term *Christian Story,* which together with *Christian Vision* makes up Movement 3, Groome says:

By 'Story' here I mean the faith tradition handed on to Christians and the contemporary understanding, celebrating, and living of it in their faith community. I use Story as a metaphor for the whole faith life and practical wisdom of the Christian community that is congealed in its Scriptures, symbols, myths, rituals, liturgies, creeds, dogmas, doctrines.[23]

In a 1994 essay, Groome gave a more precise explanation of what he means by the term "Christian Story" as he uses it in *shared Christian praxis* when he stated: "in more traditional language" the term "story" can "be called **scripture and tradition**."[24]

Explaining what he means by the term *Vision,* Groome says: "Vision is a metaphor for the possibilities and responsibilities, the promises and the demands, that are prompted by the Christian community's Story."[25]

Regarding Movement 4, Groome says it revolves around a *"Dialectical Hermeneutic"* intended *"to Appropriate Christian Story/Vision to Participants' Stories and Visions."*[26] This means "participants place their critical understanding of present praxis around a generative theme or symbol (movements 1 and 2) in dialectical hermeneutics with Christian Story/Vision (movement 3)."[27] Groome says that "essentially" movement 4 "is a dialectical hermeneutics between participants' stories/-visions and Christian Story/Vision"[28] where "both are evaluated in light of each other to discern what is true for one's life."[29]

Finally, with regard to Movement 5, Groome says: "Movement 5 creates a dynamic and dialogue that explicitly invites participants to decision about their response, individual and/or collective, as the historical outcome of this *shared Christian praxis* event."[30] He adds that Movement 5 "not only gives participants explicit opportunity to make particular praxis-like decisions but aims also to form them in the habit of making decisions conceptually and morally appropriate to Christian faith."[31]

The Relativistic Nature of Shared Christian Praxis

In *Fides et Ratio,* Pope John Paul II clarified the way in which Revelation serves to lead us to an ever deeper knowledge of the mystery of God and of human life. He said:

> Revelation has set within history a point of reference which cannot be ignored if the mystery of human life is to be known. Yet this knowledge refers back constantly to the mystery of God which the human mind cannot exhaust but can only receive and embrace in faith. Between these two poles, reason has its own specific field in which it can enquire and understand, restricted only by its finiteness before the infinite mystery of God.[32]

"Revelation", continued Pope John Paul II in *Fides et Ratio,* "stirs thought" because it enables the latter to enter into the mystery of God and of man. It is, said the Holy Father, "the ultimate possibility offered by God for the human being to know in all its fullness the seminal plan of love which began with creation."[33] Revelation communicates truth and is by this very fact addressed to reason. Hence we find that in *Fides et Ratio*, Pope John Paul II insists that reason is capable of acquiring the certitude of truth and of discerning its absolute value. In conjuction with this, the Holy Father states: "Just as grace builds on nature and brings it to fulfilment, so faith builds upon and perfects reason. Illumined by faith, reason is set free from the fragility and limitations deriving from the disobedience of sin and finds the strength to rise to the knowledge of the Triune God."[34]

After stating that "reason is by its nature oriented to the truth and is equipped moreover with the means necessary to arrive at truth," Pope John Paul II went on in *Fides et Ratio* to say that "a philosophy conscious of this as its 'constitutive status' cannot but respect the demands and the data of revealed truth."[35] The truth necessary for our salvation, and hence the truth to which our praxis should conform, has been revealed to us by God. He has revealed this truth to us through the natural moral law which he has written into our 'being'—as well as through Sacred Scripture and Tradition—all of which rely on the teaching of the Church's Magisterium for their authoritative interpretation.

In contrast to what has been said above, *shared Christian praxis* is predicated on deeply embedded relativist perceptions of reality. Heavily influenced as he is by the ideas of subjectivists such as Heidegger, Freire and Habermas, Groome's theology, which permeates and gives direction to *shared Christian praxis,* displays but scant regard for the metaphysical and doctrinal dimension of Christianity. In light of this, I now turn to examine in greater depth Movement 3 of *shared Christian praxis.*

In terms of *Christian Story/Vision* and its relevance to Movement 3, Groome says that "Revelation as doctrine" which "understands revelation as 'divinely authoritative doctrine inerrantly proposed as God's word by the Bible or by official Church teaching'...is not appropriate to movement 3 of shared Christian praxis."[36] In rejecting as an apt model of revelation a view of the "Bible and Christian tradition" which can find expression in "doctrinal propositions," Groome quotes Elisabeth Schussler Fiorenza who says that such a view of revelation is deficient in that it "takes historically limited experiences and texts and posits them as universals which then become authoritative and normative for all times and cultures."[37]

Groome applauds Fiorenza's attempts at "constructive" and "recon-structive" hermeneutics. He says that her attempts at "writing back" into the Christian "Story/Vision from clues and traces that remain in its texts" are necessary to recover the "dimensions that were 'written out'." He adds:

> Elisabeth Schussler Fiorenza's work has become a model of such reconstruction; she recreates the history of the first Christian communities to reflect more accurately the 'basileia vision of Jesus as the praxis of inclusive wholeness' in a 'disciple-ship of equals' with women as full partners.[38]

In line with his endorsement of Fiorenza's 'scholarship,' Groome holds that "to make absolute any expression or interpretation of a faith tradition is to ossify and deaden it," and that "to forget that there have been distortions and corruptions reflected in Christian Story/Vision is historically naive."[39] To ensure that educators remain alert to the pres-ence of such "distortions and corruptions" in Christian Story/Vision, Groome proffers the following advice:

> Religious educators should approach the faith tradition with a healthy suspicion and, as educators, help people to recognise that 'much that has been proudly told must be confessed as sin; and much that has been obscured and silenced must be given voice'.[40]

Groome has structured Movement 3 of *shared Christian praxis* in such a way that religious educators can approach Christian Story/ Vision with the type of "healthy suspicion" he recommends above. Consequently, Movement 3 involves educators turning "to the 'texts' of Story/Vision with a critical hermeneutics that has dialectical aspects" in order to discern by way of a "threefold schema of activities" the "mean-ing and import of the texts."[41] The threefold schema of activities are: a) "to recognize and affirm the truth of the text," b) "to question or refuse the limitations and/or errors in its dominant interpretation," and c) "as appropriate, to reformulate or construct new horizons of meaning and ethic beyond how it is currently understood and lived."[42]

In implementing the "threefold schema" of Movement 3, the educator "employs a 'hermeneutic of suspicion' to uncover mystifications and distortions in the dominant interpretations of Christian Story/*Vision* and to reclaim its 'dangerous memories'."[43] In all of this, "the educator's task in hermeneutics of suspicion" is to "look out for false consciousness and distortions in original texts and/or in their accepted interpretations, to un-cover negative consequences they may have had over history or still legitimate now."[44]

Groome says that "a hermeneutic of suspicion reflects awareness that God's revelation is always mediated in particular historical circumstances and through culturally conditioned symbols" and that consequently "people who interpret these symbols" are to refuse "all claims that human, historical, interpretative matters elude relativity and corruption."[45] Further to this, Groome adds that "this hermeneutic of suspicion is essential, if the interpretative activity of religious education is to avoid Habermas's criticism of the hermeneutical sciences."[46] According to Groome, Habermas's criticism of hermeneutics is that without the element of "suspicion" it tends to serve "the interest of 'practical control' and thus tends to maintain people 'within the walls' of a tradition by forgetting the social interests that gave rise to the original expression of the tradition and who it was intended to benefit."[47]

This "hermeneutic of suspicion," as a tool for developing a certain "critical consciousness" which is so central to the realization of the overall objectives of *shared Christian praxis,* must ultimately be applied to the definitive and dogmatic teaching of the Church itself with a view to isolating and repudiating what is perceived as "untruth" and alienating in it. In consequence of this, *shared Christian praxis* is predicated on a wide-ranging scepticism regarding the dogmatic principle in Catholicism.

Groome's understanding of Sacred Tradition is as deficient as Fiorenza's. In *Educating for Life,* Groome makes a distinction between what he terms "Tradition" with a "big T" and "tradition" with a "small t" in order to differentiate between what he believes to be essential to the Church's life and practice and what is not. He says: "A relative few aspects of Christian faith are Tradition with a capital T whereas the rest is tradition with a small t."[48] To the unwary reader, such a distinction might seem plausible, but in the context of Groome's work it is flawed. In distinguishing between "big T" and "small t," Groome fails to draw accurate lines of demarcation between the two categories with the result that at times he reduces definitive and dogmatic teachings of the Church to the level of "small t" which are then subjected to reductionist reinterpretations that contradict the teaching of the Magisterium.

In *Educating for Life,* Groome states that "Scripture and tradition are to be continually reinterpreted in light of changing circumstances and contemporary consciousness." [49] He adds that when "freedom of conscience" is taken into account, "then Catholicism has no place for fundamentalism or dogmatism in the authority it grants to tradition." [50] In speaking of the need to approach Catholic Tradition with a critical consciousness, Groome says: "Such a 'critical consciousness' seems theologically appropriate to Catholic tradition, given how much untruth is in every statement of faith." [51]

Groome's notion that there is "much untruth" in "every statement of faith" was rejected by the Sacred Congregation for the Doctrine of the Faith in a 1973 statement titled *Declaration In Defence Of The Catholic Doctrine On The Church Against Some Present-Day Errors (Mysterium Ecclesiae).* This *Declaration,* whose publication was ordered by Pope Paul VI, stated that "it sometimes happens that some dogmatic truth is first expressed incompletely (but not falsely), and at a later date, when considered in a broader context of faith or human knowledge, it receives a fuller and more perfect expression." [52] It added that "the dogmatic formulas of the Church's Magisterium were from the very beginning suitable for communicating revealed truth, and that as they are they remain for ever suitable for communicating this truth to those who interpret them correctly." [53] The *Declaration* recognized "that revealed doctrine must be maintained intrinsically identical even while it has to be presented in such a way as to take into account new problems and different mentalities." [54]

In *Fides et Ratio,* Pope John Paul II stated that "the history of thought shows that across the range of cultures and their development certain basic concepts retain their universal epistemological value and thus retain the truth of the propositions in which they are expressed." [55] After stating this, the Holy Father went on by way of a footnote to quote *Mysterium Ecclesiae* where it says:

As for the meaning of dogmatic formulas, this remains ever true and constant in the Church, even when it is expressed with greater clarity or more developed. The faithful therefore must shun the opinion, first, that dogmatic formulas (or some category of them) cannot signify the truth in a determinative way, but can only offer changeable approximations to it, which to a certain extent distort or alter it.[56]

Groome is 'convinced' that Fiorenza's understanding of the early Church as a "discipleship of equals" is soundly based. He says: "Elizabeth Schussler Fiorenza, probably more than any other New Testament theologian, has established the inclusive praxis of Jesus toward women and the 'inclusive discipleship of equals' he intended for his community."[57] The 'dogmatism' with which Groome here endorses the 'scholarship' of Fiorenza tells us more about his own poor judgement than it does about the quality of her research. There is a large body of Biblical scholarship which believes that Fiorenza's attempted reconstruction of the early Christian community as an "inclusive discipleship of equals" belongs to the category of historical fiction. For example, the section of the *New Jerome Biblical Commentary* which deals with recent developments in biblical scholarship has this to say about Fiorenza:

Through her optic of a hermeneutics of suspicion, she reconstructed an early egalitarian Jesus movement which existed before the introduction of oppressive male hierarchies. It is debatable, however, whether such a Christianity ever existed and is not a projection of current sensitivities.[58]

If the early Church was structured according to the will of Christ as a "discipleship of equals" with women holding ministerial and leadership roles similar to those of the Apostles, then such a structure would have to be a constituent aspect of the Church for all times. If this were true, then the supreme teaching and jurisdictional authority which the Pope exercises in the Church at the present time would have to be seen as an imposition foreign to the Church's nature and thereby needing to be abolished. At best, the Successor of St. Peter would be tolerated as the "first among equals." In fact, Groome understands the Papal office in such a reductionist way. In referring to papal authority in *Educating for Life,* Groome says:

In mainstream Catholic understanding of papal magisterium, however, the pope, as bishop of Rome, must teach in consultation and collegiality with the bishops of the world and represent the consensus faith of the whole Church, in fidelity to Scripture and Tradition.[59]

Before identifying the error in the statement above by Groome regarding papal authority, a few clarifications should be made. First, let us disregard Groome's statement referring to "mainstream Catholic understanding" since in having no doctrinal import it is merely extraneous matter. Secondly, Groome is right in saying that the Pope in exercising his "papal magisterium" must do so "in fidelity to Scripture and Tradition." Lest there be any confusion here, however, it should be recalled that the infallibility of the Church's Magisterium "extends not only to the deposit of faith but also to those matters without which that deposit cannot be rightly preserved and expounded."[60]

As we saw in Chapter 2, papal authority is derived from the institutional fact that the Pope has "the mission of teaching, strengthening his brothers, and guaranteeing that the Church's preaching conforms to the 'deposit of faith' of the apostles and of Christ's teaching."[61] The Pope's authority in this area stems from the conviction "developed in Christian tradition" that the "Bishop of Rome" is "the heir to Peter in the charism of special assistance that Jesus promised him when he said: 'I have prayed for you' (Lk 22:32)"—something which "signifies the Holy Spirit's continual help in the whole exercise of the teaching mission, meant to explain revealed truth and its consequences in human life."[62] It was for this reason that Vatican II in *Lumen Gentium 25* stated that the Pope's teaching—in whatever form it takes—is to be adhered to by all the faithful. Coupled with this, we saw in Chapter 2 that the Pope can teach on a matter of faith and morals in a way that commands the irrevocable assent of all the faithful either by way of the exercise of his extraordinary papal magisterium or by the exercise of his ordinary papal magisterium when he confirms or reaffirms a point of doctrine to be held definitively by all the faithful.

For the present purposes, let us take the example of the Pope exercising his extraordinary magisterium to define *ex cathedra* a doctrine of faith or morals. According to Vatican I's Dogmatic Constitution *Pastor Aeternus* which defined Papal Infallibility, dogmatic statements made by the Pope in the exercise of his extraordinary papal magisterium "are irreformable of themselves, and not from the consent of the Church." In the context of this same solemn definition, Vatican I added that "if any-

one—which God avert—presume to contradict this Our definition—
anathema sit."[63] Looking at this statement, we note that the binding
force of the Pope's *ex cathedra* teaching is derived from the institutional
fact that he is the Successor of St. Peter and not because his teaching
intervention elicits "the consent of the Church." This teaching of
Vatican I was reaffirmed by the Second Vatican Council when it stated:

> And this is the infallibility which the Roman Pontiff, the head
> of the college of bishops enjoys in virtue of his office, when, as
> the supreme shepherd and teacher of all the faithful, who con-
> firms his brethren in their faith (cf. Lk 22:32), by a definitive act
> he proclaims a doctrine of faith or morals. And therefore his
> definitions, of themselves, and not from the consent of the
> Church, are justly styled irreformable, since they are pro-
> nounced with the assistance of the Holy Spirit, promised to
> him in blessed Peter, and therefore they need no approval of
> others, nor do they allow an appeal to any other judgement.[64]

In view of Vatican I and Vatican II's dogmatic teaching on the
supreme teaching authority of the Pope as outlined above, it is clear that
Groome's statement that the Roman Pontiff in exercising his papal
magisterium "must teach in consultation and collegiality with the bishops of the world" is erroneous and contradicts the dogmatic teaching of
the Catholic Church.

Groome is also in error when he asserts that the Pope, in exercising
his papal magisterium, "must...represent the consensus faith of the
whole Church." If this were true, it would contradict Vatican I's teaching on papal infallibility which states that *ex cathedra* statements of the
Roman Pontiff "are irreformable of themselves, and not from the consent of the Church." *Mysterium Ecclesiae* expressed this truth also where
it said: "However much the Sacred Magisterium avails itself of the contemplation, life and study of the faithful, its office is not reduced merely
to ratifying the assent already expressed by the latter; indeed, in the
interpretation and explanation of the written or transmitted Word of
God, the Magisterium can anticipate or demand their assent."[65]

Groome's "consensus faith of the whole Church" cannot be the
equivalent of "the supernatural appreciation of the faith" *(sensus fidei)*.
An aspect of the *sensus fidei* is that those "People of God" possessed of
such a supernatural "appreciation" of the faith, allow themselves "to be

guided by the sacred teaching authority"—knowing that in "obeying it"—they receive "not the mere word of men, but truly the word of God."[66]

Groome follows up his attempt to 'downsize' papal authority with a similar reductionist assault on the teaching authority of the Magisterium in general. He says, "If we remember that the Church is the whole community of the Body of Christ, including all baptised Christians and not just its leaders, then we recognise that the Church's 'teaching authority' cannot be limited to the institutional magisterium."[67]

While Groome is right in saying that the Church "is the whole community of the Body of Christ" which includes all baptised Christians, he is wrong however in concluding from this that "teaching authority" in the Church "cannot be limited to the institutional magisterium." As was noted in Chapter 2, the Second Vatican Council explicitly stated that "the task of giving an authentic interpretation to the Word of God, whether in its written form or in the form of Tradition, has been entrusted to the living teaching office of the Church alone. Its authority in this matter is exercised in the name of Jesus Christ."[68] According to the *CCC,* this teaching of Vatican II means that the task of authentically interpreting the Word of God "has been entrusted solely to the Magisterium of the Church, that is, to the Pope and to the bishops in communion with him."[69]

Groome also calls into question the Catholic Church's belief that there is a direct line of succession linking the Pope to St. Peter. In *Sharing Faith,* Groome says: "The traditional Catholic assertion that there is a direct historical line of succession between the present Pope and Peter, presumed to be the first bishop of Rome, must also be nuanced."[70] He adds that "in light of New Testament scholarship, we cannot presume a line of direct succession between pope and Peter...As already noted, the function of bishop as we might recognise it today did not begin until the second century."[71] Finally on this point, Groome, with the aid of a quotation from Raymond Brown says: "In light of this, 'the supposition that, when Peter did come to Rome (presumably in the 60's), he took over and became the first bishop represents a retrojection of later church order'."[72]

In 1998, the Congregation For The Doctrine Of The Faith published a document signed by Cardinal Ratzinger titled *The Primacy of the Successor of Peter in the Mystery of the Church* which stated:

In Peter's person, mission and ministry, in his presence and death in Rome—attested by the most ancient literary and archaeological tradition—the Church sees a deeper reality essentially related to her own mystery of communion and salvation: 'Ubi Petrus, ibi ergo Ecclesia'. From the beginning and with increasing clarity, the Church has understood that, just as there is a succession of the Apostles in the ministry of the Bishops, so too the ministry of unity entrusted to Peter belongs to the permanent structure of Christ's Church and that this succession is established in the see of his martyrdom. On the basis of the New Testament witness, the Catholic Church teaches as a doctrine of faith, that the Bishop of Rome is the Successor of Peter in his primatial service in the universal Church, this succession explains the pre-eminence of the Church of Rome, enriched also by the preaching and martyrdom of St. Paul."[73]

In connection with the points made above, Vatican I solemnly declared: "What Christ the Lord, prince of pastors and great shepherd of the sheep, established in the blessed Apostle Peter for eternal salvation and for the everlasting welfare of the Church, must always perdure, by the will of the same Christ, in the Church which, founded on rock, will remain indestructible until the end of time."[74] Coupled with this, Vatican I also defined as a truth of Catholic faith that it "is by divine right that blessed Peter has endless successors in his primacy over the whole Church" and that "the Roman Pontiff is the successor of blessed Peter in the same primacy."[75] Finally, in order to remove any doubt that might remain on this question, Vatican I solemnly proclaimed: "If, then, any one shall say that it is not by the institution of Christ the Lord, or by divine right, that Blessed Peter should have a perpetual line of successors in the primacy over the Universal Church; or that the Roman Pontiff is not the successor of Blessed Peter in this primacy—anathema sit."[76]

In view of the infallible teaching set out above on the link between Peter and his successors in the Roman See, it is clear that Groome is contradicting this teaching when he asserts that "we cannot presume a line of direct succession between pope and Peter."

Groome draws 'inspiration' from Fr. Richard McBrien for his understanding of the rights he believes theologians have to dissent from the teaching of the Magisterium. He says: "Richard McBrien, writing from a Catholic perspective, is helpful on the issue of 'dissent' from official church teachings."[77] After saying this, he then goes on to quote McBrien as follows:

> Dissent is never possible against a dogma...Dissent against a non-dogmatic teaching (doctrine) is always a possibility...if (1) the teaching did not seem to make sense...(2) the teaching seems to conflict with other clearly established truths of faith; (3) the teaching conflicts with one's own Christian experience regarding the matter in question; or (4) the teaching generates dissent from other members of the Church who merit respect by reason of their scholarly competence, pastoral experience, or personal integrity and prudence.[78]

In view of his own dissent from the Church's dogmatic teaching on the nature and scope of papal authority, it appears as though Groome does not agree with McBrien that "dissent is never possible against a dogma." But since the whole context of Groome's quoting McBrien suggests that he does agree with him, then we are left with only two possibilities that might explain why Groome dissents from defined dogma: i) Groome does not know that doctrine solemnly defined by an Ecumenical Council is dogma, or, ii) he does know that it is dogma but he feels free to dissent from it.

The question of dogma aside, McBrien is wrong in stating that dissent from non-dogmatic teaching "is always a possibility." If this were true, then Catholics would not have to give irrevocable assent to a papal teaching which though not proclaimed with an *ex cathedra* definition was nevertheless presented in a definitive way. While there is no explicit mention of a so-called right of dissent in the documents of Vatican II, Professor William May points out however that the question was dealt with by the Council's Theological Commission. In response to a question on dissent from only three bishops during the Council's proceedings, the Theological Commission referred them to approved theological manuals which in no way supported a right to public dissent from magisterial teaching.[79]

In 1990, the Congregation for the Doctrine of the Faith published with the approval of Pope John Paul II an *Instruction on the Ecclesial Vocation of the Theologian (Donum Veritatis)* of which nearly one-third was devoted to "The Problem of Dissent." The document listed some reasons which are regarded as justifying dissent such as appeals to "the opinion of a large number of Christians" which is then mistakenly identified with the *sensus fidei*.[80]

The *Instruction* repudiated the claim of certain theologians to be a "parallel magisterium" in the Church.[81] It pointed out that the modern tendency of placing the teaching of the Magisterium on an equal footing with mere theological opinion served only to call the integrity of the faith into question.[82] The *Instruction* recorded that the role of the theologian is to pursue a deeper understanding of the doctrine of the Church, a role which he or she must carry out in communion with the Magisterium which has been charged with the responsibility of preserving the deposit of faith. Hence, the *Instruction* stated that arguments of theologians appealing to the right of private conscience in order to legitimate dissent had no validity. It said

> Conscience is not an independent and infallible faculty. It is an act of moral judgement regarding a responsible choice. A right conscience is one duly illumined by faith and by the objective moral law and it presupposes, as well, the uprightness of the will in the pursuit of the true good. The right conscience of the Catholic theologian presumes not only faith in the Word of God...but also love for the Church from whom he receives his mission, and respect for her divinely assisted Magisterium. Setting up a supreme Magisterium of conscience in opposition to the Magisterium of the Church means adopting a principle of free examination incompatible with the economy of Revelation and its transmission in the Church and thus also with a correct understanding of theology and the role of the theologian. The propositions of faith are not the product of mere individual research and free criticism of the Word of God but constitute an ecclesial heritage. If there occur a separation from the Bishops who watch over and keep the Apostolic Tradition alive, it is the bond with Christ which is irreparably compromised".[83]

Catholic theologians and others who are employed to teach in the name of the Church have no right to undermine its doctrine by publicly contradicting it. Instead, their duty is "to set forth the Church's teaching and give, in the exercise of their ministry, the example of loyal assent, both internal and external, to the Magisterium's teaching in the areas of both dogma and morality."[84]

Groome's dissent from the definitive teaching of the Church is relentless. For example, he posits that "the exclusion of women from ordained ministry is the result of a patriarchal mind-set and culture and is not of Christian faith."[85] Explaining how this 'oppressive' situation whereby women are debarred from the ordained priesthood came about, Groome says:

In the early church an 'inclusive discipleship of equals' was soon replaced by the metaphor of *pater familias.* Borrowed from Roman culture, in which the 'father of the household' was considered sole owner of wife, children, and slaves, it became the model for church leadership and ministry. The pater familias model prompted the assumption soon made explicit, that women could not participate equally with men in the church community, and as ministry became synonymous with priesthood, they were gradually excluded from ordination.[86]

In *Sharing Faith,* Groome tells of how in one parish where he conducted an adult education course he used the *shared Christian praxis* process to change the attitudes of Catholics to the Church's doctrine on the male-only ministerial priesthood. He says that "in a six-week Lenten program with the Altar Society of a Catholic parish, the participants had chosen the generative theme of Women in the Church with a particular focus on the issue of women's ordination." He adds that apart from himself, "the group was of women who were senior members of the congregation" and that "it became evident in the opening movements that they agreed, and I disagreed, with our church's official position of refusing ordination to women."

Regarding his implementation of Movement 3 of this particular exercise in *shared Christian praxis,* Groome says he "presented the historical praxis of Jesus as a radical critique of the sexist mores of his time, highlighting his commitment to a 'discipleship of equals'." Having said this, Groome added:

We read from and studied together the Vatican document of 1976, 'Declaration on the Question of the Admission of

Women to the Ministerial Priesthood,' and its three main arguments against the ordination of women. We also studied some
of the scholarly critiques of those arguments, and **especially
the one offered by Karl Rahner**.[87]

Regarding the 'Vision' aspect of Movement 3 and the Movements 4
and 5, Groome said:

As Vision, we reflected on the text of Galatians 3:28 ('neither
male nor female', etc) and on some of the human rights tradition of Catholicism, to propose a church of mutuality and
inclusiveness (i.e 'catholic') for all God's people. Being designated the facilitator and resource person, I made my own 'principle of selectivity' and convictions about this issue clear to participants. Movement 4 was a lively dialogue, and movement 5
brought some decisions from participants and facilitator that
none had anticipated at the beginning.[88]

Recounting the final outcome of this parish based exercise in *shared
Christian praxis,* Groome said:

Of the 'altar society' reflecting on 'women in the church,' movement 5 questions first evoked little praxislike response.
However, one of the oldest members finally announced, 'I'm
going to write to my grandaughter in California and tell her
that I think the church is sexist in many ways, and we must all
work together to see to it that women are fully included in
every aspect of Church life, including ordination'. Many others
seemed to generally agree, but her intervention was a catalyst,
and many suggestions emerged about what needs to be changed
and how they could help to make the changes. Finally, a group
decided to each write a letter to some young woman about
whose faith they cared deeply (granddaughter, grandniece,
neighbour's child, etc), telling her of their new hopes for and
commitments to an inclusive church.[89]

In recent decades, the Church's teaching regarding the impossibility
of conferring the Sacrament of Holy Orders on women was reaffirmed
on the following occasions: i) Pope Paul VI, *Response to His Grace the*

Most Reverend DR F.D Coggan, Archbishop of Canterbury, Concerning the Ordination of Women to the Priesthood, 1975; ii) *Inter Insigniores,* Sacred Congregation for the Doctrine of the Faith, 1976; iii) Pope John Paul II, Apostolic Letter *Mulieris Dignitatem* (n. 26), 1988; iv) Pope John Paul II, Apostolic Exhortation *Christifideles Laici* (n. 51), 1988; v) *Catechism of the Catholic Church* (n. 1577), 1992; vi) Pope John Paul II, Apostolic Letter *Ordinatio Sacerdotalis,* 1994; vii) *Response to Dubium,* CDF, 1995; viii) *Commentary on the Concluding Formula of the 'Professio fidei,'* CDF, (n. 11), 1998.

In *Ordinatio Sacerdotalis,* published in 1994, Pope John Paul II taught that the practice of not conferring priestly ordination on women was founded on the example of Christ as recorded in the Gospels and on the universal Tradition of the Church. In view of this, the Holy Father stated:

In order that all doubt may be removed regarding a matter of great importance, a matter which pertains to the Church's divine constitution itself, in virtue of my ministry of confirming the brethren (cf. Lk 22:32) I declare that the Church has no authority whatsoever to confer priestly ordination on women and that this judgement is to be definitively held by all the Church's faithful.[90]

In 1995, a year after *Ordinatio Sacerdotalis* was issued, Groome published a book entitled *Language for a "Catholic" Church (Revised Edition)* in which he stated that "the continued exclusion of women from ordained ministry in the Catholic Church is seen by fair-minded scholars as without theological or biblical warrant."[91] Having stated this, Groome went on to add:

Official Catholic statements usually offer three arguments against the ordination of women: 1) that there were no women among 'the twelve,' 2) that it would be contrary to the tradition; 3) that to represent Jesus, a priest must be male (the 'iconic argument'). For a fine, balanced and scholarly refutation of these arguments, see, for example, Rahner, *Concern for the Church, Chapter 3.*[92]

In 1995, the Congregation for the Doctrine of the Faith issued a *Response* to a *'Dubium'* (question) on the teaching of *Ordinatio*

Sacerdotalis which said: "This teaching requires definitive assent, since, founded on the written word of God and from the beginning constantly preserved and applied in the Tradition of the Church, it has been set forth infallibly by the ordinary and universal Magisterium (cf. Second Vatican Council, Dogmatic Constitution on the Church *Lumen Gentium,* 25, 2)." It added that in issuing *Ordinatio Sacerdotalis,* the Roman pontiff had exercised "his proper office of confirming the brethren (cf. Lk 22:32)" and thereby handed on "by a formal declaration" a teaching that was "to be held always, everywhere, and by all, as belonging to the deposit of faith."[93]

The *Response* of the CDF to the question on *Ordinatio Sacerdotalis* was issued with the approval of Pope John Paul II who ordered its publication. Despite this however, in 1998 Groome was still asserting that the Catholic Church must be concerned to eradicate "sexism and patriarchy" in its structures and the only way to do this was for it to make way "for the full inclusion of women in every aspect of its mission and ministry."[94] In saying this, Groome was implying that the Church should open up the ministerial priesthood to women as the failure to do so would mean that not "all aspects" of the Church's "ministry" is open to women.

Groome's rejection of the Church's teaching on the male-only ministerial priesthood is often couched in extreme terms. For example, he asserts that "the injustice of excluding women from priesthood debilitates the church's sacramentality in the world" and "is a counter-sign to God's reign."[95] He asserts further that the exclusion of women from the ministerial priesthood "is an injustice to the church and its people" and that it "functions as a legitimating sign for patriarchy and sexism—thus doing spiritual and moral harm to society."[96] In making such assertions, Groome is thereby implying that the male-only ministerial priesthood is not of divine origin.

The extreme manner in which Groome expresses his opposition to the Church's teaching on the male-only ministerial priesthhod reminds one of the vitriolic tones in which Martin Luther expressed his repudiation of the Catholic Church's teaching on the sacrament of Holy Orders. He said: "The Church of Christ does not know this sacrament, it was invented by the pope's Church." [97] In referring to Luther's attitude to the Sacrament of Holy Orders, Cardinal Ratzinger said: "all the bitterness of the young reformer against the existing priesthood finds expression in such shocking exclamations" as the following: "O you princes, not of the Catholic Church, but of the synagogue of Satan, yes, of darkness." [98]

Indeed, Groome cites Luther and Calvin as examples from history of people who fruitfully applied a critical consciousness to all matters pertaining to Catholic faith and life.[99] He says that "the Reformers de-emphasised the role of the Church as a mediator" and that they "championed the rights of individual Christians to read and interpret Scripture for themselves and to bypass Church control in their pieties and go directly to God." [100] In this, says Groome, the Reformers "did an extraordinary service to the emerging human consciousness of the Western world."[101]

In this Chapter, I have presented examples from Groome's published works where he has contradicted both solemnly defined and definitive teachings of the Catholic Church. Since acceptance of such teachings is an essential requirement for anyone deserving of the title 'Catholic theologian,' then, on the basis of his published works, Groome has no claim whatsoever to such a title. Also, given the anti-dogmatic orientation of his *shared Christian praxis,* it can hardly be regarded as an appropriate pedagogical method upon which to base a Catholic religious education curriculum. I will have more to say about this in Chapter 10.

Reference

1   *Webster Comprehensive Dictionary: Encyclopedic Edition.*
2   *Macquarie Dictionary.*
3   *Oxford Dictionary.*
4   Thomas Groome, *National Catholic Reporter,* December 30, 1983.
5   Thomas Groome, *Sharing Faith,* op. cit. p. 12.
6   Thomas Groome, *Educating for Life,* op. cit. p. 376.
7   Ibid. pp. 376-77.
8   Michael Bezzina, *Exercising a Preferential Option: A Reflection for Catholic Schools,* in *Catholic School Studies: A Journal of Education for Australian and New Zealand Catholic Schools,* May 1996, pp. 31-34.
9   Michael Bezzina, Peter Gahan, Helen McLenaghan, Greg Wilson, *Shared Christian Praxis* as a Basis for Religious Education, Word of Life, Journal of Religious Education, Australian Catholic University, ACT, Vol. 45(3), 1997, p. 11.
10   In pages 32-35 of *Sharing Faith,* Groome gives a comprehensive description of what he understands by the term "being" and in doing so he acknowledges his dependence of Heidegger's ideas even though he distances himself from some of them.

11 Thomas Groome, *Sharing Faith,* op. cit. pp. 26–27.
12 Ibid. p. 29.
13 Ibid. p. 73.
14 Ibid. pp. 73–74.
15 Ibid. p. 135.
16 Thomas Groome, *Sharing Faith,* Chapter 4.
17 Thomas H. Groome, *Sharing Faith,* p. 146.
18 Ibid.
19 Ibid. p. 146.
20 Ibid. p. 147.
21 Ibid. p. 189.
22 Ibid.
23 Ibid. pp. 113–114.
24 Thomas H. Groome, *Shared Christian Praxis,* A Possible Theory/Method of Religious Education, in *Critical Perspectives On Christian Education,* edited by Jeff Astley, Gracewing, Herefordshire, 1994, p. 228.
25 Thomas H. Groome, *Sharing Faith,* op.cit. p. 115.
26 Ibid. p. 147.
27 Ibid.
28 Ibid. p. 250.
29 Ibid. p. 251.
30 Ibid. p. 266.
31 Ibid. p. 267.
32 Pope John Paul II, *Fides et Ratio,* n. 14.
33 Ibid. n. 15
34 Ibid. n. 43.
35 Ibid. n. 49.
36 Thomas H. Groome, *Sharing Faith,* op. cit. pp. 218–219.
37 Ibid. p. 219.
38 Ibid. pp. 234–235.
39 Ibid. p. 232.
40 Ibid. p. 233.
41 Ibid. p. 230.
42 Ibid.
43 Ibid. p. 232.
44 Ibid.
45 Ibid.
46 Ibid. p. 502n.55.
47 Ibid.
48 Thomas H. Groome, *Educating for Life,* op. cit. pp. 254–255.
49 Ibid. p. 242.
50 Ibid.
51 Ibid. p. 142.

52 Sacred Congregation For the Doctrine of the Faith, *Mysterium Ecclesiae,* n. 5. In a statement made at a press conference for the launch Mysterium Ecclesiae, Most Rev. Joseph Schroffer, the then Secretary of the Sacred Congregation for Catholic Education said: "The term 'Declaration' indicates that the Document does not teach new doctrine, but it recalls and summarises the Catholic Doctrine which has been defined or taught in former Documents of the Magisterium of the Church; it gives the right interpretation of this Catholic doctrine and indicates its limits and scope."

53 Sacred Congregation For the Doctrine of the Faith, *Mysterium Ecclesiae,* n. 5.

54 Observations On The Declaration Mysterium Ecclesiae taken from *L'Osservatore Romano* and published with the Declaration by Saint Paul Publications, Homebush, NSW 1973 with official Vatican Translation.

55 Pope John Paul II, *Fides et Ratio,* n. 96.

56 Ibid. n. 96n. 113.

57 Thomas H. Groome, *Sharing Faith,* p. 319.

58 *New Jerome Biblical Commentary,* edited by Raymond Brown et al., Geoffrey Chapman, London 1992, p. 1145.

59 Thomas Groome , *Educating For Life,* p. 240.

60 *Mysterium Ecclesiae,* SCDF, n. 3; Cf. Vatican II, *Lumen Gentium,* n. 25.

61 Pope John Paul II, *General Audience,* March 17, 1993, in Catechesis on the Creed, Volume 4, Pauline Books & Media, Boston, 1998, p. 288.

62 Pope John Paul II, *General Audience,* March 17, 1993, in *Catechesis on the Creed,* Volume 4, Pauline Books & Media, Boston 1998, p. 288.

63 Vatican I, *Dogmatic Constitution Pastor Aeternus,* Denz. 3074–75.

64 Vatican II, *Lumen Gentium,* n. 25.

65 *Mysterium Ecclesiae,* S.C.D.F. n. 2. In making this statement, Mysterium Ecclesiae referred by way of footnote 23 to the teaching on this point contained in Pastor Aeternus.

66 Vatican II, *Lumen Gentium,* n. 12.

67 Thomas Groome, *Educating For Life,* p. 241.

68 Vatican II, *Dei Verbum,* n. 10.

69 *CCC,* n. 100.

70 Thomas Groome, *Sharing Faith,* p. 314.

71 Ibid. p. 314.

72 Ibid.

73 CDF, *The Primacy of the Successor of Peter in the Mystery of the Church, L'Osservatore Romano,* November 18, 1998.

74 Vatican I, *Pastor Aeternus, Denz.* 3056.

75 Vatican I, *Pastor Aeternus, Denz.* 3058.

76 Vatican I, *Pastor Aeternus, Denz.* 3058.

77 Thomas Groome, *Sharing Faith,* op. cit. p. 507.

78 Thomas Groome, *Sharing Faith,* p. 507n. 15, quoting McBrien (Catholicism, Vol. 1. pp. 71-72).

79 Professor William May, *An Introduction to Moral Theology (revised edition),* op. cit. pp. 236-240.

80 The Ecclesial Vocation of the Theologian, *(Donum Veritatis),* CDF 1990, nn. 34, 35.

81 Ibid. nn. 6, 34.

82 Ibid. nn. 34, 38.

83 Ibid. n. 38.

84 Veritatis Splendor, n. 110; Cf. *Humanae Vitae,* n. 28.

85 Thomas Groome, *Sharing Faith,* op. cit. p. 328.

86 Ibid. p. 319.

87 Ibid. p.247, emphasis added.

88 Thomas Groome, *Sharing Faith,* op. cit. 247-48.

89 Ibid. p. 282.

90 Pope John Paul II, *Ordinatio Sacerdotalis,* n. 4 ; see also nn. 1 and 2

91 Thomas Groome, *Language for a 'Catholic' Church: A Program of Study (revised and updated edition),* Sheed & Ward, Kansas City 1995, p. 31.

92 Ibid. page 70 footnoote n.10. In Chapter 3, I referred to Rahner's dissenting statement from Inter Insigniores. This is the statement which Groome here refers to as "a fine, balanced and scholarly refutation" of the Church's doctrine (referred to by Groome as 'arguments'). Incidentally, these same "arguments," which Groome asserts were discredited by Rahner, were presented by Pope John Paul II in *Ordinatio Sacerdotalis* as the "fundamental reasons" (n. 2) underlying the definitive (infallible) teaching of the Church on this question. We will have occasion to return to this question in a later chapter.

93 Response of CDF to the 'Dubium', *L'Osservatore Romano,* November, 22, 1995.

94 Thomas H. Groome, *Educating for Life,* p. 411

95 Thomas H. Groome, *Sharing Faith,* p. 328.

96 Ibid. p. 518.n.114.

97 Martin Luther, cited by Cardinal Joseph Ratzinger in Principles of Catholic Theology, Ignatius Press, San Francisco, 1987, p. 261. Luther made these remarks in Bablyonian Captivity, on this point see also *International Theological Commission: Texts and Documents,* 1969 -1985, Ignatius Press, San Francisco 1989, p. 14.

98 Martin Luther in Bablyonian Captivity, cited by Cardinal Joseph Ratzinger in *Principles of Catholic Theology,* Ignatius Press, San Francisco 1987, p. 261.

99 Thomas H. Groome, *Educating for Life,* pp. 186-87.

100 Ibid. p. 187.

101 Ibid.

6

The Hierarchical Church and the Ministerial Priesthood

After a meeting between a representation of the Australian Bishops Conference and the Prefects and Secretaries of six dicasteries of the Roman Curia including the Congregation for the Doctrine of the Faith in Rome in November 1998, a *Statement of Conclusions* containing proposals and directions for the mission of the Church in Australia was issued. Pope John Paul II, in an address to the Australian Bishops for their *ad limina* visit to Rome in December 1998, made reference to this *Statement of Conclusions* by saying: "I earnestly recommend to your prayer and reflection, to your responsibility and action, the document which summarizes your meetings with the various dicasteries of the Holy See."[1]

After referring to "a crisis concerning the ability to know the truth," the *Statement of Conclusions* went on to speak about "Problems of Ecclesiology" whereby Christ is presented as "anti-ecclesial...who did not create a hierarchy." In consequence of this, said the *Statement,* the Church is regarded as being "of merely human origin" which means that "along with the reinterpretation of Revelation" it "needs to be reorganised to make it more suited to the present day."[2] In this scheme of things, the *Statement* added, "Truth is no longer discovered in a

Revelation already given, but is based on the shifting sands of majority and consensus."[3]

If the hierarchical nature of the Catholic Church is not derived from Christ, or if its male-only ministerial priesthood was not instituted by him, then the Catholic Church does not speak with the authority of Christ. Therefore, to call into question the divine origin of either the hierarchical nature of the Church or its male-only ministerial priesthood, is equivalent to calling into question the integrity of the Catholic Church's claim to have been founded by Christ himself. With the seriousness of these questions in mind, let us now turn to look in more detail at what Groome and Fiorenza have to say about the hierarchical nature of the Church and about the origin of its male-only ministerial priesthood.

Christ: Priest, Prophet and King

In speaking of Jesus' ministry, Groome says: "[There] have been many attempts to schematise the central functions of Jesus' ministry. A favourite listing that emerged in later Christian tradition (perhaps crystallised first by Calvin) is of Jesus as priest, prophet and king...this threefold designation, however, is nowhere explicitly stated in the New Testament to sum up the ministry of Jesus."[4] Referring to Jesus' reading at the synagogue in Nazareth of the passage in Isaiah—"the Spirit of the Lord is upon me, because he has anointed me to bring good news to the afflicted..." (Isaiah 61:1ff; Lk 4: 18-19)—which the Lord applied to himself—Groome says:

> This incident presents the basic functions of Jesus' ministry as (1) to preach the healing and prophetic word of God to all, (2) to tend with love and justice to human suffering and alienation, (3) to call people to a community of free and right relationship with God, self, others and creation, and (4) to live as though God rules in their lives.[5]

While the New Testament may not explicitly cobble together the terms priest, prophet and king to sum up the ministry of Jesus, it does not thereby follow that the New Testament does not in fact present these as the central aspects of the role of Christ. It is clear that in so far as these functions pertain to the messianic mission of Christ, they are thereby understood by the New Testament as not only central to an understanding of Christ and his mission, but also as profoundly complementary to each other. The New Testament presents Christ as Priest, Prophet and King from a variety of perspectives. For example, the purpose of Jesus' teaching is to proclaim God's kingdom (Lk 9:11). In the words and actions of Christ, the words and mission of the Old Testament prophets are fulfilled (cf. Lk 4:15; 13:32-33). Before Pilate, Jesus reveals the kingly aspect of his power (cf. Mt 27:11; 28:18-20). Finally, of his own free will, Christ "lays down his life for his sheep" (Jn 10: 11). The Gospel sees in this spontaneous sacrifice of Christ the sacrifice of the Priest who sheds his own blood for the expiation of sins (cf. Mk 14:24; Rom 5:6; Eph 1:7; 2:3; 1 Jn 2:2; Gal 1:4; Eph 5:20-25).[6]

Any relativisation of Christ's priesthood throws into confusion our understanding of the ministerial priesthood in the Church. Bearing this in mind, I will now make a few points on the priestly role of Christ before going on to look at the wide-ranging nature of Groome's and Fiorenza's attack on the ministerial priesthood and hierarchical nature of the Church.

In stating before Pilate that he was a king by virtue of the fact that he had come into the world "to bear witness to the truth" (Jn 18:37), Jesus thereby gave testimony to the inseparable link between his royal and prophetic mission.[7] However, the word "Messiah", which means "Anointed", also includes according to the Old Testament tradition a "priestly" character.[8] This unity of the royal and priestly character in the person of the Messiah "has its earliest expression as a prototype and an anticipation in Melchizedek, king of Salem."[9] In the Book of Genesis, we read of Melchizedek that in going out to meet Abraham: "He offered bread and wine; he was priest of God Most High. And he blessed him and said, 'Blessed be Abram by God Most High, maker of heaven and earth'" (Gen 14: 18-19).

Psalm 110 reveals how the figure of Melchizedek as both king and priest entered into the messianic tradition. Here we read that God-Yahweh addresses "my Lord" (ie. the Messiah)[10] with the words: "Sit at my right hand till I make your enemies your footstool.' The Lord sends forth from Zion your mighty sceptre. Rule in the midst of your foes!" (Ps 110:1-2). Further on we read: "The Lord has sworn and will not change his mind, 'You are a priest forever after the order of Melchizedek'" (Ps.110:4). Commenting on these words of Psalm 110,

Pope John Paul II says: "As is evident, the one whom God-Yahweh addresses by inviting him to sit 'at his right hand,' will be simultaneously king and priest according to the order of Melchizedek."[11]

In the history of Israel, the priesthood was hereditary in the tribe of Levi and it traced its origin to Aaron who was the brother of Moses. In the Book of Sirach we read: "He [God] exalted Aaron, the brother of Moses...of the tribe of Levi. He made an everlasting covenant with him and gave him the priesthood of the people" (Sir 45:6-7). Further to this, we are told that God: "Chose him out of all the living to offer sacrifice to the Lord, incense and a pleasing odour as a memorial portion, to make atonement for the people. In his commandments he gave him authority in statutes and judgements to teach Jacob the testimonies, and to enlighten Israel with his law" (Sir 45:16-17).

From the passages of the Old Testament referred to above, we see that priests are selected for the purpose of worship—for the offering of sacrifices of adoration and atonement—linked to which is the responsibility to teach about God and his law.[12] In this regard, the *CCC* says that the priesthood of the Old Covenant was instituted for "liturgical service"[13] and "to proclaim the Word of God and to restore communion with God by sacrifices and prayer."[14] However, the *CCC* also points out that the priesthood of the Old Covenant was "powerless to bring about salvation, needing to repeat its sacrifices ceaselessly and being unable to achieve a definitive sanctification, which only the sacrifice of Christ would accomplish."[15]

Man's absolute dependence on God imposes on him the obligation to glorify God. In the Divine plan, however, the glory God desires can only be rendered to him by the God-man who renders it in as much as he is the Mediator between God and man. To be a mediator between God and man is to discharge the role of priest. Thus, the ultimate meaning and fulfilment of the "Messiah-king" and of the "king-priest after the order of Melchizedek" present in the Old Testament is to be found in the mission of Jesus.

While Jesus, as a descendent of David, did not come from the tribe of Levi, nevertheless in the tradition of Israel the Levitical priesthood is placed alongside the royal dignity of the future descendent of David whose kingdom would be everlasting. Thus, in the Book of Sirach we read: "For even [God's] covenant with David...was an individual heritage through one son alone; but the heritage of Aaron is for all his descendants" (Sir 42: 25).[16] It is significant that in his trial before the

Sanhedrin, Jesus replied to the high priest Caiphas who asked him if he was "the Christ the Son of God" by saying: "You have said so. But I tell you, hereafter you will see the Son of Man seated at the right hand of God..." (Mt 26: 63-64). Commenting on these words of Jesus whereby he reveals the nature of his mission, Pope John Paul II says: "It is a clear reference to the messianic Psalm 110 which expresses the tradition of the king-priest."[17]

The New Testament book that reveals most fully the priestly nature of Christ's mission is the Letter to the Hebrews. After saying that priests are "appointed to act on behalf of men in relation to God, to offer gifts and sacrifices for sin" (Heb 5:1), it goes on to present Jesus as the fulfilment of that priesthood prefigured by Melchizedek in that it tells of Christ who "being made perfect, became the source of eternal salvation to all who obey him, being designated by God a high priest after the order of Melchizedek" (Heb 5:9-10). Then, after recalling what the Book of Genesis (cf. Gen 14:18) said about Melchizedek, the Letter to the Hebrews goes on to add: "His name when translated means king of righteousness; and then he is also king of Salem, that is, king of peace. He is without father, or mother or genealogy, and has neither beginning of days nor end of life, but resembling the Son of God he continues a priest for ever" (Heb 7:2-3).

In speaking of the priesthood of Christ and its prefigurement in the Old Testament, the *CCC* says:

> Everything that the priesthood of the Old Covenant prefigured finds it fulfilment in Christ Jesus, the "one mediator between God and men" (1 Tim 2:5). The Christian tradition considers Melchizedek, 'priest of God Most High," as a prefiguration of the priesthood of Christ, the unique "high priest after the order of Melchizedek" (Heb 5:10); "holy, blameless, unstained" (Heb 7:26), "by a single offering he has perfected for all time those who are sanctified" (Heb 10:14), that is by the unique sacrifice of the cross.[18]

On coming into the world, Jesus addressed the Father thus: "Behold, I have come to do your will, O God" (Heb 10: 7). He came into the world in order to "become a merciful and faithful high priest in the service of God, to make expiation for the sins of the people" (Heb 2:17). Having offered "himself without blemish to God" (Heb

9:14), Christ thus bears in himself a "priesthood that continues for ever" (Heb 7:24). Further to this, Jesus has no need to offer sacrifice daily for the sins of the people since "he did this once for all when he offered up himself" (Heb 7:27).

In speaking of the mystery of Christ's priesthood and of the way it is linked to the Incarnation and to the ministerial priesthood in the Church, Pope John Paul II said:

> *Let us consider our call, brethren"* (cf. 1 Cor 1:26). The priesthood is a call, a particular vocation: "one does not take this honour upon himself, but he is *called by God"* (Heb 5:4). The Letter to the Hebrews harks back to the priesthood of the Old Testament in order to lead us to an understanding of the mystery of Christ the Priest: "Christ did not exalt himself to be made a high priest, but was appointed by him who said to him: ... *You are a priest for ever, after the order of Melchizedek"* (5:5-6). Christ, the Son of one being with the Father, has been made priest of the New Covenant according to the order of Melchizedek: there-fore he too was called to the priesthood. It is the Father who "calls his own Son, whom he has begotten by an act of eternal love, "to come into the world" (cf. Heb 10:5) and to become man. He wills that his only-begotten Son, by taking flesh, should become "a priest for ever": the one priest of the new eternal Covenant...Thus the mystery of the priesthood *has its beginning in the Trinity* and is, at the same time, *a consequence of the Incarnation...*The priesthood of the New Covenant, to which we are called in the Church, is thus *a share in the unique priest-hood of Christ.*[19]

Jesus Established the Hierarchical Church and He Conferred the Ministerial Priesthood on the Apostles

Fiorenza argues that St. Luke did not envision "an ordained priest-hood" and that "the twelve apostles" did not receive "any priestly ordi-nation."[20] She states that "Jesus rejected all hierarchical forms of power in his community of followers"[21] and she claims that the hierarchical

model of the Church is more determined "by Roman imperial structures than by the Christian vision of the discipleship of equals."[22] She
says "the gradual patriarchalization and hierarchalization of the church"
finally won out over the "discipleship of equals" at the time of the reign
of the emperor Constantine.[23]

Fiorenza holds that "the exclusion of women from the sacramental
ministry of the Catholic Church remains a powerful sign of the structural sin of patriarchal sexism."[24] She says it "is invalid to deny ordination to women on scriptural grounds" since "Jesus called women to full
discipleship and the Spirit empowered them as apostles, prophets, and
leaders in the early church."[25] She adds that the "exclusion of women
from the sacramental priesthood corrupts the Eucharist and the
Christian church."[26] In tandem with these views, Fiorenza states that the
hierarchical structured Church does not represent "the authority of
Jesus Christ" and that consequently we should not "submit to the patriarchal authority presently displayed by the Vatican."[27] Holding that
"equality can be reached only in and through a change and transformation of the Constantinian form of the church,"[28] Fiorenza summons
those who support her emancipatory aspirations to a "conversion"
involving "institutional disobedience."[29]

Though somewhat more nuanced, Groome's theology of the
Church and of the ministerial priesthood is as radical as Fiorenza's.
Speaking of what he calls "the traditional Catholic notion that the apostles were commissioned at the Last Supper to preside at Eucharist,"
Groome goes on to quote with apparent approval Kenan B. Osborne as
saying: "In spite of the long tradition of this view, contemporary scholars find no basis for such an interpretation. In other words, Jesus did not
ordain the apostles (disciples) at this final supper to be 'priests,' giving
them thereby the power to celebrate the eucharist."[30]

Quoting Richard McBrien, Groome says that "the present ministerial structure in the Catholic Church...is not to be found as such in the
New Testament itself."[31] By way of a quotation from Eduard Schillebeeckx, he adds that "studies of ministry in the New Testament seem to
indicate that it is next to impossible to give a clear factual description of
the state of ministries in that era."[32]

While stating that "it is far from clear" who presided at the
Eucharist in the early Church, Groome nevertheless posits that "the
community chose" certain people "to preside at divine worship" for the
sake of "holy order" and that "usually, but not invariably, this designation

fell to the community leader, not because of a sacral power, but by her or his function of leadership."[33] In respect of the person so designated "by the community" to celebrate the Eucharist, Groome says: "Power to celebrate Eucharist did not lead to community leadership, but rather leadership led to presiding at Eucharist...the notion that presiding at Eucharist is an exclusively priestly function did not become widespread until the beginning of the third century."[34] In the same context, Groome adds that "the association of priesthood with Eucharist emerged as later Christians began to allegorize the sacrifices of the Hebrew covenant, which were offered by priests." In consequence of this, says Groome, the Eucharist came to be "perceived as replacing the sacrifices no longer offered in the now destroyed temple, and thus requiring the sacerdotal function of the priest."[35]

The new covenant recognises no other priesthood other than that of Christ himself. Consequently, in conferring on the apostles the sacramental charge "do this in memory of me," Jesus thereby conferred on them a unique form of participation in his own priesthood. As presented by the New Testament and Church Tradition, the ministerial priesthood in the Catholic Church "is essentially the extension and realisation of the priesthood of Christ himself."[36] Hence, it is "impossible to understand the essence and nature" of the ordained priesthood "except in relation to Christ."[37]

In teaching that the Church is "Hierarchical", Vatican II said: "The one mediator, Christ, established and ever sustains here on earth his holy Church" which is a "society structured with hierarchical organs."[38] The CCC says that "the Lord Jesus endowed his community with a structure that will remain until the Kingdom is fully achieved."[39] Referring to the nature of this structure, the CCC adds: "Before all else, there is the choice of the Twelve with Peter as their head."[40]

According to the Letter to the Hebrews, the Church owes its very existence as a priestly people to Jesus Christ its High Priest and Head. As such, the Church of its very nature has to be hierarchical. Since Jesus was always conscious that his earthly life would end in crucifixion, and while he would always remain invisibly present in his Church ("I am with you always" Mt. 28:20), he nevertheless chose to make provision for the continuation in the Church of his visible presence as its Head. To this end, Jesus chose and carefully prepared the Twelve apostles to whom he explained the full meaning of his teaching: "The knowledge of the mystery of the kingdom of heaven has been given to you, but to them [crowd] it has not been granted" (Mt 13: 10–11).

According to Fr. Benedict Ashley O.P, the Church "is no mere mob or loose 'Jesus Movement,' but an organic, well-structured, dynamically acting community whose organisation is determined by its spiritual mission."[41] Fr. Ashley adds that the word "hierarchy" "is derived from the Greek *heros*, sacred, and *arche*, a principle of order, and hence refers to 'sacred order'."[42]

The hierarchical nature of the Church is often expressed by way of metaphor in the New Testament. In his First Letter to the Corinthians, St. Paul compared the Church to a living body with differentiated organs among which Christ is the head (cf. 1 Cor 12). Fr. Ashley says that since Paul "used this metaphor to restore order in the Corinthian church he evidently had in mind not just Christ invisibly present, but the community leaders who represented Christ in that Church."[43] Metaphors, such as the one used here by St. Paul to compare the Church to a body with Christ as its head, makes clear that "the Church is hierarchical, that is, has a sacred order in which Christ as High Priest is the *hierarch*, the principle of that organic order."[44] Also, since the Church is Christ's body by which he remains visibly present and active in the world, its leaders must also sacramentally signify his priestly presence and headship within the Church.[45]

In establishing the Church, Christ inscribed within it the ministerial priesthood as one of its constituent elements. This ministerial priesthood is bound up with the apostolic succession and hence with the hierarchical and sacramental nature of the Church. In speaking of the ministerial priesthood, Pope John Paul II said: "The ordained priesthood ought not to be thought of as existing prior to the Church, because it is totally at the service of the Church. Nor should it be considered as posterior to the ecclesial community, as if the Church could be imagined as already established without this priesthood."[46]

The Eucharist, and the ministerial priesthood which is inextricably linked to it, are grounded in the words and deeds of Jesus at the Last Supper. Here, after changing bread and wine into his Body and Blood, Christ gave it to the Apostles and said to them: "Do this as a memorial of me" (Lk 22:19). In doing this, Jesus "instituted the Eucharist as a memorial of his death and Resurrection,"[47] and in commanding the apostles to celebrate it until his return, he thereby "constituted them priests of the New Testament."[48]

In speaking of the power to celebrate the Eucharist which Christ conferred on the apostles when he addressed to them the sacramental charge "Do this in memory of me," Pope John Paul II said: "The charge to do again what Jesus did at the Last Supper by consecrating bread and wine implies a power of the highest degree; to say in Christ's name, 'This is my Body', 'This is my Blood', is to be identified with Christ, as it were, in the sacramental act."[49]

The Council of Trent, in teaching that the ministerial priesthood was instituted by Christ said: "If anyone says that by the words 'Do this in remembrance of me' (Lk 22:19; 1 Cor 11:24) Christ did not establish the apostles as priests or that He did not order (ordinasse) that they and other priests should offer His body and blood, let him be anathema."[50] Following on from this, the Council of Trent added:

Sacrifice and priesthood are so joined together by God's foundation that each exists in every law. And so, since in the new covenant the Catholic Church has received the visible sacrifice of the Eucharist from the Lord's institution, it is also bound to profess that there is in it a new, visible and external priesthood into which the old one has been changed. The sacred scriptures show, and the tradition of the Catholic Church has always taught, that this was instituted by the same Lord Our Saviour, and that power was given to the Apostles and their successors in the priesthood to consecrate, offer and administer his body and blood, as also to remit or retain sins.[51]

In setting out the Church's doctrine on the ministerial priesthood, the Council of Trent condemned the proposition that in the New Testament there is no visible priesthood possessing the power to consecrate the Eucharist and forgive sins. It said:

If anyone should say that in the New Testament there is no visible and external priesthood, or that power is not given to consecrate and offer up the true body and blood of the Lord and to forgive sins, but only the duty and mere function of preaching the Gospel...let him be anathema.[52]

The teaching of Trent on the origin of the ministerial priesthood was reaffirmed by the Second Vatican Council. After stating that in Church the "Lord has established certain ministers among the faithful in order to join them together in one body where 'all the members have not the same function' (Rom. 12:4)," Vatican II went on to add that "these men were to hold in the community of the faithful the sacred power of Order, that of offering sacrifice and forgiving sins, and were to exercise the priestly office publicly on behalf of men in the name of Christ."[53]

The ordained priesthood finds its definitive expression in the celebration of the Eucharistic Sacrifice and this would explain why its institution by Christ took place at the Last Supper.[54] Speaking of this, Pope John Paul II said: "The Eucharist is the principal and central *raison d'etre* for the sacrament of the priesthood, which effectively came into being at the moment of the institution of the Eucharist, and together with it."[55] Repeating this teaching in his *Letter to Priests* for Holy Thursday in 1996, the Holy Father said that at the Last Supper, Christ "revealed to the Apostles that *their vocation was to become priests like him and in him.*" Pope John Paul II added that in saying to the Apostles—"Do this in memory of me" (1 Cor 11:25)—Christ thereby "*entrusted to them his own sacrifice* and, through their hands communicated it to the Church for all time." By thus "entrusting to the Apostles the memorial of his sacrifice," said the Holy Father, Christ thereby made them "sharers in his priesthood" and from them "we [ordained priests] have inherited the priestly ministry."[56]

All that has been said above about the way in which the priesthood of Christ is linked to the Eucharist and the ministerial priesthood in the Church is summed up by the *CCC* where it says:

> The redemptive sacrifice of Christ is unique, accomplished once for all; yet it is made present in the Eucharistic sacrifice of the Church. The same is true of the one priesthood of Christ; it is made present through the ministerial priesthood without diminishing the uniqueness of Christ's priesthood: "Only Christ is the true priest, the others being only his ministers."[57]

The Choice of the 'Twelve'

Basing itself on the example recorded in the Sacred Scriptures of Christ choosing his apostles only from among men, the teaching authority of the Church has consistently held that the practice of excluding women from the ordained priesthood is in accordance with God's plan for His Church.[58]

Those who argue that Jesus' selection of all male apostles was a historically and culturally conditioned choice ignore the fact that everything Jesus did was done with the sovereign freedom and knowledge befitting the pre-existent Son of God. Apart from this, the charge that Jesus could not rise above the sociological and legal structures of his time ignores the internal evidence of the Gospel which clearly shows that Christ freely dispensed with social custom and religious traditions when they no longer served the cause of justice.

On the basis of his Messianic claim, Jesus set himself above even the Mosaic law in its interpretation of the Sabbath commandment (cf. Mk 2: 23-28; 3: 1-6). Coupled with this, a striking characteristic of the Gospel is the great concern Jesus shows to all who suffer, be they men or women. "Do not weep!", he says to the widow of Nain (Lk 7:13) before giving back to her the son he raised from the dead. To the deceased daughter of Jairus he showed similar compassion. The Gospel shows Jesus' kindness to several women sinners, whose repentance he asks for without humiliating them (cf. Jn 8:3-11). At times his attitude to female sinners aroused the anger of the Pharisees as for example when he allowed himself to be touched by one (cf. Lk 7:33-43). Jesus publicly expressed admiration for the faith of some women. For example, in the case of a woman with a hemorrhage, he tells her: "Your faith has made you well" (Mt 5:34). This Gospel episode is all the more significant as the woman concerned was subject to the segregation imposed by the old law.

In reconciling us with God and with each other, Jesus was concerned to uphold the dignity of those most burdened by injustice not least amongst whom were women. In first-century Palestine, women were treated as chattels whose place in the home was more or less alongside the slaves and the children rather than their husbands. Contrary to such conventions, Jesus numbered women amongst his friends and he shook the foundations of patriarchal privilege when he forbade men to divorce their wives (cf. Mk 10:1-12). In his ministry,

Jesus was accompanied by many women who followed and assisted him and the community of disciples (cf. Lk 8:1-3). This was something new in respect of Jewish tradition. In drawing those women to follow him, Jesus thus shows that he was not bound by whatever prejudices existed against women in his male-dominated world.

In a society where women were barred from the study of the Torah, the Gospel pays a profound tribute to the dignity of women and to their place in the redemptive work of Christ when it presents them as the faithful disciples who accompany the Lord to Calvary (cf. Mk 15:40-41). The radical nature of the Gospel's understanding of the role of women in salvation history is highlighted by the fact that it records that it was to women that Jesus first appeared after the Resurrection (cf. Mt 28:1-10; Jn 20:11-19). In appointing these women as the first witnesses to His resurrection, Jesus was making a radical break with social and legal convention since women were precluded from giving official public witness which meant that their evidence was not accepted in a Jewish court of law. All this clearly indicates that Jesus' relationship to women was not conditioned by the prejudice against them which was characteristic of his time.

Despite his liberating attitude towards women, the fact remains that in choosing his Twelve Apostles, Jesus did not include any women amongst them (cf. Mk 3:13-19; Mt 10:1-4; Lk 6:12-16). In conjunction with this, it is very significant that apart from the "appointment" of the "Twelve," the seventy-two disciples who Jesus sent on a mission similar to that of the Apostles were also all men (cf. Lk 10:1-12).[59]

Several New Testament texts make it clear that Jesus did not act casually in his choice of the Twelve. According to St. Luke, the Twelve were chosen after Jesus had spent a whole night in prayer: "In these days he [Jesus] went out into the hills to pray; and all night he continued in prayer to God. And when it was day, he called his disciples, and chose from them twelve, whom he named apostles..." (Lk 6:12-13). According to St. Mark, Jesus "called to him those whom he desired" (Mk 3:13). Thus in St. John we read: "You did not choose me, no, I chose you, and I commissioned you" (Jn 15: 16). After the Resurrection, it is only on the Apostles that Jesus bestows the power to forgive sins and it is to them also that he entrusts the mission to evangelise the whole world—an act in which Jesus reaffirms the Apostles and their successors as rulers over his Church (cf. Jn 20:21-23; Mt 28:16-20).

Regarding Jesus' appointment of the Apostles, Pope John Paul II says that the number "Twelve" referred to the twelve tribes of Israel and that Jesus' use of it "reveals his intention to create a new Israel, the new People of God established as a Church."[60] The Holy Father adds that Jesus' intention to create appears in the very word used by St. Mark to describe the foundation of the Twelve: "He appointed Twelve...he appointed the Twelve" (Mk 3:13-19). The word "appointed" or "made", says Pope John Paul II, "recalls the verb used in the Genesis account about the creation of the world and in Deutero-Isaiah (43:1; 44:2) about the creation of the people of God, the ancient Israel."[61]

Fr. Jean Galot S.J. sheds further light on this question of Jesus' selection of the Apostles. He says that in St. Mark's account of the appointment of the 'Twelve', the verb used which means "to make" reveals the "evangelist's intention to acknowledge" that "in the establishment of the new people, Jesus exercises a creativity" that belongs only to God.[62] Fr. Galot points out that the semitic usage of the verb "to make" with persons as objects occurs only three times in the Old Testament. These are in I Kings 13:33 and 2 Chronicles 13: 9 where we have the phrase "to make priests", and in I Samuel 12:6 where we read that God "made Moses and Aaron".[63] Fr. Galot notes that the expression "to make a priest" or "to make priests" reappears in the New Testament in Heb 3:2 and Rev 5:10 and he points out that the verb used by Mark "is particularly apt to point to the creation of the new priesthood."[64]

Returning now to the Last Supper. The New Testament makes clear that only the "Twelve" were present with Jesus: "with the Twelve" (Mk 14:17); "with the twelve disciples" (Mt 26:20); "and the apostles with him" (Lk 22:14). Jesus personally made very careful arrangements for the Last Supper which took place against the backdrop of the Passover meal (cf. Mk 14:12-16). Commenting on the significance of this decision by Jesus to invite only his Apostles to the Last Supper, Fr Manfred Hauke said:

> The Eucharist was made present in a Passover meal, or at least has a clear connection with such. Now, women and children were also admitted to the Paschal feast, and they dined at the table along with everyone else. But even though the most esteemed women among Jesus' company, and the most intimate group of his followers, were in Jerusalem at the relevant time (Mk 15:40f. par; Jn 19:25-27), no one except the Twelve partic-

ipated in the Last Supper. This fact is even more remarkable given that, with reference to all the other dining scenes during Jesus' lifetime that are described in the Gospels, we hear nothing about any similar drawing of boundaries.[65]

In view of all that has been said above, we must now ask why did Jesus choose only males to make up the group of the 'the Twelve' and why was it only they he invited to the Last Supper? The answer I believe is clear—because it was only on "the Twelve" that he wanted to confer the sacramental charge: "Do this in memory of me." In other words, intrinsic to Jesus' institution of the Sacrament of Holy Orders was his intention that it be conferred only on men.

One might object that the details given above regarding Jesus' choice of 'the Twelve' are only mere deeds which without accompanying words have no binding or normative significance. This objection fails to take account of the teaching of Vatican II which is that "Revelation is realised by deeds and words" which "are intrinsically bound up with each other."[66] Hence, the Council reminds us that Christ communicated the Gospel not by his words alone, but also "by his way of life and his works."[67] For their part, the Apostles, says Vatican II, communicated the Gospel by "their preaching, by the example they gave, by the institutions they established."[68]

Speaking of the inner unity which exists between deeds and words in Divine Revelation, Pope John Paul II stated in *Fides et Ratio* that the "plan of Revelation is realised by deeds and words having an inner unity, the deeds wrought by God in the history of salvation manifest and confirm the teaching and realities signified by the words, while the words proclaim the deeds and clarify the mystery contained in them."[69] Consequently, Jesus' example of conferring on men only the sacramental charge—"Do this in memory of me"—is of critical importance since when taken in tandem with Jesus' choice of twelve male Apostles, it constitutes an aspect of Divine Revelation whereby the 'inner unity of word and deed' point to the institution by Christ of the male-only ministerial priesthood.

St. Paul teaches that it is in accordance with "a command of the Lord" that women are not called to be "teachers" in the Church (cf. 1 Cor 14: 34-38; 1 Tim 2:12). Those who clamour for the ordination of women tend to dismiss the significance of this Pauline text by asserting that it is expressive of patriarchal bias and outdated anthropology. In arguing this way, such people rarely consider whether or not their own approach to the Pauline texts might be expressive of an extreme fundamentalism—even St. Peter himself warns that there are aspects of St. Paul's writings that are "hard to understand" and which "unbalanced people distort" (2 Pet 3:16).

Fr. Manfred Hauke argues that the ban on women "teaching" in the Church refers in fact to a prohibition against their fulfilling the role of the priest. Hauke devotes over sixty pages to an exegesis of the relevant passages from St. Paul in which he draws attention to the four reasons given by the Apostle for the prohibition. The first three are the practice of the Church, the general moral code, and the argument from Scripture, the fourth and clinching reason however is that it is "a command of the Lord" (cf. 1 Cor 14: 34–38).[70]

Inter Insigniores explicitly referred to 1 Cor 14: 34–35 and 1 Tim 2:12 as a "prohibition" on women taking up an "official function of teaching in the Christian assembly."[71] The reason for this is that the "official teaching position" in question corresponds to the authoritative "teaching" role of the apostles and their successors which is acquired via the Sacrament of Holy Orders. *Inter Insigniores* makes the intention of St. Paul clear by comparing his instruction that it is according to a "command of the Lord" that women cannot be official "teachers" in the Church with his own approval of women prophesying in the assembly (cf. 1 Cor 11:5). Moreover, *Inter Insigniores* went on to state that "for St. Paul this prescription is bound up with the divine plan of creation" (cf. 1 Cor. 11: 7; Gen . 2: 18–24) and that consequently "it would be difficult to see in it an expression of a cultural fact."[72] The teaching of *Inter Insigniores* was reaffirmed by Pope John Paul II in *Ordinatio Sacerdotalis* when he said: "the Declaration *[Inter Insigniores]* recalls and explains the fundamental reasons" for the Church's teaching on why it cannot "admit women to priestly ordination."[73]

The Apostles Remained Faithful to the Intention of the Lord

In *Ordinatio Sacerdotalis,* Pope John Paul II teaches that the Gospel witness is that Jesus acted deliberately in calling only men to the ordained ministry and that the Apostles "did the same when they chose fellow workers who would succeed them in their ministry."[74] Regarding this same point, *Inter Insigniores* said:

The apostolic community remained faithful to the attitude of Jesus towards women. Although Mary occupied a privileged place in the little circle of those gathered in the Upper Room after the Lord's Ascension (cf. Acts 1:14), it was not she who was called to enter the College of the Twelve at the time of the election that resulted in Matthias: those who were put forward were two disciples whom the Gospels do not even mention.[75]

On the day of Pentecost, it was "Peter and the Eleven" (Acts 2:14) upon whom the duty fell to give public witness to the fulfillment in Jesus of all the prophecies despite the fact that the Holy Spirit had come down upon and filled both men and women (cf. Acts 1:14; 2:1).[76] *Inter Insigniores* points out that when the apostles brought the Gospel beyond the frontiers of the Jewish world they were impelled to break with Mosaic practices and that in similar vein there was nothing in the Greco-Roman world to prevent them conferring the ministerial priesthood on women if it was not for the fact that they felt themselves restricted from doing so by the will of the Lord.[77]

Fr. Louis Bouyer has stated that the ancient world of the fertile crescent of Greece and Rome at the time of the origins of Christianity had always known of female priests alongside male priests. Indeed, says Fr. Bouyer, "if there was a particular tendency in this connection, at the time of Christ and the apostles, it was rather towards the crediting than the discrediting of female priests."[78] Coupled with this, we see from the New Testament that certain women such as Phoebe and Prescilla worked very closely with St Paul (cf. Rom 16:1; Acts 18:26). Despite this however, the fact remains that "at no time was there a question of conferring ordination on these women."[79]

Fr. Albert Vanhoye S.J., secretary of the Pontifical Biblical Commission, in taking up the point made in *Inter Insigniores* regarding the practice in the apostolic community of restricting the ministerial priesthood to men said:

When Judas had to be replaced after the Ascension, Luke states that Peter expressly limited the choice to "men" (*andres* in Greek: Acts 1:21) who had accompanied Jesus during his public life, although some women at the time had stronger claims since they had been more faithful to Jesus than his male disciples, even on Calvary and at the tomb (Mt 27: 55, 61; par.).[80]

Fr. Vanhoye also points out that later on when the community's growth caused problems requiring a more diversified organization of the apostles' ministry, the "Twelve" invited the community of the disciples to "select for the new task 'seven men (andres)' (Acts 6:3), even though the problems concerned female groups, those of the widows (Acts 6:1)."[81] Fr. Vanhoye continued:

> In this account the laying on of hands is mentioned (Acts 6:6) as the ordination gesture for a ministry. It meant—and still means—the bestowal of a spiritual power conferred by God. In the New Testament women never receive this laying on of hands. The cases mentioned concern only men: Barnabas and Saul in Acts 13:3, when at the Holy Spirit's command they were sent on an apostolic mission, and Timothy, in 1 Tim 4:14 and 2 Tim 1:6, texts which speak of a "gift of grace (charisma)" conferred by this rite. Similarly the texts that give directions for choosing presbyters (Tit 1:5-6) and the episkopos (1 Tim 3:2), state clearly that it is a question of men (andres).[82]

In contrast to the clear New Testament evidence regarding the non-admissibility of women to the ranks of the ministerial priesthood, Fiorenza and Groome cannot cite a single explicit New Testament text to substantiate their assertions that women served as presbyters and presiders at worship in the early Church. At times, Fiorenza looks for confirmation of her views in some New Testament details of disputed interpretation. For example, she asserts that the reference in Romans 16:7 to a certain "Junias" is in fact a reference to a female apostle named "Junia."[83] This is the line taken also by Hans Kung in his dissent from *Ordinatio Sacerdotalis*.[84] However, the name 'Junias,' as it appears in the Letter to the Romans, is to be understood as referring to a man. The RSV Bible specifically notes that the reference in this passage to "Andronicus and Junias" is a reference to "men." After an indepth examination of the name 'Junias' and its various Greek derivatives, Fr. Manfred Hauke concluded that the so-called female apostle 'Junia' falls into the category of a modern myth.[85]

The Bishops Are the Successors of the Apostles

Fiorenza argues that St. Luke did not envision "an 'apostolic succession' of the twelve" and that hence "the twelve apostles had no successors."[86] She states that "the elders and bishops in Acts are not understood as successors of the twelve."[87]

Speaking of "ministry" in the early Church, Groome says: "As gifts of the Holy Spirit, the many specific ministries in the New Testament church seems to have emerged from the existential situation and needs of the first Christian communities."[88] He says that as people were needed to "preside at worship" and for other ministries, the communities designated people for the various services but that in doing so they "did not understand the commissioning to confer a sacral status, but rather appointed people to specific functions in service to the apostolic mandate of the community 'to build up the Body of Christ' (Eph 4:12)."[89] Groome adds that "for the first Christians 'sacramental power' comes from the presence of the Holy Spirit in the community; then they select and designate someone with the appropriate charism to act in their name."[90] Further to this, in describing what he understands as the emergence of the priestly ministry in the Church, Groome says:

> The diversity of ministerial functions in the first communities was gradually replaced by the 'degrees' of priesthood, with emphasis on its 'sacramental powers'. This tendency gained impetus as the church began to emphasise Eucharist as a sacrifice and thus, by association, requiring a priest to preside at it. By the beginning of the third century, roles previously distinct—presiding at Eucharist and the more institutional functions of elder (*presbyteros*) and overseer (*episkopos*)—are being united in one sacerdotal function and identified as *priest* (a term not used in the New Testament).[91]

Speaking of the "Tridentine perspective" on "ministry," the most significant aspect of which was its emphasis on the traditional tripartite division of ordained ministry according to the ranks of bishop, priest and deacon, Groome says:

> In a Tridentine perspective...Ministry is synonymous with priesthood, which entails the hierarchical 'degrees' of bishop, priest,

and deacon. It is entered by ordination to Holy Orders, which also designates its recipients as 'clergy,' set aside from the 'laity'; the clergy are considered to possess in and of themselves the awesome power to consecrate Eucharist and forgive sins...yet New Testament evidence suggests this critical insight: the Tridentine perception of ministry outlined above is much more the product of history and of the sociocultural contexts in which the church found herself than of any blueprint to be found in the New Testament communities.[92]

Groome asserts that "the function of bishop as we might recognize it today did not begin until the second century."[93] He states that "equating apostle with bishop...is not in the first century" and neither is the identification of "apostle with sacerdotal function."[94] In reference to what he terms "the presumed correlation and direct lineage between apostles and bishops in Tridentine ministry," Groome approvingly quotes Raymond Brown as saying: "the affirmation that all the bishops of the early Christian church could trace their appointments or ordinations to the apostles is simply without proof'."[95]

While the words "ordained" and "ministerial" priest do not appear in the New Testament, equivalent terms such as *presbyteroi (presbyters)* do. The word "presbyteroi" initially meant "elder ones" or "elders," which in French is translated as *"prêtres,"* and hence the English word "priests." Those who received the power of the apostolic ministry from the Apostles were called "episkopoi," which primarily used to mean "overseers." The English word "Bishop" comes from this Greek term "épiskopos." In the New Testament, however, it is not always easy to distinguish between "presbyters" (elders) and "bishops" (overseers).[96]

In its teaching on the Sacrament of Holy Orders, the Council of Trent declared: "If anyone shall say that in the Catholic Church there is not instituted a hierarchy by divine ordinance, which consists of bishops, priests and ministers—*anathema* sit."[97] Commenting on the word "ministers" as used here by Trent, Pope John Paul II said: "The New Testament books already attest the presence of ministers, 'deacons,' who gradually formed a distinct category from the *presbyteroi* and *episcopoi*."[98]

Coupled with his conferral of the ministerial priesthood on the Apostles, Jesus also indicated during his earthly life his intention to establish the presbyterate. He did this by appointing "seventy-two" disciples (cf. Lk 10:1-12)—who though subordinate and distinct from the apostles—were nevertheless to be endowed with their priestly task in that the mission they received was very similar. Most importantly, they were to proclaim the Gospel with the authority of Christ himself: "Anyone who listens to you listens to me; anyone who rejects you rejects me, and those who reject me reject the one who has sent me" (Lk 10: 16).

Linking the appointment of the "seventy-two" disciples to the mission of the Apostles, Pope John Paul II stated that while this step "only prefigures the ministry that Christ will formally institute later on," it nevertheless indicates that Jesus intended them to participate "with the Twelve in the *redemptive work* of the one priest of the new covenant, Christ, who wanted to confer on them too a mission and powers like those of the Twelve." Having said this, the Holy Father added: "The establishment of the presbyterate, therefore, does not only answer one of the practical necessities of the bishops, who feel the need for co-workers, but derives from an explicit intention of Christ. In the early Christian era presbyters (*presbyteroi*) are present and functioning in the Church of the Apostles and of the first bishops, their successors (Cf. Acts 11:30; 14:23; 15:2, 4, 6, 22, 23, 41; 16:4; 20:17; 21:18; 1 Tim 4:14; 5:17, 19; Ti 1:5; Jas 5:14; 1 Pt 5:1, 5, 15; 2 Jn 1; 3 Jn 1)."[99]

In regard to the question of the male-only ministerial priesthood, a key point to note about the appointment of the seventy-two disciples referred to above is that they were all men. Pope John Paul II alluded to this when—after stating that "Jesus has entrusted the task of the ministerial priesthood only to males"—he added: "Thus the Gospels indicate that Jesus never sent women on preaching missions, as he did with the group of the Twelve, all of whom were male (cf. Lk 9:1-16), and also with the Seventy-two among whom no feminine presence is mentioned."[100] Speaking of this significant aspect of the appointment of the seventy-two disciples, Fr. Jean Galot says: "There is absolutely no doubt that Jesus chose only men for the priestly ministry he instituted. The names of the Twelve are known. As to the seventy-two disciples sent out on a mission (Lk 10:1-12), they too were men, for in the language of the gospels the term 'disciples' never refers to women."[101]

The apostles played a prominent role in the Christian communities that formed after Pentecost. In the Jerusalem community, for example, St. Paul speaks of Peter, James and John as its "pillars" (cf. Gal 2:9). Along with the apostles, however, we are also told that there were "presbyters" in the early community (cf. Acts 11:29-30; 15:2, 4) who, with the apostles, "constitute the first subordinate rank of the hierarchy."[102] In carrying out their mission, the apostles appointed ministers as their "co-workers" whose task was: i) to proclaim the Gospel (cf. 2 Tim 1:8, 13; 2:2; 4:2, 5; 1 Tim 4:11, 13; 6:20); ii) to exercise direction of the liturgical service (cf. 1 Tim 3:9; 4:13); iii) to lead and guide the community (cf. 1 Tim 3:15; 5:17-19; 1 Pet.).

The most detailed information we have on how early Church leaders were appointed comes from the account of the institution of "the Seven" in Acts 6:1-6. The initiative is taken by "the Twelve" who "called a full meeting of the disciples and addressed them" (Acts 6:1-2). It was the apostles who suggested to the "community" how the problems between the "Hellenists" and the "Hebrews" should be resolved. St. Luke tells us that "the whole assembly approved this proposal" and after electing suitable candidates to carry out the assigned tasks they then "presented these to the apostles, who prayed and laid their hands on them." (Acts 6: 5-6). Note, in this episode of Acts where the "Seven" are installed in their designated ministry, it is the apostles who confirm the "Seven" in their office—the "community" has no authority to make such an installation.

Elsewhere in the New Testament, where the institution of ministers is referred to, there is no mention of a community role in the process. For example, as the Church took root in Antioch the apostles sent a representative named Barnabas (cf. Acts 11:22). After his conversion, St. Paul went with Barnabas to Jerusalem as the "ecclesial center of authority to confer with the apostles."[103] From Antioch, Barnabas and Saul were sent out on an apostolic mission after the apostles "laid hands on them" (Acts 13:2-3). From this time on, Saul is called Paul. As the mission spread and as communities began to spring up, we are told that the apostles appointed "presbyters" (cf. Acts 24:23). The responsibilities of these presbyters "are defined in detail in the pastoral letters to Titus and Timothy, whom Paul appointed as heads of the community (cf. Tit 1:5; 1 Tim 5:17)."[104] After the Council of Jerusalem, the apostles sent to Antioch along with Paul and Barnabas two men named Silas and Judas who were considered as "leaders among the brothers" (Acts 15: 22).

Of the communities founded by Paul and Barnabas we read: "In each of these churches they appointed elders" (Acts 14:23). Coupled with this, St. Paul tells us that he left Titus behind in Crete "to get everything organised there and appoint elders in every town, in the way that I told you" (Tit 1:5). In his letters, St. Paul mentions other "co-workers" and "companions" apart from Titus and Timothy (cf. 1 Thes 1:1; 2 Cor 1: 9; Rom 16:1, 3-5).

A stage was eventually reached in the expansion of the Church when new leaders were needed to succeed the apostles. The Apostles knew that it was "Christ's will that they provide for successors, who as their heirs and representatives, would continue their mission."[105] Speaking of this, Pope St. Clement of Rome, who was the third successor of St. Peter wrote:

> Our Apostles knew through our Lord Jesus Christ that there would be strife for the office of Bishop. For this reason, therefore, having received perfect knowledge, they appointed those who have already been mentioned, and afterwards added the further provision that, if they should die, other approved men should succeed to their ministry.[106]

Speaking of how the Apostles appointed bishops as their successors, the Second Vatican Council in its *Dogmatic Constitution on Divine Revelation (Dei Verbum)* said: "In order that the full and living Gospel might always be preserved in the Church, the apostles left bishops, as their successors. They gave them their own teaching authority."[107] The same truth is reaffirmed elsewhere in the Council documents where it says: "Jesus Christ, the eternal pastor, set up the holy Church by entrusting the apostles with their mission...He willed that their successors, the bishops namely, should be the shepherds in his Church until the end of the world."[108] Further to this, *Lumen Gentium* added: "That divine mission, which was committed by Christ to the Apostles, is destined to last until the end of the world (cf. Mt 28:20)...For that very reason the apostles were careful to appoint successors in this hierarchically constituted society."[109] The Apostles, adds *Lumen Gentium*, "consigned, by will and testament, as it were, to their immediate collaborators the duty of confirming and finishing the work begun by themselves" and to these men they gave "the order that, when they should have died, other approved men should take up their ministry."[110] Finally, on the question of apostolic succession, *Lumen Gentium* stated:

> Amongst the various offices which have been exercised in the Church from the earliest times the chief place, according to the

witness of tradition, is held by the function of those who, through their appointment to the dignity and responsibility of bishop, and in virtue consequently of the unbroken succession, going back to the beginning, are regarded as the transmitters of the apostolic line. Thus, according to the testimony of St. Irenaeus, the apostolic tradition is manifested and preserved in the whole world by those who were made bishops by the apostles and by their successors down to our own time.[111]

Pope John Paul II said that the Apostles called "other men as bishops, as priests and as deacons in order to fulfil the command of the risen Jesus who sent them forth to all people in every age."[112] He added that "the writings of the New Testament are unanimous in stressing that it is the same Spirit of Christ who introduces these men chosen from among their brethren into the ministry" and that "through the laying on of hands (cf. Acts 6:6; 1 Tm. 4:14; 5:22; 2 Tm.1:6) which transmits the gift of the Spirit, they are called and empowered to continue the same ministry of reconciliation, of shepherding the flock of God and of teaching (cf. Acts 20: 28; 1Pt. 5:2)."[113]

Regarding deacons, their place in the early Church is attested in Acts 6:1-6. Coupled with this, St. Paul lists the qualities deacons should possess (cf. 1 Tim 3:8-13). The Second Vatican Council, in referring to the place of deacons in the hierarchical structure of the Church said:

At a lower level of the hierarchy are deacons, upon whom hands are imposed 'not unto the priesthood, but unto a ministry of service.' For strengthened by sacramental grace, in communion with the bishop and his group of priests they serve in the diaconate of the liturgy, of the word, and of charity to the people of God.[114]

Speaking of the presence of bishops, presbyters and deacons in the early Church, St. Ignatius of Antioch said:

When you submit to the bishop as you would to Jesus Christ, it is clear to me that you are living not in the manner of men but as Jesus Christ...Let everyone respect the deacons as they would respect Jesus Christ, and just as they respect the bishop as a type of the Father, and the presbyters as the council of God and college of Apostles. Without these it cannot be called a Church.[115]

This testimony of St. Ignatius is very important because not only was he the third bishop of Antioch (St. Peter was the first), but he was also a hearer of St. John the Evangelist. Around the year 115, St. Ignatius died a martyr's death when he was sentenced to the beasts in the arena during the reign of the Emperor Trajan.

From earliest times also, it was acknowledged that supreme power over the whole Church belonged to the Bishop of Rome as the successor of St. Peter. For example, St. Irenaeus, the martyred Bishop of Lyons, insisted that in doctrinal disputes, agreement with the Church of Rome was the test of orthodoxy. Further to this, he explained that the root of all heresy is found in deviation from the Church's teaching authority as centred in the successor of Peter. St. Irenaeus, who was a native of Asia Minor, had in his youth been a pupil of St. Polycarp, who in turn was a disciple of St. John the Evangelist. St Irenaeus, therefore, saw himself in continuity of teaching with the Apostles.

Commenting on the relationship of the Apostolic authority to the structure of the Church, Hans Urs von Balthasar said: "The Catholic Church will never be able to abandon the idea that Jesus entrusted his powers of consecration and of absolution from grievous guilt to an office in the Church that was first carried out by the 'Apostles' and then explicitly passed on to others who in turn pass it on."[116] He added that the hierarchical structure of the Church which rests on the ministerial priesthood cannot be changed by the Church herself since "it is essentially and permanently a gift of Christ to the Church, which is permitted to be what she is by virtue of this gift."[117]

After pointing out that the clear evidence of the New Testament is that "the Church is structured by office,"[118] Von Balthasar stated that it cannot have been the practice of the Apostles "to plan or even to tolerate contradictory structures: for example, next to a 'hierarchic' structure in which chosen heads, approved by the Apostles, led the community, a purely 'democratic' structure in which the community consecrated its leaders by its own authority and enabled them to perform sacramental acts."[119]

Therefore, whatever role the community may have played in the lead up to the appointment of those who would preside at the Eucharist in the early Christian communities, it was always, however, the official leaders of the Church who had the ultimate authority to appoint individuals to this and other ministries. Similarly today, while the community can testify to the suitability of a candidate for the priesthood, it cannot make the final decision as to his ordination nor can it confer the Sacrament of Holy Orders on him. This power belongs to the bishops alone, who have it by virtue of the fact that they themselves possess the fullness of the ministerial priesthood and because they are the successors of the Apostles to whom Christ granted authority to confer this sacrament.

With the above facts in mind, we can better understand the words of Pope John Paul II where he says: "The hierarchical ministerial priesthood is not a 'product' of the universal priesthood of the faithful. It does not come from a selection or delegation by the community of believers, but from a special divine call...A Christian obtains this office on the basis of a special sacrament, that of Orders."[120]

Indeed, Pope Pius VI taught that it is "heretical" to assert that "the power of the ministry and of ecclesial rule comes to the pastors from the community of the faithful."[121]

The Substantial Core of a Sacrament Cannot Change

At the Last Supper, Christ instituted the Eucharistic sacrifice of his Body and Blood and in commanding his Apostles to celebrate it until his return, he thereby constituted them priests of the New Testament.[122] This he did "in order to perpetuate the sacrifice of the cross throughout the ages until he should come again."[123] From the beginning, the Church has been faithful to the Lord's command. Of the Church in Jerusalem we read: "They devoted themselves to the apostles' teaching and fellowship, to the breaking of bread and the prayers...Day by day, attending the temple together and breaking bread in their homes, they partook of food with glad and generous hearts."[124] It was above all on "the first day of the week," Sunday, the day of Jesus' Resurrection, that the Christians met "to break bread" (Acts 20:7).

According to Pope John Paul II, the "sacred character of the Mass is a sacredness instituted by Christ" in which "the words and actions of every priest, answered by the conscious participation of the whole Eucharistic assembly, echo the words and action of Holy Thursday."[125] Speaking of how the essence of the Eucharistic celebration as it was instituted by Christ does not change, Pope John Paul II added:

Beginning with the Upper Room and Holy Thursday, the celebration of the Eucharist has a long history, a history as long as that of the Church. In the course of this history the secondary elements have undergone certain changes, but *there has been no change in the essence of the 'Mysterium'* instituted by the Redeemer of the world at the Last Supper.[126]

From the beginning of the Church "on down to our own day the celebration of the Eucharist has been continued so that today we encounter it everywhere in the Church with the same fundamental structure. It remains the center of the Church's life."[127] Speaking of the place of the Holy Mass in the ongoing life of the Church, the *CCC* says: "From the first community of Jerusalem until the parousia, it is the same Paschal mystery that the Churches of God, faithful to the apostolic faith, celebrate in every place. The mystery celebrated in the liturgy is one, but the forms of its celebration are diverse."[128]

The diverse forms in which the liturgy is celebrated in the Universal Church spring from the diverse cultures in which the Church has taken root. The liturgical traditions or rites presently in use in the Church are: the Latin and Byzantine, Alexandrian or Coptic, Syriac, Armenian, Maronite and Chaldean. These diverse liturgical traditions or rites "manifest the catholicity of the Church because they signify and communicate the same mystery of Christ."[129] Consequently, all of these liturgical rites are "of equal dignity" and the Church "wishes to preserve them in the future and to foster them in every way."[130]

The Sacred Liturgy includes divine as well as human elements. The former, "instituted as they have been by God, cannot be changed in any way by men."[131] The human components on the other hand do admit of various modifications as, "the needs of the age, circumstance and the good of souls require, and as the Ecclesiastical Hierarchy under guidance of the Holy Spirit, may have authorised."[132] Consequently, in regard to the divinely constituted parts of the Mass, the Church is merely the guardian and has no authority to change them.[133]

The divinely constituted part of each of the Sacraments is often referred to as its substantial core or essential sign. For example, the Sacrament of Matrimony can only be conferred on a man and a woman who are baptised and it is based on the mutual consent of the contracting couple who agree to give themselves to each other definitively in order to live a covenant of faithful and fruitful love.[134] The Sacrament could not, for example, be conferred on two pagans or on two members of the same sex.

The essential sign of the Sacrament of the Eucharist "are wheat bread and grape wine, on which the blessing of the Holy Spirit is invoked and the priest pronounces the words of consecration spoken by Jesus during the Last Supper: This is my body which will be given up for you...This is the cup of my blood."[135]

Inextricably bound to the essential sign of the Sacrament of the Eucharist is the fact that "only validly ordained priests can preside at the Eucharist and consecrate the bread and the wine so that they become the Body and Blood of the Lord."[136] Consequently, since it is only men that can be validly ordained, then it is only men also who can validly preside over the Eucharistic Sacrifice. Therefore, what has been asserted by Groome and Fiorenza regarding women as presbyters and presiders at "divine worship" in the early Church cannot be true if by the term "church" Groome and Fiorenza are referring to the community ruled by the apostles and their successors.

The Sacramental Sign of Holy Orders

Groome speaks in a very confused and misleading way about the origin and nature of the Sacramental Rite of priestly ordination. He says:

> In the first century, however, laying on of hands for ministerial commissioning was not practiced in all the communities, and where it was used, it designated people for a variety of ministries (not only sacerdotal) or was simply a symbol of blessing. This early practice then, is too fluid to be taken as synonymous with what we mean today by 'ordination.'[137]

The essential rite of the Sacrament of Holy Orders "consists in the bishop's imposition of hands on the head of the ordinand and in the bishop's specific consecratory prayer asking God for the outpouring of the Holy Spirit and his gifts proper to the ministry to which the candidate is being ordained."[138]

In the early Church, the transmission of Apostolic authority and the ministerial priesthood was effected through the imposition of hands by either the Apostles themselves or by those whom they appointed to succeed them in the Apostolic ministry. We have a reference to this process in the words addressed by St. Paul to his disciple Timothy: "I remind you to enkindle the gift of God that is within you through the laying on of my hands" (2 Tim 1:6), and, "If any one aspires to the office of bishop, he desires a noble task" (1 Tim 3:1). At the same time, Paul advises Timothy not to be "too quick to lay hands on any man" (1 Tim 5:22). Speaking to Titus along somewhat similar lines, St. Paul said: "This is why I left you in Crete, that you amend what was defective, and appoint presbyters in every town, as I directed you" (Titus 1:5).[139]

Regarding the consecratory prayer of ordination, while St. John does not recount the words of institution of the Eucharist, he does, however, recount the priestly prayer of Christ for his apostles upon whom he conferred the ministerial priesthood. St. John presents Christ as the High Priest of the New Covenant, who prays for the apostles that they might "be consecrated in the truth" (Jn 17:17). Regarding this consecratory prayer of Jesus—"Father, consecrate them in the truth: your word is truth" (Jn 17:17)—the 1970 document *The Priestly Ministry* produced by the International Theological Commission said: "This is truly the formula of a sacerdotal institution (cf. Ex 29:1: "You shall consecrate them to serve me in the priesthood')." [140] It added that "the apostles were consecrated *in truth;* in relation to this consecration, that of Aaron and his sons was only a shadow, as the law of Moses was itself only a shadow of the truth of the *Logos* (Jn 17:17 to be related to Jn 1:17)."[141] Like Christ, whom the Father had consecrated and sent into the world (cf. Jn 10:36), so also were the Apostles consecrated by God and sent into the world to proclaim the truth which they had received from Christ (cf. Jn 17: 18; 20:21).

As indicated above, the Apostles were the first to have the ministerial priesthood conferred on them whereby they were entrusted with a pastoral mission in regard to which they were given authority to proclaim the gospel, celebrate the Eucharist, forgive sins and rule over the community. Holy Orders is the sacrament "through which the mission entrusted by Christ to his apostles continues to be exercised in the Church until the end of time."[142] It is "the sacrament of apostolic ministry," which "includes three degrees: episcopate, presbyterate, and diaconate."[143]

The *CCC* teaches that "since the beginning, the ordained ministry has been conferred and exercised in three degrees: that of bishops, that of presbyters, and that of deacons."[144] Recalling the testimony of St. Ignatius of Antioch, the *CCC* adds: "The ministries conferred by ordination are irreplaceable for the organic structure of the Church: without the bishop, presbyters, and deacons, one cannot speak of the Church."[145] Pope John Paul II sounded a somewhat similar note when he said:

> The ordained priesthood is an irreplaceable element in the edifice of the Redemption, it is a channel through which the fresh waters necessary to life normally flow. The priesthood to which one is called as pure gift (cf. Heb. 5:4), is the nerve-centre of the Church's whole life and mission.[146]

It is sometimes asserted that there is no significant difference between the ministerial priesthood and the common priesthood of all the faithful. Speaking of the common priesthood, the *CCC* says: "The whole Church is a priestly people. Through Baptism all the faithful share in the priesthood of Christ. This participation is called the 'common priesthood of all the faithful.'"[147] In reference to the way in which this common priesthood obliges all of the faithful to bear witness to Christ in their daily life, Vatican II said: "The baptised, by regeneration and the anointing of the Holy Spirit, are consecrated into a spiritual house and a holy priesthood...Everywhere on earth they should bear witness to Christ and give an answer to those who seek an account of the hope of eternal life which is in them (cf. 1 Pet. 3:15)."[148]

In teaching that the common priesthood of all the faithful and the ministerial priesthood are interrelated, Vatican II was careful however to state that they "differ from one another in essence and not only in degree."[149] Referring to this teaching of Vatican II, Groome says:

> Concerning *designated functions of ministry,* including the ordained, I note first the sentiments of Vatican II. It claimed there is a difference not only "in degree" but "in essence" between the common priesthood of all and ordained priesthood. Though this reflects the present "mind of the church" (historical circumstances and critical scholarship may yet nuance it)...in its context (*Constitution on the Church,* par. 10) the primary intent was to affirm the close relationship between

the two and their common ground in the priesthood of Christ, and their distinction seems more parenthetical.[150]

Vatican II's teaching that the common priesthood of all the faithful and the ministerial priesthood "differ in essence and not only in degree" is of much greater importance than the mere "parenthetical" significance that Groome ascribes to it. Pope Pius XII pointed out that just as the sacrament of Baptism sets all the faithful apart from those who are not baptised, so too does the Sacrament of Holy Orders set the ordained priest apart from the rest of the faithful.[151] Speaking of this distinction between the ordained priesthood and the common priesthood of all the faithful, the *CCC* says:

> The ministerial priesthood differs in essence from the common priesthood of the faithful because it confers a sacred power for the service of the faithful. The ordained ministers exercise their service for the People of God by teaching *(munus docendi),* divine worship *(munus liturgicum)* and pastoral governance *(munus regendi).*[152]

Equality of 'Male and Female' Does Not Mean the Suppression of Differences

In arguing that the early Church was an "inclusive discipleship of equals," wherein women had the same functions as men, Fiorenza often draws on St. Paul's words in Galatians 3:27-29. She says:

> Christian feminism is fascinated by the vision of equality, wholeness and freedom expressed in Galatians 3:27-29; in Christ Jesus "there is neither Jew nor Greek, neither slave nor free, neither male and female"...Yet this vision was never realised by the Christian church throughout its history...The failure of the church to realise the vision of Galatians 3:28-29 in its own institutions and praxis had as its consequence a long sexist theology of the church.[153]

There are many ways in which the text of Galatians 3:28 can be interpreted so as to harmonise with the Church's doctrine on a male-only ministerial priesthood. Referring to Galatians 3:28, *Inter Insigniores* says: "This passage does not concern ministries: it only affirms the universal calling to divine filiation, which is the same for all."[154] Pope John Paul II in one instance interprets the passage as referring to Jesus' intention to unify humanity: "To reconcile all men through his sacrifice 'in one body' and make everyone 'one new man' (Eph 2: 15, 16), so that now 'there is neither Jew nor Greek, there is neither slave nor free, there is neither male nor female; for you are all one in Christ Jesus (Gal 3:28)." Having said this, the Holy Father added: "If Jesus Christ reunited man and woman in their equal status as children of God, he engages both of them in his mission, not indeed by suppressing their differences, but by eliminating all unjust inequality and by reconciling all in the unity of the Church."[155] The passage can also be taken to refer to how believers who respond to God's word become members of Christ's Body. The "body's unity does not do away with the diversity of its members" but rather "the unity of the Mystical Body triumphs over all human divisions."[156]

The Holy Spirit does not do away with differences but rather makes possible their fruitful development. Hence, Galatians 3:28 does not speak simply of "being equal" but rather of "being one" on the basis of a common Christian piety within the Holy Spirit.[157] Speaking of how the Letter to the Galatians and the First Letter to the Corinthians complement each other, Fr. Vanhoye says: "The Letter to the Galatians discusses the *foundation* of Christian *existence*. On this basic level only one thing counts: faithful adherence to Christ. The 'works of the law' do not matter, nor do individual differences, whether religious, social or sexual in origin. United to Christ through faith, all are 'one'."[158] On the other hand, adds Fr. Vanhoye: "The First Letter to the Corinthians considers another level, that of the various *functions* carried out in the Church, the Body of Christ. At this secondary level, St. Paul affirms the necessity of the differences. Not everyone can be an apostle, not everyone prophets or teachers (cf. 1 Cor 12:29–30). These differences, established by God himself (12:28), are to be accepted by each person for the good of the whole Body. They are the conditions for a life of effective charity."[159] Finally, regarding attempts to use Galatians 3:27-29 as a scriptural foundation to support an egalitarian Church, Fr. Vanhoye says:

Egalitarian claims, however, cannot be reconciled with authentic charity because they are in accord neither with the divine disposition contained in creation (cf. 1 Cor 12:18) nor with the example of Christ in redemption (cf. Phil 2:6). Of course, every Christian man and woman are equal in their fundamental dignity. "For through faith you are all children of God in Christ Jesus" (Gal 3:26). However, it does not follow that all have a claim to the same functions within the Church.[160]

Reference

1   Pope John Paul II, address to Bishops of Australia, December 14, 1998, *L'Osservatore Romano,* December 16, 1998.
2   Statement of Conclusions, n. 8, *L'Osservatore Romano,* December 16, 1998.
3   Ibid.
4   Thomas Groome, *Sharing Faith,* op. cit. p. 300.
5   Ibid.
6   For these points on Christ as priest, prophet and king, I have drawn on an article by Archbishop Henryk Muszynski which was published in *L'Osservatore Romano* on August 26, 1992.
7   Cf. Pope John Paul II, *General Audience,* February 25, 1987, in Catechesis on the Creed, Vol 2, p. 120.
8   Cf. Pope John Paul II, *General Audience,* February 18, 1987, ibid. p. 114.
9   Pope John Paul II, *General Audience*, February 18, 1987, ibid.
10 Pope John Paul II, *General Audience,* February 18, 1987, ibid. p. 115.
11 Pope John Paul II, *General Audience,* February 18, 1987, ibid.
12 Cf. Pope John Paul II, *General Audience,* February 18, 1987, ibid.
13 *CCC.* n. 1539.
14 *CCC.* n. 1540.
15 *CCC.* n. 1540; cf. Heb 5:3; 7:27; 10:1–4.
16 On this point see Pope John Paul II, *General Audience,* February 18, 1987, in Cathechesis on the Creed, Vol. 2, p. 116.
17 Pope John Paul II, *General Audience,* February 18, 1987, ibid.
18 *CCC.* n. 1544.
19 Pope John Paul II, Holy Thursday Letter To Priests, *L'Osservatore Romano,* March 27, 1996.
20 Elisabeth Schussler Fiorenza, *Discipleship of Equals,* op. cit. p. 115.
21 Ibid. p. 93.
22 Ibid. p. 224.
23 Ibid.
24 Ibid. p. 236.
25 Ibid. p. 87.
26 Ibid. p. 145.

27 Ibid. p. 247.

28 Ibid. p. 31.

29 Ibid. p. 145.

30 Thomas Groome, *Sharing Faith,* p. 512n. 27.

31 Ibid. p. 309.

32 Ibid.

33 Ibid. p. 310 (emphasis added).

34 Ibid.

35 Ibid.

36 Archbishop Henryk Muszynski, *L'Osservatore Romano,* 26/8/92.

37 Ibid.

38 Vatican II, *Lumen Gentium,* n. 10.

39 CCC. n. 764.

40 Ibid.

41 Fr. Benedict Ashley, O.P., *Who Is A Priest, in Catholic Dossier,* Ignatius Press, San Francisco, July–August 1998, p. 9.

42 Ibid.

43 Ibid. p. 10.

44 Ibid.

45 Cf. Ibid.

46 Pope John Paul II, *Pastores Dabo Vobis,* n. 16.

47 *CCC.* n. 1337.

48 Council of Trent, Denz. 1740; cf. *CCC.* n. 1337.

49 Pope John Paul II, *L'Osservatore Romano,* July 8, 1992.

50 Council of Trent, DS 1752, Session XXII, 1562, Canon 2.

51 Council of Trent, Session XXIII.

52 Council of Trent, Session XXIII, Canon 1.

53 Vatican II, Presbyterorum Ordinis, n. 2. Footnote number 5 appended to this statement of Vatican II recalls Canon 1 of Session XXIII of the Council of Trent which is quoted above (note 51). This insertion was made by the Fathers of Vatican II to make sure that the doctrine it was expounding on the ministerial priesthood would be interpreted in continuity with the teaching of Trent.

54 Some theologians argue that it is the proclamation of the Gospel that is central to the life of the ordained priest and not the celebration of the Eucharist. To raise such an issue is the establish a false dichotomy since the ultimate goal of evangelisation is to lead people to full and conscious participation in the Eucharistic Sacrifice of the Mass which is the "source and summit of the Christian life" (Vatican II, Lumen Gentium, n. 11; *CCC.* n. 1411).

55 Pope John Paul II, "Cf. Pope *Dominicae Cenae,* n. 2.

56 Pope John Paul II, *L'Osservatore Romano,* March 27, 1996.

57 *CCC.* n. 1545; the quotation within this passage is from St. Thomas Aquinas, Hebr. 8,4.

58 Cf. Pope Paul VI, Response to the Letter of His Grace the Most Reverend Dr. F. D. Coggan, Archbishop of Canterbury, *Concerning the Ordination of Women to the Priesthood,* 30 November 1975.

59 Cf. Pope John Paul II, *L'Osservatore Romano,* August 3, 1994. See also Fr. Jean Galot, S.J. Theology of the Priesthood, Ignatius Press, San Francisco, 1985, p. 255.

60 Pope John Paul II, *General Audience,* July 1, 1992; in Catechesis on the Creed, Vol. 4. p. 202.

61 Pope John Paul II, *General Audience,* July 1, 1992; ibid.

62 Fr. Jean Galot, *Theology of the Priesthood,* op. cit. p. 73.

63 Ibid.

64 Ibid.

65 Fr Manfred Hauke. *Women In The Priesthood: A Systematic Analysis in the Light of the Order of Creation and Redemption,* Ignatius Press, San Francisco 1988, p. 333.

66 Vatican II, *Dei Verbum,* n. 2.

67 Vatican II, *Dei Verbum,* n. 7.

68 Ibid.

69 Pope John Paul II, *Fides et Ratio,* n. 10.

70 Fr Manfred Hauke, *Women In The Priesthood,* op. cit. For the section on St. Paul's teaching see pages 340–403.

71 Inter Insigniores, SCDF., 1976, n. 4.

72 Ibid.

73 Pope John Paul II, *Ordinatio Sacerdotalis,* n. 2.

74 Pope John Paul II, *Ordinatio Sacerdotalis,* n. 2; Cf. 1 Tim 3:1; 2 Tim 1:6; Tit 1:5–9.

75 Sacred Congregation For The Doctrine Of The Faith, *Inter Insigniores,* n. 3.

76 Cf. *Inter Insigniores,* n. 3.

77 Cf. *Inter Insigniores,* n. 3.

78 Father Louis Bouyer, *L'Osservatore Romano,* January 20, 1977.

79 *Inter Insigniores,* n. 3.

80 Father Albert Vanhoye, *L'Osservatore Romano,* March 3, 1993

81 Ibid.

82 Ibid.

83 Elisabeth Schussler Fiorenza, *Discipleship of Equals,* op. cit. p. 84.

84 Hans Kung, *National Catholic Reporter,* December 15, 1995.

85 Fr Manfred Hauke, *Women in the Priesthood,* op. cit. p. 358–59.

86 Elisabeth Schussler Fiorenza, *Discipleship of Equals,* op. cit. p. 115. Here, Fiorenza also asserts that James, the leader of the Jerusalem church, "was not one of the twelve."

87 Ibid.

88 Thomas H. Groome, *Sharing Faith,* op. cit. p. 309.

89 Ibid.

90 Ibid. p. 316.

91 Ibid. p. 313.

92 Ibid. p. 311–12.

93 Ibid. p. 314.

94 Ibid. p. 314.

95 Ibid.

96 Cf. Pope John Paul II, *General Audience,* March 3, 1993, in Catechesis on the Creed, Vol. 4, op. cit. p. 302.

97 Council of Trent, *Canons on the Sacrament of Order,* Denz. 1776.

98 Pope John Paul II, *General Audience,* October 6, 1993 in Cathechesis on the Creed, Vol. 4, p. 391

99 Pope John Paul II, *General Audience,* March 31, 1993; in Catechesis on the Creed, Vol. 4, pp. 300–304.

100 Cf. Pope John Paul II, *L'Osservatore Romano,* August 3, 1994.

101 Fr. Jean Galot, *S.J. Theology of the Priesthood,* op. cit. p. 255.

102 Pope John Paul II, *General Audience,* July 8, 1992, ibid. p. 206.

103 Pope John Paul II, *General Audience,* July 8, 1992, ibid.

104 Pope John Paul II, *General Audience,* July 8, 1992, ibid. p. 207.

105 Pope John Paul II, *General Audience,* July 1, 1992, in Catechesis on the Creed, Vol. 4, p. 205.

106 Pope St. Clement of Rome, Letter to The Corinthians, cited in William A. Jurgens' *The Faith of the Early Fathers,* Liturgical Press, Minnesota, 1970, Vol. 1, p. 10.

107 Vatican II, *Dei Verbum,* n. 7.

108 Vatican II, *Lumen Gentium,* n. 18.

109 Vatican II, *Lumen Gentium,* n. 20.

110 Ibid.

111 Ibid.

112 Pope John Paul II, *Pastores Dabo Vobis,* n.15.

113 Ibid. Pope John Paul II, *Pastores Dabo Vobis,* n.15.

114 Vatican II, *Lumen Gentium,* n. 29.

115 St. Ignatius of Antioch, Letter to the Trallians, cited in William A. Jurgens' *Faith of the Early Church Fathers,* Vol. 1, p. 20, Liturgical Press, Minnesota 1970.

116 Hans Urs von Balthasar, *A Short Primer For Unsettled Laymen,* Ignatius Press, San Francisco 1987, p. 100.

117 Ibid.

118 Ibid. p. 31.

119 Ibid. p. 44.

120 Pope John Paul II, *General Audience,* July 8, 1992, in Catechesis on the Creed, Vol. 4, p. 206.

121 Pope Pius VI, *Const. Auctorem Fidei,* August 28, 1794: Denz. 1502.

122 Cf. *CCC.* n. 1337; *Council of Trent,* Denz. 1740.

123 *CCC.* n. 1323.

124 Acts 2:42, 46; cf. *CCC.* n. 1342.

125 Pope John Paul II, *Dominicae Cenae,* n. 8.

126 Ibid.

127 *CCC.* n. 1343.

128 *CCC.* n. 1200.

129 *CCC.* n. 1208.

130 *CCC.* n. 1203.

131 Pope Pius XII, *Mediator Dei,* n. 50.

132 Ibid.

133 Cf. *CCC.* n. 1205.

134 Cf. *CCC.* n. 1662.

135 *CCC.* n. 1412.

136 *CCC.* n. 1411.

137 Thomas Groome, *Sharing Faith,* op. cit. p. 311.

138 *CCC.* n. 1573.

139 Cf. *CCC.* n. 1590.

140 *The Priestly Ministry,* International Theological Commission: Texts and Documents 1969-1985, foreword by Joseph Cardinal Ratzinger, Ignatius Press, San Francisco, 1989, p. 38. The subcommission of the ITC which produced this document included Hans Urs von Balthasar.

141 Ibid.

142 *CCC.* n. 1536.

143 Ibid..

144 *CCC.* n. 1593.

145 Ibid.

146 Pope John Paul II, Address to the Congregation For The Clergy, October 15, 1998, *L'Osservatore Romano,* November 4, 1998.

147 *CCC.* n. 1591.

148 Vatican II, *Lumen Gentium,* n. 10.

149 Ibid.

150 Thomas Groome, *Sharing Faith,* p. 324

151 Cf. Pope Pius XII, *Mediator Dei,* n. 43.

152 *CCC.* n. 1592.

153 Elisabeth Schussler Fiorenza, *Discipleship of Equals,* pp. 68-69.

154 *Inter Insigniores,* n. 6.

155 Pope John Paul II, *L'Osservatore Romano,* July 13, 1994.

156 *CCC.* n. 791.

157 Cf. Fr Manfred Hauke, *Women in the Priesthood?* op. cit. p. 346.
158 Fr Albert Vanhoye, S.J. op. cit.
159 Ibid.
160 Ibid.

7

The Most Holy Trinity

The *Statement of Conclusions,* issued after the meeting in late 1998 between a representation of the Australian Bishops Conference and Prefects of various dicasteries of the Roman Curia, referred to "a crisis concerning the ability to know the truth" which it said "is also a crisis in the profession of God as Person—the God of Abraham—and of Jesus as the true God, in such wise as to be able to say 'I know God'."[1] The *Statement* pointed out also that "some aspects of feminist scholarship can lead to a rejection of the privileged place given to the scriptural language describing the Trinity and to Jesus' own teaching, and can even lead to rejection of the Trinity itself."[2]

An integral aspect of Groome's and Fiorenza's theological project is a commitment to the reconstruction of the language of Revelation and Catholic liturgy in order to make them conform to their egalitarian and inclusivist vision. They even propose the neutering and feminisation of Christ himself—something which amounts to an attempt to obliterate objective reality.

How Shall We Address 'God the Father'?

Speaking in 1993 of a perceived need to recast the language of Revelation, Fiorenza said: "We must learn to speak of God as Father and Mother, as Son and Daughter, as she and he. Unless female God-language is commonly accepted in Christian theology and worship, women will not be able to recognise themselves in the image and likeness of God."[3] Speaking on the same theme in 1998, she said: "Today the theoretical struggle over a critical deconstructive and reconstructive feminist model of interpretation for the most part does not center on theological hermeneutics but on issues of language and theory."[4]

In speaking of the Holy Trinity in *Sharing Faith*, Groome says: "One traditional (since Augustine) imaging of the inner life of the Trinity poses the Holy Spirit as the Love between God the **Father/Mother** and the Second Person, revealed in Jesus Christ."[5]

Groome's program for the transformation of the language of Catholic Faith was given extensive treatment in his 1995 book *Language for a Catholic Church (Revised Edition)*. In proposing changes to the language of both Revelation and the Creed, Groome's stated objective is to rid the Church of the "sin" of "sexism" in regard to which he believes, "Catholic congregations sin more boldly with exclusive language than do mainline Protestant ones."[6] Groome asserts that the "now common recognition of scholars" is that the "fundamental impetus of the Bible for inclusion and mutuality has been greatly diminished by its translators" and he lists Fiorenza as an example of an "outstanding" scripture scholar who has "deepened" our awareness in this regard.[7]

Inviting "faith communities" to a "conversion" that will create a more "inclusive" environment, Groome calls on religious educators to adopt programs geared at "consciousness raising," which will reflect the "values of inclusion, dialogue and participation."[8] The "overall dynamics" of such a program should, says Groome, reflect "the movements of a '*shared Christian praxis*' approach to faith education."[9] This process of "consciousness" raising begins with a "focusing activity" which uses an "opening statement establishing the theme of inclusive language as a 'generative' one (Freire) for a Christian community."[10] This focusing act "leads to an invitation to participants to name *present praxis* (i.e. what they and their communities are doing) regarding the theme, and to critically reflect on it."[11] The various movements that make up this particular exercise in *shared Christian praxis* conclude by offering participants "a more explicit opportunity for personal and communal decision-making," in regard to the use of language in the Church.[12]

In applying *shared Christian praxis* to the language of Revelation in order to reconstruct it, Groome fails to consider that some of the language he proposes to change does not permit any such alteration because of the doctrine it embodies as well as the concrete historical realities to which it sometimes refers.

In reference to Jesus' revelation of God the Father, Groome says: "A particular issue for Christians is the image of God as Father, clearly the favoured image of Jesus."[13] Having said this, Groome adds that it is "evident that Jesus' intent was to address God as *like* a loving, trustworthy, kind, and gentle parent."[14] On the basis of this assertion, Groome goes on to say: "For us the crucial issue is whether or not we can still capture all that Jesus meant then by 'Father' by simply repeating the term and without using other terms that help to complete what Jesus intended."[15]

Groome's difficulty with references to "the Father" extends into the Mass. After saying that "the present 'typical edition' of the Roman Missal was composed before consciousness about inclusive language," Groome goes on to add:

> I'm convinced that: *All presiders and ministers at mass or communion services can address and lead the assembly in prayers that are gender-inclusive for both God and ourselves. Likewise, people can pray their common prayers and responses inclusively.* No presider need address God only as 'Father' in the collects.[16]

Suggesting how the community can be conditioned to adopt inclusive language, Groome says: "Engaging people to pray and participate at liturgy with inclusive language will clearly take some educational efforts and perhaps printed suggestions for the congregation. For example, the presider can readily say, 'Pray my sisters and brothers, that my sacrifice and yours will be acceptable to God our loving parent.'"[17] The offending words in the Roman Missal which Groome here wants to expunge are: "may be acceptable to God, the almighty Father." As will become clear later in this work, these words of the Roman Missal embody great doctrinal significance.

In proposing a solution to the perceived problem of how to appropriately address God, Groome says: "All God-language is analogous and metaphorical."[18] After calling on religious educators to "help end sexism in the Church by not teaching it, and by teaching for inclusion and mutuality,"[19] Groome goes on to say:

> An issue of particular concern for catechists is the strong tradition in primary catechesis of referring to God exclusively as

'Father'. (This is often occasioned by the teaching of the Lord's Prayer, the Sign of the Cross, and the 'Glory Be')...if 'Father' is the only image used of God, and especially in early catechesis, it may no longer teach what Jesus intended to teach with this analogy.[20]

In suggesting a solution to this perceived pedagogical problem, Groome says:

One possible solution (which for this author has seemed successful with younger children) is to interchange the terms 'father,' 'mother,' and 'loving parent' for God. Then, when teaching a traditional prayer like the 'Our Father,' teachers can take care to explain in the catechesis which follows that Jesus intends us to approach God as a trustworthy, forgiving and loving parent.[21]

Proffering advice on how we might address the Persons of the Holy Trinity in order to avoid exclusivist terms, Groome says:

Terms like 'Creator, Savior and Sanctifier' seem worthy candidates, at least when speaking of the Trinity's relationship to us...A formula that might more adequately represent our faith in the triune relationship within the Godhead...is suggested by an inclusive language breviary text which prays 'Glory to you, Source of all Being, Eternal Word, and Holy Spirit'.[22]

Groome calls on religious educators to adopt concerted strategies in order to adjust their community's language patterns. Part of this strategy is to "avoid male pronouns for God—his, him, he, himself—and instead repeat the word God again in a sentence or use 'the divine,' Godself, God's very self, God's own etc."[23] Similarly, Groome advises that some biblical titles or referents for God "can be readily made gender-inclusive," such as, "Sovereign One can be used instead of Lord, or Sovereign God instead of Lord God...God as ruler can be used instead of King."[24] Groome also proposes that "some peculiar personifications along gender lines are better avoided: e.g. 'the Church...she' (use 'it')."[25]

Proper Names for the Divine Persons of the Holy Trinity

The Holy Sacrifice of the Mass is the source and summit of the Christian life as well as the primary bearer of the Church's catechesis. Consequently, all catechetical activity in the Church should have as one of its key objectives the goal of leading those being catechised to a more conscious and active participation in the sacred liturgy. The language of catechesis and religious education should reflect this objective and hence there is a need to preserve continuity between the Church's official language in the liturgy and the language used in catechetics and religious education.[26] The Holy See's current *Norms for the Translation of Biblical Texts for Use in the Liturgy* lays down the following:

4.2. The grammatical gender of God, pagan deities, and angels according to the original texts must not be changed insofar as this is possible in the receptor language.

4.3. In fidelity to the inspired Word of God, the traditional biblical usage for naming the persons of the Trinity as Father, Son and Holy Spirit is to be retained.

4.5. There shall be no systematic substitution of the masculine pronoun or the possessive adjective to refer to God in correspondence to the original text.

Groome's and Fiorenza's difficulty with the language of Revelation stems in part from their heavy reliance on philosophers such as Habermas and other exponents of critical theory. In this regard, Fiorenza and Groome have failed to discern correctly what is of value in critical theory and what is incompatible with the deposit of faith and its mode of transmission in the Church. A characteristic of critical theory is that it lacks a solid foundation in metaphysics.

In *Fides et Ratio*, Pope John Paul II stated that "reality and truth do transcend the factual and the empirical" and he insisted on the human being's capacity to know the "transcendent" and "metaphysical" dimension of reality "in a way that is true and certain, albeit imperfect and analogical."[27] Coupled with this, the Holy Father stated that philosophy needs metaphysics in order to transcend "empirical data" and "in order to attain something absolute, ultimate and foundational in its search for truth."[28] After stating that in the search for truth "we cannot stop short at experience alone," the Holy Father went on in *Fides et Ratio* to add that "a philosophy which shuns metaphysics would be radically unsuited to the task of mediation in the understanding of Revelation."[29]

Fides et Ratio stated that the importance of metaphysics becomes very evident when "we consider current developments in hermeneutics and the analysis of language."[30] While acknowledging the help that such studies can provide for the understanding of faith by bringing "to light the structure of our thought and speech and the meaning which language bears," the Holy Father cautioned, however, that some scholars working in these areas "tend to stop short at the question of how reality is understood and expressed without going further to see whether reason can discover its essence."[31] Speaking of the connection between Revelation and our ability to know the truth, Pope John Paul II stated in *Fides et Ratio* that God—"in his goodness and wisdom"—chose to reveal to us "the purpose of his will" which is that "through Christ, the Word made flesh, man has access to the Father in the Holy Spirit and comes to share in the divine nature."[32]

Regarding the connection between faith and knowledge, *Fides et Ratio* states that in the free act of faith, the human person "reaches the certainty of truth and chooses to live in that truth."[33] At the same time, "the knowledge proper to faith does not destroy the mystery; it only reveals it the more, showing how necessary it is for people's lives."[34] Consequently, the knowledge that comes with faith "refers back constantly to the mystery of God which the human mind cannot exhaust but can only receive and embrace in faith."[35] Between "these two poles," i.e. between the mystery and our knowledge of it, "reason has its own specific field in which it can enquire and understand, restricted only by its finiteness before the infinite mystery of God."[36] While faith is "a gift from God" and "is not based on reason," nevertheless faith cannot "dispense with reason" while on the other hand "reason needs to be reinforced by faith, in order to discover horizons it cannot reach on its own."[37]

While acknowledging that "human language may be conditioned by history and constricted in other ways," Pope John Paul II nevertheless stated in *Fides et Ratio* that "the human being can still express truths which surpass the phenomenon of language."[38] Coupled with this, the "word of God refers constantly to things which transcend human experience and even human thought," but these mysteries (e.g. the Holy

Trinity), "could not be revealed" nor could theology render them "in some way intelligible" were "human knowledge limited strictly to the world of sense experience."[39] Consequently, adds Pope John Paul II in *Fides et Ratio*, "faith clearly presupposes that human language is capable of expressing divine and transcendent reality in a universal way—analogically, it is true, but no less meaningfully for that."[40] Hence, what we have in the texts of Sacred Scripture is "human language" that "embodies the language of God, who communicates his own truth with that wonderful 'condescension' which mirrors the logic of the Incarnation."[41] The key truth of Christian faith that is revealed in the language of Revelation is, as Pope John Paul II expresses it in *Fides et Ratio*, that through grace Christians are enabled "to share in the mystery of Christ" who "offers them a true and coherent knowledge of the Triune God."[42]

At various stages in the Church's history, the central truths of Revelation have been summarised in its various Creeds. Speaking of these Creeds, the *CCC* says: "None of the Creeds from the different stages in the Church's life can be considered superseded or irrelevant. They help us today to obtain and deepen the faith of all times by means of the different summaries made of it."[43] In this context, amongst various Creeds cited by the *CCC* is the *Fides Damasi* (Creed of Pope Damasus I).[44] In this Creed of Pope Damasus (366-384) we read:

> We believe in one God the Father almighty and in our one Lord Jesus Christ the Son of God and in (one) Holy Spirit...We confess one God in the name of the Father and of the Son and of the Holy Spirit...The proper name for the Father is Father, and the proper name for the Son is Son, and the proper name for the Holy Spirit is Holy Spirit.[45]

Despite the fact that these proper names for the persons of the Blessed Trinity are translations from *Fides Damasi*, their use is intended to have a specific referent to whom the name applies, e.g. "Father" refers to the Father and not to the Son. Now, as we saw earlier, Pope John Paul II has stressed that language is capable of expressing divine and transcendental reality, but that it does so analogically but nevertheless meaningfully (cf. notes 27 and 40). On the other hand, Groome asserts that "all God-language" is "metaphorical".[46] This is clearly false for these reasons: a) while metaphors are analogies, not all analogies are metaphors; b) while all language **about** God is analogical, some "god-language" is not **about** God, but is addressed to him. This category includes proper names and simple prayers. Thus, the proper name "Father" is not **about** God—rather it denominates, names, indicates, points to—"the Father".

Groome would have us believe that "the Father" has been revealed to us in order that we may simply "approach God as a trustworthy, forgiving and loving parent."[47] But this not only conflates God with the first person of the Blessed Trinity, it also confuses naming and describing. "Father" does not describe the desirable characteristics of some father or other, it names this reality with the name, "Father". Since a proper name as such is not an analogy, it cannot be a metaphor. Therefore, Groome's assertion that "all God-language" is "metaphorical" is false.

Like feminist theologians such as Elisabeth Schussler Fiorenza, Mary Daly, Rosemary Reuther and Elisabeth Johnson, Groome's proposal for the restructuring of the language of Revelation is dependent on the obliteration of the critical distinction between analogy and metaphor. On the basis of such a fundamental error, he ends up proposing that we settle for a way of naming the persons of the Holy Trinity that is based on our own subjective understanding of reality (tainted as it is by the consequences of original sin) rather than accepting the names by which God has revealed himself in Sacred Scripture and Sacred Tradition.

God in the Old Testament

To understand why we are not free to refer to the First Person of the Holy Trinity as "God the Father/Mother" as Groome recommends, we must first examine the difference between the revelation of God in the Old Testament where he is sometimes referred to as 'father' and the revelation of "God the Father" in the New Testament.

The First Vatican Council taught that God "is really and essentially distinct from the world...and ineffably raised above all things which are outside of himself or which can be conceived as being so."[48] In reference to God the Creator of all things, the same Council added: The Holy Catholic Apostolic Roman Church, believes and confesses that there is one true and living God, Creator and Lord of heaven and earth, almighty, eternal, immense, incomprehensible, infinite in intellect, in will, and in all perfection; who, as being one, sole, absolutely simple and immutable spiritual substance, is to be declared as really and essentially distinct from the world, of supreme beatitude in and from himself, and ineffably exalted above all things which exist, or are conceivable, except himself.[49]

The First Vatican Council's emphasis in the passage quoted above on the transcendence, incomprehensibility and ineffability of God was "dictated by the need to withstand both the errors of nineteenth century pantheism and those of materialism, which had begun to assert themselves at that time."[50] Pantheism postulates that God is the universe or that the development of the universe is the development of God, while materialism rejects the transcendent origin of the universe.[51]

Even "if the existence of God can be known and demonstrated, and even if his essence is in some manner knowable in the mirror of creation," it nevertheless remains true that "no created image can reveal the essence of God, as such, to the human mind," for "it exceeds all that exists in the created world and all that could be thought in the human mind."[52] The essence of God—"which is the divinity"—is "found to be outside every category of genus and species which we use in our definitions."[53] Hence, the human intellect, even though "it has been elevated significantly" by revelation "to a deeper and more complete knowledge" of God's mystery, is still "unable to comprehend God adequately and exhaustively."[54]

While God is "ineffably raised above all things which are outside of himself" and hence is transcendent to his creation, he is nevertheless intimately involved with his creation and in this context we can speak of his immanence. The fact that God is neither man nor woman,[55] does not mean that the sexual symbolism applied to him does not instruct us in the mystery that he is. The sexual images applied to God can relate to either his immanence or his transcendence—thereby expressing the way he relates to his creation. A fully immanent God is contained in his creation and thus belongs to a pantheistic religious philosophy. Against this, a transcendent God is distinct from his creation—though he 'is in it' he is not 'contained in it'.

In the Old Testament, male symbolism represents God's transcendence and the concept 'father' includes the qualities of power, justice, benevolence and mercy. The female symbolism on the other hand represents God's immanence. In reference to this, the *CCC* says:

By calling God 'Father,' the language of faith indicates two main things: that God is the first origin of everything and transcendent authority; and that he is at the same time goodness and loving care for all his children. God's parental tenderness can also be expressed by the image of motherhood, which emphasises God's immanence, the intimacy between Creator and creature.[56]

God revealed his name to Moses as *YHWH* which is variously translated as "I Am He Who Is," "I Am Who Am" or "I Am Who I Am" (cf. Ex. 3:13-14).[57] God's name is mysterious as he himself is mysterious and in revealing it "God says who he is and by what name he is to be called."[58] The name *YHWH* especially designates God as creator and source of all life which means that as such he is "completely transcendent" in regard to the world.[59]

The Old Testament uses the divine name *YHWH* (translated as Lord in English) some 6800 times. Fr. Paul V. Mankowski, S.J., a specialist in ancient Semitic languages, says that the name *YHWH* is almost a Semitic verb in the imperfect tense (equivalent to the English present or future tenses) whose meaning is thought by most scripture scholars to be "a causative form of the verb *hayah,* meaning 'he causes to be' or 'he calls into being'."[60] Other scripture scholars, says Fr. Mankowski, have suggested derivation from a root meaning "to be passionate or strong." Whichever way the verb is understood, adds Fr. Mankowski, it must be "a third person *masculine* form of the verb," which implies "the form of the verb that is God's name must point to a grammatically masculine referent."[61] Fr. Mankowski says that "further corroboration is to be had from the fact that *elohim,* the word for 'God' as opposed to the proper name, is also masculine in form, as is the word *adonai,* which is the *gere* or substitute pronounced for the letters *YHWH*."[62] Finally, Fr. Mankowski points out that "every adjective, every pronoun, every participle that refers to *YHWH* is unmistakably masculine."[63]

Apart from the divine name *YHWH,* the Old Testament uses many metaphors or images to express God's relationship to his people. *YHWH* is often described as a shepherd, rock, fortress, refuge etc. Eventually, as the people of Israel became more conscious of God's merciful and providential care for them, they began to apply the title 'Father' to him. In designating God as "Father," the Old Testament is thereby identifying God as the all-powerful yet transcendent source of life who does not remain distant from man but rather approaches him out of loving concern.

In the Old Testament, God is first of all "father" to the people Israel who he regards as his firstborn son (cf. Ex 4:22). God is the "father" who gave Israel its "being" (Dt 32:6). *YHWH* continuously calls his wayward children to repentance—to cry out to him as "My Father" (Jer 3:4)—knowing that they are indeed his children: "For I am a father to Israel, and Ephraim is my first-born son" (Jer 31:9; cf. Mal 1:6; Is 63:16; 64:7). Next, God is father of orphans and of the king who rules in his name (2 Sam 7:14; Ps 68:6; 89:27). The author of the Book of Sirach addresses God as Father in his prayer: "Lord, father and master of my life...Lord, father and God of my life" (Sir 23:1, 4). The author of the Book of Wisdom addresses God in similar terms: "...taking ship to cross the raging sea...your providence, Father, is what steers it" (Wis 14: 1-3).

In the Old Testament, God is occasionally compared to a mother. In Isaiah we read: "Can a mother forget her infant, be without tenderness for the child of her womb? Even should she forget, I will never forget you" (Is 49: 15). Later in Isaiah, we read: "As a mother comforts her son, so will I comfort you" (66:13). God's providential care for his people is often compared to the way a mother bird cares for her young: "On my bed I think of you...I sing for joy in the shadow of your wings" (Ps 63:6-7; cf. Ps 17:8; 36:7; 57:2).

The two most important words used in the Old Testament to describe the mercy of God are *hesed* and *rahamim*. The word *rahamim* has a different nuance from hesed, which refers to God's mercy as reflected in his covenantal relationship with the people of Israel. Speaking of the meaning of *rahamim,* Pope John Paul II says: "*Rahamim, in its very root, denotes the love of a mother (rehem* = mother's womb)...We read in Isaiah: 'Can a woman forget her suckling child, that she should have no compassion on the son of her womb? Even these may forget, yet I will not forget you' (Is 49:15)."[64]

Despite the fact that at times the Old Testament compares God's love for his people to the love of a mother for her children, nevertheless it is the divine 'father' image which predominates. Fr. Mankowski points out that "every image that is *predicated* of YHWH, that is, every instance in which we find a statement of the kind 'YHWH is X,' the predicate is either masculine or entirely compatible with maleness."[65] Regarding the feminine attributes which the Old Testament ascribes to God, Fr. Mankowski says they "are never predicated of YHWH but only suggested in the form of similes...God is *like* a mother."[66] Contrasting this to the male referents for God, Fr. Mankowski points out that the situation is very different. He says: "In Exodus 15...we read *YHWH 'is milhamach,'* 'YHWH is a man of battle'—a male, a *vir proelii*...Of the fifty-five recorded Hebrew sentence names that are composed of the name YHWH and a verb, each shows the masculine form of the verb. The evidence is exceptionless."[67]

In the Old Testament, the 'father' image for God is reinforced by other masculine images such as 'king.' As we have already noted, in the Old Testament God is always designated by the masculine pronoun *he* and not *she.* While the Old Testament incorporates feminine imagery into the 'father' image for God, never however does it address God as 'mother' and never does it pair 'Father' with 'Mother' as a referent for God. In view of all this, it is clear that God's transcendence is a pivotal point of Old Testament theology and that this is tied up with the predominance of the masculine imagery for God. In contrast to this, Fr. Manfred Hauke points out that a study of Gnosticism in the early Christian era, Greek mythology, Near-Eastern fertility religions, the Jewish Cabala, as well as Chinese and Hindu religion, all reveal that religions with deities that are female—or both male and female—tend to be pantheistic.[68]

While God is pure spirit and is therefore "neither man nor woman," nevertheless the respective "perfections" of man and woman "reflect something of the infinite perfection of God: those of a mother and those of a father and husband."[69] Speaking of the way in which the word 'father' is used in the Old Testament to refer to God, Fr. George T. Montague, S.M., Professor of theology at St. Mary's University in San Antonio says: "Of course, the fatherhood is adoptive, and the word for 'father' in the Old Testament texts is the formal one. Even so, the metaphor was a way of conveying the intimate covenant relationship between Israel and Israel's God, a relationship that gave Israel reason to expect only the best from its covenant God."[70]

The New Testament: Revelation of the Holy Trinity

The covenant which God made with man reaches its full and definitive form in Jesus Christ. God, who "is incomprehensible to us," wished "to reveal himself, not only as the one creator and Almighty Father, but also as Father, Son and Holy Spirit."[71] This revelation of the

Holy Trinity reveals the most essential truth about the interior life itself of the one divinity in which God is "an ineffable communion of persons."[72] Hence God, as Christ has revealed him, "does not merely remain closely linked with the world as the Creator and the ultimate source of existence," but rather he desires "to give himself" to man and in doing so he "grants participation in the very life of God: Father, Son and Holy Spirit."[73]

While the truth about God's trinitarian life was not revealed explicitly in the Old Testament, it did, however, prepare the way for the revelation of the Holy Trinity "by showing God's Fatherhood in the covenant with his people, and by manifesting his activity in the world with Wisdom, the Word and the Spirit (cf. e.g., Wis 7:22-30; Prov 8:22-30; Ps 33:4-6; 147:15; Is 55:11; Wis 12: 1; Is 11:2; Sir 48:12)."[74] Since the mystery of God's trinitarian life has been revealed to us by Jesus Christ, it follows that when we move from the Old Testament to the New Testament the word 'Father' when applied to God takes on a completely new perspective—the new element being the way in which Jesus himself uses the word. At no point does Jesus imply that God the Father is simply like a 'father' to him, rather his message is that God "the Father" actually is his 'Father.'

The intimacy with which Jesus speaks of God the Father reaches its climax in the Garden of Gethsemane where he addresses him as *Abba* (Mk 14:16) which when translated into English finds its closest expression in the word 'Daddy.' In speaking of Jesus' use of this term *Abba* to address the Father, Fr. George T. Montague, says: "The fact that Mark goes out of his way to give the Aramaic *Abba* in his otherwise Greek rendering of Jesus' prayer in the garden (Mk 14:36) and Paul does the same in Galatians 4:6 and Romans 8:15 for Christian prayer makes it virtually certain that behind every use of 'Father' in Jesus' discourses lies the same Aramaic word."[75]

By addressing God as *Abba*, Jesus reveals that his relationship to God is unique. Throughout his life, Jesus' mission was focused on revealing the Father and revealing himself as the Son of the Father. In St. Luke's Gospel, the first words of Jesus recorded are "I must be busy with my Father's affairs," while his last words are: "Father, into your hands I commit my spirit"(Lk 2:50; 23:46). In teaching about "the Father," Jesus says: "All things have been delivered to me by my Father, and no one knows the Father except the Son and anyone to whom the Son chooses to reveal him" (Mt 11:27). After St. Peter proclaims Jesus to be "the

Christ, the Son of the living God," Jesus responds to him by saying: "Blessed are you...because flesh and blood has not revealed this to you, but my Father in Heaven" (Mt 16:16-17). From these passages we see that just as only the Father knows the Son and makes him known: "This is my beloved Son with whom I am well pleased" (Mt 3:17)—so also only the Son makes the Father known: "I have made your name known to the men you took from the world to give me" (Jn 17:6).

Those who contested Jesus' claim to have come from the Father "sought to kill him, because he called God his Father, making himself equal with God" (Jn 5:18). They said to him: "Where is your Father?" In reply, Jesus said: "You know neither me nor my Father; if you knew me, you would know my Father also" (Jn 8:19). On hearing this, his questioners objected further—"we have one Father God"—to which Jesus responded: "If God were your Father, you would love me, for I proceeded and came forth from God...he sent me...Truly, truly I say to you, before Abraham was, I am" (Jn 8: 41-42,58). In applying to himself the divine name "I Am," which had been revealed many centuries earlier to Moses, Jesus thereby further enraged those who did not believe in him—so much so that "they picked up stones to throw at him" (Jn 8:59).

Jesus is able to reveal the Person of the Father because he himself is the pre-existent and eternal Son of God: "He who is in the bosom of the Father, he has made him known" (Jn 1:18). In reference to Jesus' words to Philip—"He who has seen me has seen the Father"—Pope John Paul II says: "After the Incarnation, there exists a human face in which it is possible to see God."[76] On another occasion, the Holy Father said that in making the Father known, "the visible Son makes us see the Father who is invisible—'He who has seen me has seen the Father' (Jn 14:9)."[77] Having said this, the Holy Father added: "The Son lives by the Father first of all because he has been generated by him."[78] The Letter to the Hebrews goes back to the Old Testament to render intelligible the full truth regarding the fatherhood of God that has been revealed in Jesus. To this end it combines Psalm 2:7—"You are my son, today I have begotten you"—with 2 Samuel 7: 14 which says: "I will be his father, and he shall be my son" (cf. Heb 1: 4-14). Speaking of the meaning of these words in both their original setting and in the Letter to the Hebrews, Pope John Paul II says:

They are prophetic words. God is speaking to David about his descendant. While in the Old Testament context these words seem to refer only to adoptive sonship, by analogy with human fatherhood and sonship, the New Testament reveals their authentic and definitive significance. They speak of the Son who is of the same substance of the Father, of the Son who is truly generated from the Father. They speak also of the real fatherhood of God, of the fatherhood to which belongs the generation of the Son consubstantial with the Father. They speak of God who is Father in the highest and most authentic meaning of the word. They speak of God who eternally generates the eternal Word, the Word consubstantial with the Father. God is Father in the ineffable mystery of his divinity, in regard to the Word. 'You are my son, today I have begotten you.' The adverb 'today' speaks of eternity. It is the 'today' of the intimate life of God. It is the 'today' of eternity, the 'today' of the Most Holy and ineffable Trinity—Father, Son and Holy Spirit, who is eternal love and eternally consubstantial with the Father and the Son.[79]

In view of what has been said above, it is clear that the New Testament references to the Fatherhood of God "pertains first of all to the fundamental mystery of God's inner life, to the trinitarian mystery"—whereby the 'Father' is the one "who eternally generates the Word, the Son who is consubstantial with him." [80] Coupled with this, the Father in union with the Son, "is eternally the principle of the 'spiration' of the Holy Spirit, who is the love in which the Father and the Son reciprocally remain united (cf. Jn 14:10)."[81]

The mystery of the Holy Trinity is one of those "mysteries hidden in God which can never be known unless they are revealed by God."[82] It is possible to know the truth about the Triune God only by means of the New Testament revelation. Even after being revealed, the mystery of the Holy Trinity "remains the most profound mystery of Faith" which the intellect on its own "can neither comprehend nor penetrate."[83] However, "in a certain way the intellect enlightened by faith can grasp and explain the meaning of the dogma" and thereby "bring the mystery of the inmost life of the Triune God close to man."[84]

The eternal generation of the Son by the Father is a "truth of faith proclaimed and defined by the Church many times"—not only at the

Councils of Nicaea and Constantinople but also at the Fourth Lateran Council in 1215.[85] While "God is Spirit" and hence this eternal generation in God "is of an absolute spiritual nature" pertaining to "the mystery of God's inner life, which is inscrutable to us," nevertheless it follows that since it "is a truth of faith contained directly in revelation and defined by the Church, we can say that the explanation given of it by the Fathers and Doctors of the Church is a well-founded and certain theological doctrine."[86] So, "while the human intellect is not at a level to comprehend the divine essence," revelation nevertheless "unfolds for us the essential terms of the mystery" and "expresses it for us and enables us to savor it in a way well beyond all intellectual understanding, while we await and prepare for the beatific vision in heaven."[87]

The 'Father-Son' relationship which Jesus revealed regarding himself and God illuminates not only the nature of Christ himself but also that of each Christian. With one exception, Jesus is always shown in the Gospels speaking of God as Father only to the disciples. This corresponds to what St. John says in the prologue to his Gospel: "To all who received him [Jesus] he gave power to become children of God' (Jn 1:12). It corresponds also to St. Paul's understanding that "when the time had come, God sent forth his Son...so that we might receive adoption as sons" (Gal 4:4-5). Jesus impresses upon his disciples their dignity as children of God when in response to their request that he teach them to pray he gave them the prayer which begins with "Our Father" (Mt 6:9-13) or "Father" (Lk 11:2-4). Pope John Paul II says that in "the revelation of this prayer," the disciples "discover their special participation in the divine sonship."[88]

In teaching the disciples to pray "Our Father," Jesus did so in a form different from the way he prayed "Father"—he drew a distinction between "my Father" and "your Father." For example, in addressing Mary Magdalene after his resurrection he said: "Go to my brethren and say to them, I am ascending to my Father and your Father, to my God and your God" (Jn 20:17). The reason for this distinction is that Christ's filiation is different from ours: he is 'Son' from all eternity: "Now, Father, it is time for you to glorify me with the glory I had with you before ever the world was made" (Jn 17:5). Coupled with this, it is only through Jesus that access can be had to the Father: "No one comes to the Father but by me" (Jn 14:6).

The special relationship with 'God the Father' which Christians enjoy does not result from their membership of the human race but rather is a consequence of their incorporation into the Body of Christ at Baptism: "Unless a man be born through water and the Spirit he cannot enter the kingdom of God...the Son of man must be lifted up, so that whoever believes in him may have eternal life. Yes, God loved the world so much that he gave his only Son, so that whoever believes in him should not be lost but have eternal life" (Jn 3:5, 14-16). The "eternal life" which Jesus promises those who believe in him "is no less than the participation of believers in the very life of the risen Jesus and consists in their insertion into the movement of love uniting the Father and the Son who are one (cf. Jn 10:30; 17:21-22)."[89]

The Holy Spirit "is the eternal bond that unites the Father and the Son and involves human beings in this ineffable mystery of love."[90] The communion of divine life which characterises the unity of the First and Second Person of the Holy Trinity can be fully understood only by the "Spirit who scrutinises the hidden things of God" (cf. 1 Cor 2:10). The Holy Spirit who "dwells" in the disciples of Christ is the "Spirit of truth," who acts "deep within believers, making the truth that is Christ shine in their minds."[91] It is through this presence of the Holy Spirit in their minds that believers can "understand" the words of Jesus where he says: "Father, Righteous One, the world has not known you, but I have known you, and these have known that you have sent me. I have made your name known to them and will continue to make it known, so that the love with which you loved me may be in them, and so that I may be in them" (Jn 14:20; 17: 25-26). It is the Holy Spirit who teaches us to say "Jesus is Lord" (1 Cor 12:3) and who makes "us capable of speaking with God" and calling him "Abba, Father!" (Gal 4:6).[92]

The dignity to which the baptised Christian is raised "comes from the grace of God," which is "the free and undeserved help that God gives us to respond to his call to become children of God, adoptive sons, partakers of the divine nature and of eternal life."[93] Grace "is a participation in the life of God," which "introduces us into the intimacy of the Trinitarian life."[94] Through baptism, a Christian "participates in the grace of Christ, the Head of his Body" whereby "as an 'adopted son' he can henceforth call God 'Father' in union with the only Son."[95]

In St. Paul's Letter to the Galatians we read: "The proof that you are sons is the fact that God has sent forth into our hearts the Spirit of his Son which cries out 'Abba, Father'." (Gal 4:6-7; cf. Rom 8:15-17). When St. Paul calls us 'sons,' he is not making a statement about our gender but rather he is specifying the nature of the relationship baptised

Christians have with God through Christ. God "does not merely assure us of his providential fatherly care, but communicates his own life, making us 'sons in the Son'."[96] St. John emphasises this same truth when he says: "See what love the Father has given us, that we should be called children of God; and so we are" (1 Jn 3:1).

The New Testament revelation revolves around the Good News that God in his mercy has in Christ extended to us an invitation to enter into eternal communion with the Persons of the Holy Trinity. The invitation to become "sons in the Son" through baptism is made clear by Jesus when after the resurrection he says to the disciples: "Go, therefore, make disciples of all the nations; baptise them in the name of the Father and of the Son and of the Holy Spirit, and teach them to obey all the commands I have given you" (Mt 28:20). Through his gratuitous self-revelation, God wills that through baptism all should "have access to the Father, through Christ, the Word made flesh, in the Holy Spirit and thus become sharers in the divine nature."[97]

In referring to the great privilege Christians have in being able to pray "Our Father", the *CCC* says:

> We can invoke God as "Father" because *he is revealed to us* by his Son become man and because his Spirit makes him known to us. The personal relation of the Son to the Father is something that man cannot conceive of nor the angelic powers even dimly see: and yet, the Spirit of the Son grants a participation in that very relation to us who believe that Jesus is the Christ and that we are born of God (cf. Jn 1:1; 1 Jn 5:1).[98]

What of "God the Father/Mother" and of Jesus as "the Daughter of God"?

Christians are not permitted to adopt Groome's androgynous term "Father/Mother" or his other recommended terms "Parent" and "Source of all Being" as substitutes for the proper name of the first Person of the Blessed Trinity. To do so would mean the reduction of the revelation of "God the Father" to that of mere metaphor. The same principle applies to Fiorenza's recommendation that we learn to speak of the second Person of the Holy Trinity as "Son and Daughter."

Neither is it permissible to replace the revealed names of "Father, Son and Holy Spirit" with the impersonal titles of "Creator, Redeemer and Sanctifier."

Nowhere in the Bible is God ever addressed as 'Mother.' Feminine imagery is often incorporated into the Father image for God but never paired with it as a way of addressing him. Speaking of problems that arise from using "Creator" or "Source of All Being" as substitutes for 'Father' when referring to God, Fr. George T. Montague says:

> The problem with this circumlocution is that it defines God only in relation to creation, and when used along with 'Redeemer' and 'Sanctifier,' it falls into the error of modalism, that is, the divine persons are only three different ways of speaking about one God. These titles cannot serve for the Trinity, and if they are intended as such, they are erroneous for they say nothing about the relations within the Trinity.[99]

Rev. Dr. Cassian Folsom, O.S.B, who teaches at the Pontifical Liturgical Institute of *Sant' Anselmo* in Rome, points out that when, on the grounds of "alleged sexism," the standard doxology—Glory be to the Father, and to the Son, and to the Holy Spirit—is changed to "Glory be to the Creator, the Redeemer and the Sanctifier" or some such phrase, then "the meaning is thus profoundly changed."[100] To say "Father, Son and Holy Spirit," adds Rev. Folsom, is to say "something about the nature of the Trinity *in se* as revealed to us, about the relationship of the persons of the Trinity one to another, and about the manner of their procession."[101]

Also, it is erroneous to ascribe the work of creation to God the Father alone. While it is true that in the Creed we proclaim "God the Father Almighty" as the "Creator of heaven and earth," it is also true, as the *CCC* says, that "the New Testament reveals that God created everything by the eternal Word, his beloved Son."[102] Thus, in the Prologue to St. John's Gospel we read: "In the beginning was the Word: the Word was with God and the Word was God...all things were made through him, and without him nothing was made...and the world was made through him" (Jn 1:1-2, 10). This passage from St. John gives definitive meaning to the words of Psalm 33:6 which states that it was "by the word of the Lord the heavens were made." The Holy Spirit was also active in the creation of the universe. In the Book of Genesis we read:

"In the beginning God created the heavens and the earth...and the Spirit of God was moving over the face of the waters" (Gen 1:1-2). Thus, in the *CCC* we read: "The Church's faith likewise confesses the creative action of the Holy Spirit, the 'giver of life,' 'the Creator Spirit' *('Veni, Creator Spiritus'),* the 'source of every good'."[103] Indeed, it is a truth of faith that all three persons of the Holy Trinity are active not only in the work of creation, but also in the work of redemption and sanctification. Speaking of this, the *CCC* says: "The whole divine economy is the common work of the three divine persons. For as the Trinity has only one and the same nature, so too does it have only one and the same operation."[104]

In view of what has been said above, it is clear that there are serious doctrinal problems with substituting the titles 'Creator, Redeemer, Sanctifier' for the revealed and proper names 'Father, Son and Holy Spirit' when referring to the Holy Trinity. Speaking of this, Rev. Cassian Folsom says:

> The substitution version says nothing about the inner nature of the Trinity at all, since each of those titles of God (Creator, Redeemer and Sanctifier) can be attributed freely to any of three persons of the Most Holy Trinity quite indiscriminately. The Son is also creator, since 'by him all things were made.' The Spirit is also creator, for he hovered over the waters at the very beginning. The unity of the three persons of the Trinity in the act of creation is seen by the patristic tradition in the words of the Psalm: 'by his word (the Son) the heavens were made, by the breath of his mouth (the Spirit) all the stars.' Therefore, to change the doxology, or the Sign of the Cross in this way, is to seriously tamper with the very faith of the Church.[105]

Mark Brumley has also pointed to the problems that arise when we attribute the work of Creation, Redemption and Sanctification to God the Father, Son and Holy Spirit respectively. He says:

> The three Divine persons of the Trinity are not 'defined' as Persons by these actions, since Creation, Redemption and Sanctification are common to all Three. What defines them as Persons are their unique relations among one another, with the

Father begetting, the Son being begotten and the Spirit being 'spirated' from the Father and the Son. To reduce each Person of the Trinity to a particular function—Creator, Redeemer, Sanctifier—is to succumb to the ancient heresy of Modalism, which denies that there are Three Persons in God and instead holds that there is really only one Person in God who acts in three different modes—Father, Son and Spirit. Or in this case, Creator, Redeemer, Sanctifier.[106]

In reference to the Holy Mass, Groome states that "no presider need address God only as 'Father' in the collects," and he further advises that "the presider can readily say 'Pray my sisters and brothers, that my sacrifice and yours will be acceptable to God our loving parent' rather than 'acceptable to God, the Almighty Father.'[107] Groome's proposal here to expunge from the liturgy certain references to God the Father strikes deep into the heart of Catholic life and sacramentality. In Catholic faith, the decisive relationship to God is constituted **in** the Holy Spirit **through** Christ and **toward** the Father. This basic structure of our faith is indicated in various ways in the New Testament and is reflected in the Eucharistic Sacrifice of the Mass whose midpoint is formed by the high prayer: "Through him, with him and in him, in the unity of the Holy Spirit, all glory and honour is yours, Almighty Father, for ever and ever. Amen."[108]

Groome's recommendation that in the Holy Mass "presiders" should feel free to alter liturgical texts at their own discretion is not only expressive of a disregard for the proper authority of the Magisterium in this area, but it also manifests a certain lack of perception regarding the profundity of the mystery which is celebrated in every Mass. Indeed, Groome suggests that the liturgy could be made to embody greater "creativity" by subjecting it to the process of *shared Christian praxis*. He says:

It seems appropriate...to bring a shared praxis perspective to the preparation and enactment of Christian liturgy...Christian communities that enact a less rubrically regulated form of liturgy have more room for creativity if they choose to structure their Sunday worship from the perspective of shared praxis.[109]

Those who advocate addressing the first Person of the Blessed Trinity in terms such as "Mother," "Father/Mother," "Loving Parent" or "Ground of All Being" often seek to justify their position on the basis that given the high level of family disintegration today the word "father" has negative connotations for many people. This line of argument is rejected by Fr. Montague who says:

> We can readily dismiss the argument that 'father' to many today evokes painful memories of their earthly father as unloving, abusive, or simply absent. Such a painful situation signals a need for individual healing and social reform, not avoidance.[110]

Paul C. Vitz, who is a professor of psychology at New York University, warns that tampering with the revelation of "God the Father" is sure to have severe consequences for the psychological health of both men and women. Vitz says that God the Father "gives men a model with which to identify" even if their "own fathers have been inadequate."[111] In stating that the revelation of God the Father is "a fundamental psychological support" for "positive male identity," Vitz argues that it is "bizarre to the point of pathology at this time in our culture to be trying to remove God the Father from our theology" given "the increase in violence" in our society "resulting from fatherlessness in families."[112]

Vitz argues further that the fatherhood of God also enhances feminine identity. He says that the way it does this is analogous to the way in which "through love and support" a good father "enhances the sexual identity of his own daughters." In saying this, Vitz points out that "a good deal of research has shown that girls raised without fathers tend to be less sure of their lovability and femininity" as a result of which "they are more vulnerable to pathologies ranging from depression to promiscuity."[113]

We are not permitted to project onto the revelation of 'God the Father' our disfigured experiences of human fatherhood which often lies behind the push to change liturgical language whereby we would address the First Person of the Blessed Trinity as *Mother* or *Loving Parent* etc. On the contrary, it is according to the Fatherhood of God that all other forms of 'fatherhood' are to be judged: "Call no man your father on earth, for you have one Father who is in Heaven" (Mt 23:9). I "bow my knees," says St Paul, "before the Father, from whom all fatherhood in heaven and on earth is named" (Eph. 3:14).

In the relationship of Jesus to the Father, of the Father to the Son, and the love that binds them together in the Person of the Holy Spirit, there is revealed the ultimate origin of all life and of all that is good. To come to know "the Father" is to come to know something of the very depths of God: "Lord, let us see the Father and then we shall be satisfied" (Jn 14:8).

The Holy Spirit: 'He' or 'She'?

In *Language for a Catholic Church,* Groome, in referring to how we should speak of the Holy Spirit says: "The term for spirit in Hebrew and Aramaic, Jesus' native tongue, is *ruach* (also means breath or wind) and is feminine in gender, and the Greek word is *pneuma* and neuter. Thus the original texts advise that we not use male imagery or pronouns for the Holy Spirit."[114] In *Educating for Life,* Groome uses the feminine pronoun to refer to the Person of the Holy Spirit. He says that the Holy Spirit "blows where she will," and he gives John 3:8 as his reference.[115]

The Holy See's current *Norms for the Translation of Biblical Texts for Use in the Liturgy* lays down the following:

> 4.4. In keeping with the Church's tradition, the feminine and neuter pronouns are not to be used to refer to the person of the Holy Spirit.

If Groome is right in his assertion that the "original texts" of Sacred Scripture "advise that we not use male imagery or pronouns for the Holy Spirit," then the Church's tradition and its current *Norms for the Translation of Biblical Texts for Use in the Liturgy* have to be in contradiction of the message of Sacred Scripture itself. Given that this question deals with the Magisterium's instructions on the use of Scripture in the liturgy, then any error on the Holy See's part in this area would have profound ramifications. However, the problem does not lie with the Holy See's norms but rather with Groome's erroneous assertion.

In Sacred Scripture, the Hebrew term for the spirit is *ruah*.[116] The first meaning of the term is "breath" as it refers to the life principle in man. A human person cannot live without "breath" and hence its presence in man is derived from the creative action of God who can also take it away again (cf. Ps 104: 29-30). However, *ruah* can also mean "the blowing of the wind"—a great external "breath"—which could be called "God's breath." Speaking of the liberating force of this "breath of YHWH", the Book of Exodus says: "A blast from your nostrils and the waters piled high...One breath of yours you blew, and the sea closed over them" (Ex 15:8-10). Commenting on this passage from the Book of Exodus and the different translations of *ruah* as 'breath,' 'spirit,' and 'wind,' Pope John Paul II said:

> This expresses in a very suggestive way the conviction that the wind was God's instrument in these circumstances. From observations on the invisible and powerful wind one came to conceive of the 'spirit of God.' In the texts of the Old Testament one passes easily from one meaning to the other...The many meanings of the Hebrew term *ruah*, used in the Bible to designate the Spirit, seem to give rise to some confusion. Indeed, in a given text, it is often not possible to determine the exact meaning of the word. One might waver between wind and breath, between breath and spirit, or between the created spirit and the divine spirit.[117]

In the Old Testament, the meaning of *ruah* as "breath of God" expands to refer to the "spirit of God" or "wind" taking hold of a person and using him to further the divine plan (cf. Judges 13:25; 14:6; 1 Sam 10:10). Also, the creative force of the "breath of Yahweh" parallels that of the "Word" so that in the Psalms we read: "By the word of YHWH, the heavens were made, their whole array by the breath of his mouth" (Ps. 33:6). Speaking of how the Old Testament uses the terms "spirit," "word" and "wind" interchangeably to describe God's active presence in the world, Pope John Paul II said:

> Thus we can say that already in the creation narrative of the Book of Genesis, the presence of the 'spirit (or wind) of God,' which was moving over the face of the waters while the earth was formless and void, and darkness was upon the face of the deep (cf. Gen 1:2), is a remarkably striking reference to that vital force. It suggests that the breath or spirit of God had a role

in creation: a life-giving power, together with the 'word' which imparts being and order to things.[118]

From what has been said above, it is clear that in the Old Testament, the word ruah "is not expressly invested with female attributes."[119] In Hebrew, all nouns are either masculine or feminine—hence *ruah* is used as a feminine substantive and is not intended to categorise according to gender the person of Yahweh. Going beyond this, the Person of the Holy Spirit is not explicitly revealed in the Old Testament, so when it uses the term *ruah* to refer to the "breath of Yahweh" it is referring to an impersonal force of God's. This all changes when we move to the New Testament. In the Greek New Testament, *ruah* is translated as *pneuma,* which is neuter and can thus take on many meanings including wind, breath, soul and spirit. In Latin, *ruah* is translated as *spiritus* and thus becomes fully masculinised. Thus, it is clear that there is no basis for Groome's assertion that "the original texts advise that we not use male imagery or pronouns for the Holy Spirit."

St. Hilary of Poitiers cautioned that we "must not measure the Divine nature by the limitations of [our] own, but gauge God's assertions concerning Himself by the scale of His own glorious self-revelation." St. Hilary added that "the best student is he who does not read his thoughts into the book, but lets it reveal its own; who draws from it its sense, and does not import his own into it, nor force upon its words a meaning which he had determined was the right one before he opened its pages." Finally, St. Hilary said: "Since then we are to discourse of the things of God, let us assume that God has full knowledge of Himself, and bow with humble reverence to His Words. For He Whom we can only know through his own utterances is the fitting witness concerning Himself."[121]

As Catholics, it is vitally important that we adopt an attitude of reverence towards Sacred Scripture and the teaching of the Magisterium lest in succumbing to a prideful confidence in our own subjective ideas we fall into multiple errors. Since it was Jesus Himself who designated the Godhead 'Father, Son, and Holy Spirit" (cf. Mt 28:19), then there can be no ungendered equivalents of 'Father' and 'Son' for the first and second Persons of the Holy Trinity, i.e. there is no either/or choice as Groome and Fiorenza would have us believe.

Reference

1   Statement of Conclusions, n. 5, *L'Osservatore Romano,* December 16, 1998.
2   Ibid.
3   Elisabeth Schussler Fiorenza, *Discipleship of Equals,* op. cit. p. 128.
4   Elisabeth Schussler Fiorenza, *Sharing Her Word,* op. cit. p. 88.
5   Thomas Groome, *Sharing Faith,* op. cit. p. 442–43 (emphasis added).
6   Thomas H. Groome, *Language for a Catholic Faith (Revised and expanded edition),* Sheed & Ward, Kansas City 1995, p. v.
7   Ibid. p. 20.
8   Ibid. p. vi.
9   Ibid. v.iii
10 Ibid. p. viii
11 Ibid.
12 Ibid. P. ix.
13 Ibid. p. 25.
14 Ibid. p. 26.
15 Ibid. p. 26.
16 Ibid. p. 63 (emphasis in original).
17 Ibid. p. 64.
18 Ibid. p. 31.
19 Ibid. p. 36.
20 Ibid. pp. 38–39.
21 Ibid. p. 39.
22 Ibid. p. 53.
23 Ibid. p. 51
24 Ibid.
25 Ibid. p. 50
26 There has been a long-running debate amongst religious educators which revolves around a distinction they draw between 'Catechesis' and 'Religious Education' whereby the former is said to be more explicitly concerned with nurturing a deeper knowledge of the Catholic faith in those being educated while the latter is said to concern itself with religion as a historical and sociological phenomenon independent of confessional considerations. I believe that all religious education in a Catholic school should have a definite catechetical objective of leading parents, teachers and students to a more intimate union with Christ and to a greater love for his Church and for all that she teaches. In this regard, Vatican II stated that among the special functions of the Catholic school are: i) to enable "young people, while developing their own personality, to grow at the same time in that new life which has been given them at baptism," ii) to serve as a means for orienting "the whole of human culture to the message of salvation" (Declaration *Gravissimum*

Educationis, n. 8). Even in situations where students and their families become involved with Catholic schools primarily for the quality of the education they offer, the service of such schools is still always "an internal element of evangelisation of the Church" *(General Directory For Catechesis,* n. 260).

27 Pope John Paul II, Fides et Ratio, n. 83.
28 Ibid.
29 Ibid.
30 Ibid. n. 84.
31 Ibid.
32 Ibid. n. 7.
33 Ibid. n. 13.
34 Ibid.
35 Ibid. n. 14.
36 Ibid.
37 Ibid. n. 67.
38 Ibid. n. 95.
39 Ibid n. 83.
40 Ibid. n. 84.
41 Ibid. n. 94.
42 Ibid. n. 33.
43 *CCC.* n. 193.
44 *CCC.* n. 192.
45 *Fides Damasi,* Denz 71-72; cited in *The Companion to the Catechism of the Catholic Church: A Compendium of Texts Referred to in the Catechism of the Catholic Church,* Ignatius Press, San Francisco 1994, p. 56.
46 Thomas H. Groome, *Language for a Catholic Church,* op. cit. p. 31.
47 Ibid. p. 39.
48 Vatican I, *Const. Dei Filius,* Denz. 3002; cited by Pope John Paul II, General Audience, August 28, 1985; in Catechesis on the Creed, Vol. 1, p. 122.
49 Vatican I, *Const. Dei Filius,* Denz. 3001.
50 Pope John Paul II, *General Audience,* September 4, 1985; in Catechesis on the Creed, Vol. 1, p. 126; cf. Vatican I, *Const. Dei Filius,* can. 1-4, Denz. 3001.
51 Cf. *CCC.* n. 285.
52 Pope John Paul II, *General Audience,* August 28, 1985; in *Catechesis on the Creed,* Vol. 1, p. 122.
53 Pope John Paul II, *General Audience,* August 28, 1985; ibid. p. 123.
54 Pope John Paul II, *General Audience,* August 28, ibid.
55 Cf. Pope John Paul II, *Mulieris Dignitatem,* n. 8; CCC. n. 370.
56 *CCC.* n. 239
57 Cf. *CCC.* n. 206.
58 *CCC.* n. 206.

59 Pope John Paul II, *General Audience,* August 28, 1985; in *Catechesis on the Creed,* Vol. 1, p. 122.

60 Paul V. Mankowski, S.J., in *The Politics of Prayer: Feminist Language and the Worship of God,* edited by Helen Hull Hitchcock, Ignatius Press, San Francisco, 1992, p. 159.

61 Ibid.

62 Ibid.

63 Ibid.

64 Pope John Paul II, *On The Mercy of God,* n. 4, footnote 52.

65 Paul V. Mankowski, S.J., in *The Politics of Prayer: Feminist language and the Worship of God,* edited by Helen Hull Hitchcock, op. cit. pp. 159

66 Ibid.

67 Ibid. p. 160.

68 In Chapter 7 of Hauke's book, *Women In The Priesthood,* there is an in-depth analysis of the question of images of God and their metaphysical significance.

69 *CCC.* n. 370.

70 Fr George T Montague, *The Living Light,* Department of Education, U.S Catholic Conference, Washington, D.C., Fall 1998, Vol. 35–No. 1, p. 6.

71 Pope John Paul II, *General Audience,* October, 9, 1985; in *Catechesis on the Creed,* Vol. 1. pp. 151–52.

72 Pope John Paul II, *General Audience,* October, 9, 1985; ibid. p. 151.

73 Pope John Paul II, *On The Mercy of God,* n. 7.

74 Pope John Paul II, *General Audience,* October, 9, 1985; ibid. p. 154.

75 Fr George T Montague, *The Living Light,* Department of Education, U.S. Catholic Conference, Washington, D.C., Fall 1998, Vol. 35–No. 1, p. 8.

76 Cf. Pope John Paul II, *Message for 14th World Youth Day, 'God the Father Loves You,' L'Osservatore Romano,* January, 20, 1999.

77 Pope John Paul II, *General Audience,* October 23, 1985; in *Catechesis on the Creed,* Vol. 1, p. 161.

78 Pope John Paul II, *General Audience,* October, 23, 1985; ibid. p. 160.

79 Pope John Paul II, *General Audience,* October, 16, 1985; ibid. p. 156.

80 Pope John Paul II, *General Audience,* October, 23, 1985; ibid. p. 162.

81 Pope John Paul II, *General Audience,* October, 23, 1985; ibid.

82 Vatican 1, Const. Dei Filius, IV; cf. Pope John Paul II, *General Audience,* November 27, 1985; ibid. p. 180.

83 Pope John Paul II, *General Audience,* November 27, 1985; ibid. p. 180.

84 Pope John Paul II, *General Audience,* November 27, 1985; ibid. p. 180.

85 Pope John Paul II, *General Audience,* November 6, 1985; ibid. p. 170.

86 Pope John Paul II, *General Audience,* November 6, 1985; ibid.

87 Pope John Paul II, *General Audience,* November 6, 1985; ibid. p. 171.

88 Pope John Paul II, *General Audience,* July 1, 1987; in Catechesis on the Creed, Vol. 2, p. 171.

89 Pope John Paul II, *General Audience,* December 16, 1998, L'Osservatore Romano, December 23, 1998.

90 Ibid.

91 Ibid. Cf. Jn 14: 16–17; 15:26; 16:13.

92 Cf. Pope John Paul II, *Message for 14th World Youth Day, 'God the Father Loves You,' L'Osservatore Romano,* January, 20, 1999.

93 *CCC.* n. 1996.

94 *CCC.* n. 1997.

95 *CCC.* n. 1997.

96 Pope John Paul II, *General Audience,* January 13, 1999, L'Osservatore Romano, 20/1/99

97 Vatican II, Dei Verbum, n. 2.

98 *CCC.* n. 2780.

99 Fr George T Montague, *The Living Light,* Department of Education, U.S Catholic Conference, Washington, D.C., Fall 1998, Vol. 35–No. 1, p. 10.

100 Rev. Dr. Cassian Folsom, O.S.B., *Homiletic and Pastoral Review,* January 1994, p. 25.

101 Ibid. p. 26.

102 *CCC.* n. 291.

103 *CCC.* n. 291; Cf. Nicene Creed; Denz 150.

104 *CCC.* n. 258.

105 Rev. Dr. Cassian Folsom, O.S.B., *Homiletic and Pastoral Review,* January 1994, p. 26.

106 Mark Brumley, *The Catholic Faith Magazine,* July/August 1999.

107 Thomas Groome, *Language for a Catholic Church (Revised and Updated Edition),* op. cit.p. 63–64.

108 Cf. Fr. Manfred Hauke, *Women In The Priesthood? A Systematic Analysis in the Light of the Order of Creation and Redemption,* op. cit. p. 249.

109 Thomas H. *Groome, Sharing Faith,* pp. 362–363.

110 Fr George T Montague, *The Living Light, Department of Education, U.S Catholic Conference,* Washington, D.C., Fall 1998, Vol. 35–No. 1, p. 8.

111 Paul C. Vitz, *Support from Psychology for the fatherhood of God, Homiletic and Pastoral Review,* February 1997, p. 13.

112 Ibid.

113 Ibid. p. 14.

114 Thomas Groome, *Language for a Catholic Church (Revised and Updated Edition),* op. cit. p. 51

115 Thomas Groome, *Educating for Life,* p. 187.

116 Sometimes *'ruah'* is written as 'ruach' whereby the change of spelling is accounted for by different ways of transliterating the final letter in the original Hebrew word.

117 Pope John Paul II, *General Audience,* January 3, 1990; in Catechesis on the Creed, Vol. 3, pp. 151–53.

118 Pope John Paul II, *General Audience,* January 10, 1990; ibid. p. 155

119 Fr Manfred Hauke, *Women In The Priesthood,* op. cit. p. 279

120 Pope John Paul II, *General Audience,* January 3, 1990; in Catechesis on the Creed, Vol. 3, p. 152. The bracketing of "Holy Spirit" alongside "Wind" is in the original.

121 St Hilary of Poitiers, On The Trinity, 3.1 and 1. 18, pp. 62 and 45 in *Nicene and Post -Nicene Fathers of the Christian Church,* second series, vol. 9, pp. 62 and 45, cited together with this footnote by Roland Mushat Frye in The Politics of Prayer, op. cit. p. 227.

8

What Shall We Say Of Christ?

In the Incarnation, the Son of God became truly man while remaining truly God and hence we say that "Jesus Christ is true God and true man."[1] From its very beginning, the Church has had to defend this belief about Christ against various heresies which sought to falsify it. The *CCC* states that the first heresies to assail the Church "denied not so much Christ's divinity as his true humanity (Gnostic Docetism)." Consequently, says the *CCC*, "from apostolic times the Christian faith has insisted on the true incarnation of God's Son 'come in the flesh'."[2]

The *Statement of Conclusions*, which as we saw in previous chapters was drawn up in late 1998 following a meeting between a representation of the Australian Bishops Conference and Prefects of various dicasteries of the Roman Curia, after referring to "a crisis in the profession of God as Person" and "of Jesus as the true God," went on to say that throughout the world "there is evidence of a weakening of faith in Christ, as well as a distortion of some doctrines based on the Scriptures and the early Councils of the Church."[3] In conjunction with this, the *Statement* referred to "modifications to Christology" which, among other things, substitute "a pneumatological economy for the flesh and blood reality of Christ, true God and true man."[4]

The Maleness of Christ

In the 1995 edition of *Language for a Catholic Church,* Groome states that in the interests of greater "sensitivity to inclusive language," it "is helpful to reduce reliance on gender-based pronouns" when referring

to Jesus in order "to emphasize his humanity rather than his maleness."[5]
Stating his reasons for attributing little if any significance to the fact that
in the Incarnation the pre-existing Son of God took on the male gender, Groome says:

> As for all human beings, Jesus had to be one gender or the
> other, and the Gospels give no indication of any particular sig-
> nificance in his being male. Better, then, to treat this as one
> aspect of the 'scandal of particularity' that was his life: as a per-
> son, Jesus was a man, a Jew, a carpenter, from Nazareth, etc. It is
> through his divinity and humanity, not particularly his maleness,
> that Jesus is our Saviour and Liberator.[6]

In the first edition of *Language for a Catholic Church* which was published in 1991, Groome in the parallel passage to that quoted above said
that Christ's maleness was merely one of "the 'accidents' of his life."[7]

While the New Testament bears witness in many ways to the divinity of Christ, it also bears witness to the fact that he is also true man. In
the Prologue to St John's Gospel we read: "And the Word became flesh
and made his dwelling amongst us" (Jn 1:14). The Greek word for flesh
is *sarx,* which "denotes man as he actually is, with his body, and therefore its insecurity, its weakness, and in a certain sense its transitoriness."[8]
Jesus Christ is truly man in that he took flesh and a human nature from
his mother Mary. He was born at a certain time and in a certain place,
he was circumcised and given the name Jesus, he grew from boyhood to
manhood and so on (cf. Lk 2:40).

As a man of flesh, Jesus experienced exhaustion, hunger and thirst
(cf. Mt 4:2; Jn 4:6-7). He had a mortal body "that finally underwent the
torture of martyrdom through the scourging, crowning with thorns,
and eventually crucifixion."[9] Jesus' death on the Cross was followed
three days later by his resurrection from the dead when "he returned to
life in his own human body," which, although it was "transformed" and
"glorified" and "endowed with new qualities and powers," was still "a
truly human body."[10] Only a true man could have suffered and died as
Jesus did and only a true man could rise from the dead—there was
nothing illusory about it—Jesus is "not a man merely in appearance, not
a phantasm, but a true man."[11] From all this it is clear that the Eternal
Son (the Word) "assumed a perfect human nature, soul and body and
mind, and all whatever is man except sin."[12]

To be in possession of a human nature is to be either male or female, which means to be stamped to the depths of one's being by either masculinity or femininity. In his highly acclaimed book titled *Love and Responsibility,* Karol Wojtyla (Pope John Paul II), stated that "every human being is by nature a sexual being" so that from his very beginning he or she belongs "to one of the two sexes."[13] According to contemporary scientific findings, the individual is so profoundly affected by sexuality "that it must be one of the factors which give to each individual's life the principal traits that distinguish it."[14] Indeed, "it is from sex" that a human individual "receives the characteristics which, on the biological, psychological and spiritual levels" make him or her "a man or a woman."[15]

The Second Vatican Council affirms that man is "the only creature on earth whom God willed for its own sake."[16] According to Pope John Paul II, "Man's coming into being does not conform to the laws of biology alone, but also, and directly, to God's creative will, which is concerned with the genealogy of the sons and daughters of human families." Having said this, the Holy Father added: "God *'willed' man from the very beginning, and God 'wills' him in every act of conception and every human birth*...Parents, in contemplating a new human being, are, or ought to be, fully aware of the fact that God 'wills' this individual 'for his own sake.'"[17] Coupled with this, and in regard to the creation of the human person as either a "man" or a "woman," the *CCC* says:

> Man and woman have been *created,* which is to say, *willed* by God: on the one hand in perfect equality as human persons; on the other, in their respective beings as man and woman. "Being man" or "being woman" is a reality which is good and willed by God...In their "being-man" and "being-woman," they reflect the Creator's wisdom and goodness.[18]

In view of what has been said above, we cannot put aside the masculinity of Jesus Christ as though it were an insignificant part of his humanity. Since maleness or femaleness is a primal and constitutive element of true humanity, then the gender specificity of Jesus Christ is a constitutive aspect of his humanity and without it his humanity does not exist. Hence, any attempt to lay aside the maleness of Christ as merely accidental data in the mystery of the Incarnation runs the risk of falling prey to the error of Docetism, which posited that Jesus Christ was solely God and only appeared to be a man. From this position, the docetists held that Christ did not have a real flesh and blood body and hence that "in the whole sphere of the Incarnation and redemption, we are dealing merely with an illusory body."[19]

Closely related to the question of the significance of Christ's maleness is the use of the generic word man in Sacred Scripture and in the Creeds and the liturgy. In the Bible and the liturgy, the word "man" sometimes appears in an ambiguous way where it is not easy to discern whether the text is referring to *generic man* or to *gender-specific man*—an ambiguity that is not simply a fault of the English translation, since it appears also in the Greek and Latin. Referring to this ambiguity, Rev. Dr. Cassian Folsom, O.S.B., says that the primary reason for using both meanings of "man" interchangeably is christological. To demonstrate his point, Fr. Folsom takes two examples: the first being the interpretation given to Psalm 8 in the Letter to Hebrews and the second being the way the word "man" is used in reference to Jesus in John 19:5.

The RSV translation of the Bible renders Psalm 8:4-5 as follows: "What is man that thou are mindful of him, and the son of man that thou dost care for him? Yet thou hast made him little less than God, and dost crown him with glory and honour." Fr. Folsom says that here in Psalm 8 it is clear that all members of the human family are being referred to which means that "man" is being used in its generic sense. However, when we turn to the Letter to the Hebrews, the same passage from Psalm 8 is interpreted as referring to Christ. After quoting the relevant passage from Psalm 8, the Letter to the Hebrews goes on to interpret it as follows: "We see Jesus, who for a little while was made lower than the angels..." (Heb 2:9). Commenting on this interpretation of Psalm 8 by the author of the Letter to the Hebrews, Fr. Folsom says: "The entire christological argument is based on the fact that the word 'anthropos' is ambiguous: it can mean both generic man (the literal meaning of the psalm) and gender-specific man, in this case, Our Lord Jesus Christ himself (the spiritual interpretation of the psalm)."[20]

Now, in the New RSV translation, Psalm 8 is translated with inclusive language so as to read: "What are human beings that you are mindful of them, mortals that you care for them? Yet you have made them a little lower than God, and crowned them with glory and honor" (Ps 8:4-5). When this inclusive language translation is applied consistently throughout the Bible, then Psalm 8:4-5 can no longer carry the christological interpretation it receives in Hebrews 2:7-9. Commenting on this outcome, Fr. Folsom says:

> The deliberate ambiguity of *anthropos* has been rejected and the christological interpretation of the psalm is now lost. Thus, in this particular instance, an ideologically motivated 'adjustment' of the Scriptures has resulted in logical fallacy at best, and at worst, a rejection of two things: the inspired nature of the Scriptures and the NT christological explanation of OT texts.[21]

The second example Fr. Folsom draws on to highlight the deliberate ambiguity of the Greek word *anthropos* and its corresponding Latin word *homo* used for "man" in parts of the Bible is taken from St. John's account of the Passion of Our Lord where Pilate in presenting Jesus to the crowds after having him scourged says: "Behold the man" (Jn 19:5)—in Greek "Idou ho anthropos," in Latin "ecce homo." After pointing out that in this passage it is clear that generic man is being used with reference to the man, Jesus, Fr. Folsom adds that if the New RSV was consistent with its inclusive interpretations it would have to render this passage as "Behold the human being" or "Behold the mortal." However, in this case it is not consistent and renders the passage thus: "Here is the man."

In regard to the deliberate ambiguity that exists in some Biblical texts with respect to the use of generic man and gender-specific man, Fr. Folsom states that "there is a fundamental issue involved which touches upon not only the person of Christ, but also the possibility of man's salvation."[22] In reference to the teaching of Vatican II that Christ "fully reveals man to man himself and makes his exalted vocation known to him,"[23] Fr. Folsom says: "Our salvation depends on the incorporation of mankind (the species man being intended here, which includes every individual of the species) into the one man, Jesus Christ." Having said this, Fr. Folsom added that in maintaining a clear distinction between generic man and gender-specific man on the one hand, and by "insisting on the necessary ambiguity of the terms on the other, we can arrive at a certain unity of opposites, whereby the truth about God (in Christ) and the truth about man (in Christ) are held together as one single truth in all the richness of its complexity."[24] On the basis of this analysis, Fr. Folsom concludes that "to make a gender-specific word into a neuter word is to do violence to the Scriptures"—something which amounts to "a serious offense against the text" which "is all the more serious" given the fact that "it is done to the inspired text of the Scriptures, or to the venerable texts of the liturgy."[25]

The points made above regarding the ambiguity that can be inherent in the use of the word "man" in its generic and gender-specific form also have application to the use of the word "man" in the Nicene Creed. Here, in referring to the Incarnation of the pre-existent Son of God we say: "He became man." In saying this, we mean that the Word assumed a substantial human nature of male gender. In reference to the Nicene Creed and its affirmation concerning the Incarnation, Groome asserts that the expression "and became man" could be rendered in a way "more faithful to the tradition and intent of the original Creed" if it was expressed as "true God from true God...became truly human."[26]

Speaking of the impossibility of removing the term "He became man" from professions of faith such as the Nicene Creed, Msgr. Robert Sokolowski from the Catholic University of America said: "In connection with the *lex credendi,* there are some uses of the generic word 'man' that are essential to the expression of Christian doctrine and that cannot be provided by other terms." This, he went on, "is especially true for expressions dealing with the mystery of the Incarnation." Consequently translations of the Creed that renders—"*et homo factus est*" as "and became truly human" are "misleading and could be taken in a monophysite sense," meaning they "could be taken to mean that the *Logos* merely assumed the feature or the attribute or the adjectival form of being human."[27] After saying that the term "truly human" when used as an adjectival phrase "does not convey the same unambiguous sense of substantial assumption that the noun 'man' does," Msgr. Sokolowski added:

> After all, the incarnate *Logos* also became 'truly tall' or 'truly hungry', but he was not hypostatically united with tallness or hunger. They were only accidental to him, and to say merely that Christ was 'truly human' (and not 'man') is to leave open the possibility that his humanity too was only accidental. Only the use of the word 'man' conveys unambiguously the doctrine that the *Logos* assumed a substantial human nature and was hypostatically united with it.[28]

The Maleness of Christ and the Ordained Priesthood

In 1982, Groome stated that the main reasons given by the Church for the non-ordination of women are all "false".[29] In 1995, in positing that gender is irrelevant to the person who sacramentally represents Christ in the Mass, Groome stated that "it is unfortunate and misleading when the maleness of Jesus is used to favour men and exclude women in any way"—something which he said "the Church appears to do...when it uses what is called 'the iconic argument' against the ordination of women: that the one who represents Jesus in the moment of eucharist must have a 'natural resemblance' to him."[30]

In making this assertion, Groome was echoing the ideas of Karl Rahner. In Chapter 5 we saw that Groome referred to Rahner's dissenting statement from *Inter Insigniores* as "a fine, balanced and scholarly refutation" of its arguments against the ordination of women.[31] In his statement of dissent against *Inter insigniores,* Rahner also raised the question of Christ's maleness and its connection with the Sacrament of Holy Orders. He said "it is not clear that a person acting with Christ's mandate and in that sense (but not otherwise) in *persona Christi* must at the same time represent Christ precisely in his *maleness*."[32]

Elisabeth Schussler-Fiorenza holds that by using the maleness of Christ as a significant factor underpinning its teaching on the male-only ministerial priesthood, the Church is thereby risking "christological heresy in order to maintain the present patriarchal church structures and ideologies."[33] She says that the Magisterium's "insistence on the maleness of Christ" serves "not so much as an argument against the ordination of women" but rather "demonstrates that the central mysteries of Christian faith are male and exclusive of women."[34] Indeed, after quoting Mary Daly's statement that "The idea of a unique divine incarnation in a male, the God-man of the 'hypostatic union,' is inherently sexist and oppressive. Christology is idolatry,"[35] Fiorenza goes on to say that by "insisting on the maleness of Christ" as a factor barring women from priestly ordination, the Magisterium thereby "seems merely to confirm Mary Daly's assertion."[36]

In 1998, Fiorenza's criticism of the Church's teaching on the relationship between the maleness of Christ and the male-only ministerial priesthood took on a somewhat incoherent tone. She said:

The christological doctrine of male headship and kyriarchal authority both legitimates the exclusion of wo/men from ordained ministries and makes it impossible for Christian children and wo/men to resist sexual abuse by marital and ecclesial 'heads of households' by natural and spiritual 'fathers'.[37]

At issue in the debate over the Church's no to women's ordination is the question of fidelity to the ministerial priesthood as it was instituted by Christ. Pope Pius XII referred to this when he said that the Church must accept Christ's "practice of conferring priestly ordination on men alone" as normative on the grounds that "the Church has no power over the substance of the sacraments, i.e. over anything that Christ the Lord, as attested by the sources of Revelation, wanted to be maintained in the sacramental sign."[38] Despite Groome's and Fiorenza's multi-faceted attack on the Catholic Church's teaching on the male-only ministerial priesthood, this doctrine nevertheless harmonises wonderfully with the rest of the Church's sacramental and christological doctrine.

A sacramental celebration "is woven from signs and symbols."[39] The Council of Trent taught that sacraments are outward signs instituted by Christ through which He acts to confer grace.[40] The words, actions and elements used in the sacraments constitute what is called the 'sign' of the Sacrament.[41] The visible sign of each sacrament signifies the gift of grace conferred by Christ in that sacrament.[42] Hence, the actions of the sacraments are said to signify what they effect and to effect what they signify.

In speaking of the nature and role of the ministerial priesthood in the mission of the Church, Vatican II stated that through the anointing of the Holy Spirit in the sacrament of Holy Orders, priests "are signed with a special character and so are configured to Christ the priest in such a way that they are able to act in the person of Christ the head [*in persona Christi Capitis*]."[43] This means that "in the ecclesial service of the ordained minister, it is Christ himself who is present to his Church as Head of his Body, Shepherd of his flock, high priest of the redemptive sacrifice, Teacher of Truth."[44] Consequently, it is through the ministerial priesthood that "the presence of Christ as head of the Church is made visible in the midst of the community."[45]

Pope John Paul II points out that through the sacrament of Holy Orders the ordained priest "participates ontologically in the priesthood of Christ" and is truly consecrated "a man of the sacred."[46] Referring to the Holy Sacrifice of the Mass, Vatican II stated that while Christ is especially present in the Eucharistic species, he is also present in the person of the ordained priest.[47] The priest offers the Sacrifice of the Mass *in persona Christi,* which according to Pope John Paul II, means more than offering "in the name of" or "in the place of" Christ.[48] *In persona Christi* means "in specific sacramental identification with 'the eternal High Priest' who is the Author and principal Subject of this Sacrifice of his, a Sacrifice in which, in truth, nobody can take his place."[49] Consequently, in the Mass, it is Christ who is "the offerer and the offered, the consecrator and the consecrated."[50]

The efficacy of a sacrament depends on the integrity of the sign. For example, we could not use rice and lemonade in the Eucharist instead of bread and wine since it was the latter that Christ singled out as the signs of his Body and Blood. *Inter Insigniores* states that "the whole sacramental economy" is "based upon natural signs, on symbols imprinted upon the human psychology."[51] Quoting St. Thomas Aquinas, it adds that sacramental signs "represent what they signify by natural resemblance" which it says "is required for persons as for things."[52] Coupled with this, St. Thomas Aquinas pointed out that since a sacrament is a sign, then "what is done in the sacrament requires not only the reality but also the sign of the reality."[53]

Now, in the Mass, the ordained priest "takes the part of Christ, lending him his voice and gestures."[54] As such, he is a sacramental sign acting in the person of Christ "to the point of being his very image" when he pronounces the words of consecration.[55] This means that in the Mass the ordained priest serves as a sacramental *sign* of Christ who now offers in an unbloody manner the same sacrifice as he once offered on Calvary.[56]

From what has been said above, it follows that in the Mass there is a need for a "natural resemblance" between Christ and the person who is his sign.[57] If Christ's role in the Mass were taken by a woman, there would not be a "natural resemblance" between Christ and his sacramental *sign* since "Christ himself was and remains a man."[58] Barbara Albrecht touched on this point when, in commenting on St. Paul's teaching that the Incarnate Son of God has become like us in all things but sin (cf. Heb 4:15), she said:

"In all things"—that includes that the Son of God has also submitted as man to the order of creation, hence also to the order of sex. The Son of God was purely and simply a man, and that surely not by accident. There are no accidents in the Incarnation of God. The Incarnation of the Word "has been effected in the male sex. This, of course, is an issue of fact; this fact, however, is indissolubly linked with the economy of salvation, without in the least denoting a presumed natural superiority of man over woman" (*Inter insigniores,* n. 5). Since the priest represents the Lord not in his Godhead, but as the One who is incarnate, crucified, resurrected, and ascended to the Father in Heaven, the logical conclusion is that the priest, too, must be a man.[59]

In view of the doctrine of the Church expressed above that "**Christ himself was and remains a man**,"[60] Groome's recommendation—"that male identification and referents for the Risen Christ can and should be avoided since our faith is that the Risen One represents all humanity"[61]—becomes rather problematic. Even more problematic is Fiorenza's attempted annihilation of the masculinity of Christ where in referring to the Risen Christ as a female figure she says: "To embrace the Gospel means to enter a movement, to become a member of God's people who are on the road that stretches from Christ's death to **Her** return in glory."[62] This question of the identity of the Risen Christ was taken up by *Inter Insigniores* where in reference to the sacramental representation of Christ by the ordained priest in the Eucharist it said:

> Could one say that, since Christ is now in the heavenly condition, from now on it is a matter of indifference whether he be represented by a man or by a woman, since 'at the resurrection men and women do not marry' (Mt 22:30). But this text does not mean that the distinction between man and woman, so far as it determines the identity proper to the person, is suppressed in the glorified state; what holds for us holds also for Christ.[63]

Nuptial Celebration of the Bridegroom and the Bride

Human nature is not a product of random evolutionary forces but rather bears the imprint of the creative Love and Wisdom of God. The Book of Genesis affirms that man and woman were created for each other: "It is not good that the man should be alone" (Gen 2:18). The woman, Adam's counterpart, is "flesh of his flesh", she is his equal in dignity, she is complementary to him and given to him by God as a "helpmate" (cf. Gen 2:18-25). God created the couple in order that they might give themselves as a gift to each other in the totality and truth of their masculinity and femininity. In this reciprocal self-giving of one to the other, the couple thereby bind themselves indissolubly to each other so that they are no longer two but rather "one flesh" (Gen 2:24; cf. Mt 19:6).

A husband and wife are made in the image of God not just in their individuality, but also in their complementarity. The love that binds a couple together in the indissoluble bond of marriage is intended to be a reflection of the creative and redemptive love God has for man. Speaking of this, Pope Paul VI said: "The duality of the sexes was willed by God, so that man and woman together might be the image of God and, like him, a source of life."[64] St. Paul sees marriage and family life as a reflection of the Divine life: "I kneel before the Father from whom every family in heaven and on earth takes its name" (Eph 3: 14). The *CCC* says: "The Christian family is a communion of persons, a sign and image of the communion of the Father and the Son in the Holy Spirit."[65]

Speaking of how marriage reveals the Triune God, Pope John Paul II said: "In the creation of the human being as man and woman, the marital community and the family based on it are a special and privileged revelation of the Triune God and, at the same time, a revelation of the constitutive family nature of the human person."[66] The Holy Father reiterated this point in his *Letter to Families* when he said: "In the light of the New Testament it is possible to discern how the primordial model of the family is to be sought in God himself, in the Trinitarian mystery of his life."[67]

In the Bible, marital symbolism is often used to express God's relationship to his people. God's Covenant with Israel is presented as a marriage relationship between God and humanity. YHWH appears as the Bridegroom of Israel, the chosen people. As Bridegroom, YHWH is both affectionate and demanding, as well as jealous and faithful.[68] In their moments of infidelity, the prophets were sent to the chosen people to call them to conversion and to remind them of YHWH's faithful love. This marital analogy comes to the fore in the words of Isaiah directed to Jerusalem during the time of the Babylonian exile: "He who has become your husband is your maker...like a wife forsaken and grieved in spirit, the Lord calls you back, a wife married in youth and then cast off...For a brief moment I abandoned you, but with great tenderness I will take you back....with enduring love I take pity on you, says the Lord, your redeemer" (Is 54:5-8). Later in Isaiah we read: "As a young man marries a virgin, your Builder shall marry you. And as a Bridegroom rejoices in his bride, so shall your God rejoice in you" (Isa. 62:5).

The Song of Songs can be interpreted as an exaltation of ideal human marriage or as a celebration of the nuptial love between God and His people. With dramatic images, the prophet Hosea develops the theme of the spousal covenant between God and his people. Hosea's marriage and the subsequent infidelities of his wife give symbolic expression to the infidelity of the chosen people to YHWH. However, in the overflow of Divine love and mercy, YHWH will not forsake his sinful people: "Therefore, behold, I will allure her, and bring her into the wilderness, and speak tenderly to her" (Hos 2:7). God promises to overcome sin in order to give himself again to his people: "I will espouse you to me forever, I will espouse you in right and in justice, in love and in mercy; I will espouse you in fidelity, and you shall know the Lord" (Hosea 2:21-22). Through the prophet Jeremiah, God again speaks to his people as a husband to his spouse: "With age-old love I have loved you: so I have kept my mercy towards you. Again I will restore you and you shall be rebuilt, O *virgin of Israel*" (Jer 31:3-4).

The Old Testament texts cited above which tell of God's marital love for man receive their definitive fulfilment in the Incarnation and Paschal Mystery of Christ. Jesus referred to himself as the "Bridegroom" (Mk 2:19). In the Book of Revelation we read: "Let us rejoice and be glad, and give him glory! For this is the wedding day of the Lamb. His bride has prepared herself for the wedding" (Rev 19:7). Through his Incarnation and Paschal victory, Christ who is *God-the Bridegroom* is with the Church which has become *a Bride,* the Bride of Christ.[69] The Church is the spotless bride of the spotless Lamb (cf. Rev 22:17; Eph 1:4; 5:27).

The Corinthian Church is for St. Paul a virgin bride wedded to one husband, Christ (2 Cor 11:2; cf. Eph 5:25). St. Paul further speaks of the whole Church and of each of the faithful as a bride "betrothed" to Christ the Lord so as to become one with him (Cf. Mt 22:1-14; 25:1-13; 1 Cor 6:15-17). When speaking of marriage as a "great mystery," St. Paul adds that this has many implications which apply to the relationship between Christ and the Church (cf. Eph 5:32). The Church professes that Marriage, as the sacrament of the covenant between husband and wife, is a "great mystery" because "it expresses *the spousal love of Christ for his Church*."[70] In ushering in the order of Redemption, Christ lifted up the relationship of man and woman in marriage and assumed it into his redeeming life and into the action of the Church. Thus was marriage instituted as a sacrament which "signifies the union of Christ and the Church."[71]

In his book *Called to Communion,* Cardinal Joseph Ratzinger discusses St. Paul's conception of the Church as the Body of Christ which he says has three sources in the biblical tradition which are: i) the Semitic view of the corporate personality; ii) the Eucharist; and iii) the idea of nuptiality.[72] Regarding the Eucharistic significance of the term, Cardinal Ratzinger says:

[The] Lord becomes our bread, our food. He gives us his body...The body is a man's self, which does not coincide with the corporeal dimension but comprises it as one element among others. Christ gives us himself—Christ, who in the Resurrection has continued to exist in a new kind of bodiliness. The outward action of eating becomes the expression of that intimate penetration of two subjects...Communion means the fusion of existences; just as in the taking of nourishment the body assimilates foreign matter to itself, and is thereby enabled to live, in the same way my 'I' is 'assimilated' to that of Jesus, it is made similar to him in an exchange that increasingly breaks through the lines of division. This same event takes place in the case of all who communicate; they are all assimilated to this 'bread' and thus are made among themselves—*one* body.[73]

Regarding the nuptial meaning of St. Paul's image of the Church as the Body of Christ, Cardinal Ratzinger said:

[The] biblical philosophy of love...is inseparable from eucharistic theology. This philosophy of love appears immediately at the beginning of Holy Scripture: it is found at the conclusion of the creation narrative, where the following prophetic word is attributed to Adam: 'For this reason the man shall leave his father and mother and cleave to the woman, they shall become *one* flesh' (Gen 2:24). *One* flesh—hence, a single new existence...[The] Church is the Body of Christ in the way in which the woman is one body, or rather one flesh, with the man...Christ and the Church are one body in the sense in which man and woman are one flesh, that is, in such a way that in their indissoluble spiritual-bodily union, they nonetheless remain unconfused and unmingled. The Church does not simply become Christ, she is ever the handmaid whom he lovingly raises to be his Bride.[74]

Since Christ is both head and spouse of his Church, then the model for the relationship of the ordained priest to the Church is the sacrificial and spousal relationship that Christ himself has to it. In speaking of this, Pope John Paul II said: "Christ's gift of himself to his Church, the fruit of his love, is described in terms of that unique gift of self made by the bridegroom to the bride, as the sacred texts often suggest. Jesus is the true bridegroom who offers to the Church the wine of salvation (cf. Jn. 2:11)."[75] The Holy Father adds that the Church is "the bride who proceeds like a new Eve from the open side of the redeemer on the cross" and before whom he is ever standing in order to "nourish and cherish her" (cf. Eph. 5:29) by "giving his life for her."[76] In similar fashion, says the Holy Father, the ordained priest "is called to be the living image of Jesus Christ, the spouse of the Church."[77] Therefore, "inasmuch as he represents Christ, the head, shepherd and spouse of the Church, the priest is placed not only in the Church but also towards the Church."[78]

As the Sacrament of our Redemption, the Eucharist embodies the spousal relationship between Christ and the Church whereby Christ continues to sacrifice Himself for His spouse. Speaking of this, Pope John Paul II said: "Christ is the Bridegroom because 'he has given himself': his body has been 'given,' his blood has been 'poured out' (cf. Lk 22: 19-20). In this way 'he loved them to the end' (Jn 13:1)."[79] After saying that "the 'sincere gift' contained in the Sacrifice of the Cross gives definitive prominence to the spousal meaning of God's love", the Holy Father added: "The Eucharist is the Sacrament of our Redemption. It is the Sacrament of the Bridegroom and of the Bride."[80] As such, the Eucharist "makes present and realises anew in a sacramental manner the redemptive act of Christ, who 'creates' the Church, his body"—an action in which "Christ is united with this 'body' as a bridegroom with the bride."[81] All this, says Pope John Paul II, is contained in the Letter to the Ephesians where the "perennial 'unity of the two' that exists between man and woman from the very 'beginning' is introduced into this 'great mystery' of Christ and the Church."[82]

In instituting the Eucharist, Christ "linked it in such an explicit way to the priestly service of the Apostles" that it is "legitimate to conclude that he thereby wished to express the relationship between man and woman, between what is 'feminine' and what is 'masculine'"—a relationship "willed by God both in the mystery of creation and in the mystery of Redemption."[83] Pope John Paul II says that it "is the Eucharist above all that expresses the redemptive act of Christ the Bridegroom towards the Church the Bride" –something which "is clear and unambiguous when the sacramental ministry of the Eucharist, in which the priest acts 'in persona Christi,' is performed by a man".[84] On another occasion, Pope John Paul II in speaking of the relationship between marital symbolism and the requirement of a male-only ministerial priesthood said:

If a reason is sought as to why Jesus reserved admission to the ministerial priesthood to men, it can be discovered in the fact that the priest represents Christ himself in his relationship to the Church. Now this relationship is spousal in nature: Christ is the Bridegroom (cf. Mt 9:15; Jn 3:29; 2 Cor 11:2; Eph 5:25), the Church is the bride (cf. 2 Cor 11:2; Eph 5:25-27, 31-32; Rev 19:7; 21:9). Because the relationship between Christ and the Church is validly expressed in sacramental Orders, it is necessary that Christ be represented by a man. The distinction between the sexes is very significant in this case and cannot be disregarded without undermining the sacrament. Indeed, the specific nature of the sign used is essential to the sacraments. Baptism has to be performed with water which washes; it cannot be done with oil, which anoints, even though oil is more expensive than water. Analogously, the sacrament of Orders is celebrated with men, without questioning the value of persons.[85]

Related also to what has been said above is the fact that integral to the Eucharistic Sacrifice of the Mass is the symbolism of the New Adam and the New Eve. The distinction between Adam and Eve "is the sexual difference between man and woman, the primordial distinction universally present wherever human beings are found".[86] The ordained priesthood is sacramental not only because it is conferred by a sacrament and because its ministry is sacramental, but also because "the priest himself is 'sacramental', a sign of Christ."[87] Since a woman does not have that "natural resemblance" to Christ who **was and remains a man**,"[88] then a woman cannot serve as a sacramental sign of Christ the New Adam and Bridegroom of the Church in the Eucharistic Sacrifice of the Mass.

All that we have said up to now about Jesus as Head, Shepherd, Bridegroom and New Adam is consistent with the fact that the pre-existent Son of God became incarnate in the male sex. In other words, all of Christ's tasks are inseparably bound up with his male human nature. Speaking of the connection between the divine choice of the male gender for the Incarnation and Christ's establishment of a male-only ministerial priesthood, Fr Jean Galot S.J. says:

The divine choice that once singled out the male gender for the Incarnation also assigns to this gender the priestly ministry. If the priesthood is restricted to men, it is not, then, because of a casual decision predicated on contingencies, but because of an essential orientation built into the mystery of the Incarnation.[89]

The Sacrament of Matrimony is a "real symbol" of the nuptial union of Christ the Bridegroom with the Church his Bride.[90] To assert that in the Mass a woman can be a sacramental sign of Christ the "Bridegroom" of the Church is equivalent to holding that a man can be a sacramental representation of Christ's Bride the Church within the symbolism of the Sacrament of Matrimony. Such a thing is not possible since it would contradict the meaning of the Sacrament of Matrimony which is intended to be an efficacious sign of the covenant between Christ and the Church.[91] If on the other hand this assertion were true, then it would be difficult to justify objections to homosexual marriages since one could argue on the same basis that the union of "male and female" are not necessarily required for a valid celebration of the Sacrament of Matrimony.

In view of all that has been said above, it can be seen that in select-ing only men as his Apostles, Christ thereby guaranteed that those who were destined to sacramentally represent him in the Eucharistic Sacrifice would be able to do so fully in terms of his masculine identity which includes his spousal relationship to the Church—as Bridegroom to Bride and as the New Adam to the New Eve.

Christianity is based on realities that took place in history. The Sacrifice of Christ on Calvary, which is represented in every Mass, was a historic and concrete event. In the Incarnation, the Son of God became incarnate in a real flesh and blood masculine human nature, and as such he died on the Cross. The requirement of a male-only ministerial priesthood in the Catholic Church is rooted in this historical and con-crete male gender of the God-man. To assert that the Church can con-fer priestly ordination on women is equivalent to asserting that the Church can dispense with the historical, objective and normative aspects of Divine Revelation. To argue that a woman can sacramentally represent Christ the Bridegroom of the Church in the Sacrifice of the Mass is equivalent to holding that the signs used in the sacraments do not effect what they symbolise and that they do not necessarily have to comply with certain objective requirements.

Given what has been said above regarding the complementarity of "male and female" and its place in God's plan for the human family and the Church, it is obvious that any social science, philosophy or theology that seeks to gloss over the real distinctions between men and women and their respective roles in God's plan for human life is sure to give rise to severe forms of alienation in both Church and society.

As a teacher I have become aware that a failure to acknowledge real differences between boys and girls leads to an acute crisis in under-standing by young people of how best to behave as male and female. In their book *Brainsex,* Anne Moir and David Jessel state that to treat men and women as though they were the same "in aptitude, skill or behav-iour is to build a society based on a biological and scientific lie."[92] They add that men and women—"could live more happily, understand and love each other better, organise the world to better effect"—if they were to acknowledge their differences something which would then enable them to build their lives "on the twin pillars of distinct sexual identities."[93]

What is true of the relationship between the sexes in general has application also to the Church where aspects of divine revelation pertaining to it are predicated on the real distinctions between men and women. In this context, there are no "accidents" in the Incarnation of the pre-existent Son of God and consequently it is not a matter of indifference whether God's becoming man occured in the form of a male or a female. Groome's and Fiorenza's assertion that Christ's maleness has no lasting significance in the scheme of salvation has profound implications for how we understand the sacramentality of the Catholic Church.

As a reflection of the Trinitarian life of God, man and woman reflect a mysterious but profound complementarity that is at once both physical and spiritual. This complementarity is 'Real' in that it exists not as an abstract concept but as something embodied in human nature by every man and woman. It is 'Symbolic' in that it points beyond itself to God's creative and redemptive plan for the human race. Sometimes referred to as "metaphysical symbolism," this symbolism cannot be tampered with without doing great damage to man's spiritual and moral well-being. C.S. Lewis displayed a keen awareness of this when he said: "We have no authority to take the living and sensitive figures that God has painted on the canvas of our nature and shift them about as if they were mere geometrical figures."[94]

It is not possible for the Catholic Church to efface the nuptial symbolism which God has inscribed within the Eucharistic Sacrifice of the Mass without thereby altering the content of the sacramental realism that is contained there. Any "Eucharistic" celebration that would allow a woman to act as a sacramental representation of Christ the New Adam and Bridegroom of the Church could never claim to be the Holy Mass of the Catholic Church. In reference to this, Fr. Donald Keefe said:

> The Catholic understanding of orders is of ordination to offer the One Sacrifice of Christ by its Eucharistic representation in the person of Christ...As the Sacrifice is the institution of the New Covenant of the second Adam and the second Eve, Christ and the Church, its Eucharistic representation is the historical actualisation of the New Covenant by the sacrificial and sacramental presence of the Christ in union with his bridal Church, the sacrament of the eschatological Kingdom, the risen Body of which Christ is the risen Head. It is possible to offer this sacrifice only in the person and with the authority of Christ, which

is to do so as the Head, the second Adam, whose sacrifice is his nuptial union with his Body, the bridal Church. This most ancient doctrine…is resisted today on grounds both ecumenical and feminist…[If] the nuptial covenantal symbolism is taken seriously, the priest, offering the One Sacrifice in the person of the Head, must act as the Bridegroom: for this representation, masculinity enters ineluctably into the sacramental sign itself, and is indispensable to it: the ordination of a woman is then an ontological impossibility because it is first a liturgical impossibility. Any denial of the sacramental significance of sexuality of course undercuts the sacramentality of marriage as well—and not merely incidentally: the ground of that sacrament, as of all others, is the nuptial New Covenant."[95]

Pointing to a failure of modern consciousness to discern the methaphysical symbolism written into the nature of man as "male and female," Pope John Paul II in his *Letter to Families* said: "The modern age has made great progress in understanding both the material world and human psychology, but with regard to his deepest, methaphysical dimension contemporary man remains to a great extent a *being unknown* to himself." Consequently, said the Holy Father, "the family too remains an *unknown reality*" due to the "estrangement from the 'great mystery' spoken of by the Apostle."[96] Here, the Holy Father is referring to St. Paul's statement in his Letter to the Ephesians where he presents marriage as a "great mystery" (cf. Eph 5: 25-33) which sheds light on the nuptial relationship between Christ and the Church.

The Catholic Church's teaching on the male-only ministerial priesthood bears witness to the truth regarding Christ's will for the Sacraments of the Eucharist and Holy Orders. As such, it sheds light on the truth regarding God's nuptial plan for human existence—a plan written into the creation of man as "male and female" which has been lifted up by Christ into the redemption whereby marriage has been raised to the dignity of a sacrament pointing beyond itself to Christ's spousal relationship to the Church. The groundwork for a much deeper understanding of the realities that are here involved was laid by Pope John Paul II in his teaching on the nuptial meaning of the human body. This body of papal teaching, says George Weigel, "held that maleness and femaleness are not biological accidents but revelations of deep truths about the human condition that directly touched God's redemptive purposes for the world." This theology of the body, added Weigel, "challenged what Hans Urs von Balthasar once described as contemporary 'monosexism,' a leveling-out of the meaning of sexual differentiation that had ominous implications for Church and society and that had distorted the debate over women's ordination." Weigel rightly pointed out that since this question of the non-ordination of women touches "core Catholic perceptions about the sacramental nature of reality," then it is necessary to raise the level of debate regarding it above the "passions" and "cultural confusions" in which it has often got entangled.[97]

Is Christ a 'Divine Person' or a 'Human Person'?

If we fall into error in regard to the identity of Jesus Christ, then the entire ediface of Christian dogma collapses. Consequently, the Christological definitions of the early Church Councils are very important. These definitions, says Pope John Paul II, always bring "us back to the mystery of the one Christ" who "is the Word that became incarnate for our salvation, as it is made known to us by revelation, so that believing in him and loving him, we may be saved and have life (cf. Jn 20:31)."[98]

In response to problems occasioned by the spread of various heresies in the early centuries of the Christian era, the First Ecumenical Council of Nicaea (325) defined the Church's faith in Jesus Christ as follows:

> We believe...in one Lord Jesus Christ, Son of God, the only begotten of the Father, that is, of the Being of the Father, God from God, light from light, true God from true God, begotten not created, one in Being with the Father, through him all things were made, both in heaven and on earth. For us men and for our salvation he came down from heaven; he became incarnate; he was made man...[99]

Referring to this dogmatic definition of the Council of Nicaea, Pope John Paul II stated that it "reproduces the essential elements" of "biblical Christology" and that from "the beginning the Church guarded this faith and transmitted it to successive Christian generations." This definition, added the Holy Father, "reflects not only the truth about Jesus Christ inherited from the apostles and fixed in the books of the New Testament, but also the teaching of the Fathers of the post-apostolic period." [100]

The Council of Nicaea was called in order to respond to errors which contradicted the faith of the Church in Jesus Christ as true God and true man. The most troublesome of these errors was that of Arius who at the beginning of the fourth century spread the heresy that Jesus Christ was not God since, even though he existed before his birth from the Virgin Mary, he was nevertheless still created in time. Responding to this heresy with the definition that Jesus Christ is the only-begotten Son of God who is "one in Being with the Father," the Council thereby expressed in formula form and in terms of the Greek culture which prevailed at the time the truth which Jesus himself revealed concerning his relationship to the Father: "I and the Father are one" (Jn 10:30).

Some fifty years after the Council of Nicaea, Pope Damasus I issued a letter which again condemned the errors of the Arians as well as those of the Apollinarists who falsely asserted that Christ's humanity was incomplete in that it lacked a human soul—its place taken they said by the Word of God. Against the Apollinarists, Pope Damasus declared that Christ's humanity was complete in every way in consequence of which Christ had to possess a real human soul and therefore a human intellect and free will. In 381, the First Council of Constantinople, condemned all the heresies that were prevalent at the time and reaffirmed the teaching of Pope Damasus I against the Arians and the Apollinarists. [101]

In the decades after the Councils of Nicaea and Constantinople, the question arose as to how the unity of the divine and human natures in Christ was to be understood. From as early as the third century it had been usual to refer to the Blessed Virgin Mary as the *Theotokos* meaning Mother of God. [102] This invocation was challenged by Nestorius and his followers who claimed that Mary could not be called Mother of God but merely Mother of Christ. Nestorius "regarded Christ as a **human person** joined to the divine person of God's Son." [103] Nestorius held that from the moment of the Incarnation, when Christ "began to exist in the womb of the Virgin Mary," his divinity and humanity were not united as "in a single personal subject." [104] Instead, Nestorius asserted that in Christ there existed "a duality" not only of natures "but also of person, the divine and the human." [105] Consequently, argued Nestorius, Mary had to be regarded as the mother of the "Christ-Man" but not the "Mother of God." [106]

Opposing the Nestorian heresy, the Council of Ephesus in 431 confessed "that the Word, uniting to himself in his person the flesh animated by a rational soul, became man."[107] It "confirmed the unity of Christ as derived from revelation" and as something which had been "believed and affirmed by Christian tradition."[108] In defining that Christ is the eternal Word who according "to the flesh was born in time from the Virgin Mary," the Council of Ephesus in taking cognizance of the fact that Christ "is only one being" went on to affirm that Mary had the right to the title "Mother of God."[109] The *CCC* reaffirmed this truth when it said: "Mary is truly 'Mother of God' since she is the mother of the eternal Son of God made man, who is God himself."[110]

The Council of Chalcedon (451), in reaffirming the doctrinal teaching of earlier councils, defined with precision the manner of the union of two natures in Christ. It said:

Following the Holy Fathers, therefore, we all with one accord teach the profession of faith in the one identical Son, our Lord Jesus Christ. We declare that he is perfect both in his divinity and in his humanity, truly God and truly man composed of body and rational soul; that he is consubstantial with the Father in his divinity, consubstantial with us in his humanity, like us in every respect except sin (cf. *Heb. 4:15*). We declare that in his divinity he was begotten of the Father before time, and in his humanity he was begotten in this last age of Mary the Virgin, the Mother of God, for us and for our salvation. **We declare that the one selfsame Christ, only-begotten Son and Lord,** must be acknowledged in two natures without any commingling or change or division or separation; that the distinction between the natures is in no way removed by their union but rather that the specific character of each nature is preserved and they are **united in one person and one hypostasis. We declare that he is not split or divided into two persons, but that there is one selfsame only-begotten Son, God the Word, the Lord Jesus Christ.** This the prophets have taught about him from the beginning; this Jesus Christ himself taught us; this the creed of the Fathers has handed down to us.[111]

According to Pope John Paul II, the definition of Chalcedon "reaffirms, develops and explains what the Church taught in the previous Councils and what was witnessed to by the Fathers, for example, by Irenaeus who spoke of 'one and the same Christ.' (cf. Adv. Haer, III, 17, 4)."[112] The dogmatic definition of Chalcedon revolves around a clear distinction between "*nature*", "*person*" and "*hypostasis*." The term "nature" gives us the answer to the question "*what* a thing is *(quid)*", while the term "person" "tells us *who* he or she is *(quis)*."[113] According to the *Catechism of the Catholic Church,* the term "person" or "hypostasis" is used "to designate the Father, Son and Holy Spirit in the real distinction among them," while the term "relation" is used "to designate the fact that their distinction lies in the relationship of each to the others."[114] The term *hypostatic union* means that in Christ there is a "union of the divine and human natures in the one person of the Word."[115]

According to Pope John Paul II, the infallible teaching of the Council of Chalcedon is that in Christ there are two natures, human and divine, which are united without mixture "**in the one personal subject** which is **the divine Person of God the Word**."[116] Hence, in the *CCC* we read that "Christ's humanity **has no other subject than the divine person of the Son of God.**"[117] The fact that there exists in Christ not a human person—but rather a "**Divine Person**"—has profound ramifications for everything we believe as Christians. Consequently, any attempt to recast Christ as a "human person" demolishes the whole edifice of the Church's christological dogma.

The *CCC* says that after the Council of Chalcedon, "some made of Christ's human nature a kind of **personal subject**" against which the fifth ecumenical council at Constantinople in 553 confessed that "there is one *hypostasis* [or person], which is our Lord Jesus Christ, one of the Trinity."[118] Consequently, the *CCC* teaches that "everything in Christ's human nature is to be attributed to his divine person as its proper subject, not only his miracles but also his sufferings and even his death: 'He who was crucified in the flesh, our Lord Jesus Christ, is true God, Lord of glory, and *one of the Holy Trinity*'."[119]

Pope John Paul II laments a tendency in some modern christologies to speak "of the existence of a '**human person**' in Jesus Christ."[120] In listing the factors conducive to this error, the Holy Father mentions a failure to understand "the Incarnation as the assuming of human nature by a transcendent and pre-existing divine 'I'" as well as a "negation of the distinction between nature and person."[121]

In *Sharing Faith,* Groome, in reference to the teaching of the Council of Chalcedon says: "Chalcedon's statement set the parameters within which 'orthodox' Christian faith must be confessed about the divinity and humanity of Jesus."[122] Having said this, he then adds: "These parameters do not exclude diverse explanations and interpretations of its meaning. For example, some scholars now refer to Chalcedon's key words *hypostasis* and *prospon* (see note 12) other than as 'person' (e.g. Rahner's 'way of being')."[123] In footnote 12 appended by Groome to this statement, he quotes the "central dogmatic definition of the Council of Chalcedon" as being that Jesus Christ:

> is perfect both in his divinity and in his humanity, truly God and truly man...consubstantial with the Father in his divinity, consubstantial with us in his humanity...We declare that the one self-same Christ ...must be acknowledged in two natures without any commingling or change or division or separation...that the specific character of each nature is preserved and they are united in one person (prosopon) and one hypostasis.[124]

It is interesting to compare Groome's quotation from Chalcedon given above with the more complete quotation I have given earlier—both are from the same source and therefore bear the same translation. While Groome's quotation includes references to the two natures in Christ and the reference to the one person in Christ, it nevertheless omits the direct statement in the definition which declares Christ to be a divine Person, ie. "this selfsame Christ" who is the "only-begotten Son, God the Word, the Lord Jesus Christ."

As will be demonstrated presently, Groome appears to have fallen into confusion in regard to the Church's Christological dogma—which is not surprising given his reliance on Karl Rahner. In his theology, Rahner posited 'self-consciousness' as the nucleus of the notion of person. Given that there are in Christ two centres of consciousness—the human and the divine—Rahner concluded that there must also be two subjects.[125] By positing two subjects in Christ, Rahner can only reach unity "on the level of action" and hence "when the two subjects are put facing one another, the union between them will simply be a union of action, a love-relationship, in which we cannot say that Jesus is God."[126]

Fr. Jean Galot, S.J., states that Rahner, in formulating his Christology, thought "that it was not necessary that Jesus be aware during his earthly life, of the redemptive value of his death."[127] Galot points out that Rahner modified the vocabulary for speaking about the Holy Trinity by substituting the expression "three distinct modes of subsistence" for the expression "three persons."[128] Galot points out further that Rahner believed "that the modern concept of person is confirmed in the humanity of Jesus" and that "while refraining from speaking of a human person," Rahner nonetheless stressed "the autonomy of the subjective human center, a center that places Jesus vis-a-vis God." Summing up the consequence of this position for Rahner, Galot says: "Since he [Rahner] cannot admit a single subjectivity in Christ, he warns against the dangers implicit in the affirmation:'Jesus is God'."[129]

Fr. Donald Keefe, S.J., also draws attention to problems in Rahner's christology. In reference to its influence on Leonardo Boff, for example, Fr. Keefe says: "Boff, having argued that the Incarnation of the Son must have a prior possibility in humanity or it could not have happened, concludes that the possibility of a hypostatic union with a Divine Person is implicit in humanity as such. For Boff to go on to the assertion that it is a possibility also realised in Mary is then no great step beyond where Karl Rahner's transcendental Thomist anthropology has already gone." Having stated this, Fr. Keefe then referred his readers to the work of John McDermott who, he said, has "provided an extensive and most meticulous analysis of the failure of Rahner's Christological synthesis…McDermott locates Rahner's difficulty in his inadequate notion of '**person**'."[130]

We now return to Groome. Despite his reference to scholars such as Rahner who "now refer to Chalcedon's key words *hypostasis* and *prospon*…other than as 'person'," an unprejudiced reading of the dogmatic definition of the Council of Chalcedon shows how on several occasions it emphasises the unity of person between the preexistent Son of God and the man Jesus born of the Virgin Mary. In *Sharing Faith,* Groome misrepresents the teaching of St. Anselm when, in recalling the question posed by this great saint-theologian—*Cur Deus homo?*, which orthodox theologians always translate as 'Why did God become man'— Groome translates it as "Why did God become a human person?"[131] St. Anselm's Christology was steeped in the doctrine of Chalcedon and he never referred to Christ as a "human person."

Groome's tampering with the Christological dogma of the Church extends as far as the heart of the Holy Mass itself. In *Language for a 'Catholic' Church,* Groome says that in the Mass "No presider need…say of Jesus in the Fourth Eucharistic Prayer 'a man like us...' Why not 'person'."[132] So, according to Groome, there would be nothing wrong with a priest rendering the relevant part of the Fourth Eucharistic Prayer as follows: "He was conceived through the power of the Holy Spirit, and born of the Virgin Mary, **a person like us in all things** but sin." To affirm that Christ is "a person like us" we would have to hold that he is "a human person"—an affirmation that would be in conflict with the Christological dogma of the Church.

In 1997, a book was published in Australia entitled *Tomorrow's Catholic: Understanding God and Jesus in a New Millenium*. Written by Fr. Michael Morwood, M.S.C., this book repudiates several key Catholic doctrines. A 'Notice' regarding the book was issued by Archbishop George Pell on March, 10, 1998 which said:

> Archbishop Pell wishes to inform the Catholic community of Melbourne that the book *Tomorrow's Catholic: Understanding God and Jesus in a New Millenium* written by Father Michael Morwood...must not be used as a text in any of our Catholic schools and is not to be displayed, sold, or distributed in any of our Churches (cf. Canon 827, paras. 2 & 4). Defined Catholic faith holds that Jesus Christ is the Eternal Word, the Second Person of the Blessed Trinity, who became man, died on the Cross, rose for us and redeemed us. The book in question presents Christ, the Trinity and Redemption in terms which can not be reconciled with the doctrine of the Church.

In *Tomorrow's Catholic,* Fr. Morwood asserts that Jesus is merely a man approved by God and that consequently the doctrine of the Incarnation is nothing more than a mythical mode of speech designed to tell *us* that Jesus is a significant historical figure. This is all implied in Morwood's frequent assertion throughout the book that Jesus is "a human person" rather than a Divine Person. Consequently, Morwood denies the Incarnation of the preexistent Son of God, ie. the Incarnation of the Logos. Here are examples of this from the book:

> "God did marvellous deeds in and through this human person, Jesus. God has now raised this human person to the fullness of life with God".[133]

"Will the Catholic Church actively promote an understanding of Jesus as the Wisdom of God made present and visible in this human person?".[134]

"Jesus as a human person made the reality of God visible for people".[135]

The official *Report On The Doctrinal Content of Tomorrow's Catholic* produced by the Archdiocese of Melbourne highlighted its main deviations from Catholic doctrine as follows: i) "A denial of the Incarnation of the pre-existent Eternal Word, the Second Person of the Holy Trinity," ii) "A denial of the Divinity of Jesus Christ, by referring to Jesus as a "human person" and redefining "divine," iii) "A belittling of the doctrine of the Holy Trinity," iv) "A denial of Original Sin," v) "A distortion of the doctrine of the Redemption through the saving death of Jesus Christ for our sins."[136]

It is interesting to note that Thomas Groome wrote the 'Foreword' to *Tomorrow's Catholic*. Its author, Fr. Morwood, completed an MA course in Pastoral Ministry conducted by Groome and others at Boston College. Even though *Tomorrow's Catholic* eviscerates the whole Catholic tradition by removing Christ's personal divinity and thereby mutilating him, Groome nevertheless writes in his foreword to the book that:

Michael Morwood's book *Tomorrow's Catholic* is a courageous attempt to interface the ancient and rich tradition of Catholic faith 'with the great social and scientific developments of our age'. He is convinced, and rightly so, that the 'package' of Catholicism we received from the previous era is no longer adequate to the challenges of this age. Epitomised in 'blind obedience to church authority,' much of it simply won't 'work' for our time. To refashion Catholicism to meet the challenges of this new era requires imagination and courage, and Morwood demonstrates both...Tomorrow's Catholic invites us to take some bold steps in the right direction.

In 1972, the Sacred Congregation for the Doctrine of the Faith published a document on *Errors Concerning The Mysteries of the*

Incarnation and the Trinity which said: "Once the mystery of the divine and eternal person in Christ the Son of God is abandoned, the truth respecting the Most Holy Trinity is also undermined." If the person of Jesus Christ is not the Person of the Word Eternal, then Jesus is not God and he is not personally divine. If this is true, then Jesus is but a creature like us and consequently the triad of Father-Jesus-Spirit is no longer a Trinity of three equal divine persons and hence the very centre of Christianity is dissolved. Given Groome's 'Foreword' to *Tomorrow's Catholic* and his belief that Morwood is inviting us "to take some bold steps in the right direction"—which as we saw involves denying that Christ is a "Divine Person"—is Groome not thereby inviting us to acquiesce in the attempted dissolution of the centre of Christianity?

Reference

1   *CCC.* n. 464.
2   *CCC.* n. 465; cf. 1 Jn. 4: 2-3; 2 Jn. 7.
3   Statement of Conclusions, n. 5, *L'Osservatore Romano,* December 16, 1998.
4   Ibid.
5   Thomas H. Groome, *Language for a Catholic Church (Revised and Updated Edition),* Sheed & Ward, Kansas City 1995, p. 28.
6   Ibid. pp. 26-27.
7   Thomas H Groome, *Language for a Catholic Church,* Sheed & Ward, Kansas City 1991, p. 27.
8   Pope John Paul II, *General Audience,* January 27, 1988; in Catechesis on the Creed, Vol. 2, p. 297.
9   Pope John Paul II, *General Audience,* January 27, 1988; ibid.
10   Pope John Paul II, *General Audience,* January 27, 1988; ibid. p. 298.
11   Pope John Paul II, *General Audience,* January 27, 1988; ibid. p. 299.
12   The Creed of Epiphanius, *(Longer Form: Exposition of Nicene Creed proposed to certain catechumens in the Orient),* Denz. 44-45. Reference to this and other Creeds is found in the *CCC.* n. 192n.8. See also *The Companion to the Catechism of the Catholic Church,* A Compedium of Texts Referred to in the *Catechism of the Catholic Church,* Ignatius Press, San Francisco 1994, p. 47.
13   Karol Wojytla, *Love and Responsibility,* Collins, London, 1981, p. 47.
14   *Declaration On Certain Questions Concerning Sexual Ethics, Sacred Congregation For The Doctrine of the Faith,* n. 1.
15   Ibid.
16   Vatican II, Vatican II, *Gaudium et Spes,* n. 24.
17   Pope John Paul II, *Letter to Families,* n. 9.
18   *CCC.* n. 369.

19 Pope John Paul II, *General Audience,* March 9, 1988; in Catechesis on the Creed, Vol. 2. p. 323.

20 Rev Cassian Folsom, O.S.B., *The Word "man" in Bible and Liturgy, Homiletic and Pastoral Review,* January 1994, p. 22

21 Ibid.

22 Ibid. p. 23.

23 Vatican II, *Lumen Gentium,* n. 22.

24 Rev Cassian Folsom, O.S.B., The Word "man" in Bible and Liturgy, op. cit. p. 23.

25 Ibid. p. 23.

26 Thomas H. Groome, *Language for a Catholic Church (1995),* op. cit. pp. 28- 29.

27 Mons Sokolowski, Some Remarks On Inclusive Language, *L'Osservatore Romano,* March 3, 1993.

28 Mons Sokolowski, Some Remarks On Inclusive Language, *L'Osservatore Romano,* March 3, 1993.

29 Thomas Groome, *Signs of Hope,* PACE 12, Direction A, St Mary's Press, Winona 1982, p. 4.

30 Thomas Groome, *Language for a Catholic Church* (1995) op. cit. p. 27.

31 Ibid. p. 70n.10.

32 Karl Rahner, *Theological Investigations: Concern for the Church,* Vol. XX, (Darton, Longman & Todd, London, 1981), p. 43.

33 Elisabeth Schussler Fiorenza, *Discipleship of Equals,* p. 142.

34 Ibid. p. 128.

35 Elisabeth Schussler Fiorenza, *The Discipleship of Equals,* p. 92; quoting Daly in "The Qualitative Leap Beyond Patriarchal Religion,' Quest 1, 1974, p. 21.

36 Elisabeth Schussler Fiorenza, *Discipleship of Equals,* op. cit. p. 137.

37 Elizabeth Schussler Fiorenza, *Sharing Her Word:Feminist Biblical Interpretation in Context,* Beacon Press, Boston 1998, p. 149.

38 Pope Pius XII, cf. AAS 40 [1948], p. 5. Cited by Pope John Paul II, *L'Osservatore Romano,* August 3, 1994.

39 *CCC.* n.1145.

40 Cf. *Council of Trent,* Session 7, March 3, 1547.

41 *CCC.* n. 1146.

42 Cf. *CCC.* n. 1149.

43 Vatican II, *Presbyterorum Ordinis,* n. 2.

44 *CCC.* n. 1548.

45 *CCC.* n. 1549; cf. Vatican II, *Lumen Gentium,* n. 21.

46 Cf. Pope John Paul II, *General Audience,* March 31, 1993, in Catechesis on the Creed, Vol. 4, p. 304.

47 Vatican II, *Sacrosanctum Concilium,* n. 7.

48 Pope John Paul II, *Dominicae Cenae,* n. 8.

49 Ibid.

50 Ibid.

51 *Inter Insigniores,* n. 5.

52 *Inter Insigniores,* n. 5; cf. St. Thomas Aquinas, In IV Sent., dist. 25, q. 2, quaestiuncula 1a ad 4um.

53 St Thomas Aquinas, cited in Official Commentary on *Inter Insigniores,* published in *L'Osservatore Romano,* February 3, 1977.

54 Cf. Official Commentary on *Inter Insigniores,* published in *L'Osservatore Romano* on February 3, 1977.

55 *Inter insigniores,* n. 5. Cf. St. Thomas Aquinas, *Summa Theologiae,* III, q. 83, art. 1, ad 3.

56 Cf. *CCC.* n. 1367. See also: Vatican II, *Sacrosanctum Concilium,* n. 7; *Council of Trent,* Session 22: Doctrine on the Holy Sacrifice of the Mass, Ch. 2.

57 Cf. Official Commentary on *Inter Insigniores,* published in *L'Osservatore Romano,* February 3, 1977.

58 *Inter Insigniores,* n. 5.

59 Barbara Albrecht, in *The Church And Women: A Compendium,* by Hans Urs von Balthasar, Walter Kasper, Joseph Cardinal Ratzinger et al., Ignatius Press, San Francisco 1988, p. 200.

60 Cf. *Inter insigniores,* n. 5.

61 Thomas H. Groome, *Language for a Catholic Church, Revised and Updated Edition,* Sheed & Ward, Kansas City 1995, p. 51.

62 Elisabeth Schussler Fiorenza, *Discipleship of Equals,* op. cit. p. 199 (emphasis added).

63 *Inter Insigniores,* n. 5.

64 Pope Paul VI, talk to the Teams of Our Lady, Rome, May 4, 1970, n. 3.

65 *CCC,* n. 2205

66 Pope John Paul II, *L'Osservatore Romano,* November 23, 1994.

67 Pope John Paul II, *Letter to Families,* n. 6.

68 Cf. Pope John Paul II, *Letter To Families,* n. 19.

69 Ibid.

70 Ibid.

71 *CCC.* n. 1661.

72 Cf. Cardinal Joseph Ratzinger, *Called to Communion,* op.cit. pp. 35-37.

73 Ibid. p. 37.

74 Ibid. pp. 38-39.

75 Pope John Paul II, *Pastores Dabo Vobis,* n. 22.

76 Ibid.

77 Ibid.

78 Ibid.

79 Pope John Paul II, *Mulieris Dignitatem,* n. 26.

80 Ibid.
81 Ibid.
82 Ibid.
83 Ibid.
84 Ibid.
85 Pope John Paul II, *L'Osservatore Romano*, August 3, 1994.
86 Archbishop Desmond Connell, *L'Osservatore Romano*, March 7, 1988.
87 Cf. Cardinal Pio Laghi, *L'Osservatore Romano*, 18/8/93. See also Official Commentary on *Inter Insigniores*, published in *L'Osservatore Romano*, 3/2/77.
88 *Inter insigniores*, n. 5.
89 Fr Jean Galot. S.J. *Theology of the Priesthood*, Ignatius Press, San Francisco 1986, p. 262–63.
90 Cf. Pope John Paul II, *Familiaris Consortio*, n. 13.
91 Cf. *CCC*. n. 1617.
92 Anne Moir & David Jessel, *Brainsex: The Real Differences Between Men and Women*, Mandarin, London 1996, p. 5
93 Ibid. p. 8
94 C.S. Lewis, "Priestesses in the Church?", in *Undeceptions: Essays on Theology and Ethics*, London, 1971, p. 195, cited by Manfred Hauke in Women in the Priesthood, op. cit. p. 193.
95 Fr. Donald Keefe, S.J., *Covenantal Theology: The Eucharistic Order of History*, op. cit. p. 43.
96 Pope John Paul II, *Letter to Families*, n. 19.
97 George Weigel, *Witness To Hope: The Biography of Pope John Paul II*, Cliff Street Books, New York, 1999, p. 733–34.
98 Pope John Paul II, *General Audience*, March 9, 1988; in Catechesis on the Creed, Vol. 2, pp. 325–26.
99 Cf. Denz 125; cited by Pope John Paul II, *General Audience*, March 9, 1988; in Catechesis on the Creed, Vol. 2, pp. 320.
100 Pope John Paul II, *General Audience*, March 9, 1988; ibid. pp. 320–21.
101 Cf. Denz. 146, 149, 151; cf. Pope John Paul II, *General Audience*, March 9, 1988; ibid. pp. 324–25.
102 Cf. Pope John Paul II, *General Audience* March 16, 1988; in *Catechesis on the Creed*, Vol. 2, p. 327.
103 *CCC*. n. 466.
104 Pope John Paul II, *General Audience* March 16, 1988; in Catechesis on the Creed, Vol. 2, p. 328
105 Ibid.
106 Ibid.
107 Council of Ephesus, Denz. 250; cf. *CCC*. n. 466.
108 Cf. Denz. 250–266; cf. Pope John Paul II, *General Audience* March 16, 1988; in *Catechesis on the Creed*, Vol. 2, p. p. 328.

109 Cf. Denz. 251; Pope John Paul II, *General Audience* March 16, 1988; in *Catechesis on the Creed,* Vol. 2, p. 328.

110 *CCC.* n.. 509.

111 Definition of Chalcedon, Denz. 301-302; in *The Church Teaches,* prepared by John F. Clarkson, S.J. et. al., Herder Book Co., New York 1964, p. 172, emphasis added.

112 Pope John Paul II, Pope John Paul II, *General Audience,* March 23, 1988; in Catechesis on the Creed, Vol. 2, p. 331.

113 F. Ocariz et al., *The Mystery of Jesus Christ,* Four Courts Press, Dublin 1994, p. 104.

114 Cf. *CCC.* n. 252.

115 *CCC.* n. 483.

116 Pope John Paul II, *General Audience,* March 16, 1988; in Catechesis on the Creed, Vol. 2, p. 330.

117 *CCC.* n. 466.

118 *CCC.* n. 468.

119 Ibid.

120 Pope John Paul II, *General Audience,* April 13, 1988; in *Catechesis on the Creed,* Vol. 2, pp. 337-38.

121 Ibid.

122 Thomas Groome, *Sharing Faith,* op. cit. p. 261.

123 Ibid.

124 Thomas Groome, *Sharing Faith,* op. cit. p. 507n12.

125 For a critique of Rahner's ideas in this regard, see *The Mystery of Jesus Christ* by F. Ocariz et al., Four Courts Press, Dublin 1994, pp. 127-129.

126 J. A. Sayes, Jesucristo, ser y persona, Bruges, 1984, p. 87; cited in *The Mystery of Jesus Christ,* F. Ocariz et al., op. cit. p. 129.

127 Jean Galot S.J, *Who Is Christ: A Theology Of The Incarnation,* Franciscan Herald Press, Chicago 1981, pp. 31-32. Here, Galot was referring to a work by K. Rahner —W. Thusing titled Christologie—systematisch und exegetisch, Frieburg 1972, pp. 33-34.

128 Jean Galot, S. J., *Who Is Christ: Theology Of The Incarnation,* op. cit. p. 279. Galot is here recounting what Rahner said in Dieu Trinite, fondement transcendant de l' histoire du salut, Mysterium Salutis, 6, Paris 1971, pp. 121-123.

129 Jean Galot, S. J., *Who Is Christ: Theology Of The Incarnation,* op. cit. p. 279-280. The works of Rahner which Galot is here referring to are: i) K. Rahner—W. Thusing, Christologie—systematisch und exegetisch, Frieburg, 1972, pp. 55-58; ii) K. Rahner—A. Darlap, Sacramentum mundi, Frieburg 1967-1969, II, 927-929.

130 Fr. Donald Keefe, S.J., *Covenantal Theology: The Eucharistic Order of History,* op. cit. pp. 187-188 (emphasis added). The work of McDermott cited by Fr.

Keefe is: *The Christologies of Karl Rahner,* Gregorianum 67 (1986), 87–122, 297–327.

131 Thomas Groome, *Sharing Faith,* p. 22

132 Thomas Groome, *Language for a 'Catholic' Church,* Sheed & Ward, Kansas City, 1995, p. 63.

133 Fr Michael Morwood, *Tomorrow's Catholic: Understanding God and Jesus in a New Millenium,* Spectrum Publications, Melbourne 1997, p. 61

134 Ibid. p. 91.

135 Ibid. p. 115.

136 *Report On The Doctrinal Content Of Tomorrow's Catholic,* St Patrick's Cathedral, Melbourne, February 9, 1998.

9

Ancient Heresies

As conceived of by Fiorenza and Groome, the issue of "inclusive language" goes right to the heart of Catholic faith and sacramental practice. Warning against any temptation to try to rearrange the data of revelation to suit our ideological preferences, C.S. Lewis said:

Suppose the reformer stops saying a good woman may be like God and begins saying that God is like a good woman. Suppose he says that we might just as well pray to 'Our Mother which art in Heaven' as to 'Our Father'. Suppose he suggests that the Incarnation might just as well have taken a female as a male form, and the Second Person of the Trinity be as well called the Daughter as the Son...Now it is surely the case that if all these supposals were ever carried into effect we should be embarked on a different religion.[1]

Professor Paul C. Vitz has pointed out that when people change the name for God they change their religion. He says that if a small group of Christians began to refer to God as "Zeus" we would know "that something non-Christian was going on." To reject 'God the Father' as a name, says Vitz, "is to deny the basic Christian creeds," as well as to deny "the language of baptism" and the "entire theology of the Trinity upon which Christianity and its theology have been constructed." Therefore, adds Vitz, to reject the language of God as Father is to "reject Christianity."[2]

A point similar to those made above by C.S. Lewis and Paul Vitz was made by Cardinal Ratzinger when he said:

Christianity is not a philosophical speculation; it is not a construction of our mind. Christianity is not 'our' work; it is *Revelation;* it is a message that has been consigned to us, and we have no right to reconstruct it as we like or choose. Consequently, we are not authorised to change the *Our Father* into an *Our Mother:* the symbolism employed by Jesus is irreversible; it is based on the same Man-God relationship that he came to reveal to us. Even less is it permissible to replace Christ with another figure. But what radical feminism—at times even that which asserts that it is based on Christianity—is not prepared to accept is precisely this: the exemplary, universal, unchangeable relationship between Christ and the Father...I am, in fact, convinced, that what feminism promotes in its radical form is no longer the Christianity that we know; it is another religion.[3]

Fiorenza's work could be classified as hydra of heretical affirmations, half-truths and historical inaccuracies. She is particularly concerned to undercut the biblical foundations supporting the Magisterium's insistence that the Church's hierarchical nature is of divine origin. The contempt with which religious feminists regard the ministerial priesthood and the hierarchical Church was manifested at the 1995 Women's Ordination Conference (WOC) in the U.S. where the keynote speaker was Elisabeth Schussler Fiorenza. Reporting on this conference, Kathleen Howley wrote:

Four women, dressed as Catholic bishops, made their way slowly down the aisles of the Women's ordination Conference (WOC), held Novemeber 10-12 at a hotel just outside Washington, DC. The lights in the auditorium were dimmed. The 1000-plus crowd was hushed, and the music, dominated by beating drums, was loud. The "bishops" solemnly blessed the audience as they made their way to a stage that was filled with dancing women.

It was the climax of the opening ritual of the conference, at the tail end of two hours filled with songs, speeches, and other dances, including one that featured women dressed as Roman Catholic priests. Finally, using the symbols of the office of bishop, the event's planners were about to illustrate, without words, the meaning of their theme: "A Discipleship of Equals."

When the "bishops" reached the stage, the dancers began groveling in front of them—some pretending to lick their feet. Then the dancing became more frenetic, the faces of the groveling women contorted in pain. Finally the "bishops" slowly began to cast off their miters and robes, and got on their knees to embrace the women.

It ended with everyone sitting in a circle, happily holding hands—all the actions denoted that the office of bishop had been cast away..."Ordination means subordination," said Elisabeth Schussler Fiorenza, the author of *A Discipleship of Equals,* the book that inspired the conference theme...Working to achieve any office in the authority structure of the Church only perpetuates a system that is inherently unjust, said Schussler Fiorenza. In her Saturday morning speech, she argued that feminism and a hierarchical Catholic Church are incompatible.[4]

Fiorenza also repudiates the Catholic Church's doctrine on the sacrificial nature of Jesus' death. She says: "The notion of an atoning sacrifice does not express the Jesus movement's understanding and experience of God but is a later interpretation of the violent death of Jesus in cultic terms...the death of Jesus was not a sacrifice..."[5] She adds: "The Sophia-God of Jesus does not need atonement or sacrifices. Jesus' death is not willed by God but is the result of his all-inclusive praxis as Sophia's prophet."[6]

Jesus' whole life was oriented toward the redemption of the human race through his sacrificial death on Calvary. In recounting the redemptive action of Christ, the New Testament does so in terms of its sacrificial nature. This is brought out in the words of Jesus himself when at the Last Supper he speaks of his blood "to be poured out on behalf of many for the forgiveness of sins" (Mt 26:28). Speaking of Christ's sacrifice, the *CCC* says: "Christ's death is both the *Paschal sacrifice* that accomplishes the definitive redemption of men...and the sacrifice of the *New Covenant,* which restores man to communion with God by reconciling him to God through the 'blood of the covenant, which was poured out for many for the forgiveness of sins'."[7]

The Holy Mass, the Catholic Church's central act of worship, is based on the belief that it represents Christ's sacrificial death on Calvary. Speaking of how Christ offered himself in sacrifice on Calvary and of how this is sacramentally made present in the Mass, Pope Pius XII said: "The august sacrifice of the altar, then, is no mere empty commemoration of the passion and death of Jesus Christ, but a true and proper act of sacrifice, whereby the High Priest by an unbloody immolation offers Himself a most acceptable Victim to the Eternal Father, as He did upon the Cross".[8]

The *CCC* says that the Mass is called a Holy Sacrifice "because it makes present the one sacrifice of Christ."[9] It adds that in the Eucharist, Christ "gives us the very body which he gave up for us on the cross, the very blood which he poured out for many for the forgiveness of sins."[10] Consequently, the Eucharist is a sacrifice "because it re-presents (makes present) the sacrifice of the cross".[11] If, as Fiorenza says, Christ's death was not sacrificial, then the Catholic doctrine on the sacrificial nature of the Mass falls apart and with it the Church itself since its unity is rooted in the Eucharistic Sacrifice which is the source and summit of its life.

In regard to the Blessed Virgin Mary, the Mother of God, Fiorenza says that in the "search for new feminist myths integrating the personal and political, the societal and religious, women are rediscovering the myth of the mother goddess, which was partially absorbed by the Christian myth of Mary, the mother of God".[12] She adds that "as the 'queen of heaven' and the 'mother of God', Mary clearly resembles and integrates aspects of the ancient goddess mythologies, e.g., of Isis or the Magna Mater." Therefore, adds Fiorenza, "the myth has the tendency to portray Mary as divine and to place her on an equal level with God and Christ."[13] Fiorenza asserts that "the Mary-myth has its roots and development in a male, clerical, and ascetic culture and theology" and as such has "very little to do with the historical woman Mary of Nazareth."[14]

Fiorenza states that "even though the New Testament writings say very little about Mary and even appear to be critical of her praise as the natural mother of Jesus (Mark 3: 31-35), the story of Mary was developed and mythologised very early in the Christian tradition."[15] Fiorenza holds that "even though the Mary-myth has emancipatory elements, it has not served to promote the liberation of women."[16] In contrast to this, Fiorenza posits that "a radical feminist spirituality proclaims wholeness, healing, love, and spiritual power not as hierarchical, as *power over,* but *as power for,* as enabling power." She adds that this radical feminist spirituality "proclaims *the Goddess* as the source of this power" and that this "Goddess is the giver and nurturer of life, the dispenser of love and happiness."[17] After positing that "the Goddess of radical feminist spirituality is not so different from the God whom Jesus preached and whom he called 'Father',"[18] Fiorenza adds:

> The more the Christian understanding of God was patriarchalized and the more God became the majestic ruler and stern judge, the more people turned to the figure and cult of Mary. The more Jesus Christ became divinized, the more it was necessary to have a mediator between the Christian community and the transcendent God and his majestic Son...The cult of Mary thus grew in proportion to the gradual repatriarchalization of the Christian God and of Jesus Christ.[19]

In speaking of the "women question" facing the Catholic Church, Fiorenza says that it "is not just a question of ordination but that it requires an intellectual paradigm shift from an androcentric world-view and theology to a feminist conceptualisation of the world, human life, and Christian religion."[20] In her 1998 book *Sharing Her Word,* Fiorenza is quite open about the fact that she sees her theological labours as part of a "spiritual struggle for a **different religion**" which in seeking to realise "the dream and vision of **G★d-Sophia's** [sic] alternative community" will be "inspired and compelled by **Her** gospel of liberation."[21]

Worship of the "Goddess" is nothing new in human history. A distinctive feature of all idolatry is that it inevitably leads to human sacrifice. An integral aspect of Fiorenza's political agenda is her implacable support for abortion. She publicly defended the U.S. Supreme Court's decision of Roe v Wade which effectively delivered abortion on demand in the United States. She welcomed the Supreme Court's decision on the grounds that it "means freedom for women."[22]

In voicing her support for abortion, Fiorenza washes her hands of the humanity of the pre-born child by saying: "Since I am neither a philosopher nor a moral theologian, I do not want to discuss here the difficult question of when personal human life begins."[23] She states that liberalised abortion laws are an expression of "justice, mercy and faith" which are necessary to "protect women's civil right to self-determination" and "to create a social situation where the interests of the mother and those of the fetus do not compete with each other."[24]

Fiorenza is opposed to adoption as an alternative to abortion. She says "we must stop advocating adoption as the moral solution to the problem of abortion" and she adds that "the adoption business of bartering 'white babies' is morally more offensive than the termination of pregnancy in the first weeks after conception."[25] Fiorenza views the question of abortion in terms of spiritual warfare between men and women: "How can we proclaim 'mutuality with men' in the Body of Christ as long as men curtail and deny reproductive freedom and moral agency to us?."[26] She adds that "at the heart of patriarchy is the control of women's reproductive powers and their economic dependency."[27] Fiorenza views the Catholic Church's teaching on contraception and abortion in this same oppressive context. She says:

> Moreover, the official stance of the Roman Catholic Church on birth control and abortion demonstrates that woman in distinction from man has to remain dependent on her nature and is not allowed to be in control of her biological processes. According to the present church 'fathers', as long as woman enjoys the sexual pleasures of Eve, she has to bear the consequences.[28]

Ancient Heresies Revisited

Groome's and Fiorenza's multi-faceted assault upon Catholic doctrine is in many respects expressive of resurgent heresies which plagued the early Church. One of these heresies was Gnosticism which took many forms all of which were based on a religious syncretism involving Eastern religions, Christianity, Greek philosophy, the Jewish Cabala and Babylonian religion. We have already noted in an earlier chapter how Fiorenza relies on gnostic writings to establish her case for the early Church as "a discipleship of equals."

Devotees of gnosticism were promised salvation through the possession of secret knowledge and understanding. Most gnostics believed in a remote and Supreme Being and that there was a necessary antagonism between the body and the soul. The most perilous aspect of gnosticism was its adaptability. It appropriated doctrines and rites from other religions and refashioned them to fit its own particular cult. It attempted to express itself in Christian forms from the very beginning of the Church. Gnosticism made contact with Christianity for the purpose of reshaping and assimilating Christian doctrines to fit its own syncretistic system. In attacking the early Church, gnosticism denied Jesus' physical body, his real suffering on the Cross and his Resurrection from the dead. It also forbade marriage. The most influential form of gnosticism was Valentinianism which denied the Resurrection and that Mary was the Mother of God. Coupled with this, the Valentinians denied free-will, they taught justification by faith alone, and they invented an absurd genealogy of eons and gods.

The basic dualisms that characterised gnosticism, between faith and experience, between spirit and matter, and between the soul and the flesh led it to adopt divergent moral positions—from extreme asceticism to over-indulgence and promiscuity. Archbishop (now Cardinal) Francis Stafford, stated that gnosticism in its more libertine form "manifested itself in an unbridled licentiousness, a conscious effort to free oneself of the law of the flesh by flouting it."[29]

As a religious and moral system, gnosticism never really disappeared. It had a significant influence on Manichaeism which incorporated into its religious system a contempt for the flesh which was based on an irreconcilable conflict between spirit and matter. Even though the Manichaeans believed that matter was evil, this did not prevent them indulging their self-centred permissiveness in all things sexual. In doing so however, they avoided human conception through whatever means possible. In his 1994 *Letter To Families,* Pope John Paul II branded as "neo-Manichaean" the present day practice of regarding the human body as material to be used and manipulated in the same way as the bodies of animals are.[30] As examples of this the Holy Father cited the trend towards the manipulation and exploitation of human sexuality as well as destructive experimentation on human embryos and fetuses.[31]

Apart from Manichaeism, gnosticism also influenced many other heresies such as Albigensianism and Catharism. The Cathars celebrated non-procreative sexual union; they regarded the conception of a child as the bringing of another "son of the Devil" into the world. While people today may not use such terms to express their contempt for childbearing, they have however embraced the "contraceptive mentality" which views the procreative meaning of marital intercourse as a subhuman activity that needs to be overcome in whatever way possible.

Fiorenza's view that adoption is more "offensive" than abortion is arguably expressive of such neo-Manichaean perceptions.

Western societies are now experiencing a deep crisis of religious and moral consciousness. A key indicator of this is the increasing rupture of the natural linkages which bind marriage, love, sexuality and procreation together. The greater acceptance of perverse sexual practices such as sodomy is in effect expressive of a rejection of "marital symbolism" as this has been stamped on our human nature in God's good creation of man as 'male and female.' This failure in moral and religious consciousness has given rise amongst 'progressive' Catholics to a litany of objections to certain aspects of the Church's teaching—in particular to its teaching on sexuality and marriage, its prohibition against the reception of the Eucharist by the divorced and remarried, as well as its doctrine on a male-only ministerial priesthood. It is striking that in general we will be able to predict what a Catholic will hold on any of these matters once we know what he or she holds on one of them. Why should this be so?

Cardinal Ratzinger has pointed out that the above litany of objections to the Church's doctrine is rooted in a faulty vision of man. He says that this faulty vision is, amongst other things, "closely associated with the inability to discern a spiritual message in the material world."[32] He adds that men and women of today cannot understand that "their bodiliness reaches the metaphysical depths and is the basis of a symbolic metaphysics whose denial or neglect does not ennoble man but destroys him."[33] For those whose vision of man is based on such a faulty anthropology which fails to recognise in the "being" of the human person the handiwork of the Creator, there is "no difference whether the body be of the masculine or the feminine sex: the body no longer expresses being at all."[34] Consequently, the difference "between homosexuality and heterosexuality as well as that between sexual relations within or outside marriage have become unimportant".[35] Likewise divested of "every metaphysical symbolism" is the "distinction between man and woman" which is to be "regarded as the product of reinforced role expectations."[36]

Coming back to gnosticism, it too rejected the "metaphysical symbolism" the Creator has stamped upon the nature of man as 'male and female'. Consequently, it tended to be marked by an androgynous anthropology whereby the differences between the sexes were seen in some instances as a limitation from which it was necessary to be liberated. Many gnostic cults worshipped an androgynous deity who was addressed as "Mother and Father God." In the "eucharistic" celebrations of several gnostic groups, the Holy Spirit was regarded as the "mother of all" and praise of "God as mother" constituted the theme of many of their chants and invocations.[37]

Following the gnostics, the Arians of the fourth century also challenged the traditional Christian doxology for God—"Father, Son and Holy Spirit." They too wanted to call the first Person of the Blessed Trinity "Creator" rather than "Father." According to Deborah Belonick, the "Arians claimed that Jesus Christ was not the Son of God but merely a superior creature; therefore, 'Father' was a fleshly, foolish, improper term for God."[38] One of St. Athanasius' great contributions to the defeat of Arianism was his defence of the traditional names of the Trinity. As well as demonstrating that it is wrong to refer to the Father alone as Creator since the Bible teaches otherwise (cf. Gen 1:1-2; Jn 1:1-3), St. Athanasius also pointed out that when we refer to God as "Father" we thereby mean something higher than his relation to creatures which is what the term "Creator" signifies. If creation did not exist, asked St. Athanasius in his tract *Against the Arians*, would this Creator-God cease to be?[39]

Turning again now to the question of "women priests". Bishop Patrick Dunn and Fr. Manfred Hauke both point out that the Church in the era of the Fathers and beyond saw the ban on women priests as a secure truth of the faith.[40] It was only within some heretical sects of the early centuries, principally gnostic ones, that attempts were made to confer the priesthood on women by allowing them to "preside" over "eucharistic" celebrations. St. Irenaeus identified the practice with Valentinian gnosticism.[41] Whenever the subject of ordaining women was raised it was rejected not simply as a breach of Church discipline but rather as heresy. There are explicit references to this in the writings of Tertullian (d. 220), St. Epiphanius of Salamis (d. 403), St. Augustine (d. 430) and St. John Damascene (d. 749).

In speaking of the practice amongst heretical sects of conferring the "priesthood" on women, Fr. Louis Ligier, S.J. said: "It is united with the corrupted eschatology and pneumatology of Montanism. It is met with, furthermore, in the corrupted Marian cult of the Coliridians, who admitted the offering or *prosfora* in Mary's name." After saying this, Fr. Ligier added: "Such a heretical milieu was in itself and still remains for us today, a sign of a considerable alienation from the genuine Christian tradition."[42] Fr. Donald Keefe sees the question of the ordination of women in the same historical context as Fr. Ligier. He says: "It should not be supposed that the issue of women's orders is novel: it dates back to the Montanist heresy of the second and third centuries, and since then has surfaced intermittently in association with comparably gnostic and anti-historical interpretations of Christianity."[43]

In his outstanding work entitled *The Early Liturgy To The Time of Gregory the Great,* Josef Jungmann, S.J. devoted an entire chapter to the way in which the early Church had to struggle to protect its doctrine and liturgy from contamination by gnostic concepts and practices.[44] Cardinal Francis Stafford has stated that gnosticism in all its varied presentations consists "in a reversion to paganism under pseudo-Christian auspices."[45] In reference to contemporary expressions of gnosticism, Cardinal John Wright stated: "All the Gnostics are not yet dead. They publish articles regularly and have 'renewed' their theology for our generation and our age in the life of the Church."[46] Dr. Germain Grisez has warned that Gnosticism has risen like the phoenix from the ashes and taken up residence in the Church. He has stated that "in many places...[Gnosticism] has become institutionalised so that it constitutes the establishment, while genuine Catholicism exists only as a dissident remnant."[47]

Reference

1   C.S. Lewis, *'Priestesses in the Church?',* Time and Tide XXIX, August 14, 1948.
2   Paul C. Vitz, *Support From Psychology For The Fatherhood of God,* Homiletic and Pastoral Review, February 1997, p. 7.
3   Cardinal Joseph Ratzinger, *The Ratzinger Report,* Ignatius Press, San Francisco, 1985, p. 97.
4   Kathleen Howley, *Catholic World Report,* January 1996, Vol. 6, No. 1.
5   Elisabeth Schussler Fiorenza, *In Memory of Her,* op. cit. p. 130.
6   Ibid. p. 135.
7   *CCC.* n. 613.
8   Pope Pius XII, *Mediator Dei,* n. 68.
9   *CCC.* n. 1330.
10 *CCC.* n. 1365.
11 *CCC.* n. 1366.
12 Elisabeth Schussler Fiorenza, *Discipleship of Equals,* op. cit. p. 72.
13 Ibid. p. 73
14 Ibid. pp. 73–74.
15 Ibid. p. 74.

16 Ibid. p. 55.

17 Ibid. p. 93.

18 Ibid. p. 93.

19 Ibid. p. 93–94.

20 Elisabeth Schussler Fiorenza, *The Power of Naming, Orbis Books,* New York, 1996, p. 167.

21 Elisabeth Schussler Fiorenza, *Sharing Her Word,* op. cit. p. 183, emphasis added.

22 Elisabeh Schussler Fiorenza, *Discipleship of Equals,* op. cit. p. 50.

23 Ibid. p. 51.

24 Ibid. p. 51.

25 Ibid. p. 52.

26 Ibid. p. 204.

27 Ibid. p. 218.

28 Ibid. p. 75.

29 Archbishop J. Francis Stafford, *The 'New Age' Movement: Analysis Of A New Attempt To Find Salvation Apart From Christian Faith,* published in L'Osservatore Romano, 27/1/93. In this excellent article, Cardinal Stafford examines the relationship between contemporary attacks on Catholic doctrine and New Age religious syncretism which he sees as a contemporary expression of ancient Gnostic heresies.

30 Cf. Pope John Paul II, *Letter To Families,* n. 19.

31 Pope John Paul II, *Letter To Families,* n. 19.

32 Cardinal Joseph Ratzinger, *L'Osservatore Romano,* July 24, 1989.

33 Ibid.

34 Ibid.

35 Ibid

36 Ibid.

37 Cf. Manfred Hauke, *Women in the Priesthood,* op. cit. pp. 161–164.

38 Deborah Belonick, in *The Politics of Prayer,* edited by Helen Hull Hitchcock, Ignatius Press, San Francisco, 1992, p. 298.

39 Ibid.

40 Cf. Bishop Patrick Dunn, *Priesthood,* Alba House, New York, 1990, p. 193; Fr Manfred Hauke, *Women in the Priesthood,* op. cit. p. 478.

41 Cf. St. Irenaeus, *Adversus Haereses,* 1,13,2.

42 Fr Louis Ligier, S.J., *L'Osservatore Romano,* 2/3/78.

43 Fr. Donald Keefe, S.J., *Covenantal Theology: The Eucharistic Order of History,* op. cit. p. 42.

44 Cf. Josef A. Jungmann, *S.J., The Early Liturgy To the Time of Gregory the Great,* Chapter 10 entitled The Defense Against Gnosticism, University of Notre Dame Press, Indiana 1959.

45   Archbishop J. Francis Stafford, *L'Osservatore Romano,* January 27, 1993.
46   Cardinal John Wright, *L'Osservatore Romano,* March 20, 1976.
47   Germain Grisez, cited by Fr. Tom O'Mahony in *Gnosticism: A Perennial Heresy,* Challenge Magazine, Canada, February, 1992, p. 20.

10

Shared Christian Praxis: Fatally Flawed

I began this book by noting the "concerns of Australian Catholics" which found expression in the *Instrumentum Laboris* which was prepared in advance of the Synod of Bishops for Oceania held in Rome during Nov–December 1998. These concerns extended to "teachers in Catholic schools" who "often have lives or ideas that are publicly in conflict with church teaching" and which "can be truly harmful for youth." Other problems referred to in *Instrumentum Laboris* included the difficulty faced by the Church in attracting young people, opposition in the Church to the Magisterium and confusion about the teaching of Vatican II, as well as decline in Sacramental practice and poor understanding of the Church's teaching on the sanctity of life.

It is against the backdrop of the catechetical challenge the problems listed above pose for the Catholic Church in Australia that in this chapter I will attempt to demonstrate why Groome's *shared Christian praxis* has to be considered as a totally inappropriate catechetical method to use in any Catholic setting.

Nature and Content of Catechesis

Truth can be communicated in propositional form and be presented to the intellect with a view to eliciting its assent. In this context, it is interesting to note that in *Fides et Ratio*, Pope John Paul II pointed out that "there are in the life of a human being many more truths which are simply believed than truths which are acquired by way of personal verification."[1] In this Encyclical, the Holy Father also pointed out that Revelation does not undermine freedom or reason. He quoted St. Augustine as saying: "To believe is nothing other than to think with assent. Believers are also thinkers: in believing they think and in thinking they believe. If faith does not think, it is nothing."[2]

Catechesis refers to all efforts made within the Church "to help people to believe that Jesus is the Son of God, so that believing they may have life in his name, and to educate and instruct them in this life and thus build up the Body of Christ."[3] The definitive aim of catechesis "is to put people not only in touch but in communion, in intimacy, with Jesus Christ: only he can lead us to the love of the Father in the Holy Spirit and make us share in the life of the Holy Trinity."[4] Placing the Person of Christ and his revelation of the Holy Trinity at the centre of catechesis, the *General Directory for Catechesis* published in 1997 said:

> The internal structure of catechesis: every mode of presentation must always be christocentric-trinitarian. Through Christ to the Father in the Holy Spirit. If catechesis lacks these three elements or neglects their close relationship, the Christian message can certainly lose its proper character.[5]

A good religious education process should contain a variety of pedagogical techniques that will engage both the analytical and affective modes of consciousness. It should make use of role-plays, drama, music, art, video and media resources, etc. No matter how good the method or process of religious education is, however, it will serve little purpose if it is not based on the foundation of a systematic treatment of Catholic doctrine which is sequentially programmed and appropriate to the stages of development of the students.

Catholic faith is first and foremost concerned with facts and not with notions and concepts. For example, we believe in realities such as the Incarnation of God's Eternal Word, the Virginal Conception, Christ's Bodily Resurrection and his Real Presence in the Eucharist. According to Cardinal Newman, Gospel faith is "a definite deposit, a treasure common to all, one and the same in every age, conceived in set words, such as to admit of being received, preserved, transmitted."[6] In Newman's understanding of how a vibrant faith develops, doctrinal knowledge was not seen as something which only the intellectual needed to be in possession of. He said:

[Gospel] faith is what even the humblest member of the Church may and must contend for; and in proportion to his education will the circle of his knowledge enlarge...and according as his power of grasping the sense of [the Creed's] articles increases, so will it become his duty to contend for them in their fuller and more accurate form.[7]

While it is true that greater knowledge of the doctrine of the faith does not necessarily confer greater sanctity, it is also true however that "the blossoms" of faith and piety "do not grow in the desert places" of a memory empty of doctrinal content.[8] In this regard, Catholic educators should bear in mind what Cardinal Newman said of his own spiritual journey: "When I was fifteen (in the autumn of 1816) a great change of thought took place in me. I fell under the influences of a definite Creed, and received into my intellect impressions of dogma, which, through God's mercy, have never been effaced or obscured."[9] Later, Newman added: "From the age of 15, dogma has been the fundamental principle of my religion: I know no other religion: I cannot enter into the idea of any other sort of religion...What I held in 1816, I held in 1833, and I hold in 1864. Please God, I shall hold it to the end."[10]

In speaking of how doctrinal knowledge is a constituent aspect of personal integration, Newman said:

[Doctrinal] propositions may and must be used, and easily can be used, as the expression of *facts,* and they are necessary to the mind in the same way that language is ever necessary for denoting facts...Again, they are useful in their dogmatic aspect as ascertaining and making clear for us truths on which the religious imagination has to rest. Knowledge must ever precede the exercise of the affections.[11]

From what Newman has stated above, it is clear that doctrinal content should be the centre about which a catechetical or religious education curriculum revolves. Doctrinal formulas provide young people with something their minds can grasp and they provide teachers with coherent lessons which are free of deceptive ambiguities and error. Consequently, a good religious education program should seek to have the students commit to memory certain words of Jesus as well as the

Ten Commandments, doctrinal formulas, Creed, essential prayers and liturgical texts.[12] Coupled with this, good school liturgy which is faithful to the liturgical law of the Church is important for cultivating in the students a love for the Holy Mass.

In the twenty six years I have been involved with religious education in Catholic high schools in Ireland, New Zealand and Australia, I have always found that young people appreciate solid doctrine when it is presented to them in an interesting way. Coupled with this, it is essential that those responsible for catechetical or religious instruction in Catholic schools see their role as that of "serving divine truth in the Church," which means they must love and seek "the most exact understanding" of that truth "in order to bring it closer" to themselves and to others.[13]

Young people thirst for authenticity in those who teach them about ultimate realities. In *Evangeli Nuntiandi,* Pope Paul VI highlighted this need for authenticity in the one who teaches the Catholic Faith when he said: "Modern man listens more willingly to witnesses than to teachers, and if he does listen to teachers, it is because they are witnesses."[14] The question that needs to be addressed to all religion teachers is this: "Do you really believe what you are proclaiming? Do you live what you believe? Do you really preach what you live?"[15]

In 1988, Archbishop Eric D'Arcy called for "a renaissance in the doctrinal dimension of education-in-faith." He stated that the catechetical method in vogue for the two decades up to 1988 had "failed badly in the doctrinal dimension." As a result, "Australian pastors, parents and teachers have been expressing strong and constant dissatisfaction about the 'Experientialist Model Catechetic' which became dominant in Catholic high schools." Archbishop D'Arcy added that as this experientialist model catechetic became "entrenched" in the Catholic school system, "great numbers of young Catholics were coming away from twelve years of Catholic schooling, ignorant of the reasons that support those doctrines: vulnerable to even the most elementary and hackneyed secularist objections to Catholic beliefs."[16]

In *Fides et Ratio,* Pope John Paul II pointed out that when faith stresses "feelings and experience" at the expense of reason and Revelation, it then runs "the risk of no longer being a universal proposition."[17] Archbishop Daniel Buechelin, head of the U.S Bishops' Ad Hoc Committee to oversee the use of the *Catechism of the Catholic Church,* issued a report to the National Conference of U.S Catholic

Bishops at their June 1997 meeting in Kansas City. In referring to texts used for religious education, the report stated: "When the methodological starting point is predominantly human experience, the texts at times easily leave the impression that human initiative is the prerequisite for divine action. God's initiative appears subordinate to human experience and human action." Sean Innerst, who is the Director of the Office of Religious Education in the Diocese of Rapid City, South Dakota, in commenting on this statement by the U.S. Bishops' Ad Hoc Committee, said that it drew attention "to the almost universal methodology called 'experience-based' catechesis" which he added "is one of the root causes" of many of the deficiencies which have characterised religious education in recent decades.[18]

An overemphasis on experientialism in religious education overlooks the fact that we believe there is an objective basis to our faith which requires us to believe that certain things are true and others false. Consequently, there is an important place in religious education for memorising, understanding, knowing, interrelating and accepting on trust the doctrine of the Church. Archbishop D'Arcy gave an example of why it is necessary to go beyond mere experiential considerations when teaching religion when he said:

> I do not *experience* the changing of the bread and wine into our Lord's body and blood at Mass, any more than I *experience* the neuronal changes constantly occurring in my own brain. But a knowledge of the latter is an item of every educated person's general knowledge; a knowledge of the former is an item of every well instructed Catholic's faith-knowledge; and in both cases one acquires the knowledge not through experiencing it, but by being taught it by those who already possess it.[19]

A doctrinally based catechesis does not have to conflict with a pedagogy that seeks to take account of the lived experiences of those who are to be educated in the faith. Jesus himself constantly drew on his hearers' daily experience in order to build a bridge from it to what he intended to instruct them in concerning the Kingdom of God. Consequently, a wise teacher will always have in the forefront of his mind's eye the type of background his students come from and what may be of concern to them at a particular stage in their development.

In *Catechesi Tradendae,* Pope John Paul II said that Catholic youth have "a right to receive 'the word of faith' not in a mutilated, falsified or diminished form but whole and entire, in all its rigour and vigour."[20] The Holy Father added that "unfaithfulness on some point to the integrity of the message means a dangerous weakening of catechesis and putting at risk the results that Christ and the ecclesial community have a right to expect from it."[21] Also, it is naive to claim that in order to make religious education appealing to youth, it is necessary to sacrifice doctrinal content in order to give sufficient weight to the students' life experience. It must not be forgotten that "no one can arrive at the whole truth on the basis solely of some simple private experience."[22]

The overarching pupose of a Catholic school or college is that it exists to foster the growth in holiness of all who are associated with it. In pursuing this objective, the Catholic school has a responsibility to help its students train and purify their reason in order to accept all that the Church teaches. In this regard, Pope John Paul II has said that "the mission of the Catholic teacher is to train the mind to accept the truths of faith."[23] On another occasion, while describing the type of teaching that should form the younger generations, the Holy Father said: "This teaching must seek to provide students with a clear, solid and organic knowledge of Catholic doctrine, focused on knowing how to distinguish those affirmations that must be upheld from those open to free discussion and those that cannot be accepted."[24]

While it is true that in the process of growth to maturity, propositions which the intellect once held as true may in the course of "critical enquiry" be "cast into doubt," it is also true that the human being is "one who seeks the truth" and who simultaneously "lives by belief."[25] Consequently, in the religious education of Catholics, it is important to help students develop a "critical consciousness" that will enable them to examine all that is presented to them as true in order that they assimilate it more deeply.

On the basis of what has been said above, it is clear that a doctrinally-based religious education program will necessarily include the objective of helping those being educated to acquire a critical consciousness that will enable them to better defend the doctrines of the faith by always having their "answer ready for people" who call them to account "for the hope" that is in them (cf. 1 Pet 3:15). To illustrate what is involved in this, I will give an example from my own experience as a teacher. Several years ago, I was teaching a unit of work on the Sacrament of Holy Orders to senior high school students. In order to prepare them to withstand the slogans and propaganda of those who campaign for the ordination of women, I first gave the students an outline of the main arguments of those who believe the ordination of women is possible. Next, I presented the case for the Church's doctrine on the male-only ministerial priesthood. When the unit was completed, there was unanimous agreement amongst the students that the Church's teaching was true and soundly based in Sacred Scripture and Tradition.

As the above example indicates, the purpose of helping students acquire a critical consciousness in the area of their faith-development is to strengthen their conviction about the solidity and truth of the Church's doctrine. When students leave our Catholic schools with such sharpened critical faculties, they will be less likely to succumb to those values in their secularised culture which are opposed to the doctrines of the faith.

The Importance Of An Appropriate Methodology

While orthodox content is of critical importance in the construction of a Catholic religious education curriculum, the pedagogical methodology that is used to transmit the doctrines of the faith is also important.

Cardinal Newman held that a fundamental cause of radical differences of belief was that of different *starting points*—which is to say in fundamental assumptions. Any chain of reasoning, any religious or theological position, any pedagogical method, must in the last analysis begin with certain starting points that are not themselves the product of reasonings. Coupled with this, in all effective education, the methodology adopted is intimately connected with the particular discipline involved. For example, there are particular methodologies that would be suitable for the teaching of science but not for literature.

The word 'method' is derived from the Greek word *methodos* which literally means "a way or path of transit." Rev. Professor Robert J. Henle, S.J., has pointed out that St. Thomas Aquinas expressly developed a view of methodology whereby the methodological principles as well as the starting points of any discipline determine its character and its conclusions.[26] Hence, in the field of education, a discipline involving objective truth must imply a methodology intrinsically determined by it. It follows from this that a doctrinally based religious education curriculum must include a pedagogical methodology which is suitable for receiving and transmitting the various truths of faith. In speaking to a group of U.S. Bishops in 1998, Pope John Paul II touched on this important question of methodology when he said:

> Young Catholics have a right to hear the full content of that message [Gospel] in order to come to know Christ, the One who has overcome death and opened the way of salvation. Efforts to renew catechesis must be based on the premise that Christ's teaching, as transmitted in the Church and as authentically interpreted by the Magisterium, has to be presented in all its richness, **and the methodologies used have to respond to the nature of the faith as truth received** (cf. 1 Cor 15:1).[27]

The Meaning of Praxis

In order to explain what he means by *praxis,* Groome in a 1994 essay went back to Aristotle, who, he pointed out, identified three ways of knowing called *theoria, praxis* and *poiesis.* In this essay, Groome states that *theoria* "amounts to a spiritual type of contemplation of ideas, objects and events." He explains *poiesis* (also referred to as techne or technique) as "the activity of making artefacts and the knowledge... upon which such activity was based." [28] Groome adds that *praxis* "is a combination of the theoria dimension (reflection) and the poiesis dimension (action)."[29] He adds that Aristotle understood *praxis* as "the twin moments of reflection and participation" so that: "Praxis was action that was reflectively done or was reflection upon the action that was being done. It was only in being reflectively done that it was known."[30]

In the essay referred to above, Groome stated that "praxis as a way of knowing was greatly overshadowed by theoria in Western philosophy from Aristotle to the recent past." He added that it was Karl Marx who through "a dialectical relationship with Hegel's concept of Geist" that "reunited theory and praxis and reintroduced praxis as the primary way of knowing."[31] Coupled with this, I have quoted Groome elsewhere in this book as having stated that Marx's "insight that our 'knowing' and thus our very 'being' is powerfully shaped by our socio/cultural context must be honoured in a pedagogy for conation."[32]

In Chapter 5, we saw that Groome believes an overriding objective of religious education to be the development of a critical consciousness that will foster an emancipatory praxis aimed at the creation of a more egalitarian Church and society. In tandem with this, we noted also how he perceives all education as eminently political in nature: "I contend that the essential characteristic of all education is that it is *a political activity*."[33] Also in Chapter 5, we noted that Groome endorsed "liberation theologies" on the grounds that they "heighten the emancipatory intent of Christian faith" in a way that "unmasks what has been used to oppress and victimize."[34] In reference to feminist liberation theology, for example, Groome is of the view that it "reflects and contributes to the rising feminist consciousness throughout the world" and that it "mounts a devastating criticism of the patriarchy of the Church and challenges the ways Jewish and Christian traditions have been interpreted to legitimate the oppression of women and domination by men."[35]

Again in Chapter 5, we noted that two philosophers who have significantly influenced Groome are Heidegger and Habermas. It is interesting to compare Heidegger with Aristotle and other leading philosophers of ancient Greece. If we trace a line of philosophical development from Aristotle to Heidegger, we will notice that there is a shift from a priority of theory to a priority of *praxis* which is parallelled by a shift from the priority of the infinite to a priority of the finite. On the basis of this perceived priority of praxis over theory and of the finite over the infinite, Heidegger "saw Christianity not as a body of contents but as a performance" which meant that it derived "its significance not from its contents but from the 'factical' experience of life."[36]

As regards Habermas, Groome states that "for Habermas knowledge is by praxis."[37] After quoting Habermas as saying that "Self-reflection is at once intuition and emancipation, comprehension and liberation from dogmatic dependence,"[38] Groome goes on to say: "My description of both critical reflection and action draws heavily on Habermas."[39]

Groome does not understand well enough the notion of *praxis* in either its Aristotelian or Marxist form, nor does he properly understand Liberation Theology. He is simply adopting popularised forms of these ideas and harnessing them to the propagation of his own agenda. He is using them to drive his educational philosophy (which as we saw earlier he understands as essentially a *political* activity) in the direction of his emancipatory and egalitarian vision.

For Aristotle, *praxis* is not a combination of theoria (theory) and poisis. Rather, *praxis* is guided by a moral desire to act truly and rightly—something which the Greeks called *phronesis*. In the thought of Aristotle, theory provides the general principles that should govern *praxis* (action) and thus it is a form of knowledge. Consequently, for Aristotle, *praxis* is not simply action based on reflection but rather is action that embodies certain qualities including a commitment to conform one's actions to the truth and to all that is perceived as good.

In contradistinction to Aristotle, Marx inverted the relationship between theory and *praxis*. For him, there is no objective truth. Asserting that the human vocation is not to understand the world but to transform it,[40] Marx posited that the principle objective of human thought and action should be the creation of the classless society on earth in which would emerge a "new man". With the 'Idea of God' dismissed as something invented as a mere symbol for human ideals, the way of social perfection and harmony lay, according to Marx, not through conversion to God and his will but rather through revolutionary praxis aimed at the realisation of the "new man" living in a classless society. The only truth that existed in the marxist system was that which emerged from revolutionary praxis—something that was always relative and contingent.

From its very beginning, marxist thought "has become divided and has given birth to various currents which diverge significantly from each other."[41] Western Marxism based itself on the thesis that man creates himself through his own work (praxis). The distinguished philosopher, Rocco Buttiglione, refers to this fact by saying that the "idea of the self-creation of man through praxis constitutes the authentic core of Marx's thought."[42] Consequently, Marxism can be understood as a philosophy of praxis whereby Marx erroneously conceived and defined *praxis* by dissolving "the subjectivity of the concrete man in praxis" with the result that "the concrete human subject is lost in social work."[43]

Building on the idea "that men are the products of circumstances and upbringing, and that, therefore, changed men are products of different circumstances, and changed upbringing,"[44] Marxist revolutionary praxis sets out to gain control of material surroundings and social relationships in order to transform them.[45] Buttiglione says that it is evident "that the insufficiency of this notion of praxis is at the root of the totalitarian character which Marxism has assumed in practice, as also of the bloody and violent way in which it has pursued its achievement in history." Buttiglione posits further that it is in "the radical negation of the metaphysical subjectivity of man" that it is impossible to speak of "human rights" within a Marxist context. He adds that Marxism's "one-sided attention to the transformation of our surroundings" implies that "any price in terms of human value and of the individual's suffering is acceptable in order to achieve that revolutionary change of objective structures which will in the future bring about a completely new humanity."[46]

In contemporary culture, the understanding of the meaning of freedom is in crisis. This situation has occurred largely because moral relativism has separated the notion of freedom from its foundation in truth. Looking at this same problem from another angle, we can say that the crisis of relativism in both religion and morality is expressive of an erroneous conception of *praxis,* whereby the latter is not understood in terms of its relationship to truth. In other words, in order to discover the obligations of freedom, ie. correct *praxis,* we must first set our minds on the discovery of truth since it is only by having its foundation in truth that we can say our actions are expressive of a *praxis* that is in keeping with the dignity and vocation of the human person.

In his philosophical work titled *The Acting Person,* Karol Wojtyla (now Pope John Paul II), sought to set forth a Christian understanding of the idea of *praxis* which Marx had failed to explain in an integrally human way. In his introduction to the third Polish edition of this work by Wojytla, Rocco Buttiglione pointed out that for Wojtyla the relationship between *praxis* and truth was so critical that the "sovereignty of the person is expressed in the decision for truth and the imposition of the law of truth on one's own passions."[47] Further to this, Buttiglione pointed out that, while Wojtyla took cognisance of the fact that the human person is profoundly conditioned by his culture and circumstances of life, he is nevertheless "able to transcend such a conditioning in order to obey the truth," and that therefore the "transcendence of the person and obedience to the truth are two sides of a single dynamic reality which is the free action of the person." Consequently, says Buttiglione, the free person is the one who "acknowledges himself as responsible for the good, and the first good which is given to him and for which he is objectively responsible is his own self-realisation in the truth."[48]

On the other hand, the Marxist philosophy of *praxis* was false and dehumanising. Having repudiated objective truth and objective being, it was thereby incapable of providing an ethical judgement on all the crimes that were committed in the name of the "class struggle" and in the birthing of "the new man". It could not provide an objective or immutable foundation for the evaluation of human acts.

Wojytla's insistence on the necessary link between *praxis* and truth is a feature of all his writing. We see this very clearly for example in his book *Sign of Contradiction* which is a compilation of reflections he gave to Pope Paul VI and members of the Roman Curia at a Lenten Retreat in the Vatican in March 1976. Here, after first stating that "if we wish to remain faithful to a correct analysis of the human person, we must assert very clearly that self-fulfilment, or self-creation, has its source in man's moral conscience, his spiritual centre," Wojtyla went on to add: "The dignity of the human person has its foundation in conscience, in the inner obedience to the objective principle which enables human 'praxis' to distinguish between good and evil...Obedience to conscience, which in its turn is obedient to the divine law of love, is what equates 'serving Christ in others' with 'reigning' (cf. Lumen Gentium, n. 36)."[49]

In *Sign of Contradiction,* Woytyla anchored his reflection on the relationship between the human vocation and truth in the teaching of Vatican II which says: "Christ, who is the new Adam, by revealing the mystery of the Father and his love, also fully reveals man to man himself and makes his vocation known to him."[50] Having thus recalled this central teaching of Vatican II, Wojtyla then referred to how Jesus himself testified to the way in which his own mission was bound up with truth: "I was born for this, I came into the world for this: to bear witness to the truth; and all who are on the side of truth listen to my voice" (Jn 18: 37). Following on from this, Wojytla added:

Thus it is truth that makes man what he is. His relationship with truth is the deciding factor in his human nature and it constitutes his dignity as a person...Christ, the great prophet is the one who proclaims divine truth; and he is also the one who shows the dignity of man to be bound up with truth: with truth honestly sought, earnestly pondered, joyfully accepted as the greatest treasure of the human spirit, witnessed to by word and deed in the sight of men. Truth has a divine dimension; it belongs by nature to God himself; it is one with the divine Word. At the same time it constitutes an essential dimension of human knowledge and human existence, of science, wisdom and the human conscience. Every man is born into the world to bear witness to the truth according to his own particular vocation...For man, truth is vital. True knowledge of himself, of the world, of God; truth in conscience, truth in knowing, truth in believing. Jesus said very clearly that truth must not be denied to men or concealed from them (cf. Mt 5: 14-15) but must be openly professed (Mt 10:32). Truth has a social, a public dimension. Therefore man's right to the truth must never be denied.[51]

Since his elevation to the Chair of Peter, Pope John Paul II has continued to stress the link between truth and liberation understood as human freedom in its integral dimension. In his first encyclical he said:

Jesus Christ meets the man of every age, including our own, with the same words: 'You will know the truth, and the truth will make you free' (Jn 8:32). These words contain both a fundamental requirement and a warning: the requirement of an honest relationship with regard to truth as a condition for authentic freedom, and a warning to avoid every kind of illusory freedom...every truth that fails to enter into the truth about man and the world. Today...we see Christ as the one who brings man freedom based on truth, frees man from what curtails, diminishes and as it were breaks off this freedom at its root, in man's soul, his heart and his conscience.[52]

On another occasion, the Holy Father again took up the question of the integral nature of human freedom when he said:

Liberation means man's inner transformation, which is a consequence of the knowledge of the truth. Truth is important not only for the growth of human knowledge, deepening man's interior life in this way; truth also has a prophetic significance and power...Liberation also in the social sense begins with knowledge of the truth.[53]

In a life that is authentically Catholic, "praxis comes from the faith and is a lived expression of it."[54] By restoring "man's true freedom," Christ assigns to the human person a task: "Christian practice, which is the putting into practice of the great commandment of love."[55] Consequently, "Faith inspires criteria of judgement, determining values, lines of thought, and patterns of living which are valid for the whole human community."[56] Hence, "the Christian is called to act according to the truth (cf. Jn 3: 21), and thus to work for the establishment of that 'civilisation of love' of which Pope Paul VI spoke."[57]

In his actions, man expresses who he is, and thus through his inter-action with the outside world, he expresses his interior self. It is only by way of such an integration of faith and action that we can speak of that "unity of faith and life" which lies at the centre of Christian disciple-ship. Consequently, in this Catholic understanding of praxis, the good, and the knowledge of it, is immanent in the doing. Speaking of this integral meaning of *praxis*, Pope John Paul II said:

> The truth and everything that is true represents a great good to which we must turn with love and joy...Knowledge of truth has its meaning in itself. It is an accomplishment of human and per-sonal character, an outstanding human good. Pure 'theory' is itself a kind of human 'praxis,' and the believer is waiting for a supreme 'praxis,' which will unite him forever with God: that 'praxis' which is vision, and therefore also 'theory'.[58]

Praxis and Liberation Theology

Since 'liberation' understood as liberation from the "slavery of sin" is a Gospel theme, the expression 'theology of liberation' is a thoroughly valid term.[59] However, there are forms of liberation theology that are not in harmony with Catholic faith, especially those which seek to lace the Gospel revelation with Marxist analysis. Such Marxist-based libera-tion theologies emphasise the primacy of praxis over theory, where *praxis* is taken as the starting point of theological reflection. In particu-lar, such theologies tend to focus on a notion of praxis as something forged in dialogue with what is perceived as revolutionary action on behalf of the poor. The Marxist notion of a priority of *praxis* over the-ory often appears in liberation theology as a priority of *orthopraxis* over *orthodoxy*. For example, in speaking of *orthopraxis*, Gustavo Guttierez said:

The intention...is not to deny the meaning of *orthodoxy,* under-stood as a proclamation of and reflection on statements consid-ered to be true. Rather, the goal is to balance and even to reject the primacy and almost exclusiveness which doctrine has enjoyed in Christian life and above all to modify the emphasis, often obsessive, upon the attainment of an orthodoxy which is often nothing more than fidelity to an obsolete tradition or a debatable interpretation. In a more positive vein, the intention is to recognise the work and importance of concrete behaviour, of deeds, of action, of praxis in the Christian life.[60]

In a 1996 address to the presidents of the Doctrinal Commissions of the Bishops' Conferences of Latin America, Cardinal Ratzinger spoke of a newly emerging religious syncretism which was becoming popular in the West and which, like Marxism, puts praxis above knowledge and is thus based on a single principle which is "the primacy of orthopraxis with regard to orthodoxy."[61] In view of the threat posed to orthodox belief by this emerging religious relativism, Cardinal Ratzinger said that the moment was ripe for an "examination of the notion of ortho-praxis." As a contribution to this examination, Cardinal Ratzinger went on to say:

The previous history of religion had shown that the religions of India did not have an orthodoxy in general, but rather an orthopraxis. From there the notion probably entered into mod-ern theology. However, in the description of the religions of India, this had a very precise meaning: it meant that those reli-gions did not have a general, compulsory catechism, and belonging to them was not defined by the acceptance of a par-ticular creed. On the other hand, those religions have a system of ritual acts which they consider necessary for salvation and which distinguish a 'believer' from a 'non-believer'. In those religions, a believer is not recognised by certain knowledge but by the scrupulous observance of a ritual which embraces the whole of life. The meaning of orthopraxis, i.e., right acting, is determined with great precision: it is a code of rituals. On the other hand...To be orthodox thus meant to know and practice the right way in which God wants to be glorified.[62]

Continuing his discussion regarding this new faith with its emphasis on a priority of orthopraxis over orthodoxy, Cardinal Ratzinger said: "The new foundation of religion comes about by following a pragmatic path with more ethical and political overtones."[63] Having said this, Cardinal Ratzinger added: "A faith which we ourselves can decide about is not a faith in the absolute...The faith, together with its praxis, either comes to us from the Lord through his Church and the sacramental ministry, or it does not exist in the absolute."[64]

A Fatally Flawed Method

Having thus looked at some of the varying interpretations the idea of *praxis* can have, let us now return to Groome's *shared Christian praxis.*

As we saw in Chapter 5, Groome has clearly stated that "in more traditional language" the meaning of the term "Story" as it is used in *shared Christian praxis* can "be called scripture and tradition."[65] Again in Chapter 5, we noted how Groome asserts "that there have been distortions and corruptions reflected in Christian Story/Vision"[66] something which he said requires that "religious educators should approach the faith tradition with a healthy suspicion and, as educators, help people to recognise that 'much that has been proudly told must be confessed as sin; and much that has been obscured and silenced must be given voice'."[67] In conjunction with this, we also noted that, according to Groome, "such a 'critical consciousness' seems theologically appropriate to Catholic tradition, given how much untruth is in every statement of faith."[68] Groome posits further that such a "critical consciousness" needs to be applied also to the sacramental life of the Church whereby: "sacramental imagination should 'see' both what is 'there' as gift and what should not be at all and should conceive of creating what ought to be."[69]

In Chapter 5, we noted that Groome does not accept as "appropriate" for use in movement 3 of *shared Christian praxis* a view of "Revelation as doctrine," which he says "understands revelation as 'divinely authoritative doctrine inerrantly proposed as God's word by the Bible or by official Church teaching'."[70] Also, we saw that in rejecting as an apt model of revelation a view of the "Bible and Christian tradition" which can find expression in "doctrinal propositions," Groome quoted Elisabeth Schussler Fiorenza who said that such a view of revelation is deficient in that it "takes historically limited experiences and texts and posits them as universals, which then become authoritative and normative for all times and cultures."[71]

Coupled with his recommendation that religious educators approach "Christian Story" (read Scripture and Tradition) from the perspective of "a hermeneutic of suspicion," Groome also lends his support to Gabriel Moran's concept of "Revelation As a Continuing Process".[72] In his concern to avoid looking at revelation as something "static", Moran argued that "revelation in its most basic sense is neither a word coming down from heaven to which man assents nor an historical event manifesting a truth."[73] "It would be better," said Moran, "to begin by conceiving of revelation as an historical and continuing intersubjective communion in which man's answer is part of the revelation."[74] He posited that Catholic doctrine "with its insistence upon the closing of revelation, seems committed to the past over the present and exposed to the charge of not taking history seriously." In saying this, Moran added that Catholic theology "is trying to escape" from "a revelation that is a collection of truths, teachings, and historical facts."[75] In speaking of "the way in which Christ's consciousness attained to the knowledge of God," Moran asserted that "it is possible for him [Jesus] to have been ignorant of objective facts."[76]

In making reference to Moran's theory of revelation as a continuing process, Groome in his 1994 essay said:

Gabriel Moran's argument *(The Present Revelation)* that one's concept of revelation determines how one does theology has much truth in it...I believe one's concept of revelation has an equally determining effect on how we do Christian education. If we have a static concept of revelation and understand it is [sic] something given only in the past, then the theologian's and the educator's job is simply to explain and teach, respectively, how that revelation applies to our present life. This is a theoria approach to knowing in that it begins with a theory and attempts to apply it to practice. A static concept of revelation gives rise to a theoria approach to knowing, in this case, to knowing God's will for us. If, however, revelation is seen as an ongoing process, then Christian education ought to begin with critical reflection on the present events where God is actively revealing self. The critical reflection must be done in the light of the story of God's self-revelation in the events of the lives of our forebears but it should begin in our present...If one accepts a process concept of revelation, as I do (and as Vatican II tended toward), then I believe this points us to a praxis epistemology for our Christian education task.[77]

In speaking of Revelation, the *CCC* says: "By love, God has revealed himself and given himself to man. He has thus provided the definitive, supernatural abundant answer to the questions that man asks himself about the meaning and purpose of his life."[78] The *CCC* adds: "God has revealed himself fully by sending his own Son...The Son is the Father's definitive Word; so there will be no further Revelation after him."[79]

Vatican II stated that "God graciously arranged that the things he had once revealed for the salvation of all peoples should remain in their entirety, throughout the ages, and be transmitted to all generations."[80] In order that "the full and living Gospel might always be preserved in the Church," added Vatican II, "the apostles left bishops as their successors" and in doing so "gave them their own position of teaching authority."[81] This teaching authority is transmitted in the Church through the process of apostolic succession. In consequence of this, "the task of giving an authentic interpretation to the Word of God, whether in its written form or in the form of Tradition, has been entrusted to the living teaching office of the Church alone,"[82] that is, "to the Pope and the bishops in communion with him."[83]

Since the doctrine of the faith provides *praxis* with its principles, then any authentic catechesis basing itself on the notion of *praxis* must be rooted in the Word of God correctly interpreted. In contradistinction to this, Catholic doctrine and Groome's theology and pedagogical system are mutually exclusive in many areas and indeed posit mutually antagonistic views of reality. Catechesis, like liberation theology, must have as its "indispensable pillars: the truth about Jesus the Saviour, the truth about the Church, and the truth about man and his dignity."[84] At the root of Groome's theological and pedagogical project is a flawed Christology, ecclesiology and anthropology. In presenting Jesus primarily as one who preached a radical egalitarianism that ended all political, social and religious hierarchies, Groome's "reconstructed" Catholicism has little to do with the real and historical Catholic faith.

In Groome's system, the "hermeneutic of suspicion" functions as a determining principle. As such, the doctrines of the faith are treated like mythic putty to be reshaped at will. Under the weight of Groome's "hermeneutic of suspicion," practically everything the Church teaches becomes contingent matter subject to neverending and contradictory reinterpretations. Within the "meta approach" of *shared Christian praxis,* fashionable notions drawn from academic and political life become a corrective to Church dogma and, in the process, the Church becomes the plaything of ideologues. Groome's reconstructionist agenda in regard to the Church is clearly manifest in the title of his book *Language for a Catholic Church* where he uses the indefinite article "a" rather than "the" with the word "Catholic." In this scheme of things, the Church of the ages past is "replaced" by a 'church' of and for today. For Groome, "yesterday's truth" becomes something to be contradicted by "today's truth."[85]

Groome's methodology opens up the possibility for a repudiation of all doctrine. The content of the deposit of faith enters into Movement 4 of *shared Christian praxis* only in the context of "a dialectical hermeneutics between participants' stories/visions and Christian Story/Vision,"[86] where "both are evaluated in light of each other to discern what is true for one's life."[87] Given the case of the 'Altar Society' referred to in Chapter 5 of this book—where, according to Groome's own testimony, he felt no compunction about using the *shared Christian praxis* process to lead a group of Catholics away from a position of support for the Church's teaching on the male-only ministerial priesthood to a position of active opposition to it—then it is clear that Groome's pedagogical method is based on a relativistic understanding of the Catholic faith.

Groome's work, like that of Fiorenza, exhibits a deep-seated anti-Roman attitude, something traditionally associated with Protestantism. Groome manifests this attitude with an air of condescension he frequently adopts towards whatever comes from Rome. He filters the teachings of the Magisterium through a critical sieve after which he repudiates those teachings that do not conform to his personal opinions. After doing this, he then encourages others to do the same.

Groome's dissent from various Catholic doctrines implicitly denies that such doctrinal propositions embody certainty. In *Catechesi Tradendae,* Pope John Paul II warned of catechetical methods which posit "that faith is not certainty but questioning" and he pointed out that while in this life we are not yet "in full possession" of what we hope for, nevertheless we have "an assurance and conviction" which "is based on the Word of God who cannot deceive or be deceived." In this light, added the Holy Father, "one of the aims of catechesis" should be to give young people "the simple but solid certainties that will help them to seek to know the Lord more and better."[88]

In *Fides et Ratio,* Pope John Paul II again took up this point of the need for certainty in regard to the doctrines of the faith and their communication. Speaking of how the Word of God and the dogmatic statements of the Church are forever current, he said: "The word of God is not addressed to any one people or to any one period of history. Similarly, dogmatic statements, while reflecting at times the culture of the period in which they were defined, formulate an unchanging and ultimate truth."[89] Coupled with this, the Holy Father drew attention to the fact that "recent times have seen the rise to prominence of various doctrines which tend to devalue even the truths which have been judged certain."[90] These doctrines, said Pope John Paul II, can leave those exposed to them "with a sense that they have no valid points of reference."[91] Further to this, the Holy Father pointed out that since the human being is "one who seeks the truth," then life "can never be grounded upon doubt, uncertainty or deceit"—since "such an existence would be threatened constantly by fear and anxiety."[92] In view of all this, the Holy Father concluded by saying that today's most urgent task is "to lead people to discover both their capacity to know the truth and their yearning for ultimate and definitive meaning in life."[93]

In regard to the deposit of faith, Cardinal Ratzinger has pointed out that if its objective content "**is no longer trusted**," then "**new content slips in unnoticed**."[94] Given *shared Christian praxis'* foundation in the subjectivism of Habermas, Heidegger, Freire and Marx, it is not surprising that at times Groome seeks to change the content of the faith. *Shared Christian praxis* is a pedagogical method whose nature is such as to render it ideally suited to the pursuit of ideological objectives that seek to bring about a break with the tradition of Catholic doctrine in various areas.

As we have already seen in this chapter, the word *praxis* has a long history stretching back to classical Greece. However, in contemporary thought, the term has come to be associated mostly with Marxist philosophy. Despite its pretensions to the contrary, Marxist philosophy sought not so much to explain reality and so arrive at truth, but rather sought to change reality and so create the truth. In the Marxist framework, the self-creation of man is sought via a material dialectic which progresses from thesis and antithesis to a synthesis, ie. progresses from one opposite to the other opposite. Insofar as he has repudiated the dogmatic principle in Catholicism, Groome has left himself little option but to adopt the Marxist concept of "praxis" which demands "putting praxis above knowledge" with the result that "praxis" comes to be equated with "light."[95]

Every methodology presupposes certain metaphysical principles. The end result of attempting to integrate the doctrines of the faith with Groome's methodology is that the former are reduced to abstract ideology. In short, it is impossible to harness Groome's *shared praxis* to an effective catechesis, for of its nature it tends to create the truth and not discover or transmit it. Consequently, *shared Christian praxis* can hardly be regarded as a method capable of responding "to the nature of the faith as a truth received."

The question of the relationship between *orthodoxy* and *orthopraxis* and how it relates to catechesis was resolved by Pope John Paul II in *Catechesi Tradendae*. In Pope John Paul II's thought, orthodoxy and orthopraxis, as we have already seen, refer essentially to the same realities—an objective truth which permits us to access an objective reality—God and his self-revelation. Orthodoxy and *praxis* in this case coincide with 'being' and hence reality. In regard to this, we read in *Catechesi Tradendae:*

> It is useless to play off orthopraxis against orthodoxy: Christianity is inseparably both. Firm and well thought out convictions lead to courageous and upright action...This revelation [Divine Revelation] is not however isolated from life or artificially juxtaposed to it. It is concerned with the ultimate meaning of life and it illumines the whole of life with the light of the Gospel, to inspire it or to question it.[96]

In speaking of the problems inherent in trying to play off "orthopraxis" against orthodoxy in Christian life, Cardinal Ratzinger said:

> For if the word 'orthopraxis' is pushed to its most radical meaning, it presumes that no truth exists that is antecedent to praxis but rather that truth can be established only on the basis of correct praxis...Theology becomes then no more than a guide to action, which, by reflecting on praxis, continually develops new

modes of praxis. If not only redemption but truth as well is regarded as *'post hoc'*, then truth becomes a product of man. At the same time, man, who is no longer measured against truth but produces it, becomes himself a product.[97]

Given Groome's starting position that some of the solemn and definitive teachings of the Church are simply the products of the mindset of a particular age and hence no longer require the irrevocable assent of all Catholics, then this *starting point* renders his *shared Christian praxis* incapable of serving as a suitable methodology for imparting religious education in a Catholic school since it does not "**respond to the nature of the faith as truth received.**"[98] Rather than starting with "Scripture and Tradition"(Groome's "Story") as "truth received," *shared Christian praxis* posits that it be introduced to the students as something to be critically dismantled ("hermeneutic of suspicion") in order to identify its "distortions" and "untruth".

Groome's disciples in Australia have sought to defend their use of *shared Christian praxis* by positing that it is capable of a 'creative adaptation' for use in Catholic Schools. These educators do not seem to understand that the theoretical underpinnings of Groome's "Christian Story/Vision" contradict the Catholic understanding of Divine Revelation and its mode of transmission in the Church. Neither do these disciples of Groome seem to understand that Movement 3 and its use of a "hermeneutic of suspicion" to sift out what is perceived as erroneous and oppressive in the doctrine of the Church is a non-negotiable component of *shared Christian praxis*. Groome insists on this point when he says that if the educator bypasses Movement 3 the process "would not then be shared Christian praxis."[99] Consequently, religious educators who insist on using Groome's method in Catholic precincts are intent on embracing a religious education methodology whose criterion for the interpretation of Divine Revelation is opposed to the teaching of the Church. In continuing along this path, these educators are involving themselves in terrible contradictions.

Reference

1   Pope John Paul II, *Fides et Ratio*, n. 31.
2   Ibid. n. 79.
3   Pope John Paul II, *Catechesi Tradendae*, n. 1.
4   Ibid. n. 5

5   *General Directory For Catechesis,* n. 100.

6   Cardinal Newman, *Parochial and Plain Sermons,* II, cited by Archbishop Eric D'Arcy in *The New Catechism and Cardinal Newman,* Communio 20, Fall 1993, p. 499.

7   *Cardinal Newman, Parochial and Plain Sermons II,* cited by Archbishop Eric D'Arcy, op. cit. p. 496.

8   Cf. Pope John Paul II, *Catechesi Tradendae,* n. 55.

9   Cardinal John Henry Newman, *Apologia Pro Vita Sua,* Penquin Books, London 1994, p. 25.

10 Ibid. p. 61.

11 Cardinal John Henry Newman, *Grammar of Assent,* cited by Archbishop Eric D'Arcy, op. cit. p. 499.

12 Cf. Pope John Paul II, *Catechesis Tradendae,* n. 55.

13 Pope John Paul II, *Fides et Ratio,* n. 2 (cf. footnote n. 1 where the Holy Father quotes Redemptor Hominis, n. 19).

14 Pope Paul VI, *Evangeli Nuntiandi,* n. 41.

15 Ibid. n. 76.

16 *Archbishop Eric D'Arcy,* Australasian Catholic Record, October 1988, pp. 392-393.

17 Pope John Paul II, *Fides et Ratio,* n. 48.

18 *Sean Innerst in The Catholic* Faith, Vol. 3. No 6, Published by Ignatius Press, San Francisco, Nov/Dec 1997, p. 17.

19 Archbishop Eric D'Arcy, *Communio,* Fall 1993, p. 492.

20 Pope John Paul II, *Catechesi Tradendae,* n. 30.

21 Ibid.

22 Ibid. n. 22.

23 Pope John Paul II, *L'Osservatore Romano,* April 22, 1985.

24 Pope John Paul II, *L'Osservatore Romano,* January 11, 1995.

25 Pope John Paul II, *Fides et Ratio,* n. 31.

26 Cf. Fr. Robert J. Henle, S.J., *Transcendental Thomism: A Critical Assessment,* in *One Hundred Years of Thomism,* op. cit. pp. 93-94. Fr. Henle points out that St. Thomas developed this understanding of the importance and nature of methodology in his general epistemological doctrine on the division of the disciplines and in his Via Platonica and the Via Aristotelis.

27 Pope John Paul II, *L'Osservatore Romano,* June 3, 1998 (emphasis added).

28 Thomas H. Groome, *Shared Christian Praxis: A Possible Theory/Method of Religious Education,* in *Critical Perspectives On Christian Education,* edited by Jeff Astley and Leslie J Francis, Gracewing, Herefordshire, 1994, p. 218.

29 Ibid.

30 Ibid.

31 Ibid.

32 Thomas Groome, *Sharing Faith,* op. cit. p. 73.

33 Thomas Groome, *Sharing Faith,* op. cit. p. 12.

34 Thomas Groome, *Educating for Life,* op. cit. p. 376.

35 Ibid. pp. 376–77.

36 Cf. Ricoeur and Practical Theology by John Van Den Hengel, S.C.J., *Theological Studies,* Vol. 55, No. 3, 1994, p. 475. See analysis of Heidegger's lectures entitled "Einfuhrungin die Phanomenologie der Religion" in Otto Poggeler, Martin Heidegger's Path of Thinking, tr. Daniel Magurshak and Sigmund Barber, *Contemporary Studies in Philosophy and the Human Sciences* (Atlantic Highlands: Humanities Press International, 1987) 24–34.

37 Thomas H. Groome, *Shared Christian Praxis: A Possible Theory/Method of Religious Education,* in Critical Perspectives On Christian Education, op. cit. p. 223.

38 Ibid.

39 Ibid. p. 227.

40 Cf. Karl Marx, *11th Thesis on Feurbach.*

41 Sacred Congregation For The Doctrine Of The Faith, *Instruction On Certain Aspects of the Theology of Liberation,* Section VII, n. 8.

42 Rocco Buttiglione, *Karol Wojtyla: The Thought of the Man Who Became Pope John Paul II,* Erdman's Publishing Co., Michigan, 1997, p. 293.

43 Ibid. pp. 296–297.

44 Karl Marx, *3rd Thesis on Feurbach.,*

45 Cf. Rocco Buttiglione, *Karol Wojtyla: The Thought of the Man Who Became Pope John Paul II,* op. cit. pp. 297–298.

46 Ibid. p. 298.

47 Rocco Buttiglione, *Introduction to Karol Wojtyla's The Acting Person,* Lublin 1994—reproduced in English translation as an Appendix to *Buttiglione's Karol Wojtyla: The Thought of the Man Who Became Pope John Paul II,* op. cit. 352–380. See also, *The Acting Person,* pt. 2 , ch. 4.

48 Ibid. p. 358

49 Karol Wojytla, *Sign of Contradiction,* Geoffrey Chapman, Australia, 1979, p. 36.

50 Vatican II, *Gaudium et Spes,* n. 22.

51 Karol Wojtyla, *Sign of Contradiction,* op. cit. pp. 119–121; Cf. Karol Wojtyla (Pope John Paul II), *Toward a Philosophy of Praxis: An Anthology,* edited by Alfred Bloch and George T. Czuczka, Crossroad, New York, 1981, pp. 111–112.

52 Pope John Paul II, *Redemptor Hominis,* n. 12.

53 Pope John Paul II, *General Audience,* February 21, 1979.

54 Sacred Congregation For The Doctrine Of The Faith, *Instruction On Certain Aspects of the Theology of Liberation,* Section X, n. 3.

55 Ibid. n. 71.

56 Ibid. n. 96.

57 Ibid. n. 99.

58 Pope John Paul II, Address to teachers and university students in Cologne Cathedral, November 15, 1980.

59 Cf. Sacred Congregation For The Doctrine Of The Faith, *Instruction On Certain Aspects of the Theology of Liberation,* Section III, n. 4 and Section IV, n. 2.

60 Gustavo Gutierrez, *A Theology of Liberation,* (Maryknoll, NY: Orbis Boooks, 1988), translation by Sister Caridad Inda and John Eagleson, p. 8.

61 Cardinal Joseph Ratzinger, address during meeting of the Congregation for the Doctrine of the Faith with the presidents of the Doctrinal Commissions of the Bishops' Conferences of Latin America, Mexico, May 1996, L'Osservatore Romano, November 6, 1996.

62 Ibid.

63 Ibid.

64 Ibid.

65 Thomas H. Groome, *Shared Christian Praxis: A Possible Theory/Method of Religious Education,* in Critical Perspectives On Christian Education, op. cit. p. 228.

66 Thomas H. Groome, *Sharing Faith,* op. cit. 232.

67 Ibid. p. 233.

68 Thomas H. Groome, *Educating for Life,* op. cit. p. 142.

69 Ibid.

70 Thomas H. Groome, *Sharing Faith,* op. cit. pp. p. 218–219.

71 Ibid. p. 219.

72 Gabriel Moran, *Theology of Revelation,* Herder and Herder, New York, 1966, p.46.

73 Ibid. p. 50.

74 Ibid.

75 Ibid. p. 55.

76 Ibid. p. 69. For a perceptive analysis of the destructive consequences for catechetics of Moran's "continuing-revelation theory" see Msgr. George A. Kelly's *The Battle for the American Church,* Doubleday, New York 1979, p. 238.

77 Thomas H. Groome, *Shared Christian Praxis: A Possible Theory/Method of Religious Education,* in Critical Perspectives On Christian Education, edited by Jeff Astley and Leslie J Francis, Gracewing, Herefordshire, 1994, p. 226.

78 *CCC,* n. 68.

79 Ibid.

80 Vatican II, *Dei Verbum,* n. 7.

81 Vatican II, *Dei Verbum,* n. 7.

82 Vatican II, *Dei Verbum,* n. 10.

83 *CCC,* n. 100.

84 Cf. Pope John Paul II, Address at the Opening of the Conference at Puebla, AAS 71 (1979), cited in *Instruction On Certain Aspects of the Theology of Liberation,* SCDF, Section XI, n. 5.

85 On such trends in theology and catechesis, see *Principles of Catholic Theology* by Cardinal Joseph Ratzinger, Ignatius Press, San Francisco 1987, p. 25.

86 Thomas Groome, *Sharing Faith,* p. 250.

87 Thomas Groome, *Sharing Faith,* p. 251.

88 Pope John Paul II, *Catechesi Tradendae,* n. 60.

89 Pope John Paul II, *Fides et Ratio,* n. 95.

90 Ibid. n. 5.

91 Ibid. n. 6.

92 Ibid. n. 28.

93 Ibid. n. 102.

94 Cardinal Joseph Ratzinger, *Principles of Catholic Theology,* op. cit. p. 319 (emphasis added).

95 Cf. Cardinal Joseph Ratzinger, *Current Situation of Faith and Theology, L'Osservatore Romano,* November 6, 1996; cf. Ratzinger *On The Modern Mind,* by Fr. James V. Schall, S.J., Homiletic and Pastoral Review, October 1997.

96 Cf. Pope John Paul II, *Catechesi Tradendae,* n. 22.

97 Cardinal Joseph Ratzinger, *Principles of Catholic Theology,* op. cit. p. 318.

98 Pope John Paul II, *L'Osservatore Romano,* June 3, 1998.

99 Thomas H. Groome, *Sharing Faith,* p. 218.

11

Chaos In Religious Education and Theology: Four Case Studies

From various places throughout the English-speaking world, reports are coming to hand which indicate that a decline in Eucharistic faith is occurring amongst Catholics. Some of these reports indicate that there is a decline also in regard to other key Christian dogmas involving the Holy Trinity and the Divinity of Christ. The same is true in regard to the Church's moral doctrine.

Referring to the decline of Eucharistic faith in the United States, Bishop William Weigand of Sacramento said:

> According to results of a Gallop survey taken in December 1991 and January 1992 on U.S. Catholic understanding of Holy Communion, only 30% believe 'they are really and truly receiving the Body and Blood, Soul and Divinity of the Lord Jesus Christ, under the appearance of bread and wine.' Some 29% think they 'are receiving bread and wine, which symbolise the spirit and teachings of Jesus and in so doing are expressing their attachment to his person and words'. Another 10% understand that they are 'receiving bread and wine, in which Jesus is really and truly present'. Twenty-three per-cent say they 'are receiving the Body and Blood of Christ, which has become that because of their personal belief. [1]

These results, said Bishop Weigand, "are terribly alarming because only the first formulation is orthodox Catholic doctrine. The others are all variations of the 16th century Protestant teachings from Luther, Calvin, Zwingli and others. We have every reason to ponder how this most central teaching of our Catholic faith got so watered down and distorted over the past 25 years."

This loss of faith in the Real Presence of Christ in the Eucharist by U.S. Catholics was further borne out by a Spring 1994 New York Times/CBS poll which showed that 70% of Catholics in the 18-44 age group think that at Mass the bread and wine serve only as mere "symbolic reminders" of Jesus rather than being changed into his Body and Blood. Commenting on these findings, Fr Kenneth Baker, S. J. said:

I can think of nothing that so indicts the quality of religious instruction in our Catholic Schools and colleges during the past thirty years as the sad results of these polls. They also indict the preaching of us priests who have failed in our duty to instruct the faithful on the basics of the faith, especially on such things as the Trinity, the Incarnation, Grace, the Sacraments and the Mass.[2]

In also expressing concern about these findings on the loss of Eucharistic faith, Germain Grisez and Russell Shaw said: "In the general crisis of the Church in the United States, no individual crisis is more serious and urgent than this one. This is not least because, as we shall see, this collapse of eucharistic faith is related, as both cause and effect, to the broader crisis".[3] Included in the causes listed by Grisez and Shaw as contributing to this loss of eucharistic faith were: erroneous theological theories; unauthorised changes in the words and gestures of the Mass; an overly casual approach to the consecrated elements; virtual elimination of Benediction and other Eucharistic devotions outside the Mass; removal of the tabernacle to an obscure place in some churches; and subversion of the sense of the sacred through sexual immorality.

In Britain, trends amongst Catholics reveal a significant decline in weekly Mass attendance. A major new survey, *The English Church Attendance Survey*, reveals that between 1988 and 1998 the percentage of Catholics attending Mass regularly at the weekend has fallen by 22 percent, i.e. from 1,715,900 in 1988 to 1,230,100 in 1998.

In Australia, the absence of young people at weekend Mass now seems to be a key issue facing the Catholic Church. In November 1996, over 100,000 Catholics were surveyed in parishes throughout Australia on a wide range of religious beliefs and practices. On the basis of an analysis of this survey by Fr. Michael Mason CSsR of the Catholic Church Life Survey, and other research contained in a book titled *Taking Stock*,[4] it now appears that only about 18 percent of Australian Catholics attend Mass regularly at the weekend. Those in the 20-29 age group have the lowest Church attendance rate with only 7 percent of them attending Mass regularly.

The research referred to above in regard to Australian Catholics shows that of the 18 percent of Catholics who regularly attend Mass, only 63 percent of those aged 15-39 accepted the article of faith that "there is one God, Father, Son and Holy Spirit," while 83 percent of those over 60 accept it. The same research showed that 83 percent of those over 60 affirmed that in the consecration of the Mass, the bread and wine "Truly become the sacred Body and Blood of Christ," while only 50 percent of those under 40 did so. When compared with the 21 other Christian denominations who were surveyed, Catholics ranked second last on the proposition: "Strongly agree Christ was God, human, rose from the dead." Only 57 percent of Mass-attending Catholics accepted these articles of faith.

While the reasons for the problems outlined above are many and complex, there can be no doubt but that a major reason is a failure in religious education in many of our Catholic schools and in the toleration of dissent in the teaching of theology-based subjects at Catholic Universities. I will now present four case studies to illustrate the type of problems I have just mentioned. While the material I present refers to Australia, I believe there are similar problems in other parts of the English-speaking world. The second case-study I will be presenting relates to a diocesan religious education curriculum based on Groome's *shared Christian praxis*.

Case Study No. 1

THE AUSTRALIAN CATHOLIC UNIVERSITY

In 1999, there was made public the results of a survey conducted by Professor Dennis McLaughlin of the beliefs, values and practices of student teachers at the Australian Catholic University (ACU).[5] According to Professor McLaughlin, the ACU is "the largest single supplier of teachers for Catholic schools" in Australia. Administered to 647 first and final year student teachers at ACU campuses in Sydney, Melbourne and Brisbane, McLaughlin's most significant findings were:

- Only one-third of student teachers interviewed believed that the bread and wine truly becomes Christ's body and blood in the Eucharist;
- 2 percent said they accepted the Church's teaching on contraception and divorce;
- 14 percent said they accepted the Church's teaching on abortion;
- 10 percent accepted the Church's teaching on premarital sex;
- 50 percent of students understood God as referring to the Blessed Trinity;
- 62 percent believed that the Church should ordain women.

The results of Professor McLaughlin's survey are not surprising given the fact that several ACU lecturers are known for their dissent from the Church's doctrine. In this regard, I have already cited in Chapter 1 the example of Kevin Treston who teaches in the School of Religious Education at the ACU in Brisbane. Many more examples could be given but in what follows I will cite just a few.

The problems regarding dissent that exist at the ACU are not confined to Australia. In this context, the outcome of the struggle going on at present in the United States over the implementation of *Ex Corde Ecclesiae* which seeks to ensure that Catholic universities are in reality what they claim to be is of vital importance and will have repercussions around the world.

The Divinity and Resurrection of Christ

The Head of the School of Theology at the ACU in Sydney is Dr. Laurie Woods. The work I am now going to cite, *The Christian Story,* was prepared by Dr. Woods for use in various Scripture units conducted at the ACU in Sydney as part of its Religious Education courses since 1995.[6]

While at times Woods speaks of Jesus as divine, he does so in a very confusing way. In reference to the passage in 2 Cor 2:5 where St. Paul says that he proclaims "Christ Jesus as Lord," Woods says: "The title Lord certainly indicates the early Christian belief that Jesus was more than human even though it is not an explicit statement of belief in the divinity of Christ."[7] In regard to the "I am" and the "bread of life" statements attributed to Jesus in St. John's Gospel, Woods asserts that "the probability is that Jesus never used such language…"[8] Regarding the relationship between Jesus and God, Woods says: "Jesus Christ was seen as being one with God without being regarded as Yahweh, the God of Hebrew history."[9] Woods asserts further that "whether Jesus saw himself as divine is a question of debate" and he adds that the Gospels "do not solve the problem because they reflect the faith of the Gospel writers and do not give us undiluted insights into the very mind of Jesus."[10]

In reference to the title "Lord" as used by St. Paul to refer to Jesus, the *CCC* says: "The title 'Lord' indicates divine sovereignty. To confess or invoke Jesus as Lord is to believe in his divinity. 'No one can say 'Jesus is Lord' except by the Holy Spirit' (1 Cor 12:3)".[11] In regard to the divine name *Yahweh* or *YHWH* and the "I Am" statements of Jesus in St. John's Gospel, the doctrine of the Church is that "Jesus reveals that he himself bears the divine name…'I Am'."[12] Jesus referred to himself as the "only Son of God" (cf. Jn 3: 16; 10: 36) and in doing so he "affirms his eternal preexistence."[13] All of this is compatible with the fact that Jesus is a **Divine Person.** Since Jesus' humanity was totally assumed by his divinity, the teaching of the Church is that from the first moment of his human existence he knew in his human mind that he was true God.

Indeed, Christ's Resurrection confirms the truth of the statements he made during his public ministry concerning his divinity: "When you have lifted up the Son of man, then you will know that I am he" (Jn 8: 28). Commenting on this, the *CCC* says: "The resurrection of the crucified one shows that he was truly 'I Am,' the Son of God and God himself."[14]

Woods casts doubt on the physical aspect of the Resurrection of Jesus. In analysing St. Paul's answer to the question—"How are people raised, and what sort of body do they have…" (cf. 1 Cor 15:35-53)—Woods says: "He [Paul] affirms that a physical body cannot enter into the glory of heaven…"[15] "By obvious implication," says Woods, "*the body of the risen Christ is also non-physical*" adding that "confirmation of this view is present in the resurrection narratives of all four Gospels."[16] In regard to Jesus' Resurrection and the account of the

Empty Tomb which appears in all four Gospels, Woods says that while "the disciples were convinced that Jesus had been raised from the dead" they "did not commit themselves to belief in an empty tomb." Having said this, Woods adds: "*The empty tomb stories were part of their belief in the resurrection but not an essential condition for it to happen.*"[17] Woods states that "Paul's idea of the transformation of the resurrection body does not require a person's physical corpse or mortal remains as necessary ingredients."[18] In the 1995 edition of The Christian Story, Woods prefaced the last sentence quoted above with this statement: "*[It] was not necessary for the tomb of Jesus to be empty in order for the disciples to believe that he had been raised from the dead.*"[19]

Christ's Resurrection "is an object of faith in that it is a transcendent intervention of God himself in creation and history" in which "the three divine persons act together as one" and "manifest their own proper characteristics."[20] In raising up "Christ his Son," the Father's power "perfectly introduced his Son's humanity, including his body, into the Trinity."[21] Therefore, Christ's Resurrection "was not a return to earthly life" as was the case with those such as Lazarus and Jairus' daughter whom Jesus raised from the dead during his public life. Instead, the resurrected body of Jesus, "authentic" and "real" though it be, "possesses the new properties of a glorious body…"[22] Consequently, "in his risen body," Christ "passes from the state of death to another life beyond time and space…his body is filled with the power of the Holy Spirit: he shares the divine life in his glorious state…"[23]

However, the *CCC* teaches that "the mystery of Christ's resurrection is a real event, with manifestations that were historically verified…"[24] It adds that the Risen Christ appeared to the disciples in "the same body that had been tortured and crucified" and that it still bore "the traces of his passion."[25] The New Testament accounts of the appearances of the Risen Christ stress the physical reality of Jesus' presence. The fact that it is really Christ himself that is present is often stressed by actual physical contact: his feet are embraced by the women (Mt 28:9), Thomas was invited to probe his wounds (Jn 20: 24-29), the other apostles were invited to touch him and see that he had indeed "flesh and bones" unlike a ghost (cf. Lk 24:39), he even had a meal with the disciples (Lk 24:30, 24: 42-43; Jn 21:12). Bearing witness to the resurrection faith he had received from the apostles, St. Ignatius of Antioch said: "I know and believe that He was in the flesh even after the Resurrection. And when he came to those with Peter He said to them: 'Here, now, touch Me, and see that I am not a bodiless ghost'. Immediately they touched Him and, because of the merging of His flesh and spirit, they believed."[26]

Consequently, from what it has been said above, it is clear that despite the transcendent dimension of Christ's Resurrection, Christian faith does not allow us to regard his resurrected body as something "non-physical" as Woods asserts. In this regard, the *CCC* states that "Christ's Resurrection cannot be interpreted as something outside the physical order."[27] Consequently, Pope John Paul II can speak of man's entry into the glory of the resurrection as a state whereby "the body will return to perfect unity and harmony with the spirit: man will no longer experience the opposition between what is spiritual and what is physical in him."[28] Having said this, the Holy Father added: "The resurrection will consist in the perfect participation of all that is physical in man in what is spiritual in him. At the same time it will consist in the perfect realisation of what is personal in man."[29] In light of this, we can say with Cardinal Ratzinger that faith in the resurrection of the body is a "profession of the real existence of God and a profession of his creation, the unconditional 'Yes' with which God stands before Creation, before matter."[30]

In view of all that has been said above, it is clear that the question as to whether or not Christ's body remained in the Tomb after his Resurrection is not one that Christians are free to answer in the affirmative. The Empty Tomb, while not in itself "a direct proof of Resurrection"—"the absence of Christ's body from the tomb could be explained otherwise"—is nonetheless "the first step toward recognising the very fact of the Resurrection."[31] Had the tomb not been empty, how could there have been continuity between the crucified body of Christ that was laid in the tomb after his death and his resurrected body?

The teaching of the Church on the relationship between the Resurrection of Jesus and the Empty Tomb is this: "The physical remains of Jesus, placed in the tomb after his death, were raised in the Resurrection. Hence, the empty tomb."[32] Consequently, in the *CCC* we read: "The empty tomb and the linen cloths lying there signify in themselves that by God's power Christ's body had escaped the bonds of death and corruption. They prepared the disciples to encounter the Risen Lord."[33]

Returning now to Dr. Woods' statements about Christ's resurrection and the Empty Tomb. The issue in all that has been said above is whether Christ rose in his body or whether he rose purely spiritually, ie. in his Spirit alone with his body remaining in the tomb. In this context, we are not discussing the precise state of Christ's risen body. This is a mystery of faith, and the Church uses various terms such as 'transformed' and 'glorified' to speak of it. By asserting that the Empty Tomb "was not an essential condition" for Christ's Resurrection "to happen", Woods is asserting that Christ's Resurrection does not exclude the possibility that his body remained in the tomb. This is a contradiction of Christian dogma.

Before I leave Woods' *The Christian Story*, I will cite just one more example where the Church's dogma is compromised. In regard to the origin of the ordained priesthood and the celebration of the Eucharist in the early Church, Woods says:

Initially there were no ordained priests...There is not enough information for us to know how certain individuals came to preside over the Eucharist in the first decades of Christianity. We can only say that they performed this function with the approval of the community. There is certainly no evidence to suggest that there was a class of professional presiders equivalent to today's priesthood.[34]

I have already dealt at length with this question in Chapter 6 where I recalled the teaching of the Council of Trent where it condemned the proposition that in the New Testament there is no external and visible priesthood instituted by Christ with the power to celebrate the Eucharist. The above assertion by Woods on the celebration of the Eucharist in the early Church is similar to the position taken by Elisabeth Schussler Fiorenza on the same question. Indeed, Woods includes Fiorenza's book *In Memory of Her* in his list of 'Further Reading'.[35]

The Origin of the Seven Sacraments and Women Priests?

In a 1997 article titled *A New Relationship Between The Ministerial and Baptismal Priesthoods,* Dr. Gideon Goosen, Associate Professor of

Theology and religious Education at the ACU in Sydney, proposed "a new conceptual framework" with which to understand the nature of the ministerial priesthood. He stated that "all ministries are sacraments" and he posited that in the future "the possible pool of candidates" for ordination will be "broadened to include the married and women." Further to this, in relying heavily on the ideas of Luther and Calvin, Goosen contradicted the solemn teaching of the Church on the origin of the Seven Sacraments. He said: "The seven sacraments...do not all go back to the historical Jesus."[36] As against this, the *CCC* in citing the solemn teaching of the Council of Trent says:

> "Adhering to the teaching of the Holy Scriptures, to the apostolic traditions, and to the consensus...of the Fathers," we profess that "the sacraments of the new law were...all instituted by Jesus Christ our Lord."[37]

Christian Ethics

Turning now to the teaching of *Christian Ethics* at the ACU in Sydney. A book that has been used as prescribed reading for several courses in Christian Ethics run at the ACU in Sydney since 1995 is titled *Freedom and Purpose: An Introduction To Christian Ethics*. This book is authored by Robert Gascoigne who is an Associate Professor and Senior Lecturer in the Department of Theology and Philosophy at the ACU in Sydney.

In referring to mortal sin, Gascoigne says: "The traditional understanding of mortal sin defined it in terms of full knowledge, full intent and grave matter. The defect of this understanding lay in its tendency to equate the degree of subjective sinfulness with objective gravity of matter, coupled with an understanding of sin in terms of individual actions."[38]

Gascoigne argues that mortal sin should be understood in terms of a "fundamental option" which he says "is a state of personal being which rejects the love of God and neighbour at the deepest and freest core of the person."[39] To illustrate what he considers to be the "defect" in the Church's teaching on mortal sin, Gascoigne cites the example of a husband who he suggests may not have committed mortal sin by freely and knowingly engaging in an act of "sexual infidelity." He says:

> "Let us consider an example: a husband who is normally faithful to his wife commits an act of sexual infidelity. He knows what he is doing and is aware that he is being unfaithful to his wife. It is an untypical action, and one that he quickly and sincerely repents of in word and deed…Clearly from the perspective of most ethical traditions what this man has done is seriously wrong. He has been unfaithful to his wife in the most intimate sphere of their relationship. He has abused the physical language of sexual relations by using it without the commitment of love."[40]

From the context in which the above quotation appears, it is clear that in using the term "sexual infidelity", Gascoigne is referring to a violation of the moral law in grave matter such as adultery. He says: "From the perspective of the traditional theory of mortal sin, this man would have been in a state of mortal sin prior to repenting of his action: one deliberate action, done with awareness, constitutes mortal sin." Having said this, Gascoigne adds: "What is highly implausible about this traditional account is how one action can totally reverse the character of someone's life. This is what the traditional account claimed, since it held that an essentially good man could make himself worthy of eternal damnation in one action."[41]

In his 1983 Apostolic Exhortation Reconciliatio et Paenitentia, Pope John Paul II rejected the theory of fundamental option as it is presented in Gascoigne's book. The Holy Father said that mortal sin cannot be reduced to a "fundamental option" in such wise as to assert that mortal sin cannot be committed through a single action in which one freely and consciously chooses to act contrary to God's commandments in a grave matter.[42] The Holy Father reaffirmed the same teaching in his encyclical Veritatis Splendor where he cited the Council of Trent which in its solemn teaching repeated St. Paul's warning in 1 Cor 6:9 that one sins mortally whenever he or she deliberately and knowingly engages in certain specific kinds of behaviour including adultery.[43] The essential content of this teaching is found also in the CCC where it says: "To choose deliberately – that is, both knowing it and willing it – something gravely contrary to the divine law and to the ultimate end of man is to commit a mortal sin. This destroys in us the charity without which eternal beatitude is impossible. Unrepented, it brings eternal death."[44] Consequently, if one "knowingly and willingly" chooses an act of intrinsic evil such as adultery, then "such a choice already includes contempt for the divine law, a rejection of God's love for humanity and the whole of creation: the person turns away from God and loses charity."[45]

Gascoigne states that "the magisterium has no unique competence or authority in the detailed knowledge required for developing specific moral norms."[46] He says that the magisterium's moral teaching "is an exercise of its ordinary, non-infallible, teaching authority"[47] and hence that "public dissent from non-infallible Church teaching can contribute to progress in the Church's understanding and can be an expression of the Christian's responsibility to conscience."[48] He adds: "The moral teaching of the magisterium calls for respect and serious reflection by members of the Church, and should only be departed from after conscientious and self-critical consideration of the relevant question."[49]

In his discussion of infallible teaching and specific moral norms, Gascoigne does not mention the fact that it is the ordinary universal magisterium that is the normal channel for the expression of the Church's infallible teaching.[50] Distinguished moral theologians such as Germain Grisez and William May argue that the core of Catholic moral teaching regarding the specific precepts of the Decalogue as these have been set forth by the teaching authority of the Church have been taught infallibly by the ordinary universal magisterium. Indeed, in condemning procured abortion and euthanasia as intrinsically evil, Pope John Paul II in *Evangelium Vitae* invoked the formula used by Vatican II to identify the infallible teaching of the ordinary universal magisterium.[51]

In *Veritatis Splendor,* Pope John Paul II stated that "circumstances or intentions can never transform an act intrinsically evil by virtue of its object into an act 'subjectively' good or defensible as a choice."[52] Gascoigne's assertion that Catholics "should only" depart from the Church's moral doctrine once they have given it serious consideration implies that a choice by such Catholics to engage in acts such as the sexual abuse and torture of children could be regarded as subjectively defensible in certain situations. To accept such a line of reasoning is equivalent to saying that the human person is a totally autonomous creator of his or her own moral truth. As opposed to such absurdity, Pope John Paul II stated in *Veritatis Splendor* that "in proclaiming the commandments of God and the charity of Christ, the Church's Magisterium also teaches the faithful specific particular precepts and requires that they consider them in conscience as morally binding."[53]

Case Study No. 2

'SHARING OUR STORY'
(A RELIGIOUS EDUCATION CURRICULUM)

The second case study I will look at is the Parramatta Diocesan Religious Education Curriculum entitled *Sharing Our Story* which is based on Groome's *shared Christian praxis.* Published in late 1991, *Sharing Our Story* was the first religious education curriculum developed in Australia spanning K-12, ie. covering all the years of primary and secondary schooling.[54] Apart from the diocese of Parramatta, the *Sharing Our Story* curriculum is used also in the dioceses of Canberra-Goulburn and Wilcannia-Forbes. Sr. Patricia Malone and Maurice Ryan have revealed that an ex-student of Groome "was a key influence on the development of the first draft of *Sharing Our Story.*"[55]

Dr. Michael Bezzina, the current Director of Religious Education and Educational Services at the Parramatta Catholic Education Office, has stated that "Parramatta's Kindergarten to Year 12 guidelines, *Sharing Our Story*, are the only ones in Australia which explicitly build on Groome's *shared Christian praxis*, albeit with a slightly modified approach."[56] Dr. Bezzina said that, according to survey work conducted as part of a 1996 review of *Sharing Our Story,* teachers, religious education coordinators and school principals in the Parramatta diocese believe that "of all the strengths of *Sharing Our Story*...the praxis method was the most commonly identified, while only 2 of the 397 respondents saw it as a weakness."[57]

Since its inception, there have been many concerns raised about *Sharing Our Story.* Bishop Kevin Manning, who was appointed Bishop of Parramatta in 1997, is now overseeing the final stages of a rewriting of *Sharing Our Story* which it is hoped will be completed sometime in 2001. In an address to the Parramatta Diocesan Schools Board in February 1999, Bishop Manning said: "A primary duty of the Bishop is to ensure that the Word of God is faithfully taught, that moral teaching is faithfully handed down, and that the faithful are guarded from every doctrine and theory which is contrary to Catholic teaching."[58]

In a paper delivered to a meeting of clergy and Catholic Education Office personnel of the Parramatta Diocese in June 1998 regarding the diocesan religious education curriculum, Fr. Peter Connelly likened Groome's *shared Christian praxis* to a "Trojan Horse" with the potential to do great damage to the faith of Catholic youth. Fr. Connelly stated that Groome's "meta approach" is "an instrument for the politicisation of the religious education process" whereby "dogma is subordinated to the political ends of shared praxis." Fr. Connelly added that given the "subjectivism and relativism" which underpins shared praxis, it is thereby "fatally flawed" and "has no place in a Catholic school system."[59]

Inclusive Language and the Holy Trinity

For the purposes of the rest of this case-study, all subsequent references to *Sharing Our Story* will be to the first edition of this religious education curriculum which was used in Parramatta and other dioceses over the period 1991- 99.

Sharing Our Story revolved around four movements:i) Life Experience; ii) The Christian Story; iii) Critical Reflection; iv) Response.[60] While some aspects of *Sharing Our Story* were praiseworthy —such as its emphasis on the need for a religious education program that will "contain a substantial intellectual component that is as rigorous in content and methodology as any other part of the curriculum"[61]—it lacked precision and clarity however in the area of doctrine.

The first area of concern is the way *Sharing Our Story* promoted inclusive language. Sometimes it did this is by inserting "inclusive" terminology into texts of Vatican II documents. For example, page 5 of the curriculum document stated:

Since everyone of whatever race, condition and age is endowed with the dignity of a person, each has an inalienable right to an education corresponding to her/his proper destiny and suited to her/his native talents...(*Declaration on Christian Education.* n.1).

Apart from this tampering with Vatican II texts, *Sharing Our Story* recommended that teachers from kindergarten onward "present God to the students through a variety of images."[62] After stating that God is "tender and affectionate, like a loving mother and father," it added that "in the Old Testament, the image of God as father and creator is complemented by the image of God as mother and nurturer."[63] Coupled with this, the document avoided using male pronouns to refer to God, e.g "God continues to reveal God's love to the world."[64]

However, when it came to teaching about the Holy Trinity, something which did not receive any systematic treatment in the document until Year 7, the topic was introduced as follows:

> There is one God.
> There are three persons in the one God:
>> Father—Creator
>> Son—Redeemer
>> Spirit—Sanctifier.[65]

Speaking about the Persons of the Holy Trinity, the Year 8 section of *Sharing Our Story* stated: "God is revealed as Creator, Son and Spirit."[66] On many occasions when *Sharing Our Story* used quotations from Sacred Scripture and Magisterial documents which contained male pronouns to refer to God or which referred to the Church as "she", it inserted the word "sic" at the end of the quotation.[67] For example, in the introduction to the Year 5 component 1 John 1:3 was quoted as follows:

> "We are declaring to you what we have seen and heard, so that you may share our life. Our life is shared with the Father and with his Son Jesus Christ. (sic)."[68]

In A.J.Bliss' *Dictionary of Foreign Words and Phrases in Current English,* the word "sic" is explained thus: "sic. (Lat. 'thus') 'thus in the original,' a parenthetic insertion in a printed quotation and citation, indicating that an error or anomalous form is exactly reproduced from the original. Sometimes used as a discreet method of calling attention to the ignorance or carelessness of an earlier writer."[69]

The Person of Christ and the Origin of the Church

When discussing questions involving doctrine, Groome often does so by making conflicting affirmations. On other occasions, he embodies dissenting opinions in deceptively ambiguous terms. Not surprisingly, then, the same type of linguistic problems appeared in the *Sharing Our Story* curriculum document. For example, in reference to the mystery of Christ we read on page 201 the following correct affirmation: "Jesus is fully God and fully human." However, on page 203 we read the following: "[It] is important that Jesus be seen as a normal Jewish person; not as a superman." Jesus was not a "normal Jewish person." Jesus was and is a "Divine Person" while his contemporaries were "human persons." Consequently, as the statement stands, and even allowing for the inaccurate use of the word 'person' often applied to Christ, contextually it still implies that there is a human person and not a divine person in Christ.

Sharing Our Story was most ambiguous in its treatment of the origin and structure of the Church. In one place it stated that "Stories precede and produce the Church."[70] To reinforce this notion of the Church as the product of subjective phenomena, *Sharing Our Story* quoted with obvious approval the following statement of William Bausch:

> The story exists first, then people are caught by it, savor it, reflect on it, retell it, preserve it, and pass it on (tradition). When many people are caught by, believe in, and celebrate the same story, you have a church.[71]

Since the Catholic Church was founded by the will of Christ, then it is contrary to Catholic doctrine to locate its origin in subjective phenomena such as stories being "caught" and "savored" as is asserted by Bausch in the passage quoted above.

In reference to the Church of Christ, *Sharing Our Story* stated: "The Church of Jesus Christ is preserved in a unique way in the Catholic Church but is not exclusively present there."[72] This statement could possibly give rise to much confusion. For example, it could be interpreted as meaning that the "Church of Jesus Christ" exists as an "entity joining together by an invisible link a number of communities of Christians in spite of their differences of faith"—a proposition which was condemned by Pope Pius XII as "an aberration of divine truth."[73] Or it could be taken to mean that the Church of Christ "is nothing more than a collection (divided, but still possessing a certain unity) of Churches and ecclesial communities"—again a proposition that has been condemned by the Magisterium.[74]

When treating of the origin and nature of the Church, it needs to be stated clearly that there exists but a single Church of Christ which "subsists in the Catholic Church, governed by the Successor of Peter and by the Bishops in communion with him."[75] In regard to other Christian denominations, a distinction needs to be drawn between those Churches (Orthodox) which have preserved a valid Episcopate and Eucharist even though they reject the Catholic doctrine of Primacy which belongs to the Bishop of Rome, and those ecclesial communities which have failed to preserve a valid Episcopate and Eucharist and who also reject the doctrine of Primacy. While the Church of Christ is present and operative in the former (Orthodox Churches) even though they lack full communion with the Catholic Church, and while the other ecclesial communities are not without "elements of sanctification and truth,"[76] nevertheless it must be stated that these other Churches and ecclesial communities "derive their efficacy from the very fullness of grace and truth entrusted to the Catholic Church."[77]

The Petrine Office

Sharing Our Story referred to St. Peter's role in the early Church in ambiguous terms. It stated that "St. Peter shared his gift of leadership in the early Church."[78] The New Testament gives many examples of Peter exercising his leadership, but to my knowledge it says nothing about him "sharing" his leadership. *Sharing Our Story* stated that "Peter was one of the chief leaders in the Jerusalem community."[79] This statement too would have needed clarification since the "Jerusalem" community was part of the Church founded by Christ and ruled by Peter.[80]

Also needing clarification would have been this statement: "The college of bishops, united with the Pope, and the General Councils, constitute the highest authority in the Church."[81] As it stands, this is an incomplete statement about authority in the Church. Regarding this, Vatican II teaches: "The Roman Pontiff, by reason of his office as Vicar of Christ, namely, and as pastor of the entire Church, has full, supreme and universal power over the whole Church, a power which he can always exercise unhindered."[82]

The Origin of the Sacraments

Sharing Our Story presented conflicting affirmations on the origin of the Sacraments. For example, in reference to the Eucharist it said: "Jesus instituted the Eucharist at the Last Supper."[83] In another place it added: "A sacrament is a sign, instituted by Christ..."[84] However, elsewhere it appeared to contradict both of these correct statements by stating: "The sacraments had their origins in the early Christian community's celebration of Jesus' presence among them."[85]

Sharing Our Story's treatment of the origin of the ministerial priesthood was somewhat similar to Groome's treatment of it. For example, in reference to the early Church it said:

> In the Early Church there was a variety of ministries which arose out of the needs of the Church of the time. St. Paul lists some of these ministries in his letters. These included: apostles, evangelists, prophets, teachers, wonder-workers, helpers, elders, overseers.[86]

The ministry of the "apostles" did not arise "out of the needs" of the early Church. Rather the apostles were placed in the Church by Christ himself who at the Last Supper conferred on them the ministerial priesthood. *Sharing Our Story* contained practically no systematic development of the sacrament of Holy Orders. When describing the various ways in which Jesus is present in the Mass, it frequently failed to mention his presence in the person of the ordained priest.[87] Nowhere in the document was it stated that in the Mass and in the sacrament of penance the ordained priest acts in the person of Christ the Head.[88] This is an area of Catholic doctrine senior high school students are well capable of studying and if treated properly could enhance their appreciation for the sacrament of Holy Orders.

Speaking of the Sacrament of Penance, *Sharing Our Story* said: "In the Sacrament of Penance the priest proclaims the forgiveness of sins in the name of the Church."[89] Later it added: "Absolution—the priest assures and proclaims to the penitent God's love and forgiveness."[90] This last statement represented something of a reductionist interpretation of the efficaciousness of absolution. Certainly the priest "assures" and "proclaims" God's love and forgiveness as part of the spiritual direction that should go with the Sacrament of Penance, but the actual absolution is both a sacramental and juridical act in which the priest acting "in the person of Christ the Head" absolves the penitent.

Binding Moral Norms

In *Sharing Our Story*, there was no mention of binding moral norms but only of "ideals."[91] Neither was there any reference to the binding force of the Church's moral doctrine. A strong case could be made that one section of *Sharing Our Story* dealing with "Decision Making" and the resolution of "moral dilemmas" was proportionalist and consequentialist in its orientation.[92]

Sharing Our Story stated that Jesus called us to "a radical questioning rather than a radical obedience."[93] Cardinal Joseph Ratzinger says: "The principle by which a club develops is personal taste; but the principle on which the Church is based is obedience to the call of the Lord as we see it in the Gospel: 'He called them, and immediately they left the boat and their father and followed Jesus' (Mt 4:21f.)."[94]

Original Sin was never mentioned in *Sharing Our Story*. While the document did mention "social sin" it did not explicitly mention "mortal sin" or "venial sin." The document stated that for the early Christians, "the normal means of obtaining forgiveness of post-baptismal sins was in the Sacrament of the Eucharist."[95] This was certainly not true for mortal sins such as adultery, murder and apostasy.

Sharing Our Story presented the three rites of the Sacrament of Penance in such a way as might easily suggest that the practice of either rite can be valid for any situation.[96] That *Sharing Our Story* should have presented such an incompetent catechesis on sin and sacramental penance is not surprising since Groome asserts that the Catholic doctrine which ordinarily requires private confession of sins to a priest for purposes of absolution is expressive of a lack of awareness of the social dimension of sin.[97]

The "Teacher References" section of the *Sharing Our Story* curriculum document was heavily laden with authors noted for their dissent from the Church's teaching. The list included: Thomas Groome, Richard McBrien, Karl Rahner, William Bausch, Hans Kung, Edward Schillebeeckx, Leonardo Boff, Bernard Haring, Anthony Kosnik, Timothy O'Connell and Tad Guzie.

Sharing Our Story: 1993 Support Units

The *Sharing Our Story* project which had such an influence on religious education in Australia for the whole of the 1990s cannot be viewed in isolation from the *Support Documents* that were produced to help with its implementation. A 1997 article co-authored by members of the R.E Department of the Parramatta CEO reveals that a review of *Sharing Our Story* conducted in 1996 by members of the R.E Department at Australian Catholic University, pointed out that one of the "strengths" of the *Sharing Our Story* Curriculum was "the collaborative process used in developing the support documents based on *shared Christian praxis*."[98] In saying this, the CEO personnel also revealed that "inexperienced teachers" tended "to be too dependent" on the support materials which "became largely the material teachers used" for the "critical reflection movement."[99]

In the review of the Support Units which follows, I will confine my attention to the ones for Years 11 and 12. The release of the first edition of these Years 11 and 12 Support Units in 1993 gave rise to much public controversy. In the Units dealing with Christology, Ecclesiology (Church), Human Relationships and Decision Making, correct doctrinal statements were muddled up with ones that were erroneous and in many cases contradictory.

Christology

One exercise, a Quiz on page 15 of the *Who Is Jesus* Support unit, asked the students to answer True (T) or False (F) to the following proposition: "Because Jesus was God, he knew from his earliest years what lay in store for him?" The answer required as correct by the authors of the Support Unit was "F" (**False**). This official answer is wrong—it bases itself on the theories of some contemporary theologians who are simply repeating the Agonite heresy which attributed ignorance to the humanity of Christ.[100]

On page 25 of the same Support Unit we read: "It took many years of reflection on this [Resurrection of Jesus] for them [disciples] to be able to say in words: JESUS IS GOD. They began to speak of Jesus' earthly life in terms of this realization." From what was stated here, it can only be concluded that in Christ there took place an apotheosis, meaning that man becomes God as distinct from the Christian belief that through the possession of the gift of sanctifying grace man enters "into communion with the Word" through which he becomes "a son of God" and hence "a partaker in the divine life."[101]

Some other items of serious concern in the Christology and Ecclesiology parts of the 1993 Support Units included the following:

- the definition of Christ's Divinity by the Council of Nicaea was described as the official mythologisation of Christianity;

- the material implicitly denied that the Church was founded by Christ;

- the material asserted that the teaching of the Church whereby we are ransomed and reconciled with God through Christ's death on the Cross is merely a historical model for interpreting the Crucifixion which no longer "holds sway,"

- the claim that the Second Vatican Council redefined the role of the Pope as the "first among equals,"

- a suggested activity wherein students consider possible future trends in the Church including women priests, a female Pope, and the abolition of the Church's hierarchical structure.

Morality

The morality section of the 1993 *Sharing Our Story* Support Units was spread largely across the *Human Relationships* and *Decision Making* topics. The Support Units listed Anthony Kosnik's book *Human Sexuality* as a teacher reference. The book was written by a committee of the Catholic Theological Society of America under the leadership of Kosnik. The book sought to justify many forms of sexual perversion on the grounds that they may be conducive to "*creative growth towards integration.*" For example, it sought to justify under certain conditions the following: artificial insemination by a donor (cf. p. 139), adultery and mate swapping (cf. pp. 151-152), premarital sexual intercourse (cf. pp. 159-165), homosexual acts (cf. p. 215), sterilization and contraception even if it is abortifacient (cf. pp. 114-136).[102]

The Committee on Doctrine of the U.S. Conference of Catholic Bishops issued a statement in November 1977 condemning the Kosnik book. The Sacred Congregation for the Doctrine of the Faith also issued a statement condemning *Human Sexuality* and it ordered Paulist Press to stop publication and distribution. Despite this, however, one suggested activity in the *Sharing Our Story* Support Units involved giving the students a handout comprised of several pages taken from the Kosnik book. Entitled *The Virtue of Chastity*, these pages contained the following statement:

> Chastity calls one to a generous pursuit of that creative growth toward integration that is the purpose of human sexuality. This remains true for any way of life, that is for the married, unmarried, celibate, or homosexual...Only in the context of one's state of life can the expression of human sexuality be evaluated properly. This approach bespeaks the conviction that, morally speaking, attitudes, patterns, and habits that reflect a continuing lifestyle are far more significant than individual, isolated acts.[103]

The Support Units also gave an inadequate explanation of conscience. In the *Human Relationships* Unit, one suggested activity entailed giving a handout to students containing two pages on Church teaching about conscience supplemented by four pages from Kosnik. In these pages, Kosnik states that intrinsically evil acts such as masturbation, direct sterilisation, contraception, and premarital sex cannot be regarded as prohibited by universal and absolute moral norms (cf. pp. 78-83).

In late 1993 and early 1994, several priests in the Parramatta Diocese expressed concern about the contents of the Support Units and called for their withdrawal. Eventually, news of the Support Units found its way into the national media in response to which one of the priests who had earlier expressed concern about them received a letter dated 10th March 1994 from the Secretary of the Association of Secondary School Principals in the Parramatta Diocese which said:

> The Association publicly expresses its confidence in the Department of Religious Education and Educational Services of the CEO, commending its team for the curriculum programme, *Sharing Our Story,* and its support documents which

have been so warmly and enthusiastically received in the schools of the Diocese. These have enabled our students to approach our Catholic tradition in an intelligent, informed and faithful way.

Sharing Our Story: 1995 Support Units

In response to the controversy that was occasioned by the appearance of the 1993 Years 11 and 12 *Support Units,* the Parramatta CEO undertook a review of the materials and issued a new edition of them in February 1995. While some of the most objectionable material in the 1993 Support Units did not appear in the 1995 edition, there was still much in the new edition that was of concern.

Christology

The 1995 *Who Is Jesus?* Support Unit asserted as a matter of fact that the words of Jesus recorded in the Gospels are simply retrojection by the Evangelists. In relation to the Gospel of St. Matthew, we read:

Students may have trouble with the idea of Jesus 'predicting' conflict in the community because of him. The author, of course, is 'writing back' the very real conflicts that were happening in his community, between the Pharisees and the followers of Jesus, as if they were being predicted by Jesus. (p. 30).

In reference to St. John's Gospel, the Support Unit states:

The Apostle John whose name the Gospel bears was not the author, but the work comes from the traditions of his community. In reading John's Gospel, the question of what theologians call *Low* and *High Christology* arises. *A High Christology* such as we find in John, shows the earthly Jesus as he was later recognised to be: the divine, all-knowing, glorious saviour and Messiah. For example John puts the words into Jesus' mouth: *Before Abraham was, I am* John 8:48 [sic]. On the other hand, a

Low Christology depicts Jesus as he would have been during his life (p. 31).

The 1995 *Who Is Jesus?* Support Unit relied heavily on a biblical studies approach to Christology. It "especially recommended" for student use a book called *Jesus, Mystery and Surprise: An Introduction to the Study of the Gospels* by Gideon Goosen and Margaret Tomlinson.[104]

This Goosen/Tomlinson book contradicts the doctrine of the Church. For example, in regard to Jesus' consciousness of the salvific meaning of his Crucifixion, Goosen/ Tomlinson ask: "Did Jesus himself know the saving (soteriological) power of his death?"—to which they answer: "We do not know" (p.125). The Support Units themselves reproduced this error in somewhat different form. On page 48 par. 5 of the *Who Is Jesus* Unit we read: "Jesus, as he became more aware of his call, gravitated to the poor and marginalised".

In casting doubt on the truth that Our Lord was always fully aware of the implications of his mission, Goosen/Tomlinson are reducing Christ to the condition of a mere man—they are presenting us with an Arian Christ. This particular form of "Christological humanism" has been condemned by the Magisterium of the Church. On 24 July 1966, the Sacred Congregation for the Doctrine of the Faith, citing erroneous interpretations of Vatican II's Christological teaching declared:

> It is regrettable that bad news from various places has arrived of abuses prevailing in interpreting the teaching of the Council, and of strange and bold opinions arising here and there which greatly disturb the souls of many of the faithful...There creeps forth a certain Christological humanism in which Christ is reduced to the condition of a mere man, who gradually acquired consciousness of His divine Sonship.

Contrary to Goosen's and Tomlinson's remarks about Christ's limited knowledge, the *CCC* says: "The human nature of God's Son, *not by itself but by its union with the Word,* knew and showed forth in itself everything that pertains to God."[105] To this, the *CCC* adds: "By its union to the divine wisdom in the person of the Word incarnate, Christ enjoyed in his human knowledge the fullness of understanding of the eternal plans he had come to reveal".[106] On the basis of this truth, the

CCC goes on to say: "Jesus knew and loved us each and all during his life, his agony, and his Passion and gave himself up for each one of us: 'The Son of God...loved me and gave himself for me'(Gal 2:20)."[107]

The 1995 Support Units make many confusing and erroneous assertions. For example, on page 26 of the *Who Is Jesus?* Unit we read: "At the Resurrection the disciples experienced Jesus. He had died. He was now alive. He was changing them, because his Spirit was with them and in them. It took many years of reflection on this for them to be able to say in words: Jesus is God."

From its very beginning, the Church has acknowledged the Divinity of Christ.[108] For example, in St. John's Gospel we hear the Apostle Thomas make a profession of faith in Jesus as "My Lord and my God" (Jn 20:28-29). Explaining the relevance of the term "Lord" as applied to Jesus in the New Testament, the *CCC* says: "In the Greek translation of the Old Testament, the ineffable Hebrew name YHWH, by which God revealed himself to Moses, is rendered as *Kyrios,* 'Lord'. From then on, *'Lord'* becomes the more usual name by which to indicate the divinity of Israel's God. The New Testament uses this full sense of the title 'Lord' both for the Father and—what is new for Jesus, who is thereby recognised as God Himself."[109] Having said this, the *CCC* then adds: "By attributing to Jesus the divine title 'Lord,' the first confessions of the Church's faith affirm from the beginning that the power, honour, and glory due to God the Father are due also to Jesus."[110]

As the above examples indicate, a striking characteristic of the biblical sections of the 1995 Support Units was that there was little if any mention of inspiration, inerrancy or historicity. The Units implied that form criticism and biblical criticism are exact sciences. At best, the conclusions reached from applying the tools of scientific analysis to the interpretation of the Bible are more or less acceptable opinions depending on the extent to which they agree with the teaching of the Church. At worst, they are a vehicle whereby preconceived ideas are given legitimacy.

The general impression given by the 1995 Support Units was that the Bible is just another ancient text. Also, the emphasis in the Unit on "experience" and "meaning" betrayed a heavy dependence upon Groome's *shared Christian praxis* and on the principles underlying Liberal Protestantism. The use of the term "faith" tended to underline subjective rather than objective content..

Ecclesiology

Other authors referred to in the Christology and Ecclesiology sections of the 1995 Support Units were Leonardo Boff, Albert Nolan and Paul Collins. The *Who Is Jesus* Unit contained an entire chapter from one of Boff's books which it recommended be given to the students. In these pages, Boff refers to Jesus' mission as a "utopic project."[111] Coupled with this, he equates the coming of the Kingdom of God with the process of class struggle.[112] He places his model of Church based on a "Communitarian Christianity" in opposition to the historical institutional Church founded by Christ. In doing this, he casts doubt on the truth that the hierarchical structure of the Church was established by Christ. He says:

> Communitarian Christianity, fruit of the new evangelisation, rests on 'witness persons' far more than on institutions. Therefore it is more like a movement of Jesus and the apostles than the ecclesiastical structurization that began in the third century and has predominated in conventional Christianity down to our own day, under the hegemony of the clergy.[113]

Boff's anti-hierarchical attitude was further reinforced in the student handouts taken from Fr. Paul Collins' *Mixed Blessings.* Here Collins locates the origin of the hierarchical Church in the 11th century.[114] In *Mixed Blessings,* Collins asserts that "the priesthood as we know it today did not emerge as a separate ministry in the Church until the fourth century."[115] He asserts that "although it has never been admitted, the basis of discrimination against women playing any part in the Church's liturgical ministry lies largely in the concept of ritual purity."[116]

Morality

In the 1995 Support Units, the treatment of conscience in the *Decision Making* Unit was again inadequate. In defining conscience it says: "Conscience can be said to be 'a general sense of values, an awareness of personal responsibility, which is utterly characteristic of the human person" (p.17). This definition of conscience was taken from the 1976 edition of Timothy O'Connell's book on moral principles. In 1990, O'Connell published a revised edition of this book in which he repudiated the proportionalism of the earlier edition referred to here in the Support Unit.[117] On page 3 of the *Decision Making* Unit we read: "Conscience provides the main focus in any discussion of morality. Conscience is the capacity to make responsible decisions for oneself in relation to others and in relation to one's environment."

In *Veritatis Splendor*, Pope John Paul II gives a proper definition of conscience where he says it is not a "creative" decision but rather a "judgement" drawn from moral truths, including the negative precepts of the Decalogue which oblige in every case.[118] It is interesting to note that while *Veritatis Splendor* was listed once in a resource section of the 1995 Support Units, there was no mention of it elsewhere in the materials.

In conjunction with the inadequate presentation of the Church's teaching on conscience, the 1995 *Decision Making* Unit contained eight pages on Kohlberg's moral development theory (cf. pp. 24-31). Kohlberg divided moral development into six stages. When one finally arrived at the famous stage six, moral development was said to have peaked. Kohlberg designated this the stage of *Universal Principle Orientation* wherein he defined right as a decision in conscience which accorded with self-chosen ethical principles.

It is interesting to note that Groome held Kohlberg's six stage moral development theory in such high regard that he even hypothesised "that there are six corresponding stages in the ability of a person to engage in critical reflection." In consequence of this, Groome held that it was appropriate "to ground the very earliest efforts at formal Christian education in an approach that causes children to reflect on their lives as critically as they can in order to promote authentic Christian engagement in the world."[119] Hence did Groome claim that a *shared praxis* approach to religious education can begin from the first moment of formal education.[120]

Kohlbergian moral development theory is now generally rejected by both educators and moral philosophers.[121] It is inherently relativistic and exposure to educational techniques based upon it tend to leave people with the false impression that morality is only a question of personal opinion rather than right reason and Divine Law. Kohlberg committed suicide by drowning himself in Boston Harbour in 1987. Before his death, he admitted that there were serious defects in his moral development theory.

Due to the relativistic nature of his moral development theory, Kohlberg could not offer any reproach to his feminist colleague Carol Gilligan when she ranked the decision to abort as a Stage 6 choice. We can note that Groome speaks with praise of Gilligan's contribution to moral discourse. In noting the contribution of "feminist" ideas to the development of an "intentional ethic of care that emphasises relationship and responsibility rather than individual rights and rational certainty," Groome attributes the "classic expression of this ethic" to Gilligan.[122]

A great weakness of the morality section of the 1995 Support Units was that the moral doctrine of the Church was reduced to the level of mere "ideals." In the Unit on *Human Relationships* we read: "The official teaching of the Church always aims to set the ideal before people, giving guidance and support to achieve this ideal..." (p. 79). For many people today, the word 'ideal' denotes something which is capable of existing only as a mental or imaginary concept. In *Veritatis Splendor,* Pope John Paul II rejected the notion that the moral doctrine of the Church can be reduced to mere "ideals". He said:

> It would be a very serious error to conclude...that the Church's [moral] teaching is essentially only an 'ideal' which must then be adapted, proportioned, graduated to the so-called concrete possibilities of man...But what are the 'concrete possibilities of man'? And of which man are we speaking? Of man *dominated* by lust or of man *redeemed* by Christ? This is what is at stake: the *reality* of Christ's redemption. *Christ has redeemed us!* This means that he has given us the possibility of realising the *entire* truth of our being; he has set our freedom free from the *domination* of concupiscence.[123]

The adverse consequences of reducing the Church's moral doctrine to mere 'ideals' in the 1995 Support Units became all too apparent in the *Human Relationships* Unit which dealt with the question of the reception of the Eucharist by the divorced and remarried. In regard to the case of a person who, after a failed petition for annulment, contracts a second marriage on the basis of a personal conviction that the first marriage was invalid, the Support Unit material said:

Where a case cannot be proved—for lack of witnesses, for instance—but the person feels convinced that the marriage was not valid, the Church fully respects a conscience decision to remarry, although it will not publicly authorise the remarriage. It recognises the right of such a remarried person to receive Holy Communion in good conscience, scandal being avoided (p. 80).

The statement above—based as it is on the so-called *Internal Forum* solution to the question of divorce, remarriage and the reception of the Eucharist—contradicts Catholic sacramental and moral doctrine. The Church, basing itself on the words of Jesus in the Gospel, teaches that marriage according to the design of the Creator is of its nature indissoluble so that no human power can dissolve it. Consequently, the Church teaches that attempts to "remarry" after a divorce are not efficacious and therefore sexual relations of divorced persons who have attempted remarriage are not marital but rather are adulterous.[124] In *Familiaris Consortio,* Pope John Paul II explicitly mentioned the most difficult case—those who are "subjectively certain" in conscience that their previous marriage was not valid.[125] He said:

[The] Church reaffirms her practice, which is based upon Sacred Scripture, of not admitting to Eucharistic Communion divorced persons who have remarried. They are unable to be admitted thereto from the fact that their state and condition of life objectively contradict that union of love between Christ and the Church which is signified and effected in the Eucharist.[126]

In 1994, the Congregation for the Doctrine of the Faith issued with the approval of Pope John Paul II a Letter to the Bishops of the world calling on them to defend and explain the teaching of the Church on marriage. In this Magisterial statement we read:

In fidelity to the words of Jesus Christ, the Church affirms that a new union cannot be recognised as valid if the preceding marriage was valid. If the divorced are remarried civilly, they find themselves in a situation that objectively contravenes God's law. Consequently, they cannot receive Holy Communion as long as this situation persists. [127]

I think I have described enough of the *Sharing Our Story* project to demonstrate what can happen to a religious education curriculum that bases itself on Groome's *shared Christian praxis.* Referring to Movement 3 of *shared Christian praxis,* Dr. Michael Bezzina stated in 1997 that a "close reading" of Groome reveals that it "does not, in fact, rely on simplistic assertions of faith." Quoting Groome, Bezzina added that the *shared Christian praxis* approach is one which "advises religious educators to approach the faith tradition" from the perspective of a "hermeneutics of suspicion" that will "help people to recognise" that much that "has been proudly told must be confessed as sin; and much that has been obscured and silenced must be given voice'."[128]

Case Study No. 3

'Out Of The Desert' (A Series of Religious Education Texts for Secondary Students)

This case-study deals with a popular series of religious education text books entitled *Out of the Desert.* To date, three books covering Years 7-9 have been published. There have been several authors involved in writing the series: Books One and Two have been authored by Janet Morrissey, Peter Mudge and Adam Taylor; while Book Three has been authored by Greg Wilson, Janet Morrissey and Peter Mudge. Both Morrissey and Taylor have held positions as Religious Education coordinators in Catholic schools, while Mudge is a Religious Education officer at the Parramatta Catholic Education Office where Wilson is also employed as Head of the Religious Education and Spiritual Formation Division. Wilson co-authored the article referred to in Chapter 1 which stated that *shared Christian praxis* is "by far the most admirable faith forming religious education model available today because of its educational and theological precision." This was the same article which called for professional development of teachers which would allow for an "implementation" of *shared Christian praxis* which would be "faithful to Groome's thinking."[129]

Mudge states that while the *Out of the Desert* series "is based on the sequence of modules for the Sydney Archdiocesan program Faithful to

God, Faithful to People," it is at the same time "equally inclusive of other Catholic curricula in use throughout Australia, stretching from Brisbane, Parramatta and Melbourne, through Adelaide and Perth." Mudge adds that the series are "even cognisant of cross Tasman interests such as the Australian version of the New Zealand Understanding Faith series."[130]

Mudge says that the title *Out of the Desert* "connotes a liminal zone" that "has flavoured the biblical accounts of the desert which, like the liminal Australian beach, is both a barrier and a means of communication."[131] He says that the "liminality that the desert metaphor evokes is also reflected in the text itself —at once a territory of danger and new life, mainstream and margins, old and new wineskins."[132] In stating that "the series is written with the Catholic school market in mind," Mudge adds that some of the features of the series is its focus on "Australia's multicultural society; the nature of an Australian spirituality; the spirit of Vatican II and other contemporary movements in theology; an integrated vision of future church and society; and practical activities for reflection and action."[133]

In an article describing the methodology underpinning *Out of the Desert,* Mudge says that the series is "committed to the importance of connected knowing" and he adds that the "academic literature on 'connected knowing' posits that the most trustworthy knowledge comes from personal experience rather than the pronouncements of authorities."[134] This, says Mudge, explains "the emphasis throughout the series on really understanding the personal experiences behind a topic, both those of the people involved and the students themselves."[135] In reference to the various ways of knowing, Mudge states that the *Out of the Desert* series "embodies a clear rejection" of "what Freire terms 'the banking model of education', lamented by him as that process by which students store isolated fragments of knowledge rather than an interconnected synthesis of the topic."[136] Mudge concludes this article with a lengthy quotation from Groome's *Sharing Faith.*

The Foundation of the Church By the Will of Christ

Regarding the foundation of the Church, Book One (Year 7) of *Out of the Desert* states:

In the beginning there was Jesus' ministry of preaching and healing. Jesus did not set out on purpose to found 'the church' in person. Those who followed Jesus formed the church. Instead, Jesus had gathered a group of disciples who went about with him and whom he sent to preach and heal as he himself had done (see Matthew 10:1, Luke 6:13-16). After the death and resurrection of Jesus, there were gradual moves to form a more organised group which we today call the early church.[137]

The Catholic Church was universal from its very beginning. This, says Cardinal Ratzinger, "is obviously the message Saint Luke wants to convey in his account of Pentecost, where he tells us that even before there were congregations, there was already the Catholic Church, the Church of all peoples."[138] In speaking of the way Christ is related to the Church, the scholarly Cardinal added: "Christ is not related to the Church the way the founder of some association or other is bound to the association he has founded. He did not found the Church as an association; he did not found her by a series of separate actions, but by being, himself, the grain of wheat that dies."[139]

In speaking of the foundation of the Church, the First Vatican Council declared: "The eternal Shepherd...decided to establish his holy Church in which the faithful would be united, as in the house of the living God, by bonds of the same faith and charity."[140] In its turn, the Second Vatican Council stated: "The one mediator, Christ, established and ever sustains here on earth his holy Church, the community of faith, hope and charity, as a visible organisation through which he communicates grace to all men."[141] Elsewhere in the teaching of Vatican II we read: "The Catholic Church was founded by Christ our Lord to bring salvation to all men."[142] The *CCC* points out that while the Church was prepared for in the Old Covenant, it was nevertheless "Christ who instituted the New Covenant" and thus "the Church is born primarily of Christ's total self-giving for our salvation, anticipated in the institution of the Eucharist and fulfilled on the cross."[143]

That Christ purposely set out to found the Church is an article of Catholic faith. The *Commentary on the Concluding Formula of the 'Professio fidei,'* which was published by the Congregation for the Doctrine of the Faith in 1998 in order to shed light on the significance of some sections in Pope John Paul II's *Ad Tuendam Fidem*, stated that "the foundation of the Church by the will of Christ" is an article of Catholic faith.[144] This

CDF Commentary also pointed out that anyone who "obstinately" places in doubt or "denies" dogmas such as that which declares the Church to be founded by the will of Christ thereby falls "under the censure of heresy, as indicated by the respective canons of the Code of Canon Law."[145]

The Origin of the Church's Hierarchical Structure

Book Three of *Out of the Desert* distorts the teaching of the Magisterium on the hierarchical structure of the Church. Referring to the role of Peter in the early Church it says:

> Peter's was a communal leadership, as he consulted with and sent out the other apostles to proclaim the Gospel (Acts 8:14) and acted as a team with John (Acts 3:1-11, 4:1-22), 'the disciple Jesus loved' (Jn 13:23-25). So although centred around Peter, John, James and eventually Paul, the young Church was a model of 'unity in diversity'.[146]

Since the Church has never been acephalous, is *Out of the Desert* not confusing collegiality with common-ism (the taking of decisions by a common vote) in the passage quoted above? Book Three of *Out of the Desert* goes on in another throw-away statement to say that "the church is primarily a mystery or sacrament, not primarily a hierarchical organisation."[147] To oppose the Church as an hierarchical organisation to the Church as a mystery or sacrament is to introduce a false dichotomy; the Church is inextricably all three by virtue of her origin in Christ.

Indeed, Book Three of *Out of the Desert* goes on to repudiate entirely the teaching of the Magisterium that the hierarchical nature of the Church is of Divine origin. Referring to changes that took place in the Church under Pope Gregory VII, and taking its clue from Paul Collins' *Mixed Blessings,* it states: "Pope Gregory VII (1073-85) and his successors introduce a hierarchical, centralised church, aspects of which still remain to day."[148] We have already seen in previous chapters that it is the infallible teaching of the Magisterium that it was Christ who established the hierarchical Church. Consequently, Pope Gregory VII did not introduce the "hierarchical church" but instead he merely reasserted papal authority.

Cardinal Ratzinger points out that a characteristic of early gnosticism was its anti-hierarchical and anti-institutional orientation.[149] The notion that Christ did not set out on purpose to found an hierarchically structured Church was also one of the heresies propagated by the modernists during the nineteenth and early twentieth centuries. Modernism, in its Catholic form, was a movement that rejected the dogmatic principle in Catholicism, as well as many of the historical elements upon which it was founded, in order to adapt it to new directions being set by post-Enlightment thought.

The leading figures of Modernism were Loisy in France, Tyrrell in England, Schell in Germany, Murri and Fogazzaro in Italy. Alfred Loisy (1857-1940) postulated that Christianity had no fixed core of beliefs that were independent of historical and cultural conditioning. Arguing that it was not possible to say definitely that Christ was God and that nowhere in the New Testament did Christ display any consciousness whatever of his being divine, Loisy eventually lost his faith in Christ's divinity. He ridiculed Catholic dogma on the Eucharist and rejected the Church's teaching on the Virgin birth and bodily resurrection of Jesus. Most importantly for our present discussion, Loisy stated that "the Church was not instituted by Jesus during his lifetime but was born of faith in the glorified Christ."[150]

Modernism was condemned by the Church in two principal documents: the decree *Lamentabili* in July 1907 and the Encyclical *Pascendi* of Pope St. Pius X in September of that same year. In *Pascendi*, Pope Pius X defined Modernism as the "synthesis of all heresies."[151] In order to prevent the spread of modernism, the Church in 1910 introduced an *Oath Against Modernism* which had to be taken by priests, theologians and bishops. Amongst other things, this *Oath Against Modernism* stated "that the Church, the guardian and teacher of the revealed word, was established immediately and directly *[proxime ac directo institutam]* by the true and historic Christ while he lived among us." In conjunction with this, the Decree *Lamentabli* condemned the modernist error which asserted that "it was far from the mind of Christ to establish a Church as a society that would last on earth for a long succession of centuries."

It is perplexing to read the interpretation the authors of *Out of the Desert* place on the actions of the Church in responding to the Modernist threat. They say:

Modernism emerged at the beginning of the twentieth century as a major threat to traditional Catholic orthodoxy ('correct belief') and brought with it the classic tension between old and new. Modernism was condemned by Pope Pius X (1902-1914) in 1907, and from 1910 onwards for many years, bishops, pastors and theologians were required to swear an oath against modernism The effects of anti-modernism continued to discourage research and educated enquiry. As a result, Catholic scholarship fell into a fifty-year depression—broken only by some encyclicals of Pius XII—and only began to recover before Vatican II (1962-65).[152]

The statement above displays a certain lack of understanding of the real questions involved in the Modernist crisis. On the occasion of St. Pius X's death in 1914, an editorial in the *London Times*, representing an Anglican view in regard to the pontificate of the late Pope, praised him for having defended the basic tenets of Christianity against Modernist heresies. It said:

The sweeping condemnation of 'Modernism' was the most conspicuous act of his pontificate within the domain of dogma...Few persons familiar with the elementary doctrines of the Roman Church would suppose that the tendencies of the new school were compatible with them. To the downright plain sense of the Pope the desperate efforts of men who had explained away the content of historical Christianity to present themselves as orthodox Roman Catholics were simply disingenuous.[153]

Modernism never died out in the Church. In the decades following the publication of *Lamentabli* and *Pascendi*, there were some Catholics who reviled Pope St. Pius X to the point of impugning his personal sanctity on the grounds that he overreacted to the modernists by condemning them prematurely and too harshly. However, in *Fides et Ratio*, Pope John Paul II remarked that in publishing his encyclical *Pascendi*, Pope St. Pius X thereby performed a great service for the Church and society by condemning modernist errors on the grounds of their "phenomenist, agnostic and immanentist" claims.[154]

Development of Doctrine

In places, *Out of the Desert* misrepresents the way doctrine develops in the Church. For example, in one place we read:

> The articles of the Creed do not have meaning apart from Scripture, and while we could spend years arguing about what is meant by 'incarnate from the Virgin Mary' and 'on the third day he rose again,' what it is really all about is how we as individuals and as a community of believers communicate 'God is love' to each other and to the whole world.[155]

What are we to make of the statement quoted above? Does it mean that Sacred Scripture and Tradition do not refer us to objective realities? For example, does not the expression "incarnate from the Virgin Mary" not mean that Jesus' "virginal conception is a biological fact"?[156]Consequently, does this credal statement not mean that Jesus "was conceived 'by the Holy Spirit without human seed" in the womb of the Virgin Mary and that consequently in the Revelation of this great mystery it is made known to us "that it truly was the Son of God who came in a humanity like our own"?[157]

Death's Entry Into Human History

In a section dealing with the story of the 'Fall' in the early chapters of Genesis, Book Two of *Out of the Desert* says:

> The story is not strictly a myth of falling into sin and guilt— only what has been elevated can fall! Nor is it about the tragic fall of an innocent first couple, a once-upon-a-time story when our ancestors were perfect, aware of themselves and of God. Then they made a sinful choice, and because of it little children are already guilty in their mother's womb: we have all become bad.[158]

Instead, says *Out of the Desert*, the story of the 'Fall' in the book of Genesis "is about losing our freedom by not trusting in God" and "nowhere in the story does it say that our first parents sinned!"[159] Having said this, it adds:

> It should also be noted that no one dies in the story. The Bible is not interested in questions about the theory of sin, death or evil. It is concerned instead with the right way to respond to God. Death is part of God's design for human life. 'You are dust and to dust you shall return' (Gen 3:19) does not mean that death is a punishment for sin.[160]

To lend substance to their assertion that death was from the beginning intended by God as a necessary part of human experience, the authors of *Out of the Desert* state: "Death is natural and necessary, otherwise the world would become overcrowded. We have to leave room for those who follow us."[161]

The doctrine of Original Sin and its effects has great significance for our understanding of the doctrine of the Redemption. Given that man was created in the supernatural order, death is a consequence of Original Sin and in this sense not intended by God. On the hypothesis that man was created simply in the natural order, then death would be natural.

The *CCC* states that "The account of the fall in Genesis 3 uses figurative language, but affirms a primeval event, a deed that took place at the beginning of the history of man."[162] The Council of Trent defined it as an article of Catholic faith that through Adam's sin at the beginning of human history, justice and holiness were lost and the punishment of death was incurred. It said:

> If anyone does not confess that the first man, Adam, when he transgressed the commandment of God in paradise, immediately lost the holiness and justice in which he had been constituted, and through the offence of that prevarication incurred the wrath and indignation of God, and thus death with which God previously threatened him...let him be anathema.[163]

The dogmatic teaching of Trent that death is a consequence of original sin is based on the teaching of Sacred Scripture. In the Book of

Wisdom we read: "God did not make death, and he does not delight in the death of the living...It was through the devil's envy that death entered the world." (Wis 1:13; 2:24). In the New Testament, the principal text on the doctrine of Original Sin and its relationship to the entry of death into human history is found in St. Paul's Letter to the Romans where it says: "sin came into the world through one man, and death came through sin, and so death spread to all because all have sinned." (Rom 5:12).

The solemn teaching of Trent that death was incurred as a result of original sin was repeated by Vatican II when it said man must suffer "bodily death from which he would be immune had he not sinned."[164] This teaching was also reaffirmed in the *Catechism of the Catholic Church*.[165]

From what has been said above, it is clear that the authors of *Out of the Desert* are in contradiction of the dogmatic teaching of the Catholic Church when they assert that "death is part of God's design for human life" and that "death is not a punishment for sin."

Given the significance of the doctrine of Original Sin and the way in which it is contradicted in *Out of the Desert*, what then can we say of Mudge's claim that *Out of the Desert* is "committed to the importance of connected knowing" which posits "that the most trustworthy knowledge comes from personal experience rather than the pronouncements of authorities."[166] Given *Out Of The Desert*'s contradiction of the Church's dogmatic teaching on original sin and its consequences, is it not true that the series as a whole rests not on a process of "connected knowing" but rather on subjectivist and relativist perceptions which "disconnect" the interpretation of the Word of God from the teaching of the Magisterium?

The 'Inerrancy' of Sacred Scripture

Out Of The Desert erroneously claims that the Bible can contain errors of an "historical and scientific" nature. It says:

All Christians reverence the Bible as the Word of God and believe it to be a source of God's revelation in matters of faith and morals. For fundamentalist Christians, who focus on the literal meaning of biblical texts, the bible is true in every sense—historically and scientifically, as well as morally and religiously.

Other Christian churches, including the Catholic Church, advocate an approach to the interpretation of the Bible that focuses on both the text and its context. Using this approach, Christians can admit that the bible contains historical and scientific errors, while continuing to believe in the essential religious and moral truth of the Bible as the Word of God.[167]

Paul Y. Taguchi, the late Cardinal Archbishop of Osaka in Japan, stated that "inerrancy" means that the Sacred Books of the Bible "are totally free from error." He added that the Church's teaching on inerrancy "is very closely linked to the belief in inspiration, for, if sacred Scripture has God for its author, and God is the supreme truth, then, obviously, there can be no error in the sacred books, for otherwise it would be tantamount to imputing the authorship of error to God himself.[168]

In order to shed light on some of the more important doctrinal and pastoral implications of Pope John Paul II's apostolic letter *Ad Tuendam Fidem*, the Congregation for the Doctrine of the Faith, issued in July 1998 a *Commentary on the Concluding Formula of the 'Professio fidei.'* Here, in giving examples of Church teachings which "require the assent of theological faith by all members of the Church," the CDF listed that Church doctrine which insists on "the absence of error in the inspired sacred texts." Indeed, the CDF *Commentary* pointed out that anyone who obstinately places "in doubt or denies" doctrines such as this one on the inerrancy of Sacred Scripture "falls under the censure of heresy."[169]

Throughout the history of the Church, and especially since the Enlightenment, many scholars both inside and outside the Catholic Church, have expended much energy in attempting to document examples of alleged inconsistencies and contradictions in the Bible. This question was taken up by Pope Leo XIII in Providentissimus Deus (1893) where he recalled the great work that had been carried out by the Fathers and Doctors of the Church who with "no less skill than reverence," sought "to reconcile with each other those numerous passages" from Sacred Scripture "which seem at variance" and which have been taken up by the "higher criticism."

In recalling the teaching of the First Vatican Council (1869-70) which stated unequivocally that the "books of the Old and New Testament...have God for their author,"[170] Pope Leo XIII sought in *Providentissimus Deus* to reaffirm the received Catholic teaching on the inspiration and inerrancy of Sacred Scripture. In regard to the CDF *Commentary* on the *'Professio fidei'* cited earlier, which reaffirmed the Church's teaching regarding 'the absence of error in the inspired sacred texts," the first reference given by the CDF was to Pope Leo XIII's *Providentissimus Deus* where he gave the following definition of biblical inspiration:

> Hence, the fact that it was men whom the Holy Spirit took up as his instruments for writing does not mean that it was these inspired instruments—but not the primary author—who might have made an error. For, by supernatural power, He so moved and impelled them to write—He so assisted them when writing—that the things which He ordered, and these only, they first rightly understood, then willed faithfully to write down, and finally expressed in apt words and with infallible truth. Otherwise, it could not be said that He was the Author of the entire Scripture. Such has always been the persuasion of the Fathers.

In thus upholding in *Providentissimus Deus* the received Catholic teaching on the inerrancy of Sacred Scripture, Leo XIII simultaneously acknowledged the contribution modern historical science can make to biblical exegesis. However, in doing so, Leo XIII reminded Catholic biblical scholars that in carrying out their work in fidelity to the teaching of the Magisterium, they need not fear the possibility of a clash between the contents of Sacred Scripture and historically demonstrated truth. This conclusion, said Pope Leo XIII, was based on the fact that God—who is the author of all truth—does not contradict himself.[171] In regard to this very point, Leo XIII condemned the view that the inerrancy of Sacred Scripture extends only to religious and moral truths. He said:

> It is absolutely wrong and forbidden either to narrow inspiration to certain parts only of Holy Scripture or to admit that the sacred writer has erred. **As to the system of those who...do not hesitate to concede that divine inspiration regards the things of faith and morals, and nothing beyond,** because (as they wrongly think) in a question of the truth or

falsehood of a passage we should consider not so much what God has said as the reason and purpose which He had in mind in saying it—**this system cannot be tolerated**...For all the books which the Church receives as sacred and canonical are written wholly and entirely, with all their parts, at the dictation of the Holy Spirit; and so far is it from being possible that any error can coexist with inspiration, that inspiration not only is essentially incompatible with error, but excludes and rejects it as absolutely and necessarily as it is impossible that God Himself, the supreme Truth, can utter that which is not true.[172]

The 1907 Holy Office decree *Lamentabili,* which was strongly confirmed by Pope St. Pius X,[173] condemned the proposition which asserts that "Divine inspiration does not extend to the whole of Sacred Scripture in such a way that it protects each and every part of it from all error."[174] In order to commemorate the occasion of fifteenth centenary of the death of St. Jerome, Pope Benedict XV issued in 1920 an encyclical titled *Spiritus Paraclitus* in which he stated that it is an error to arbitrarily restrict scriptural inerrancy to religious matters alone. He said: "The teaching of Jerome strongly corroborates and illustrates what Our predecessor of blessed memory Leo XIII solemnly declared to be the ancient and constant faith of the Church about the complete immunity of the Scriptures from error of any kind."[175]

In 1943, in an encyclical titled *Divino Afflante Spiritu,* Pope Pius XII again reaffirmed the solemn teaching of the Church on the inerrancy of Sacred Scripture. He stated that the human authors of Sacred Scripture did not always use the forms of speech with which we are accustomed today, but rather that they used modes of expression common to the people of their times. He noted that the sacred authors of the Bible had certain fixed ways of narrating, as well as certain idioms and forms of expression which they used to record history and formulate laws or rules for living.

Scriptural inerrancy does not imply that every sentence in the Bible should be interpreted in a fundamentalist or 'literalist' way. Regarding this, Pope Pius XII, in *Divino Afflante Spiritu,* called on Catholic scholars to become familiar with all the literary modes used in the Bible in order that they be able to correctly interpret it and uphold its immunity from error. He said:

Not infrequently—to mention only one instance—when some persons reproachfully charge the Sacred Writers with some historical error or inaccuracy in the recording of facts, on closer examination it turns out to be nothing else than those customary modes of expression and narration peculiar to the ancients which used to be employed in the mutual dealings of social life and which in fact were sanctioned by common usage. When then such modes of expression are met with in the sacred text, which, being meant for men, is couched in human language, **justice demands that they be no more taxed with error** than when they occur in the ordinary intercourse of daily life.[176]

In his 1950 encyclical *Humani Generis,* Pius XII again condemned the notion that the inerrancy of Scripture extends only to questions of "faith and morals." He said:

A number of things are proposed or suggested by some even against the divine authorship of Sacred Scripture. For some go so far as to pervert the sense of the Vatican Council's [Vatican I] definition that God is the author of Holy Scripture, and **they put forward again the opinion, already often condemned, which asserts that inerrancy extends only to those parts of the bible that deal with God himself, religion, or morals.**[177]

The Second Vatican Council also reaffirmed the received Catholic teaching on the inerrancy of Sacred Scripture. It said:

Since, therefore, all that the inspired authors or sacred writers affirm should be regarded as affirmed by the Holy Spirit, we must acknowledge that the books of Scripture firmly, faithfully, and without error teach that truth which God, for the sake of our salvation, wished to see confided to the Sacred Scriptures.[178]

Since Vatican II, there has been much conflict over the meaning of the sentence containing the term "that truth..." in the passage quoted above from *Dei Verbum 11*. In order to forestall such conflict, the Fathers of Vatican II attached footnote 5 to *Dei Verbum 11* which directs us to several Magisterial references which are to be used as interpretive keys that will ensure that the teaching of *Dei Verbum 11* will be interpreted in continuity with the received Catholic doctrine on the inerrancy of the Bible.[179] The references given in footnote 5 of *Dei Verbum* are:

i) Session IV of the Council of Trent where it refers to "the Gospel's very purity from all error" whose "saving truth and moral discipline" have been "handed over to us by the Apostles at the dictation of the Holy Spirit" (Denz. 1501). This decree has been understood by the Church as referring to the Bible's unrestricted inerrancy.

ii) First reference to *Providentissimus Deus* where Pope Leo XIII pointed out that the Holy Spirit did not intend in the Scriptures "things in no way profitable unto salvation", but rather "described and dealt with things in more or less figurative language, or in terms that were commonly used at the time."

iii) Second reference to *Providentissimus Deus* where Pope Leo XIII declared that "it is absolutely wrong and forbidden either to narrow inspiration to certain parts of Holy Scripture or to admit that the sacred writer has erred."

iv) Third reference to *Providentissimus Deus* where Pope Leo XIII stated that "the divine writings, as left by the hagiographers, are free from all error," even in those passages which have come in for most attention from "higher cricism."

v) Reference to *Divino Afflante Spiritu* where Pope Pius XII quoted and reaffirmed what Pope Leo XIII stated in the references given above.

In the case of the Gospels, the Magisterium unequivocally calls for our belief in their historicity.[180] In this regard, Vatican II said:

Holy Mother Church has firmly and with absolute constancy held, and continues to hold, that the four gospels just named, whose historical character the Church unhesitantly asserts, faithfully hand on what Jesus Christ, while living among men, really did and taught for their eternal salvation until the day he was taken up into heaven.[181]

In *Divino Afflante Spiritu,* Pope Pius XII encouraged Catholic exegetes to work at seeking solutions to questions of biblical interpretation which will accord with the Church's teaching on the inerrancy of Sacred Scripture. In *Humani Generis,* Pope Pius XII, in opposition to those who assert that "immunity from error extends only to those parts of the Bible that treat of God or of moral and religious matters," stated that such erroneous biblical scholarship takes "no account of the analogy of faith and the 'tradition' of the Church."[182] This point was reaffirmed by Vatican II when it said:

> But since sacred Scripture must be read and interpreted with its divine authorship in mind, no less attention must be devoted to the content and unity of the whole of Scripture, taking into account the Tradition of the entire Church and the analogy of faith, if we are to derive their true meaning from the sacred texts.[183]

The Gnostic Gospel of Thomas

Book Three of *Out of the Desert,* which contains the erroneous comments outlined above on the inerrancy of the Bible, is intended for use by Year 9 students whose average age is 14–15 years. This book also contains the following student activity:

1. Find out the meaning of 'canon' when used in speaking about the Scriptures.
2. Research the structure, authorship, contents and literary style of the Gospel of Thomas. Why was it not included in the canon of the Christian Scriptures?
3. Using a Sunday missal or lectionary, find out which gospels form the basis of the Sunday readings in the liturgical years A, B and C?[184]

At this juncture, a question needs to be raised about the wisdom of setting 14–15 year-old students a research project on the gnostic Gospel of Thomas. The exercise becomes all the more questionable when we consider that the only reference given in *Out of the Desert* to the students to faciltate their research into the Gospel of Thomas is the following internet site: www.neoism.org/squares/thomas/_index.html.

The gnostic Gospel of Thomas dates from sometime in the late-second to fourth century. Like other gnostic texts, it compromises the truth about Jesus—no redemptive death etc. In referring to this 'Gospel', St. Cyril of Jerusalem said that while "being touched on the surface with the fragrance of an evangelic title," it nevertheless "corrupts the souls of the simple."[185]

When we go to the website on the Gospel of Thomas given in *Out of the Desert*, we find that its main focus is a presentation of the two forms of this gnostic text: one a translation from the (full) Coptic text, the other a translation of the (partial) Greek text. Verse-by-verse comparisons are offered. The Gospel of Thomas is a collection of 114 verses (in the Coptic version) of which most begin: "Jesus said...." Prior to verse 1, it states: *"These are the secret sayings which the living Jesus spoke and which Didymos Judas Thomas wrote down."* They are alleged sayings of Jesus, and are presented as the transmission of secret knowledge which requires correct interpretation, presumably by initiates. For example, verse 1 states: *"And he said, 'Whoever finds the interpretation of these sayings will not experience death.'"*

The invitation in *Out of the Desert* to 14–15 year-old students to enrich their Catholic education by visiting the website www.neoism.org/squares/thomas/_index.html, if accepted by the diligent, would yield further invitations via the website's own links. The unsuspecting children may click onto the Gnosis Archive, where they are asked to "Take a moment to reflect on a brief meditation and readings from the Gnostic scriptures, selected from this week's Gnostic liturgy."

Next, these students browsing this Gnostic website, could through its links, visit pages dedicated to luminaries such as Heidegger, existentialist devotee of Nazism; the nihilist philosopher Nietzsche so admired by Hitler, or rampant homosexual author Proust. At Kafka's page, they are invited to experience a spiritual renewal through his exuberantly hope-filled influence. Students with proficiency in the French language can visit a page dedicated to the noted sodomite, pervert and pornographer, the Marquis de Sade. As for those interested in comparative religion, Rosicrucian Fellowship and Masonic links are provided, as are Kabala links, "Festival of Plagiarism" and the site "Hyper Weirdness by WWW."

The invitation into this website associated with their assignment to explore the gnostic Gospel of Thomas, runs the risk of producing for some of these 14-15 year old students an excursion into the Gnostic world of secret "knowledge", witchcraft, fringe religion, bizarre philosophies and perversions. Their parents, I am sure, would not approve of such exposure, even if some Catholic educators recommend it.

I have already noted how Peter Mudge, one of the authors of *Out of the Desert*, has stated that the focus of the texts is "the spirit of Vatican II."[186] In like manner, Book Three of *Out of the Desert* claims that the series includes a focus on "the spirit of Vatican II as expressed in the *Catechism of the Catholic Church*."[187] In all the three texts being reviewed here, however, we find contradictions of the explicit teaching of both Vatican II and the *CCC*. Given that these contradictions of Church teaching are mingled in the texts with accurate quotations from Church documents, then there is a greater likelihood that the unwary reader will be led to regard everything in the texts as a faithful rendering of Catholic doctrine. This form of catechetical and theological writing, i.e. the intermingling of orthodox and heterodox ideas and presenting the whole mishmash as a work inspired by the 'the spirit of Vatican II,' is a characteristic mark of the work of many well known dissenters such as Thomas Groome and Richard McBrien.

When parents send their children to Catholic schools, there is an implicit contract that the school will provide what the Church says it should provide: namely an education in Catholic faith and morals and not indoctrination in the subjective opinions of dissidents. When students in Catholic schools are called upon to use religious education texts such as *Out Of The Desert* without their parents being first alerted to the contradictions of Catholic doctrine such books contain, there arises a question of professional malpractice.

Senior religious education officers in Catholic education offices command salaries which can range from between $70,000 to $85,000 per annum on top of which they draw royalties on any textbooks they may publish. Also, given their positions of authority within the religious education bureaucracies, such authors frequently have responsibility for organising inservices for religion teachers and hence they are placed in a very advantageous position in regard to the promotion of their books.

Case Study No. 4

'STUDIES OF RELIGION' (A SENIOR HIGH SCHOOL PROGRAM IN COMPARATIVE RELIGION)

Increasingly, the majority of Catholic senior high school students in New South Wales no longer study a systematic Catholic Religious Education programme in Years 11 and 12. Instead, they take a Board of Studies (State Government Department of Education) directed course in comparative religion called *Studies of Religion.*

Introduced in the early 1990s, this *Studies of Religion* Course is divided into three sections: Foundational Studies (35%), Depth Studies (50%) and Interest Studies (15%). According to the Board of Studies Syllabus document: "Foundation Studies introduces students to the essential concepts of the courses. It seeks to provide an understanding of the nature of religion and the expression of religious thought and practice in various belief systems".[188] The Syllabus document adds that in this initial study students are "required to achieve outcomes that are about the general nature of religion, rather than those specific to particular religious traditions".[189] Foundation Studies are expected to make substantial references to Christianity and Aboriginal Spirituality as formative and enduring influences on Australia.

The Foundation Studies serve as an introduction to the five religious traditions of the depth studies. In the Depth Studies section, students have to pick one topic from each of two groups. Group 1 is called *Religious Traditions* and is comprised of Buddhism, Christianity, Hinduism, Islam and Judaism. Group 2 is called *Cross Religion Studies* and is comprised of Rites of Passage, Sacred Writings and Stories, Teachers and Interpreters, Ways of Holiness, Women in Religion. In the Interest Studies section of the course, there is a wide range of options that can be studied such as Religious Biography, Religion and Literature, Religion and Ecology, Confucianism, Sikhism, Taoism etc.

In 1994, the NSW Board of Studies issued a Support Document to provide guidelines for the teaching of *Studies of Religion* in Years 11 and 12. Teachers place a lot of emphasis on these Support Documents issued by the Board of Studies as they give important directions for the inter-pretation of syllabus statements and they list resources which have been deemed useful in teaching a particular course or topic.

The relativistic nature of the NSW *Studies of Religion* course was clearly demonstrated in the 1994 Support Document. In one section dealing with teaching *Studies of Religion* in schools that do not have a specific religious affiliation (mostly State Schools), the Support Document says that "there may be times when students may seek the views of their teacher or when the teacher may state private views in order to illustrate a process or help students express their own views." The Support Document adds that on such occasions the teacher should present their personal view "with no special status but entitled to the same respect as the views of any other person."

However, in a section dealing with the teaching of *Studies of Religion* in schools that do have a religious affiliation (most of which are Catholic), the Support Document refers to "variants" within religious traditions (e.g. Catholicism as a 'variant' within Christianity) and says: "[The] variant must not be set up as the norm by which other variants of the tradition are to be judged. In any comparisons of variants or ref-erence to individuals, beliefs, practices or issues within them, teachers and students should strive to be objective and non-judgmental."[190] Then, in regard to different religious traditions, the Support Document says:

> "[The] religious tradition (or its variant) must not be set up as the norm by which other religious traditions are to be judged. All religious traditions must be treated and respected on their own terms. Any references to other religious traditions or to individuals, beliefs, practices or issues within them should be objective and non-judgmental."[191]

If the above recommendations regarding the treatment of "variants" in and between religious "traditions" are being implemented in Catholic schools, then our youth are being indoctrinated in religious relativism and being encouraged to adopt a false tolerance in regard to religious differences. If the question of truth is forsaken in this *Studies of Religion* course, then the whole exercise is reduced to an exercise in absurdity. Catholic youth have to be taught that there exists one true religion and that according to the teaching of the Second Vatican Council: "We believe that this one true religion continues to exist in the Catholic and Apostolic Church, to which the Lord Jesus entrusted the task of spreading it among all people."[192]

Not only is it imperative that Catholic youth be encouraged to openly profess that they belong to the "one true religion" while at the same time respecting what is good and true in other religions, but in the same context they need to be taught about those aspects of other religions which being based on various superstitions and errors give rise to rituals and moral perceptions which constitute an obstacle to human advancement and salvation.

The 1994 Support Document provides some background material on the various religious traditions including Christianity. Coupled with this, it has separate sections on Anglicanism, the Greek Orthodox Church and the Catholic Church. In the section on Christianity, the Support Document promotes an heretical understanding of the Person of Christ by referring to the reality of the post-Resurrection Jesus as "Jesus deified."[193] In the section on the Catholic Church, the Support Document says: "Scripture scholars indicate that the historical Jesus did not leave 'blueprints' for a Christian church. It was originally a diffuse movement within Judaism rather than a formal new religion."[194]

The lists of recommended texts that appear in the various parts of the 1994 Support Document dealing with Catholicism are heavily skewed towards dissent. Alongside the documents of Vatican II are listed the Dutch Catechism (New Catechism: Catholic Faith for Adults), Richard McBrien's Catholicism, Albert Nolan's Jesus Before Christianity, and controversial Episcopalian (Anglican) Bishop J.S. Spong's *Rescuing the Bible from Fundamentalism*.

That the published works of Bishop Spong should appear in the recommended resources section on Catholicism in the Support Document is surprising to say the least. Some examples of Spong's heterodoxical assertions are: i) that it is non-sensical to try to understand Jesus as the incarnation of a theistic deity; ii) that the virgin birth, understood as literal biology, makes Christ's divinity, as traditionally understood, impossible; iii) that the miracles recounted in the New Testament should not be understood as supernatural events performed by an incarnate God; iv) that Christ's resurrection is non-physical and non-historical; v) that an understanding of the crucifixion of Christ as a sacrifice for the sins of the world is a barbarian idea based on primitive concepts of God and must be dismissed; vi) that so-called 'same-sex' marriages are morally licit.

Finally, Spong asserts that: "Both papal infallibility and biblical inerrancy require widespread and unchallenged ignorance to sustain their claim to power. Both are doomed as viable alternatives for the long-range future of anyone."[195]

In another section recommending resources for use in a "Women in Religion" part of the *Studies of Religion* course, the Support Document reads like a 'Who's Who' of radical religious feminism. In particular, in recommending Elisabeth Schussler Fiorenza's *In Memory of Her*, the Support Document says: "This book has become a classic in the few years since its publication. It is difficult reading but teachers need to have access to it for reference."[196]

In the year 2000, the Board of Studies introduced a new HSC *Studies of Religion* syllabus which was set down to be tested for the first time in October-November 2001. This course is not substantially different from its predecessor. To assist with the implementation of the new course, the Board of Studies produced a Support Document in 1999. This document gave the same advice on the treatment of variants in and between religious traditions as did the 1994 Support Document. Indeed, it even recommended that the 1994 Support Document be again made use of in teaching the new syllabus.

Not long after the *Studies of Religion* course was introduced into Catholic high schools in the early 1990s, evidence became available that some Catholic youth who took the course were adopting a syncretistic mentality in regard to religious belief. In 1993, for example, Gideon Goosen of the Australian Catholic University, conducted a survey of 330 students who had completed the course in that year. He found that the students "were more inclined to agree that what people believe is not important as long as they believe something and that all religions are equally good or bad". In saying that the students "were more relativistic about religions," Dr Goosen stated that the students' increased openness to Aboriginal spirituality was "very gratifying". In expressing a desire "to stress the positive things," Dr Goosen said that "the relativism is just one negative thing that's got to be investigated further." Describing the educational process by which the course is conducted, Dr Goosen said: "You stand back from your own faith commitment". That, he added: "leads to people saying they [religions] are all much the same. They've all got a prophet. They've all got sacred writings. They've all got ritual".[197]

One of the more popular textbooks used for the *Study of Religions* course is called *Living Religion: Studies of Religion* for Senior Students. The book is written by a team of authors which includes Peter Mudge, Adam Taylor and Janet Morrissey—all of whom were involved with the writing of the *Out of the Desert* series referred to earlier. There is no room here for an in-depth review of *Living Religion*—I will merely highlight a few passages from the two chapters on the Christianity Depth Study section of the book.

In relation to Jesus, *Living Religion* says: "Jesus was considered a lay person both from a Jewish and Christian perspective (Hebrews 8:4). His background is reflected in the moral struggle between him and his adversaries, with elements such as Galilean versus Judean...and lay versus priestly."[198] As I have already pointed out in Chapter 6, the *Letter to Hebrews* bears clear testimony to the priesthood of Christ. Elsewhere in *Living Religion* we read:

> Some scholars have stressed the 'Abba' experience of Jesus' ministry. This experience stresses intimacy with God as 'Abba' or 'my own dear father'. Yet other scholars view this form of address as less important. 'Abba' occurs only once in Jesus' addresses (Mark 14:36) where Jesus is alone. Nevertheless, this **image of God as Father** blends well with the rest of Jesus ministry...Many of the titles for Jesus' ministry such as Messiah, Christ, Son of God and Lord, **probably evolved during early Palestinian Christianity and not during Jesus' ministry**.[199]

In regard to Jesus' knowledge of the Church which he founded, we read in *Living Religion*:

> It appears that Jesus' intention was to preach the Gospel to all, at the same time knowing that only some would accept it. Yet it is extremely doubtful that Jesus planned or had our understanding of 'church'."[200]

Living Religion abounds in ambiguities and false dichotomies. For example, in regard to what it sees as Vatican II's impact on spirituality and devotion, it says: "Today, identifiable 'signs of devotions' are less clear. Council reforms have led to better education, a search for meaning and relevance beyond **dogma** and **ritualism**."[201] Later it adds:

> Christianity is not just or even primarily a list of beliefs and practices. The experience of being a Christian begins with a person's lived experiences. Theologians are quick to remind us that the Christian experience of oneself as a person, that person's *encounter* with Christ, and the faith that results, all come before Christian practices, creeds, rules and regulations.[202]

It is a disavowal of the truth to suggest that the Second Vatican Council was concerned to lead us "in a search for meaning and relevance beyond dogma." In his opening address to the Council, Pope John XXIII recalled that "the principal task" being entrusted to the Council was "to guard and present better the precious deposit of Christian doctrine in order to make it more accessible to the Christian Faithful and to all people of goodwill."[203] The Documents of Vatican II reveal how well the Council Fathers fulfilled this task. However, the equivocating references to "dogma" in *Living Religion* suggests a near total ignorance by the authors of the major themes of Vatican II's key document *The Dogmatic Constitution On The Church* (Lumen Gentium).

Continuing with the same type of reductionist notions as those which appear in the quotation above, *Living Religion* says:

> Although there are core beliefs held by all Christians (such as the humanity and divinity of Christ), the range and interpretation of these beliefs are as vast as they are numerous...No Christian is expected to accept any mode of church teaching uncritically. Any believer has the freedom both to receive teaching and to question and explore it. The primary function of dogma and doctrine is not legalistic. Their main purpose in whatever form they take (preaching, liturgy, church pronouncements, the lives of believers) is to allow each person to take on and actively express their Christian beliefs.[204]

Living Religion has much to say about 'Images of God' and 'Feminist theology'. In regard to the latter it states:

The typical approach of feminist theology is to uncover and name the ways in which Christianity has been 'infected' by patriarchy. Elisabeth Schussler Fiorenza, for example, sees this patriarchy as a male pyramid of various ranks which has the effect of oppressing and exploiting women according to the class, race, country or religion of the men to whom the women 'belong'.[205]

Describing feminist theological method, *Living Religion* mentions how it provides: i) "a demonstration of the negative effects of **androcentrism** and misogyny on the Christian tradition," ii) "an attempt to discover alternative sources and guidelines to challenge these biases," iii) "a reinterpretation or reconstruction of the main themes and sources that will help remove these biases against women," iv) "a celebration of the faith, courage and talents of women."[206]

As an example of a theologian who has produced such a reconstructionist theology, *Living Religion* cites Elisabeth Schussler Fiorrenza and it quotes her as saying:

Much of women's 'her-story' in early Christianity is lost. The few references which survived in the New Testament records are like the tip of an iceberg indicating what we have lost. Yet at the same time they show how great the influence of women was in the early Christian movement...A survey of the scattered references to the participation of women in the early Christian missionary endeavour shows that the missionary work of women was equal to that of men like Barnabas, Apollo or Paul.[207]

Alongside Catholic women such as Blessed Mary McKillop and Mother Theresa of Calcutta, *Living Religion* places Elisabeth Schussler Fiorenza and Elaine Wainwright as subjects for a student research task on women who "interpreted and transformed Christianity."[208] Coupled with this, *Living Religion* has a section on Patricia Brennan, founder of MOW (Movement for the Ordination of Women) whose work is presented in a very positive light. In this context, *Living Religion* sets out in tabular form the "Arguments for" and the "Arguments against" the ordination of women (7 for ordination, 5 against).[209] Taken in context, it is highly unlikely that students reading this text will conclude that the Church's doctrine on the male-only ministerial priesthood is well grounded in Christian anthropology and Divine Revelation.

Finally, on the question of 'Images of God,' *Living Religion*, after stating that "We have already referred to the range of female, male and neuter God images in the Bible and the medieval image of 'Jesus as Mother'," goes on to say how "in recent times, theologian Sallie McFague has suggested some alternative models of God for what she calls today's 'ecological, nuclear age." Among the titles listed are: "God as Mother, lover and friend" and "The world as God's body."

While I have no doubt that a knowledgeable and committed Catholic teacher could use the *Studies of Religion* course to strengthen in some way the Catholic faith of his or her students, I am convinced nevertheless that the decision to introduce it into the Catholic school system was ill-conceived. The new orientation which the course gives to religious education in Catholic schools has profound implications for the long-run role of Catholic schools in evangelisation. I recall one teacher telling me how he thought it was ridiculous for him to have to teach a unit on the Hindu Scriptures to Year 11 students who after 10 years of Catholic schooling could not be relied on to write a coherent sentence on the difference between the Old and New Testaments, or between Catholicism and Protestantism.

With its focus on religion from a comparative and sociological perspective, *Studies in Religion* promotes a syncretistic view of religion which is willing to accommodate many different spiritual traditions on an equal level with Catholic faith and practice. It places the foundational writings of different religions on the same level by labeling them all as "sacred". Similarly, different deities are subsumed under the general category of the Transcendent, and various rituals are all considered to serve the same function of contacting and establishing unity with the Transcendent. In this setting, Christ and Krishna are presented as merely two different ways of breaking through to the divine. This contradicts Catholic doctrine since Jesus is not just one of several names for the divine drawn from human experience of the transcendent. For Catholics, Jesus Christ is "the Word Made Flesh", ie. the Second Person of the Holy Trinity who has taken on our human nature so as to lead us to share eternally in the Trinitarian life. Our Lord did not say that he was *one of the ways,* instead he said *"I am the Way"*.

Given the relativist mood that informs the *Studies of Religion* syllabus, together with the non-confessional orientation of the most popular texts that are used to teach the course, young Catholics can be easily led to subscribe to the proposition that the experience of Christ and of Krishna are equally valid experiences of the divine. In this syncretistic perspective, Christ is no longer the definitive way through which God has made contact with and come to save his people.[210]

Why Are Catholic Youth Giving Up The Practice Of The Faith

A common thread running through the four case studies I have cited is a deficiency in the treatment of Catholic doctrine even to the point of contradicting it. In this regard, we noted that Groome does not accept as "appropriate" for use in movement 3 of *shared Christian praxis* a view of "Revelation as doctrine" which he says "understands revelation as 'divinely authoritative doctrine inerrantly proposed as God's word by the Bible or by official Church teaching'."[211] We have seen that the *Out of the Desert* series contradicts several dogmatic teachings of the Catholic Church. We have noted how the *Studies of Religion* text *Living Religion* calls into question the historical reliability of the Gospels by asserting that "many of the titles for Jesus' ministry such as Messiah, Christ, Son of God and Lord, probably evolved during early Palestinian Christianity and not during Jesus' ministry."[212] The case study on the Australian Catholic University follows the same pattern.

As indicated in the introductory part of this Chapter, a noticeable characteristic of religious trends in the Western world is a growing disregard for the place of doctrine in Christian faith. This is accompanied by an increasing tendency to call into question the historical reliability of the Gospels. At the same time, this trend is accompanied by a growing interest in ancient heretical movements such as gnosticism—something which in turn has sparked renewed interest in heretical texts such as the Gospel of Thomas.

Now let us consider the effect of all that has been said above on the religious education of Catholic high school students in New South Wales, which is Australia's most populous state. Many of these students are following a religious education curriculum that is in some way based on Groome's *shared Christian praxis*. They are possibly using the *Out of the Desert* religious education texts in Years 7-9, while in Years

11-12 the same students will take the *Studies of Religion* course where they will use defective texts such as *Living Religion*. Coupled with this, some of these students will go on to take courses in Religious Education at the Australian Catholic University where after exposure to a program of study likely to involve the treatment of orthodoxy and heterodoxy as equal partners, they will subsequently be channeled back into the Catholic school system as teachers of religion.

In view of all that has been said above, it is not unfair to say that at least some of the blame for the decline in the practice of the faith amongst Catholic youth has to be attributed to the poor state of religious education at all levels of Catholic education in Australia. Perhaps one is justified in stating that it is not so much a question of Catholic youth giving up the practice of the faith, as it is a case of many of these young people having come to us for bread and instead we gave them stones.

Reference

1   Bishop W. K. Weigand, AD2000, *A Journal of Religious Opinion,* Melbourne, June 1994.

2   Fr Kenneth Baker, S. J. Editorial, *Homiletic and Pastoral Review*, February, 1995.

3   Germain Grisez and Russell Shaw, *The Crisis of Eucharistic Faith,* Homiletic and Pastoral Review, February 1995, pp. 16-21.

4   Cf. Taking Stock (1999), a profile of Australian Church attenders based on statistics from the 1996 National Church Life Survey (NCLS) and the 1996 Catholic Church Life Survey (CCLS). The study was supported by the Australian Catholic Bishops Conference, ANGLICARE (NSW) and the Uniting Church Board of Mission (NSW).

5   Professor Dennis McLaughlin, *The Beliefs, Values and Practices of Catholic Student Teachers: A Research Project,* Australian Catholic University, 1999.

6   The first edition of The Christian Story was published by the ACU in 1995 and a revised edition in 1996. In what follows I will be quoting almost exclusively from the 1999 reprint of the 1996 revised edition. In one instance where I do refer to the 1995 edition, I will make this clear. Everything I quote from the 1999 reprint was contained also in the 1995 edition.

7   Laurie Woods, *The Christian Story,* Australian Catholic University, Sydney 1999, p. 118.

8   Ibid. p. 148.

9   Ibid. p. 159.

10 Ibid. p. 158.

11 *CCC*. n. 455.

12 *CCC.* n. 221, cf. Jn 8: 28.

13 *CCC.* n. 444.

14 *CCC.* n. 653.

15 Laurie Woods, *The Christian Story,* op. cit. p. 182.

16 Ibid. p. 182, bold print and italics were inserted by Woods.

17 Ibid. p. 183, bold print and italics were inserted by Woods.

18 Ibid. p. 184.

19 Laurie Woods, *The Christian Story,* Australian Catholic University, 1995, p. 139, bold print and italics inserted by Woods.

20 *CCC.* n. 648

21 Ibid.

22 *CCC.* n. 645.

23 *CCC.* n. 646.

24 *CCC.* n. 639.

25 *CCC.* n. 645.

26 St. Ignatius of Antioch, Letter to the Smyrnaeans [ca. AD 115], cited in William Jurgens' *The Faith of the Early Church Fathers,* op. cit. Vol. 1, pp. 24–25.

27 *CCC.* n. 643.

28 Pope John Paul II, *General Audience,* December 9, 1981, L'Osservatore Romano, December 14, 1981.

29 Ibid.

30 Cardinal Joseph Ratzinger, *Journey Towards Easter,* Ignatius Press, San Francisco, 1988, p. 117.

31 *CCC.* n. 640

32 This is the teaching given by the Congregation for the Doctrine of the Faith in 1988 in response to an erroneous interpretation of Christ's Resurrection propagated by Fr. David Coffey in the early 1980s. Fr. Coffey asserted that the bodily Resurrection of Jesus "does not require or even allow the reinvolvement of a corpse" (Studies in Faith and Culture No 4, Catholic Institute of Sydney, 1980, p. 114). This ruling of the CDF was made public by Cardinal Clancy and published in the Sydney Catholic Weekly on September 28, 1988.

33 *CCC.* n. 656.

34 Laurie Woods, *The Christian Story* (1999), op. cit.

35 Ibid. p. 128.

36 Gideon Goosen, *Compass: A Review of Topical Theology,* Winter, 1997.

37 *CCC.* n. 1114 citing Council of Trent (1547): DS 1600-1601; see also CCC. nn. 1117, 1210.

38 Robert Gascoigne, *Freedom & Purpose: An Introduction To Christian Ethics,* E. J. Dwyer, New South Wales, 1993, p. 86. At the time of writing, Gascoigne's book is still being reproduced by the ACU where it is being used for a courses in "Christian Theological Ethics" and in Religious Education Certification courses for teachers in Catholic schools in Sydney.

39 Ibid. p. 84

40 Ibid. p. 83

41 Ibid.

42 Cf. Pope John Paul II, *Reconciliatio et Paenitentia,* n. 17.

43 Cf. Pope John Paul II, *Veritatis Splendor,* n. 49

44 CCC. n. 1874

45 Pope John Paul II, *Reconciliatio et Paenitentia,* n. 17.

46 Robert Gascoigne, *Freedom & Purpose,* op.cit. p. 190

47 Ibid. p. 192

48 Ibid. p. 194

49 Ibid. p. 196

50 I have dealt with meaning of the terms "infallible" and "definitive" teaching in Chapter 2.

51 Cf. *Evangelium Vitae,* nn. 57, 62, 65; Vatican II, *Lumen Gentium,* n. 25.

52 Pope John Paul II, *Veritatis Splendor,* n. 81.

53 Ibid. n. 110.

54 *Sharing Our Story,* Curriculum Document, Catholic Diocese of Parramatta, Rotary Offset Press, Sydney 1991.

55 Sr. Patricia Malone and Maurice Ryan, Sound The Trumpet: Planning and Teaching Religion in the Catholic Primary School, Social Science Press, Wentworth Falls (NSW) 1994, p. 54. As was pointed out in Chapter 1, Malone is Associate Professor of Religious Education at the Australian Catholic University in Sydney while Ryan lectures in Religious Education at the ACU in Brisbane.

56 Dr Michael Bezzina, *Word in Life,* Vol. 45 (3), Australian Catholic University 1997, p.19.

57 Ibid.

58 Bishop Kevin Manning, *Catholic Outlook,* Diocesan Newspaper of the Parramatta Diocese, March 1999, p. 7.

59 Fr. Peter Connelly, *"Further to my paper 'Is Shared Christian Praxis A Trojan Horse?"*—paper delivered to a gathering of clergy and religious educators, June 16, 1998.

60 *Sharing Our Story* (1991), op. cit. 19.

61 Ibid. p. xix.

62 Ibid. p. 54.

63 Ibid. p. 54, 59, 286.

64 Ibid. p. 59.

65 Ibid. p. 198.

66 Ibid. p. 221.

67 Cf. *Sharing Our Story,* pp. 39, 89, 120, 126, 171, 172, 175.

68 *Sharing Our Story,* p. 129.

69 A.J. Bliss, *Dictionary of Foreign Words and Phrases in Current English,* p. 323.

70 *Sharing Our Story,* p. 167.

71 Ibid.

72 *Sharing Our Story,* p. 280.

73 Pope Pius XII, *Mystici Corporis Christi,* n. 14.

74 Cf. *Mysterium Ecclesiae,* n. 1.

75 Vatican II, *Lumen Gentium,* n. 8.

76 Cf. Pope John Paul II, Ut unum sint, n. 13; *Lumen Gentium,* n. 15; Decree on Ecumenism (Vatican II), n. 3.

77 Vatican II, *Decree on Ecumenism,* n. 3.

78 *Sharing Our Story,* p. 118.

79 *Sharing Our Story,* p. 222.

80 Cf. The Primacy of the Successor of Peter in the Mystery of the Church, *Reflections Of The Congregation For The Doctrine Of The Faith, L'Osservatore Romano,* November 18, 1998.

81 *Sharing Our Story,* p. 263.

82 Vatican II, *Lumen Gentium,* n. 22.

83 *Sharing Our Story,* p. 93.

84 Ibid. p. 138.

85 Ibid. p. 95.

86 Ibid. p. 159.

87 For example, compare pages 108 and 219 with 217 of *Sharing Our Story.*

88 Cf. Vatican II, Presbyterorum ordinis, n. 2; *Lumen Gentium,* n. 10.

89 *Sharing Our Story,* p. 241.

90 Ibid. p. 243.

91 Cf, *Sharing Our Story,* p. 261.

92 Cf. *Sharing Our Story,* pp. 297-98.

93 *Sharing Our Story,* p. 234.

94 Cardinal Joseph Ratzinger, *Called to Communion,* Ignatius Press, San Francisco, 1996, p. 159.

95 *Sharing Our Story,* p. 242.

96 Ibid.

97 Cf. Thomas H. Groome, *Christian Religious Education: Sharing Our Story and Vision,* op. cit. p. 93.

98 Michael Bezzina, Peter Gahan, Helen McLenaghan, Greg Wilson, S*hared Christian praxis* as a basis for *Religious Education Curriculum, Word of Life* 45(3),1997, p.7.

99 Ibid.

100 On this point of Christ's human knowledge, see Pope Vigilius, *Constitutum,* 14. 5. 553, DS 419; Pope Gregory the Great, *Letter to Euogius,* DS 475-476;

Decree of the Holy Office of 1907 and 1918, DS 3432, 3424, 3435, 3645–3647; Pope Pius X, *Miserantissimus Redemptor,* 8.5. 1928, AAS 20, 174; Pius XII, Mystici Corporis, 2.6. 1947; Pius XII, *Sempiternus Rex,* 8.9. 1951; Pius XII, *Haurietas Aquas,* 25. 8. 1956; SCDF, 24.7.1966, AAS 58(1966) 650–660; *Catechism of the Catholic Church,* nn. 473–474.

101 Cf. *CCC.* n. 460; 2 Pet. 1:4.

102 For a penetrating review of Human Sexuality see *On Understanding Human Sexuality* by William May and John Harvey O.S.F.S., Synthesis Series.

103 Cf. Support Units Years 11 and 12, Parramatta CEO, 1993, *Suggested Activity 2.22, Human Relationships,* pp. 47–49.

104 Gideon Goosen and Margaret Tomlinson, *Jesus Mystery and Surprise: An Introduction to the Study of the Gospels,* E. J. Dwyer, Sydney, 1989. As I have already indicated, Goosen is an Associate Professor in the Theology and Religious Education department at the ACU in Sydney where Tomlinson also lectures in Culture and Creation Spirituality.

105 *CCC.* n. 473.

106 *CCC.* n. 474.

107 *CCC.* n. 478

108 Cf. Acts 9:20; Jn 20:31; Mt 16:18; *CCC.* 441–445.

109 *CCC.* n. 446. Cf. 1 Cor 2:8.

110 *CCC.* n. 449.

111 Support Units (1995), *Who Is Jesus,* p. 61.

112 Ibid.

113 Ibid. p. 63.

114 *Cf. Historical Approach to Contemporary Expressions of Church Unit,* p. 28.

115 Paul Collins, *Mixed Blessings,* Penquin Books Australia, 1986, p. 79.

116 Paul Collins, *Mixed Blessings,* Penquin Books Australia, 1986, p. 80.

117 The 1990 edition of O'Connell's book still had problems of ambiguity and confusion.

118 Pope John Paul II. *Veritatis Splendor,* nn. 56, 59.

119 Thomas H. Groome, *Christian Religious Education,* op. cit. p. 238.

120 Ibid.

121 Cf. Dr. Bernadette Tobin, *Australasian Catholic Record,* Oct. 1994, p. 412.

122 Thomas H. Groome, *Sharing Faith,* op. cit. pp. 84 and 472.n205.

123 Pope John Paul II, *Veritatis Splendor,* n. 103.

124 Cf. Mk 10:11–12; Mt 5:32; 19:9; Lk 16:18; *Council of Trent,* Session XXIV, 11 Nov. 1563, canon 7; Pius XI, Enc. Casti Connubii.

125 Pope John Paul II, *Familiaris Consortio,* n. 84.

126 Ibid.

127 *Sacred Congregation for the Doctrine of the Faith (CDF). Letter To The Bishops Of The Catholic Church Concerning The Reception of Holy Communion* by Divorced and Remarried Members of the Faithful, n. 4.

128 Dr Michael Bezzina, *Word in Life,* Vol. 45 (3), Australian Catholic University, 1997, p.19.

129 Michael Bezzina, Peter Gahan, Helen McLenaghan, Greg Wilson, *Shared Christian Praxis as a Basis for Religious Education, Word of Life, Journal of Religious Education,* Australian Catholic University, ACT, Vol. 45 (3), 1997, pp. 3, 11.

130 Peter Mudge, Word in Life 45 (1), Australian Catholic University, 1997, p. 13.

131 Ibid.

132 Ibid. p. 13.

133 Ibid. p. 14.

134 Ibid. p. 15.

135 Ibid.

136 Ibid.

137 Janet Morrissey, Peter Mudge, Adam Taylor, *Out of the Desert*, Book One, Longman Publishers, Melbourne, 1997, p. 101 (emphasis added).

138 Cardinal Joseph Ratzinger, *Co-Workers of the Truth,* Ignatius Press, San Francisco, 1992, p. 193.

139 Ibid.

140 Vatican I, *First Dogmatic Constitution on the Church of Christ,* Denz. 3050.

141 Vatican II, *Lumen Gentium,* n. 8.

142 Vatican II, *Inter Mirifica,* n. 3

143 *CCC.* n. 766; see also CCC. nn. 761-62.

144 *Commentary on the Concluding Formula of the 'Professio fidei,'* n. 11, Congregation for the Doctrine of the Faith, *L'Osservatore Romano,* July 15, 1998.

145 Ibid.

146 Janet Morrissey, Peter Mudge, Greg Wilson, *Out of the Desert, Book Three, Longman,* Melbourne, 1998, p. 148.

147 Ibid. p. 162.

148 Ibid. p. 144.

149 Cf. Cardinal Joseph Ratzinger, *Called to Communion,* op. cit. p. 68.

150 Alfred Loisy, *My Duel With the Vatican,* pp. 241-242; cited by Msgr. George A. Kelly in *The Battle for the American Church,* Doubleday, New York, 1979, p. 42

151 Pope St Pius X, *Pascendi dominici gregis,* n. 39

152 Janet Morrissey, Peter Mudge, Greg Wilson, *Out of the Desert*, Book Three, Longman, Melbourne, 1998, p. 161.

153 London Times, August 21, 1914; cited by Msgr. George *A. Kelly* in *Battle for the American Church,* op. cit. p. 45.

154 Pope John Paul II, *Fides et Ratio,* n. 54.

155 Janet Morrissey, Peter Mudge, Greg Wilson, *Out of the Desert, Book Three, Longman,* Melbourne, 1998, p. 135.

156 Pope John Paul II, *L'Osservatore Romano,* July 17, 1996.

157 *CCC.* n. 496.

158 Janet Morrissey, Peter Mudge, Adam Taylor, *Out of the Desert, Book Two, Longman,* Melbourne, 1998, p. 2.

159 Ibid. p. 2. The acknowledgments section at the front of this book expresses gratitude to "RECs, RE teachers and students of the Parramatta and other dioceses who trialled materials and supported this project."

160 Ibid. p. 2.

161 Ibid.

162 *CCC.* n. 390.

163 Council of Trent, *Decree Concerning Original Sin,* Fifth Session, June 17, 1546, n.1, in *Canons and Decrees of the Council of Trent,* trans. Rev. H. J. Schroeder, O.P., Herder, London, 1941, p. 21.

164 Vatican II, Gaudium et Spes, n. 18; cf. *CCC.* n. 1018

165 Cf. *CCC.* n. 1018

166 Peter Mudge, *Word in Life* 45 (1), Australian Catholic University, 1997, p. 15

167 Janet Morrissey, Peter Mudge, Greg Wilson: *Out of the Desert,* Book Three, Longman, Melbourne, 1998, p. 21

168 Cardinal Paul Y. Taguchi, *The Study of Sacred Scripture, L'Osservatore Romano,* May 15, 1975.

169 *Commentary on the Concluding Formula of the 'Professio fidei,'* nn. 5, 11, L'Osservatore Romano, July 15, 1998.

170 Vatican I, Denz. 1787.

171 Cf. Denz. 1947.

172 Pope Leo XIII, *Providentissimus Deus,* Part II, Section D, par. 2c, emphasis added.

173 *Cf. Motu Proprio Praestantia* (November 18, 1907).

174 Denz. 2011.

175 Denz. 2128.

176 Pius XII, *Divino Afflante Spiritu,* Part II, Section 3, par. 38–39, emphasis added.

177 Pope Pius XII, encyclical *Humani Generis.*

178 Vatican II, *Dei Verbum,* n. 11.

179 In regard to footnote 5 attached to *Dei Verbum 11,* in what follows I am drawing heavily on an essay titled *Historical Criticism of the New Testament* written by Msgr. John F. McCarhty of the Roman Theological Forum. This is contained in an excellent Study Program in Sacred Scripture which can be accessed on the internet at: http://www.rtforum.org/study/It/-It59.html. On this same internet address, there is also an excellent essay written by Rev. Dr. Brian W. Harrison, O.S. titled *The Truth and Salvific Purpose of Sacred Scripture According to Dei Verbum,* Article 11.

180 Cf. the replies from the Pontifical Commission for Biblical Studies dated June 19, 1911; June 26, 1912; May 29, 1907.

181 Vatican II, *Dei Verbum,* n. 19.

182 Pope Pius XII, *Humani Generis,* n. 22. The expression "analogy of faith" refers to the harmony of revealed truths with one another.

183 Vatican II, *Dei Verbum,* n. 12.

184 Janet Morrissey, Peter Mudge, Greg Wilson: *Out of the Desert, Book Three, Longman,* Melbourne, 1998, p. 64

185 St. Cyril of Jerusalem, *Catechetical Lectures,* cited in William A. Jurgens' *The Faith of the Early Fathers,* Vol 1, Liturgical Press, Minnesota, 1970, p. 352.

186 Peter Mudge, *Word in Life 45 (1),* Australian Catholic University, 1997, p. 14.

187 *Out of the Desert,* Book Three, p. xiii.

188 Board of Studies, *Studies of Religion* 1/2 Unit Syllabus, 1991, p. 13

189 Ibid.

190 *Studies of Religion: Preliminary and HSC Courses,* Draft Support Document, Board of Studies NSW, 1994, pp. 15-17.

191 Ibid. p. 17.

192 Vatican II, *Declaration On Religious Liberty,* n. 1.

193 *Studies of Religion: Preliminary and HSC Courses,* Draft Support Document, op. cit. p. 33.

194 Ibid. p. 46.

195 Bishop John Shelby Spong, in *Resurrection: Myth or Reality?* p. 99.

196 Ibid. p. 93.

197 Gideon Goosen, Catholic Weekly, 8/12/93

198 Peter Mudge et.al., *Living Religion: Studies of Religion* for Senior Students, Longman, Australia, 1993 (republished several times since then), p. 155.

199 Ibid. p. 156, emphasis added.

200 Ibid. p. 163.

201 Ibid. p. 188, emphasis in original text.

202 Ibid. p. 190.

203 Pope John XXIII, Discourse at the Opening of the second Vatican Council II, October 11, 1962; Cf. Pope John Paul II, *Apostolic Constitution Fidei Depositum,*.

204 Peter Mudge et.al., *Living Religion.*, op. cit. p. 190

205 Ibid. p. 268.

206 Ibid.

207 Ibid. p. 260.

208 Ibid. p. 266.

209 Ibid. p. 272.

210 The descriptions of religious syncretism which I have used here have been adopted from an excellent article on the subject written by Fr Bernard Green which was published in the April 1994 edition of The New Oxford Review.

211 Thomas H. Groome, *Sharing Faith,* op. cit. pp. p. 218-219.

212 Ibid. p. 156, emphasis added.

CONCLUSION

As we saw in Chapter 9, Fiorenza is in the vanguard of a "spiritual struggle for a different religion." This new religion seeks to realise "the dream and vision of G★d-Sophia's alternative community" that will be "inspired and compelled by **Her** gospel of liberation."[1] It is a fundamental tenet of Christianity that God's self-revelation in the person and redemptive work of Jesus Christ is a unique and normative event which is constitutive for the Christian faith and for the Church founded by Christ. In attempting to relativise this, Fiorenza is perilously close to placing herself outside of all that Christianity is. With her attempted reconstruction of the canon of Scripture, her strident support for abortion and her enthronement of the "Goddess", this "different religion" to which Fiorenza is committed represents a rejection of Christianity and a return to ancient paganism.

At issue in the debate about *Shared Christian Praxis* is the authentic transmission of the faith "delivered once and for all to the Apostles," as well as the spiritual birthright of innocent children to receive that faith free of corrupt ideological distortions. Groome's use of the concept "Story" as a replacement term for "scripture and tradition", and the "critical" sieve through which he processes it, leads at times to a relativising of the objective foundations of Catholic faith in order to uphold ideological imperatives. Thus, for example, the fact that the *Logos* took to himself a human nature of male gender—the reality of which underpins other elements in the mystery of the Redemption—becomes for Groome nothing more than mere "accidental" matter to be dispensed with in order to appease radical feminist sensibilities.

The Revelation of the Holy Trinity is the central mystery of Christian faith and life.[2] Hence, the crowning devotion of the spiritual life is devotion to the Blessed Trinity. In view of this, surely all Catholic educators will agree that it is good and proper to make God known to the children as he has manifested and revealed Himself. Consequently, when, following Groome's advice, teachers replace the revelation of God as Father, Son and Holy Spirit with the vague trinitarianism of Creator, Redeemer and Sanctifier; or when they teach children to address the First Person of the Holy Trinity as "Father/Mother," they thereby discount the truth they are obliged to pass on to Catholic children. In acting thus, they are drying up the streams of sanctity, since truth is the source of all love and devotion.

Through Baptism, Catholic children have received a special instinct for God as well as the germ of the gifts of Wisdom and Understanding. If taught properly by teachers who think with the mind of the Church as this is given voice through the teaching of the Magisterium, Catholic children are capable of grasping and spiritually enjoying the great truths of Catholic doctrine.

To begin to overcome the chaos that has overtaken Catholic religious education, it will be necessary to return to doctrinally-based religious education curricula. Such curricula will need to use the most up-to-date pedagogical techniques while simultaneously shunning methodologies such as *Shared Christian Praxis*. It will need to provide students with attractive text books that are faithful to Catholic doctrine in every respect. Coupled with all of this, those who direct religious education in Catholic schools and in Catholic education offices, should be beyond reproach in regard to the question of their fidelity to all that the Church teaches.

Most importantly, bishops will have to exercise their responsibility to protect children in Catholic schools from exposure to error. In order to defend the faith of the "least among their brethren," bishops have a responsibility to publicly refute error—even when it emanates from those comfortably ensconced in Catholic tertiary institutions and education offices. When it comes to the religious education of Catholic youth, the slightest compromise or dallying with error amounts to nothing less than a betrayal and acquiescence in the scandalisation of the young—something Our Lord threatened with grave punishment (cf. Lk 17: 1-3).

Let us all pray to Mary, the Mother of God and Mother of the Church, that all of us who have been called to work for the transmission of the Catholic faith to future generations, will do so with a degree of conviction and integrity that will enable us to say at the end of our days: "We are only servants, we have done no more than our duty."

Reference

1 Elisabeth Schussler Fiorenza, *Sharing Her Word,* op. cit. p. 183, emphasis added.
2 CCC. n. 234.